MOVEMENTS OF THOUGHT
IN THE
NINETEENTH CENTURY

MOVEMENTS OF THOUGHT
IN THE
NINETEENTH CENTURY

GEORGE H. MEAD

EDITED BY
MERRITT H. MOORE

UNIVERSITY OF CHICAGO PRESS
Chicago & London

THE UNIVERSITY OF CHICAGO PRESS, CHICAGO 60637
The University of Chicago Press, Ltd., London

© 1936 by The University of Chicago. All rights reserved
Published 1936. Ninth Impression 1972. Printed in the
United States of America

International Standard Book Number: 0–226–51662–8 (clothbound)
Library of Congress Catalog Card Number: 36–9407

PREFATORY NOTE

AS YET, comparatively little has been done by way of synthetic studies of nineteenth-century thought as a whole. This situation is aggravated in that what is available for the use of the student, or other interested persons, is of relatively little value because of lack of time, lack of training, or other reasons. To date, the most extensive single work on this period is Merz's four-volume work *History of European Thought in the Nineteenth Century*. But of this work the length alone makes its widespread use unlikely, and in some instances unfeasible, except for specific problems considered apart from their wider significance. Added to this is the difficult nature of the text. It is so detailed, so complex, as of course the thought of the century was, that the uninitiated are apt to find it more baffling than helpful. On the other hand, some work of a more popular nature has been done, but largely by French and German writers. Much of this material is untranslated, and so relatively unavailable to a large number of persons who would otherwise make use of it. Again, not a small part of the bibliography on the nineteenth century relates to works on particular phases of the thought of the period. Among these are Royce's *The Spirit of Modern Philosophy*, Lévy-Bruhl's excellent work on the *History of Modern Philosophy in France*, and Ruggiero's *European Liberalism*. These are limited in scope.

Thus Professor Mead's lectures on the "Movements of Thought in the Nineteenth Century" are peculiarly apt, for a number of reasons. They are inclusive. Even a brief perusal of the Table of Contents is sufficient to indicate the catholicity of their scope. I think it may truly be said that few significant thought developments have been neglected. The lectures are also relatively simple. Being designed, as they were, for undergraduate students in the University of Chicago, they are presented from a point of view which such students can readily grasp. This is a great boon to the general reader who wishes a picture of the thought of the century as a whole. Again, their development does not go into such detail as to hide general tendencies. Finally, Mr. Mead's penchant for turning old problems around in such a way as to bring new light on them keeps his lectures from being repetitious. These factors all lead to the cumulative value which these lectures have as one goes through them. One cannot read them with any care without having a real sense of what went on in the century immediately before our own.

Of course, when these lectures were given, Mr. Mead had not designed them for publication. They are classroom lectures, reported in the form of student notes—but of an exceptionally complete and exact nature. They have the value and deficiencies of the purpose for which they were intended. In this case, however, the former completely outweigh the latter. Perhaps, had Mr. Mead himself prepared them for publication, they might have been presented in a somewhat different form. It is, I think, unlikely that he would have made any significant changes—the material is too good as it stands. These lectures make up a course that was presented numerous times. In this process they were subject to constant growth of insight and consequent revision. Thus, it is no idle statement to say that they represent their author's mature views. As the reader of them in their present form will discover for himself, these views are worthy of conscientious study.

At least in part, the publication of this volume grows out of Mr. Mead's untimely death. He had, during his life, been peculiarly unwilling to solidify his thought in the form of published works. It seemed regrettable, however, that a mind of such penetration, such power, one that had such an influence on colleagues, students, and friends, should be left without record for posterity. Thus, under the instigation of his son, Dr. Henry Mead, and his daughter-in-law, Dr. Irene Tufts Mead, plans were made to collect available material suitable for publication. This was undertaken in conjunction with the Drs. Mead and, at their request, by Professor Arthur E. Murphy. At his suggestion I was asked to co-operate with the plan through the editing of notes on the nineteenth century.

With the exception of the second half of the chapter on Bergson, the material of the book is taken from stenographic notes prepared for Mr. Alvin Carus. It is one of a number of sets of such notes taken for him in various courses offered by Mr. Mead. No one could have asked for better material with which to work. Changes of content were almost wholly unnecessary. The bulk of the problem was one of mechanical rearrangement of material into chapters. This presented some difficulty. Mr. Mead had a very effective teaching habit of advancing cyclically through his subject matter. The result was a good deal of repetition. But each time he came back to a problem it was set in a slightly new frame. In editing the material, there has been a question as to how far this repetition should be retained and to what extent the notes should be condensed and carried along without backtracking. Both methods have been used, I trust with some degree of success.

Half of the material for chapter xiv on Henri Bergson is from notes of Mr. George A. Pappas. These were not stenographic, and the difficulty in regard to their use was increased. It was necessary to fill them out, to complete unfinished sentences, and, in some cases, to guess at the meaning and significance of brief notations. This led to a dual difficulty. On the one hand, I wished to be true to Mr. Mead's point of view. At the same time I had to remember that it was Bergson who was being interpreted and that it was necessary to avoid obvious misrepresentations of his position. I trust I have had reasonable success in meeting these demands. In so far as possible, I have tried to phrase this material as Mr. Mead would have.

The character of these notes very aptly brings us to a discussion of the value of student notes in general as we have utilized them in this volume and in the preservation of other of Mr. Mead's material. The problem hardly arises in connection with

Mr. Murphy's preparation of the Carus Lectures. These lectures were given with the intention of expansion and later publication. This Mr. Mead's untimely death precluded, and it was necessary that the task be completed by another. No such situation existed in the case of the series of which this is a part. It is true that after his death great quantities of notes and papers in various stages of completion were found among Mr. Mead's effects. There was no indication that any of them were being arranged for publication, however. What justification is there, then, for our having undertaken their preservation in this form, other than that of sentimentality?

My answer to that question is dual. On the one hand, there is the matter of historical precedent. It is a fact more or less widely known among students of philosophic works that, but for the utilization of student notes and other material prepared primarily for classroom purposes, many of our philosophical classics would not exist. This is the case specifically with at least part of our collections of the works of Epictetus, Aristotle, Leibnitz, Kant, Fichte, and Hegel. Certainly, then, to utilize such notes is not to exceed the bounds of decorum. Furthermore, it is doubtful if much, or any, of the subject matter gathered from the material of the writers mentioned above had the great virtue of being stenographic. With the single exception referred to, all the notes utilized in the preparation of this volume, and most, if not all, that composing the contents of the others of this series, may be regarded as verbatim recordings of Mr. Mead's lectures. The amount of error in such transcription is relatively slight, consisting primarily in such details as misspelled names, and so on, which a little care enables one to detect and to correct. I think we may ignore any criticism of our procedure, so far as this ground is concerned.

The other justification for the preservation of the material in published form is to be found in its worth as throwing light on the problems with which it deals. Here our evaluation cannot be so objective. In this connection I can simply repeat what I have said earlier in this Preface. It is a fact that Mr. Mead did not specifically intend the publication of this material as it now stands. It was the consensus of opinion among his students and his colleagues that it should be published. In this opinion his family and friends concurred. This is, I concede, not an unimpeachable argument for proceeding with their publication. It certainly gives an initial probability to the judgment that they contain material which is, and will continue to be, of value to students of philosophic problems. The nature and source of the contents has been specifically indicated. Having this in mind, the reader must make his final evaluation for himself. There is no question about this being the work of an original mind. We might wish Mr. Mead himself had put it in final form. That wish is vain. Even in its present form, the material has that suggestive and interpretative value of which I have spoken above.

My debt to Drs. Henry and Irene Mead and to Mr. Murphy for considering me in connection with this undertaking I cannot estimate. If, when I first started on the work, I was not as great an admirer of Mr. Mead as were some others of his students and colleagues (both of which it was my good fortune to be), my rereading and re-working of these lectures has made me that. I am also grateful to Mr. Charles W. Morris, particularly for placing at my disposal material that he gathered after he took up the work when Mr. Murphy left the University of Chicago, and for valuable assistance and corrections in the preparation of the manuscript.

I wish also to acknowledge my debt to my wife and to Miss Edna Lorraine Evans for assistance in preparing the manuscript. The preparation of the final typewritten copy was the work of Miss Lucille Hogan and Miss Gertrude Venable. The Index is the work of Mr. Vincent Tomas.

To my friend and colleague, Dr. L. W. Elder, I wish to express an especial indebtedness.

MERRITT HADDEN MOORE

KNOX COLLEGE

INTRODUCTION

WHILE it would certainly be an oversimplification, it would not be a misstatement to say the thesis which underlies these lectures, and which Mr. Mead is most interested in bringing home to his reader is this: Science, with its demand for freedom, with its demand for the substitution of rational authority for the arbitrary authority which characterized the medieval period, is the outstanding fact not simply of the nineteenth century but of all thought since, and including the Renaissance, for modern science brought in the Renaissance itself. If one gets the full import of what is meant by this statement, one will have discovered the key through which entry may be made into the new approaches which Mr. Mead brings to the study of the movements of thought and also to his original, and sometimes abstruse, contributions to philosophic thought. One finds a continuous flow of such statements as this: Science is the surest knowledge we have. A striking feature of his analysis of social movements is his analogy between procedure in these fields and in what we regard as the sciences properly so-called. For example the doctrines of Hobbes, Locke, and Rousseau are dealt with as alternative hypotheses in the effort to give a scientific theory of the state. In each case departure is made from laws thought to be universal. To these, exceptions are found. In the light of these exceptions we must make a modification of our hypotheses. The genius of the research thinker is, however, that, instead of waiting to have the exceptional instance turn up, he bends his whole energy to ferreting out particular cases for an explanation of which our accepted theory is inadequate. A swift review of the development of Mr. Mead's analysis of the correlation of thought movements in the century with which our immediate study is concerned will indicate that he neatly exemplifies his thesis.

I

Since I have indicated the central place of research science in Mr. Mead's thought, the reader will not be surprised if I point out that in this particular set of lectures the development centers around the problem of methodology. A traditional story about Mr. Mead's courses that was handed down from one generation of students to another at the University of Chicago was that he always went back to Aristotle and, if any particular class was lucky, it might have the good fortune of having him finally get through to contemporary problems, the implication clearly being that he seldom did so. Needless to say, that was an exaggeration. However, his analysis of movements in the nineteenth century does begin with medieval thought, and it might quite as well have gone back to Aristotle, for it begins with a statement of the substance-attribute relation which was the foundation of Aristotelian science. This concept plays the dual rôle of a background against which the nineteenth-century metaphysics is developed, founded, as it is, on the subject-object relation, and as the ground of serious problems which serve as the soil in which the thought of the last century took root and found nourishment.

The rationalism which colors European thought since 1600, and which pervades our contemporary scientific period through the assumptions of the knowability of nature, of the uniformity of nature, and, consequently of the universality of natural laws, is rooted in medieval theology. Picturing the universe as carrying out the purposes of a divine, rational being, any irrational element was excluded automatically, since God not only was intelligent but had the power to make his intelligence effective. From this source come the rationalistic characteristics of modern science. Galileo, Copernicus, Kepler, and Newton, to mention only four, applied mathematics to the universe with an almost naïve trust. Mathematics, the most rational of our disciplines, would fit a rational world.

This worked in two directions. On the one hand it led to a rather remarkable success in the study of physical processes. On the other hand it led to the bifurcation of nature. The church was unconcerned with the physical world. This world was merely the stage on which the drama of man's salvation was played. And the play was the thing. The scientist could muddle around with the material to his heart's content so long as his theories did not trespass on the domain of the soul, did not carry over into the realm of values. Methodologically, Galileo and his successors found values were irrelevant to their study. They ignored them as subjective. Under the double impulsion referred to above, values were taken from the world and made subjective, put into men's heads. This attitude, which made the physical world rational and mathematical, but which left the realm of values, including man's moral life and freedom, as attributes of soul stuff, was made into a philsophy by Descartes. But what had been started was not to be so easily stopped. Carrying the logic of the situation through to its inexorable conclusion, the empiricist reduced the attributes of the physical world to the same status that Descartes had reduced values. Primary, as well as secondary, qualities became attributes not of physical but of spiritual substance. Ending with the annihilating skepticism of Hume, the rational universe of science, with its universal and necessary principles, and the soul, the bearer now of all attributes, became nothing more than the habitual association of certain ideas of a perceiver. The substance of the soul having been wiped out, the attributes no longer had any ground to adhere to.

To this problem, Immanuel Kant proposed an answer, but it did not take the form of a reinstatement of substances. The basis for the universality and necessity required by a rational science is found in the mind itself. Man, the subject having certain experience, not a substance bearing certain attributes, imposes on his experiences certain forms which make them rational. True, Kant limited the application of these forms to phenomena and was himself a skeptic, as far as the possibility of knowledge of the noumena was concerned. We can—indeed, our practical, active needs require that we must—postulate certain things of the realm which lies behind the experienced. The formal character of phenomenal knowledge saved science, for, on the basis of the forms of the mind, it was again possible to defend the notion of universal and necessary truths as applied to experience. But such a science is phenomenalistic.

What of values? Kant felt impelled to make judgments in this field as universal as our phenomenal judgments. It is this aspect of his system that brings Mr. Mead to speak of him as the philosopher of the revolution, a rather startling thing to say of the staid and orderly little German professor.

Let us go back a moment. When the scientist of the Renaissance carried over from the teachings of the church the notion of a rational universe, he posited this as an assumption. He set it up as a postulate for the guidance of his thinking. But he came more and more to realize its postulational character. When the church had set up this same concept, it had framed it in the form of an arbitrary dogma. As such it was imposed on the thought of the time. The essence of the conflict which is referred to in the general term "the revolution" is the conflict between the rational authority of the budding science and the arbitrary authority of the church.

Applied to society, this means simply that man tried to find in human nature itself the rational basis for the state and all correlative human institutions. The older theory was that kings served by divine right. The church was God's agent on earth. Therefore the church could dictate on social and political matters. Its authority was arbitrary, it rested on the church's relation to God. There was no basis for an appeal above that authority; it was arbitrary. The revolution challenged that authority and endeavored to substitute in place of it a rational authority; it attempted to show that the order of society flowed from the rational nature of man, and from the rational character of society itself. This is the way out for Hobbes, Locke, and Rousseau. Such a solution is impossible, however, unless it can be shown that man's volitions have a rational character. When Hume seemingly destroyed the universal character of such volitions by reducing to a set of habitual associations the rational substance in which such values and volitions inhered, he sounded the death knell of the revolution. Man could not build a rational state on the basis of his own rational nature because his so-called "universal and necessary" principles were mere habits of thinking. Therefore, when Kant gave new foundation to the universality of scientific judgments, he saved rationalism; when he went on to give universality to man's volitions, to values, he saved the revolution. On the basis of Kant's philosophy, a rational order or society became possible, and for the arbitrary authority of the church or any other institution could be substituted a rational authority based on human nature.

In making man a sovereign, in making him a lawgiver, Kant not only justifies a movement that had gone before and was rapidly coming to a head in the French Revolution, he also laid the basis for future development. Historically, the political revolution failed. With this failure came the endeavor to turn the clock back, to recapture the past with its values, its order, its seeming stability. This attempt is romanticism. The failure to build an actual society on the foundation of liberty, equality, and fraternity led to a sense of defeat. To offset this, efforts were made to transplant the past into the present.

In the field of thought this took the form of an attempt to interpret the present in terms of what had gone before. Men could not get back to the past because, for better or for worse, they had lived through the experience of revolution. They could not see the old order as it had been seen by those who lived in it. That made them aware of two things. On the one hand, they became sensitized to themselves; they became self-conscious of their predicament. On the other hand, they saw themselves as the outgrowth of what had gone before.

When they attempted to formulate this position in theoretical terms, they found that Kant offered suitable concepts. In the first place, Kant re-established the objectivity of experience through the nature of the self. The self legislates; it makes its world. Men had lost their moorings in the defeat of the revolutionary hope. They no longer felt at home in their world. They were strangers to the present and sought solace in the old order which, though arbitrary, was nevertheless rational. But lo— were one to follow Kant, he could have a rational world, for the world is what we make it to be. We, as selves, determine what the world is; it is the objectification of ourselves. In the words of Schelling, man and nature are identical. Thus man is as much at home with the universe as he is at home with himself, and since man is rational the universe will be also.

In the second place, with the emphasis on the self the notion of activity, of process, of development and evolution, begins to replace the earlier picture of static forms. The categories of subject and object replace those of substance and attribute as the ultimate metaphysical concepts; the notions of change and development replace those of static forms and universal types. This latter is beyond Kant. We are now in the company of the romanticists. Yet, it was Kant's emphasis on the rôle of the self as giving universality to experience that made this development possible. That he rejected it in the repudiation of his disciple Fichte simply indicates he failed to see the implications of his own position. The problem posed by the skepticism of Hume, and which Kant met with his critical philosophy, was answered by the romanticists through the identification of the object of knowledge with the self in the very process of knowing. Nature and man are one. The self and the not-self, reason and nature, are one whether regarded from the point of moral experience, as in Fichte, or of the aesthetic experience, as in Schelling, or of the logical experience, as in Hegel. Nature develops through processes identical to those through which the self develops.

The transition from Kant to Hegel is a shift from an explanation of the world in terms of static forms to one utilizing the notion of an evolutionary process. For Hegel, the formal principles through the medium of which experience becomes intelligible give way to a process through which the forms themselves arise in the course of experience. The logic of the new direction in thinking is one of a dynamic process rather than one of fixed quantities. In other words, the Romantic idealists were doing within the field of philosophy what Lamarck and Darwin were doing for biology.

The science of the Renaissance was based upon the problem of the juxtaposition of simple physical particles as these were brought together and torn apart as a result of motion. That these combinations were manifest in groupings having the characteristics of common objects distinguishable from one another through their forms was entirely irrelevant to this earlier statement. The forms of trees, stones, persons, are imposed on the physical elements arbitrarily. They have no significance in the interpretation of physical reality. What the theory of evolution gives is a description of the process through which the forms themselves arise. As Mr. Mead points out, the title of one of Darwin's books was *The Origin of Species*, in other words, the origin of forms. The earlier science based on the ultimates of matter and motion was saved, after Hume's destructive blast, by Kant, who said that the form of objects is a projection in experience of certain forms native to the mind itself. This leaves us with the possibility of a phenomenal science but without any clue as to the nature of things-in-themselves. The Romantic and absolute idealists who follow Kant find the nature of the thing-in-itself in the unfolding of our experience. Darwin and Lamarck carry the same general idea over into the problem of the appearance of forms in the biological world as a consequent of a life-process which is constant but which adapts itself from time to time in such a way as to enable it to persist under changed conditions. Each of these men has his own theory as to how the adaptation occurs. They agree in the fact of a constant life-process with the particular forms of any given era dependent upon the conditions under which the life-process goes on at any given time.

This same general notion receives further philosophic development in vitalism, the most recent comprehensive statement of which is to be found in the position of the contemporary

French philosopher Henri Bergson. Thus the idea of evolution gradually becomes completely general and bids fair to supplant in all fields of thought both the Aristotelian science of fixed forms and the early mechanical science of matter and motion; it becomes a basic assumption applicable to every problem from the development of the physical world to that of political societies.

II

Turning to another phase of the development of ideas in the nineteenth century, Mr. Mead traces the correlation between problems in the field of social and economic phenomena and other phases of scientific development. Here particularly we find exemplified the author's ability to restate the relations among the various factors of a movement in such a way as to throw the whole problem into a new perspective. Rejecting the common association of the Industrial Revolution with the discovery of large deposits of easily available coal and iron, coupled with the unaccountable increase of inventive genius, Mr. Mead shows us these diverse roots of the movement: the expansion of markets, due, on the one hand to the opening of new fields through the explorations that marked the early modern period and continued through the movements toward empire, and, on the other hand, to a sudden rather unaccountable increase in the population of Europe; changes in the agricultural practices of England which released numerous peasants from the land and made them available for labor of other types; the appearance of factory towns as a result of taking production out of the home and bringing the means of production together in plants where the division of labor and the application of increasingly adequate machinery made it possible to turn out goods in sufficient quantities to meet the growing demand.

Out of the new situation two expressions of the scientific temper of the modern age arise. One of these is the development of an economic theory and a social theory capable of accounting for the new phenomena; the other, the appearance of new scientific concepts which meet needs arising in the invention of new processes of production.

In the work of Adam Smith and of Malthus we find the roots from which the orthodox economic theory flowered. According to the former, the market is a point of exchange of goods in which each party to the exchange profits, in the sense that he gives something he has but does not want for something the other party to the bargain has and in turn does not want. With their release from the land an increasingly large number of men had their ability to work (their labor) to exchange for money (for wages). No longer being bound to a lord or to the land, as he had been in the feudal society, the individual could sell his labor in the market in return for the money which he needed and wanted. Theoretically, this was a situation in which a bargain was reached which was to the advantage of both parties. But Malthus indicated this: the tendency is for population to increase geometrically while the increase in the food supply is only arithmetical. Thus, since labor is one of the costs of production, and since, in the interests of profits, the cost of production must be reduced as much as possible, the tendency is for labor to underbid its competition, with the result that soon the price of labor has been forced down to a starvation level. The outlook from the point of view of orthodox theory was, therefore, very dismal.

However, this theory is inadequate. It breaks down at two points: man can consciously control population increase and the production of food; through voluntary organizations of workers it becomes possible also to keep wages above the starvation level. Out of these inadequacies of the orthodox view arise two social philosophies of significance—utilitarianism and the socialistic theory of Karl Marx. In these Mr. Mead sees the attitude of research science at work again. Science advances through the conflict of universals, "theories," with "brute facts." This relationship is discoverable in this problem. The difference between the two suggested answers lies mainly in their direction. The utilitarians, with the background of English empiricism, which had reduced scientific laws to the psychological habits of association, was an opportunistic philosophy of society which gave a very practical rule of thumb for distinguishing what of that carried over from the past should be retained and what should be rejected. Marx's theory is more ambitious. A fusion of Hegelian metaphysics and the orthodox economic doctrine, Marx's position points to the dialectic of the economic process. This process leads inevitably to a revolution in which workers, aware of the international character of their problems, unite throughout the world to set up a new social order. As Mr. Mead points out, that movement lost ground seriously in the nationalistic disaffection of socialists in 1914. He also indicates the scientific inadequacy of this movement by calling attention to the fact that socialism never accurately depicted either the actual conditions or the actual wishes of the laborer. It thus becomes one more social theory, perfectly legitimate as such, which breaks down against particular facts. Out of this breakdown arises a new conception and the replacement of revolutionary socialism by the liberal doctrine of social evolution.

What Mr. Mead especially wants us to see in this connection is that our thinking takes the same form whether in the field of economic or political theory or in that of science properly so called. In each case we start with some theory, some universal. This we retain and extend until such time as we find some particular fact which does not conform to the law, or the hypothesis as it is given. The result is a modification of the theory so that it deals adequately with the exceptional instance, where this is possible, or, if such modification is impossible, to the rejection of the theory.

Laws of this sort are clearly of a type distinct from those formulated under the inspiration of absolutism and authority. The laws of science are not dogmas: they are postulates. The method of research science always conflicts with fixed dogmas; and, as Mr. Mead is anxious to have us see, so far the former has always been successful whenever these two methods have had occasion to lock horns.

The Industrial Revolution touches science in another way too. When the entrepreneur began to use the extensive application of machinery to meet his productive needs, he found that he was in want of some concept which would enable him to discover the comparative efficiency of different machines, various forms of power, and so forth. In other words, he needed a general concept of the unit of work. With this incentive, the problem was attacked by the scientists of the period; and the outcome of their activity was the formulation of the idea of energy. This concept, now one of the most significant and extensively applied in the whole gamut of scientific notions, made its appearance as a bookkeeping conception of the physical world! It enabled the producer to compare his alternative means of production, his sources of power, in terms of the units of work available in each.

Instances might be pointed out at some length of this sort of reciprocal stimulus in which the scientist has found his incentive in a problem posed by the producer, and, on the other hand, where the entrepreneur has applied to his problems information discovered by the scientist in the solution of his problems. These we will disregard, for there remain two other ramifications of modern scientific thought which must be indicated.

As was pointed out when we indicated that the roots of our idea of a rational world go back to the Middle Ages, the modern scientist is committed to the thesis that the world can be understood. The most common formulation of this commitment is found in the statement and acceptance of laws of nature. The success which has attended the reduction of natural phenomena to basic uniformities has led to the postulation of an explanation of the world in which each event is determined by its relation to others. This has led commonly to the assumption that the extension of scientific knowledge implies a mechanistic philosophy which reduces man, as everything else, to a phase in a process carried on inevitably and unavoidably. At this point Mr. Mead protests with the rather unique, and somewhat paradoxical, view that the more the processes of nature can be described in terms of laws, the greater is man's freedom. This follows from the fact that our control over nature is proportionate with our understanding of it. Mechanical science does not mechanize human conduct. Rather, it gives man freedom; for the more we know of the processes governing our environment, the greater is our ability to get control over it. Thus, instead of being the end of attempts to explain man and his institutions in terms of ends, mechanical science becomes a guaranty of the successful attainment of those ends. The reason this seeming paradox can be maintained carries us back to an appreciation of what modern science is doing. Research science approaches problems. In its attempt to solve its problems, it uses certain postulates. It does not, however, present these postulates as a systematic account of the world in any particular aspect. The concepts it employs are recognized solely because of their fruitfulness.

Out of this phase of the scientific attitude develops the second point of influence mentioned above. Science has given rise to philosophic movements. In the nineteenth century both pragmatism and realism arise out of science. The former relates to the method of science. In the preceding paragraph it was said that science recognized certain concepts because of their fruitfulness. Couple with that another characteristic of science since the Renaissance, the utilization of observation to discover the "brute fact" which makes necessary the modification of scientific concepts, and you have the background out of which developed William James's radical empiricism on the one hand and John Dewey's instrumentalism on the other. Such other forms of Pragmatism as that of Hans Vaihinger spring more directly from previous philosophical movements, notably the metaphysic of English empiricism and the phenomenalism of Immanuel Kant's theory of knowledge. Among these various forms of the pragmatic position, Mr. Mead's own thought attaches definitely to those which spring from an analysis of what is involved in research science.

But, besides pragmatism, another type of philosophy—modern realism—springs directly from modern science. Here an attempt of a definitely philosophic sort is made to supplement scientific conclusions. It has already been indicated that the scientist as such makes no attempt to give any systematic account of the universe as a whole or of any particular aspect of it based on his postulates, on his observations, or on his conclusions. But the human mind has always wished to know more; it has always sought some statement of the nature of the universe either as a whole or in its different aspects. The realist of the nineteenth century and of our own generation is among those who make the attempt to supply the answer to this reputedly more ultimate question.

In the lecture in which he deals with realism Mr. Mead stresses particularly a rather special phase of this movement, its interest in logic, an interest reflected especially in the work of Mr. Bertrand Russell and Mr. Alfred North Whitehead. The logic of traditional rationalism had been concerned with formal, classificatory aspects of reality. This goes back to Aristotle. During the nineteenth century, however, the question of logic became a matter of vital concern as reflecting central hopes and ends of various movements. Romanticism, for example, comes to an articulate head in the idealistic, dynamic logic of Hegel; pragmatism finds its intellectual feet in the utilitarian or instrumentalistic logic of Mr. John Dewey.

Realism is interested in a very different approach to the problem of reality than either of the movements just mentioned. Recognizing the two phases of experience, the formal and the material, the realist proposes to deal with the formal without reducing it, as the English empiricists and Kant had, either to associated states of consciousness or to forms characteristic of, and projected by the mind itself. The realist conceived of the forms as relations existing objectively. These relations are "out there" quite as much as the object related. We think them; but that would be impossible if there were not something there to be thought. The logical interest of the realist becomes, therefore, an interest in breaking up the object of knowledge into its various elements, together with the connections or relations that hold them together. The logical forte of realism is analysis. Thus appears again the problem of the individual. To the consideration of this problem Mr. Mead devotes the last chapter of the book, making it also the point of introduction of the contemporaneously important idea of relativity. Here Mr. Mead leans toward Mr. Whitehead rather than toward Mr. Russell.

III

So I have attempted to indicate some of the ways in which Mr. Mead's analysis of the thought movements of the nineteenth century centers around the scientific movement of the period, the movement which gives the key for interpreting this rich and complex period. In the following sections of this Introduction two things remain to be noted. In the first place, we must discover what phases of the thought of the period have not been included. Secondly, and primarily for those who read this volume without having read *The Philosophy of the Present*, edited by Mr. A. E. Murphy, and *Mind, Self, and Society*, edited by Mr. C. W. Morris, some hint must be given as to what is involved in Mr. Mead's notion of the past and his theory of the self, both of which are significantly referred to in the present work.

Perhaps the most important of the omissions is the lack of any mention of the pessimists, Nietzsche and Schopenhauer, and of the movement known as "positivism." The latter omission is somewhat cared for in the material which forms the Appendix of this volume. In the analysis of French philosophy August Comte, at least, is given a fairly adequate treatment. Of course, it is, to a certain extent, true that positivism exerted a rather local and temporary influence. Yet, as expressed by Saint-Simon and Comte, it indicated a live interest in the philosophic implications of the success of the methods of science, particularly as these bore on the possibility of a true scientific approach to the problems of society. These interests are congenial to Mr. Mead; and yet for some reason, on which speculation would be both in vain and useless, he neglected this doctrine in his analysis of nineteenth-century movements as a whole.

It is trite to indicate that the present volume makes no pretense of such catholicity as is found in Merz's monumental, four-volume work on *History of European Thought in the Nineteenth Century*. Apparently, Mr. Mead saw the purpose of his course as twofold. On the one hand, he wished to demonstrate the organic continuity of ideas. Therefore he emphasized the significance of the thought of the Renaissance for the period we are considering. He also wished to select from the numerous fields and developments in the last century the tendencies which particularly demarcated the genius of that period and which carry over into the present scene. To do this in a course of approximately forty-five lectures is something of a task. On the other hand, as I had already indicated, Mr. Mead's thought centers primarily around the development of research science and the ramifications of this discipline in other fields. These limits are indicated not with an intention to censure but only to assist the reader in his orientation to the material which follows.

Nonetheless, one is struck with the absence of any mention of Nietzsche and Schopenhauer. As reflecting the negative side of Romantic and absolute idealism, the least that can be said is that they exerted a widespread influence in the last century. If one may apply the Hegelian dialectic to the question, one may say that Schopenhauer is the antithesis which carries Hegelianism itself into a position demanding a new synthesis. No doubt both thinkers would have rebelled at being thus intimately linked together in the inexorable logic of a system. Within limits, it is no doubt true that Hegel thought of his own philosophy as the crowning synthesis. On the other hand, Schopenhauer did not take kindly to his neglect by the optimistic idealists who were his contemporaries. Yet, it is not an injustice to treat his pessimism as Romantic idealism's negative side.

A further significance of Schopenhauer's thought is indicated succinctly by Mr. De Witt H. Parker in the Introduction to his little volume of selections from Schopenhauer's writings.[1] In this statement he indicates a very real influence of Schopenhauer on the contemporary representative of the philosophy of irrationalism, M. Henri Bergson. Whether or not there is direct influence of the sort indicated by Mr. Parker, irrationalism is a persistent tendency and is deserving of a consideration usually minimized by those sharing the more usual predilection to rationalism. To have failed to deal with Schopenhauer seems like a real oversight.

Mr. Mead mentions neo-Kantianism and the newer idealistic movements in Germany, England, and America, only to indicate that Hegel remained a force in the latter two countries after his influence had died out in Germany. Fechner, Paulsen, Windelband, Eucken, Münsterberg, T. H. Green, Bradley, and Bosanquet are scarcely mentioned. Wundt appears in his rôle as one of the founders of modern, experimental psychology, a movement to the consideration of which Mr. Mead devotes a considerable amount of space. Along with these individuals may be cited the neglect of the study of value which is rooted in this period and is a focal point of heated discussion in our generation. The field of aesthetics is scarcely touched, and then primarily as related to the metaphysical connotations of Schelling's philosophy. Ethical theory is mentioned only where it appears as an adjunct of considerations of dominant social and political theories. The development of French philosophy receives attention only in the material incorporated as an Appendix.

As a treatise dealing with movements of thought other than philosophic, as it does wherever these illustrate the genius of research science, the following omissions should be noted. Beyond the use of their material to indicate the advance of scientific method, Mr. Mead does not trace the details in the development of physical and biological theories of the period.

[1] *Schopenhauer: Selections*, edited by De Witt H. Parker (New York: Charles Scribner's Sons).

INTRODUCTION

The philosophic offshoot of the emphasis on evolutionary ideas —vitalism—is dealt with significantly only as it appears in the work of M. Henri Bergson. This is a little odd, for in some ways this movement, centering around Eucken, Fechner, and Driesch on the Continent, and appearing also in England in the latter part of the century, is significantly and peculiarly related to certain forces at work during this era. Mathematical theory is unmentioned except as related to recent developments in logical theory. Theories of education and of the state appear only as related to social, political, and economic ideas. Movements in literature and art in general receive attention only as illustrative material.

Again let me indicate that these omissions are mentioned, not as criticisms, but solely to indicate to the reader points at which the present work will need to be supplemented.

IV

We come now to the final sections of this Introduction, in which we shall attempt to give some indication of the meaning of Mr. Mead's doctrines in regard to the nature of the self and of the past. These are treated respectively in the volumes edited by Mr. Murphy and by Mr. Morris, which were mentioned above. Since they both play a part in the development of the ideas of the present volume, some attention must be given them here. Had one asked Mr. Mead what problems were of peculiar interest to him, and with which he found himself led to deal in something other than the usual way, he might well have indicated the problem of the nature of the self and the problem of the past.

As a study dealing with thought in the preceding century, this volume must reflect, at least by implication, Mr. Mead's theory of the past. The pursuit of history brings one inevitably into intimate grips not only with the past as a fact but also with the whole question of evidence, of divergent interpretations, of the continuity of movements from one period to another, and so on. True to the basic approach to the problem with which this series of lectures is concerned, he treats the problem of the past as an instance of the application of the methods of research science. At least in the primary conception of his theory on this matter, the statement that each generation recreates the past, that for each age a new and different Caesar crosses the Rubicon, must have come to Mr. Mead from his awareness that theories of historical interpretation are broken on the same type of exception, of "brute fact," that gives rise to problems in scientific research. Our knowledge of the past is transmitted in the form of theories, of universals, just as the knowledge of nature is transmitted under the form of natural laws. In each field the discovery of new data, the uncovering of new monuments, bring exceptional cases which require that our concepts be reconstructed. The study of history, the problem of the past, thus becomes nothing more or less than a single instance of the scientific approach to any problem whatsoever.

Perhaps in the present volume this character of the past is best evidenced in the treatment of romanticism. In its attempt to turn the clock back, to catch again and give living expression to the spirit of the Middle Ages, romanticism illustrates Mr. Mead's contention that the past exists for either an individual or an age only in so far as they project themselves back into the period in which they are interested. Now, such projection always presupposes a present experience. Thus, in the case of the romanticists, the return to the past carried with it the sense of defeat which followed the collapse of the revolution. Whether they liked it or not, they returned to the past sadder and wiser men. Having lived through the revolution and its failure, the men of the new day saw the earlier period as it was impossible for the medievalists themselves or for the exemplars of the life of reason, who followed them, to have seen it. Thus we see, first, that the romantic interpretation of the Middle Ages is different from the experience of that age by those who lived in it; secondly, that the romantic interpretation of the Middle Ages is markedly different from that of the Age of Enlightenment, which immediately preceded the period of the revolution.

INTRODUCTION

In this single case we not only see the impossibility of an identical past for successive ages; we also see that the process through which each period determines the nature of the past is simply the method of research science applied to a type of problem with which we do not ordinarily associate it. In other words, the problem of the past and of research science are one—the novelty being the particular, exceptional event which requires modification of our theory; the form being the theory, the universal which we posit as the condition of our having a thread, a guiding idea in our interpretation.

The position indicated here is not a denial of the past in the sense of a solipsistic absorption of the past and the future in the momentary experience of an instantaneous, "knife-edge" present. Just as the scientist recognizes that his researches deal with real objects, although admitting he does not know their nature completely, that his theories about them will be subject to continuous modification as new data are presented, and that in the end the object will be distinctly different from the object with which he started, so the student of the past, the historian in particular, is dealing with a series of events really antecedent to any particular present, but a series of events which is successively described in quite different terms as our interpretative theories change, as the experience of the race is accumulated, and as new data present themselves. In this process the new past is different from the old, just as for the scientist the new object differs from the one it replaces. In neither case is the problem simply that of seeing what is "out there." Seeing, in any significant sense, depends upon our looking, and looking reflects the whole system of interests, theories, purposes, and ideals that leads us to seek one, rather than another, nature in the thing under consideration. This is true of all phases of scientific research as it is of all human endeavor. Completely impartial observation is never achieved. The dice are always loaded in favor of some preference. No matter how rigidly we may attempt to check and counterbalance the personal equation, our considerations are guided by theories which we expect to have to modify or to completely reject. Indeed, Mr. Mead indicates one aspect of the research method as involving conscientious efforts to break down the very theories which guide our investigations at any given time. In connection with the theory of the past, Mr. Mead does not deny the fact of pastness. He never suggests any alternative to the fact that a real Caesar crossed a real Rubicon. What he does insist upon is that for each age there is a different Caesar and a different Rubicon, because of divergent ideational backgrounds with the resultant projection on the past of different interpretative hypotheses.

Belonging, as he does, to the group closely associated with Mr. Dewey, and having been deeply influenced by the early works of Mr. Whitehead, Mr. Mead had no place for an absolute, static time composed of an infinite number of distinct and separate "knife-edge." moments. Time is a process. As process, it is change. The past is a part of time. Since what is true of the whole is true also of its parts, the past, too, must be characterized by fluidity, by change. If one agrees with Mr. Mead in giving up the absolutistic notion of time which we inherit from the nineteenth century, one has no alternative but to accept the consequences of this shift of position; one must acquiesce to some sort of relativism. It is in part this substitution of relativism for absolutism in the interpretation of concrete temporal experience that makes Mr. Mead's doctrine seem, at least at first, so strange and difficult to understand. Most of us have not caught the full implications in the shift of point of view. Or we may see and accept rationally what is involved in the change without having as yet made our emotional peace with the new approach. Relativism is not, as yet, a part of our unconsciously accepted assumptions. We still fit into the absolutistic niche of the preceding century. Should the new movement, which was so strong in the first quarter of our century, permeate our thinking as that of Newton did the thinking of our forebears, a new *Zeitgeist* will become manifest which will accept, as self-evident, theories which give us pause.

In any case, we can admit the practical significance of

INTRODUCTION

Mr. Mead's doctrine: history exists only to the extent that individuals put themselves back into the past; this being the case, there is no alternative to the conclusion that the past as an object of historical study differs from age to age, for the individuals of any given period never bring to their criticism the same background, the same interests, the same accumulation of racial experience as do the individuals of different periods.

V

We come now to Mr. Mead's treatment of the problem of the self. This problem is the subject matter of the volume edited by Mr. Morris as the first of the group of which this is the second. The problem is also considered at some length in the material composing the present volume, where we meet it in two connections, first in the analysis of the Romantic movement, which, as we have just seen, also throws light on the problem of the past, and in a later chapter dealing with the problem of society, for in Mr. Mead's mind the processes of social movement and that of the development of selves were inseparable.

The crux of the author's doctrine of the self is the portrayal of the process through which the self appears as a result of the assumption of various rôles, first of one person, then of another, then of another. Out of this procedure one comes gradually to see one's own rôle as it is demarcated from those of other persons whose rôles one has temporarily assumed. Thus, self-awareness is achieved, for, by distinguishing its own rôle, its own part from the rôle of others, the self becomes conscious of itself as distinct from other selves. In this statement we see that Mr. Mead carries over into the study of this problem the modern emphasis upon a dynamic process as over against the ancient static statement. Just as he rejects the atomistic notion of "knife-edge" presents in the analysis of time, so he rejects the notion of isolated, atomic selves. Selves come into being through a process of self-conscious interaction and interpenetration with other selves.

At first sight this process may seem as difficult to understand as was the theory of the past in its first statement. As in the case of the latter, illumination comes through the exemplification of the process in the movement of thought; and once again, as I have already indicated, the Romantic movement is the point of departure.

The essence of romanticism is its attempt to turn back the clock, to clothe itself in the forms and ideas of the medieval period, to assume and play out the rôle of another age. This was achieved to the extent that a considerable amount of the trappings of the earlier period was brought out to be admired and worn again—if not actually, then vicariously through the literature and through the general ideas and ideals of the later period. The revolution had not brought about many physical changes in Germany; but the conquering armies of France, under the leadership of Napoleon, did bring them. At first, as a result of the infectious force of the enthusiastic and conquering Frenchmen, who, on their march away from Paris, enjoyed one sweeping victory after another, these changes were regarded as being all for the good. But, when the tide of battle turned, when the staggered, broken, bewildered horde moved back toward Paris after the defeat at Moscow, a very different feeling was engendered by their presence. The ideal had collapsed. The revolution had failed, together with all that it had set into motion. The present turned out to be a mean age, one of disillusionment, of disappointment. The sense of defeat weighed heavily on all those who had so recently given their souls to the forces emanating from France. With both their immediate past and their newborn hopes shattered and stripped away, men staked what hope remained on a return to a still more distant past, that of medieval feudalism.

Much as they desired this old order, much as they attempted to identify themselves with it, an inevitable difficulty stood in their way—they came back to this old order with different eyes. The revolution had failed; and the men who had seen this failure, who had shared in the defeat, could not have been unmarked by their experience. And they were not unmarked.

INTRODUCTION

They might put on medieval garb, they might emulate and eulogize the troubadours, they might in any number of ways attempt the desired identification; but they failed to attain it. They could put on the clothes, but they could not make them fit. The garments had been cut to the form and stature of another age, and they hung ill-fitting and awkward from new shoulders. It was like the play of children ransacking old trunks and putting on the finery, playing the rôles of another era. The result of such activity may be quaint, it may stir one's memory, but it remains incongruous—the old clothes do not belong. So the romanticists could turn back the clock, they could dig into the forgotten past and attempt its resurrection, but they could not belong to it. Yet, having made the experiment, having played the rôle of another time, they came back to their own age with a self-consciousness of their own position, of their own rôle that they would not otherwise have had. In trying to be someone else, they had collectively discovered themselves.

Here, in this historical movement, we find reflected what for Mr. Mead is the basic element in the development of the self. The self is a process. It is not an entity; it is an achievement. Not only do we become aware of ourselves, but we become selves only by assuming rôles, by playing the part of others. When a self has done this, it not only is in a position to criticize the self whose rôle it has taken, but—and this is the important point—it is also in a position to criticize itself. The other self becomes a standard of comparison, so to speak. When playing at being someone else, the self realizes its own nature at the same time it realizes the nature of the person whose rôle is being played.

In this connection one important difference between the philosophy of Mr. Mead and that of the romanticists must be noted. The latter found in this process a metaphysical theory in which the ultimate identification of the self and non-self in an absolute spirit became possible. For them this is not only the process of individual development but is identical with the movement which permeates and governs the whole universe.

The individual self thus becomes the universe writ small. Mr. Mead is not interested in the metaphysical connotations of the process. His interest is in the implications this view may hold for social psychology. He turns to the process indicated to discover the genesis of persons as distinct from biological organisms, to find the root of the socially important virtue of sympathy, and to indicate the development through which we as individuals become aware of social life. Again, as in his theory of science and in his doctrine of the past, he posits the existence of objects. The not-self, the other selves through the assumption of whose rôles the new self is generated, are not objects dependent upon the processes of a subject which plays its part. Indeed, it cannot be, for there must be other selves whose rôles can be taken before the business of taking rôles is conceivable. At this point the position we are considering breaks cleanly away from metaphysical doctrines.

In his treatment of the self Mr. Mead makes a great deal of what in grammar is called the "reflexive mood." This is the mood of self-awareness. The self has no significance unless it can turn back upon itself, can become its own object, distinguish itself in a milieu of other selves. Until this can be done, the self cannot be made significant for the psychological and sociological problems which are Mr. Mead's major concern at this point. That this self-awareness is not only possible but a fact he finds indicated in the achievement of a reflexive form in language, the form which recognizes the self as both subject and object of an experience.

Whatever one may finally come to think of this doctrine, one must recognize it as a fruitful hypothesis. With Mr. Mead's profound respect for the scientific method and for the technique and successes of research science, not only would he himself have thought of this position as a hypothesis, but he would have wished criticism of it to be made in this light. Its fruitfulness as a hypothesis is indicated especially in chapters xvi and xvii of the present volume.

The immediate implications of this theory for social psychology are at once apparent. It is only through the utilization of social media that selves appear at all. Indeed, it is not an overstatement to speak of the self as a society of selves. In the process of "playing at" one rôle and then another we not only become aware of our own rôle but find that we are potentially any one of the selves whose part we have been taking. This is shown overtly in the commonly recognized fact that in shifting from one social group to another we become "different" persons. This does not involve any elaborate theory of the dissociation of personality. The thing is much more common, much more normal, than the phenomenon indicated by that phrase. We notice in others and in ourselves that, in moving from one group to another, responses so divergent from those we call "normal" are induced that we say, with literal truth, the person in question is hardly recognizable as the same person in these various manifestations of his self, in the different rôles which divergent situations call out.

The ability to be a new person in this sense, however, goes back to the fact that the self involved has already become familiar with the part to be played. Each rôle has been taken previously in play, in mimicking, as a result of esteem or for some other reason, until the self gets the "feel" of a rôle and it may be assumed becomingly when circumstances call it forth. In this way the self is both enriched and made more flexible. Being a social milieu in miniature, the self can adapt itself to new situations in such a way as to make adequate social responses.

This matter of assuming rôles is significant in another connection also. Not only does "playing at" one person and then another enrich the social experience of the self involved; not only is this the medium through which the self becomes aware of its own nature in opposition to those other selves whose rôles it takes; it is also the basis for the sympathy which every social theory requires as the basis of co-operative effort toward socially desirable ends, a sympathy for which every theory of social psychology must give an account. The traditional device at this point is to have recourse to a social instinct, or to bifurcate behavior into acts motivated either by selfish or by altruistic desires. Each of these theories involves serious difficulties, as the history of personal and social ethics shows. On the basis of Mr. Mead's theory we have a possible solution of this difficulty also. In the process he describes, we not only play the part of other selves; we also become aware of their significance, of their difficulties, and of their limitations. Having at least vicariously put ourselves in the other person's shoes, we are in a position to sympathize with him. We have played his part, and we know what he has to face. We can put ourselves in his position again and again, and each time see how we would be affected by it, see what we would be likely to do if we were in his place. Consequently, we can understand his behavior. The more rôles we can assume in this fashion, the wider will be our sympathy, and the more significant will be our social responses. To be able to deal with this aspect of our behavior without having to have recourse to special instincts or other devices seems a real contribution to the social psychology of our times.

VI

There is one further point to be advanced as showing the worth of these various doctrines of Mr. Mead. One criterion commonly agreed upon for testing scientific theories is the way in which they correlate the findings of various fields. We have already indicated that the position developed in this group of lectures indicates a certain identity between the interpretation of historical movements and of social phenomena. For example, we pointed out that, historically, the social process is graphically represented in the Romantic movement. In the chapter on individualism this same theory of the development of selves is significantly applied to the problem of the individual. Furthermore, the same movements which indicate his social theory have done double service through illuminating Mr. Mead's doctrine of the past. One might go still further to indicate that these may all be related in two directions: first, through his acceptance of the method of research science as underlying all

INTRODUCTION

significant developments in thinking; and second, through his basic assumption that the description of experience in every field is to be made in terms of processes rather than in terms of absolutes. In this further step a still more pertinent unity is introduced into his whole thought structure, and such special unities as have been indicated above are derived rather than ultimate. In any case, the fact remains that the views presented in this volume do stand together in such a way that a grasp of that which pertains to one field will illuminate one's endeavor to see what Mr. Mead is driving at in some other connection.

MERRITT HADDEN MOORE

TABLE OF CONTENTS

CHAPTER I

FROM RENAISSANCE TO REVOLUTION

THE general political, social, and institutional background of the period of the Enlightenment is the Renaissance. The former falls in a general way in the eighteenth century. Immediately back of it lies the Renaissance and the philosophy of Descartes, Spinoza, and Leibnitz. The philosophy of the eighteenth century gathers particularly about a published presentation of Leibnitz' philosophy made by the German philosopher, Wolff. It was a somewhat superficial statement, and it presented the world from the point of view of what is termed "rationalism." There is one phase of this rationalism to which I particularly want to call your attention, namely, that it is an inheritance from an earlier period and came into European thought by way of Christianity. The conception of the world as a rational order came through the theology of the church. The doctrine was built around the gospel of Jesus and the conception of St. Paul when he undertook to formulate the Jewish theory in such a form that it would be made universal.

With the advent of Christianity came the conception of a world created by a God who was infinitely intelligent and who had infinite power. Everything that such a deity created, everything that he did, must be the expression of that intelligence, and nothing could resist its expression. You can see that there could be nothing accidental or irrational in such a world. Of course, it might not be rational to us. An infinite mind would have purposes and methods of which we could not conceive with our finite intelligence. Particularly there would be purposes which would be carried out in later periods. We cannot see what these purposes are. Therefore the world may appear to us to be irrational; but actually, having been created by an intelligence that has infinite power and an infinite understanding, it must be rational clear through.

This conception, as I have said, was of a world which was fashioned to carry out God's purposes. The first expression of these purposes was found in bringing into existence men with souls, who were free to sin and who were condemned to death because of their sin. Back of this view lay the philosophy and history of St. Augustine. The world was thrown up, so to speak, as the scene in which the drama of the fall and the salvation of man was to be enacted. It had just the relation to the drama that the theater has. It had no purpose except as the scene in which the drama could be enacted. After it was enacted, the heavens were to be rolled up like a scroll. The history of the world was simply a device of the Deity for the carrying-out of this program. We have expression of this picture in the poetry of Milton. God determines to replace the fallen angels by human souls, and for this purpose he takes out of the chaos matter from which he fashioned the world. The value of the world centered in men's faith, in their souls, in what they experience.

In the light of this view St. Augustine, who lived at about the time of the fall of Rome, undertook, as Milton did later, to justify the ways of God to man on the basis of what he conceived to be the inspired scriptures. He undertook to show what God had tried to do, in so far as God revealed it to man.

As we have seen, the history of the world constitutes a sort of drama. It begins with the creation of the world as depicted in Genesis. Here man is presented as a free moral agent. He falls from grace, he sins, and the punishment of sin is death; but God elects to offer salvation to man through the ultimate sacrifice of his son, if man will accept the means of grace. On that authority St. Augustine undertakes to arrange the whole of human history: it advances from the fall of man up to the appearance of Christ, and his crucifixion, suffering, and mediation. From that time on, the world presents the opportunity for man's salvation. It was created for that purpose.

This much we know about the world and about God's intention: he made the world out of nothing; he created it in six days and placed man in it; man sinned, fell from grace, and God in his infinite mercy set up his plan of salvation through the appearance of Christ. From that time on, the world existed in order that the sons and daughters of Adam and Eve might have the opportunity of being saved. When this opportunity had been offered, the drama, so to speak, would be completed. Then the world was to be burned up, the scroll prepared, and those lost in hell were to go on suffering through eternity. That is the picture which St. Augustine portrayed.

But it assumes a perfectly definite end. And it assumes another power besides that of God, and one which runs counter to God, and that is man's free will. This is present because God saw fit to create it. Of course, he created it with the possibility of man sinning. Even the devils in hell speculated; but the assumption was that God had infinite knowledge, and he knew what the result of his creation would be. But there was in the world a principle which could oppose itself even to the infinite power because God placed it there. He saw fit to create individuals with such powers. There should be suffering and misery due to man's sinning. It was part of God's chastisement for sin. The world was, on the face of it, irrational. It was a world created by an infinite God, a perfect deity, but still one in which evil and imperfection could appear because man could exercise his choice. Man was responsible for the evil and for the accompanying suffering which came with sin. He could elect to use the means of grace which God gave him to be saved, or he could refuse and be lost. The picture of the world from that standpoint was most comprehensively given by Dante; but we have the same picture of it in Milton's *Paradise Lost* and *Paradise Regained*, having therein beings that were able to choose contrary to God's law, consequently introducing the element of evil into the world. It was natural, then, that the world should, on the face of it, be irrational.

The medieval world was conceived of as being inhabited not only by men and women but by evil and good spirits. It was a world shot through with what we might call "magic." The science of the Middle Ages is simply a history of magic, but here again the conception was that God was utilizing these spirits for his purposes. You have a fitting picture of it in Goethe's *Faust*. That world, as we look back on it, was all shot through with magic and historiology. There was the conception of it as seeming to be absolutely irrational. Yet this evil is overcome in the end by God, and everything which is for the highest glory of God is fully rational.

This attitude was entirely different from that of the ancient world. If we look back to the great systematic philosopher of the ancient world, Aristotle, we find that he regarded the world as provided with "forms." That is an Aristotelian technical term which answers in a certain way, on the biological side, to our term "species"; on the logical side, to our term "concept." It answers to the nature of things, that about things which is known. For example, it is that which goes to make up a tree, that which constitutes the nature of a spade, a house, or a chair. A spade is any object which we recognize as having a certain nature. Aristotle recognized such noble objects, such forms, in nature in so far as nature was rational. Objects which have certain exact characters, certain qualities by means of which we can make them out and from which we can deduce certain consequences, can be defined. In this way we find objects in the world from which we can deduce logical consequences.

But Aristotle recognized also that there was a great deal in the world which was not rational. A tree, for example, seldom reaches its proper symmetry. Animals are subject to all sorts of defects and monstrosities. His explanation of this, in so far as he did explain it, was that the "matter" in the world somewhat resisted the "forms." In any case he recognized not only that there was a rational character but that some things were irrational, accidental—something was present that could not be accounted for.

The ancient world assumed that there was absolute perfection in the heavens. But the ancient scientist and philosopher recognized an accidental character of affairs on the surface of the earth. They accepted a world in which there was not only a rational order but an irrational something that could not be explained, something that just happened. If the assumption were pushed far enough, we should find it to be resolvable into contingent elements. Hume later made this the basis for his skeptical philosophy.

The medieval world, as over against Aristotle's, had nothing in it that was irrational. It was this medieval view which passed down through the Renaissance to the world of modern science. Galileo in particular drew upon this conception of the absolute rationality of the world, that is, the view that everything that happens can be explained. The assumption which he used was that God works through natural forces. As an infinitely rational being he must act uniformly in accordance with what Galileo terms the "rational law of nature"; and he must act in a most perfect fashion, that is in a mathematical fashion. God is conceived of as the supreme mathematician. Objects have certain ways in which they move in reference to one another. These must be expressed and carried out in accordance with mathematical law. If we find out what the important processes of nature are, we also discover the laws which represent their various relations; we find out the laws by means of which God works. For example, one can look at a highly complicated machine without understanding it or knowing its purpose, and yet one can be confident that everything in it was arranged by a mechanic in accordance with natural law. Now God has a perfect mind; and the most rational manner in which to exercise a mind, from the point of view of the physicist of the Renaissance period, was to make mathematical use of it. It was thought, then, that laws could be found in the world which could never be broken, that uniformities could be discovered which would be absolute, because that must be the way in which a perfect mind would work.

The attitude of Galileo and also of the early modern philosophers was that God inevitably presented a world to man which was so devised that man could understand nature. This marks the passage from what we might call the "theological dogma" to the basic postulate of modern science. We state this postulate in terms of the uniformity of nature; we assume that nature may be comprehensively arranged in uniform series. We still have that confident faith. Our knowledge comes back to nature. We assume that there is a world in which there are the laws of nature, but we have no assurance of it. This is one of the great contributions of the medieval period to the modern world, and it is a contribution which has been of increasing importance as science pushed its investigations further and further into nature.

The eighteenth century was the century of the triumph of mathematical analysis. The Copernican theory had been accepted by the scientists, and thus mathematical analysis was carried both to the heavens and to the earth. This analysis, which Galileo really initiated, was carried further and further and always with distinguishing success. Men had found a language in which they could read the world; it was a mathematical language. The point I am emphasizing is that the plan of things was devised by an infinitely intelligent being who did everything in a most perfect fashion. Every detail would be carried out in the manner of a perfect mechanic. If God were a mechanic, he would construct a world perfectly worked out.

This medieval faith in the uniformity of nature became, as I have said, the background of the thinking of the modern world. It did not belong to the ancient world. From the point of view of the former there is nothing in the world which is accidental. Everything is taken care of by God, and everything he does is done in an absolutely perfect fashion. His methods are those which express themselves in mathematical form. It was to that faith that the scientist of the Renaissance period turned to unravel the facts of nature. We talk sometimes about the uniformity of nature being demonstrated by the law of probabilities; and if we try to find what the line of the argument is, we discover a number of uniformities. Together they represent the uniformity of nature. If we ask why we find them, it is because we have already assumed the uniformity; we have taken it as our major premise that nature is uniform. If nature is not uniform, of course our argument falls to the ground. But you cannot prove the uniformity of nature by assuming it in advance. It is a postulate; it has never been proved. If we look for the origin of the concept, we find it not in Greek philosophy but in Christian theology. At the present time science does not go back to a theological doctrine; it accepts the postulate of uniformity on a pragmatic basis. We state natural laws; our modern science assumes the world is rational in the sense that we can explain that which we find in terms of the uniformities of the laws of nature. We go on with perfect confidence because so far this view has always worked. It is a postulate which cannot very well be overthrown. If the laws of nature break down, we can assume that there is some other uniformity which we have not found as yet. It is a postulate for us since we have taken over the fundamental assumption of an infinite creator who has fashioned the world in a perfect way with a purpose of his own. That was definitely the attitude of Renaissance science; and, if you want an interesting account of it, you will find it in Mr. Whitehead's *Science and the Modern World*. In the early part of the book you will find a very adequate and admirable presentation. In this period the world had become more and more definitive and scientific in its attitude. This is one of the things that we do not think of; and consequently, because we do not think of it, we do not realize that it is there. But it has had a very profound effect.

When men in the Renaissance period turned to an intensive study of nature, they found that their most efficient tool was mathematics; it was that which enabled them to reach simple elements and to discover what the uniformities were in the events in which these simple elements appeared. Thus, if the world was perfectly ordered, it was ordered by a perfect mathematician. God was the great mechanic, not because his ethical or his moral ends were at all of a mechanical character, but because the means by which these were carried out were inevitably the most perfect. If God created the world for the fall and the salvation of man, as he did from the point of view of the Middle Ages, he would create it in a mathematical fashion so that a mathematical statement of it could be given.

This rationalistic conception of a mathematically ordered world was a postulate which was almost a dogma. Those of you who have followed the development of the philosophy of Descartes, Spinoza, and Leibnitz, know how they gave to the mathematical interpretation of nature an almost religious value. Descartes' conception was of a world in which reality was that which was clearly and distinctly perceived; in which truth was that of which the mind had immediate and clear conception. Clearness and distinctness were his criteria for truth. He pushed his analysis further than it had ever gone before, carrying it over into analytical geometry. Here he used the mathematical statement of the process of motion itself, dividing motion up into an infinite number of accelerations. Galileo showed that bodies fall with a uniformly increasing velocity. Descartes carried on this mathematical conception in order to reach elements which could be arranged into uniform series. Scientists were occupied with this analysis for a century and a half.

This general attitude freed the scientist; it freed him from the dogma of the church. He was studying the indefinite matter in which the church was not interested. The church was interested in man's soul and its salvation, and the material scene in which the drama took place was of no value itself.

I want to call your attention at this point to the fact that in the ancient world the atomic doctrine was fully presented but was not made use of. Our science has gone ahead through the use of this atomic conception of matter. Not only do we have atoms, but we divide the atoms up into electrons and protons. The avowed purpose of Epicurus in his presentation of this idea was to free men's minds of superstitions. There was no reality outside of weight, size, and shape. That was all there was.

Through this doctrine he hoped to free the minds of his disciples from the fear of death. But the philosophers who undertook to find values in the world were unwilling to adopt this theory. In fact, no other school did adopt this Democritean doctrine.

Trees and houses, and other things, as our science conceives of them, are made up of electrons. But a tree is not simply a definite number of ultimate physical particles. Something else is responsible for the tree. There is, as Aristotle says, a certain nature in the tree which brings about its development into a tree. When various phenomena in the world are taking place around us, we try to analyze them in order to understand them. We are always seeking simplicity in our modern scientific method. But what has been done with the unities in the content of the world? There is something more than atoms. What right have we to take the particles of the tree and say that they constitute the tree itself? These particles are really connected with the climate, the solar system, and other things. All the particles have relationships with all the other particles in the universe. A field of force surrounds every particle in the universe. There is no justification for our taking a particular group of them and saying that these constitute a tree. To make this clear we have to go back again to the medieval period, to the time of Abelard. There is a certain nature of the tree which develops in the tree itself, until it takes on the form of the fully actualized tree. What Abelard substituted for this was the concept which we have of the tree. The tree is the matter. You can conceive of the tree as made up of just matter. But our concept of the tree, or the value that it has for us, with its color, its leaves and foliage, and its bark, is a concept which we form. That concept we find in the tree in so far as it is in our mind to begin with. Then there are certain likenesses which exist. The philosophers of the Renaissance were more or less free to deal with the physical world as made up of physical particles. They could seek after this simplicity. If they were asked what the other attributes of the so-called physical world were, they would say that they were put into men's minds as impressions, colors, sounds, tastes, and odors. The atoms and molecules had no color in themselves. What you have there, what you conceive of, are vibrations. When you strike the retina, you arouse color; it comes from the mind itself. The secondary qualities exist in the mind. Space, form, and motion—these alone were supposed to belong with the objects themselves. The secondary qualities, those which come through the eye, the ear, and the palate belong to the mind. We transfer these qualities to things, and so more and more of the world is put into the consciousness of individuals. This is particularly true of the meanings of things, e.g., that which goes to make up a tree. The characters which we state in terms of the concept of a tree exist in the minds of men, and they had previously existed in the mind of God. The determination of other characters, those which Aristotle found in nature, could be put into the consciousness of individuals.

One of the reasons why it was relatively easy to transfer these attributes to the consciousness of the individual is another of the gifts of Christianity. The whole universe is created simply as scene in which the drama of the soul, which is independent of the setting, could be enacted. Would this human soul act virtuously or viciously? Would it use the means of grace provided for it, or would it fall from grace? Everything bore upon the fall and salvation of man. The human soul had an infinite life, a life of blessedness or a life of suffering. It was essential even to the perfection of God. It was thus relatively easy to carry over the important characters of the world into the consciousness of man, and the work of the scientist was made easy. First of all he comes to realize that God is a great mathematician. In the second place the indefinite world, the indefinite matter, in themselves have no value except in so far as they express the laws of God. And in the third place the consciousness of individuals is the very reason for the existence of the world. The world is there only for the sake of the individual.

Going back to the point which I have already made: the world was created for a specific purpose, and this purpose was to be carried out by the agencies which God placed on the earth. Those agencies were centered in the church. It was a living source of inspiration. God spoke through this agency as he had spoken through the Holy Writ. The church was inevitably the source of authority. The period in which the medieval world expressed itself most completely was during the twelfth and thirteenth centuries. We have the picture of the world as the theologian, the philosopher, the churchman, and the layman conceived it. It was a world created for a certain definite purpose. The salvation carried out by God and, after the sacrifice of his son, by the institution of the church itself was passed on to man through the church. This was an outside authority. It was an authority which came from an infinite deity; it was an authority which was not to be comprehended in its operation. God did not explain what all his purposes were; he told only enough to guide men in their conduct. Aside from that, his purposes transcend men's conduct. The institutions of the family and of the state themselves came from God. He established them and all other institutions. The schools and the universities were the means by which man could comprehend the will of God. This will is arbitrary. When you call in a physician, his comprehension is presumably better than yours; otherwise you would not call him in. He speaks with authority, but he does not speak with an arbitrary authority. When you call upon the engineer who builds a bridge or a skyscraper, you are not making use of an arbitrary authority, because the ground of the authority lies in the knowledge which you yourself can in some sense grasp. But the authority of the church came from an infinite deity, an infinite mind, whose knowledge you could not comprehend. You had to accept it simply because God spoke and gave his authority through the church. This authority got its expression not simply in the church but in the state. The sword was placed in the hands of the king by God himself. All institutions were conceived of as established by God. In so far as the institution reflected God's purpose, man had to accept the institution; it spoke with the authority that came to it from the church itself. This embodied itself in the so-called Holy Roman Empire. The Holy Roman Empire had at its head the emperor, who was crowned by the pope. We know that empire died out and went to pieces; it became, as it were, neither holy, nor Roman, nor an empire. But that conception belonged to practically all men's minds during that period.

The points which I have been bringing out are points which we are apt to overlook in the background of the thought of the later Renaissance period. It was a period of fundamental revolution—a period of breaking away from the conceptions of the authority of the church, an authority which was arbitrary. It is this latter which makes revolutions almost necessary. The attitude of revolution which marks the early modern period was one against the arbitrary authority of the medieval institutions, an authority which came to them as supposedly inspired by God, given by God, and given with reference to ends and purposes which lay beyond the purview of man so that he was unable to criticize those institutions or to reform them: he had to receive them as they were. This was the fundamental conception which belonged to the medieval period; its institutions were fundamentally church institutions. In the mind of the medieval period the state derived its authority from the church and from God through the church. The transcendent character of the divine purpose also carried with it the necessarily arbitrary character of the institution as such. Men could not determine what the authority of the institution should be from its function in the community. One could not say that the administration of the institution should have such and such authority in order to bring about certain results which men presented as desirable. They had to look to the purposes of God in the establishment of these institutions, and so the authority of the institutions was necessarily arbitrary. The reaction against this came on the basis of a description of human nature as having in it a rational principle from which authority could proceed. This rational principle was presented by Rousseau as the recognition of rights which were the end of the individual and which could be made universal because in asserting his rights the individual recognized them as belonging to others also.

The reaction against arbitrary authority is one which took place, on the political side, in the French Revolution; and we shall see that Rousseau expressed the gospel of this revolution in his *Contrat social*. He undertook to find in man's own nature the basis for the institutions of society. He undertook to find in man's rational nature the basis for the state as the sovereign authority. It was not necessary to go outside of man's own nature to get the basis for such an authority. On this ground, in so far as a member of the community both enacts and obeys the laws of the community, a rational state is possible. If laws express the will of the whole community, the individual is able both to enact them and to obey them as a member of the community. And such laws could express the will of the whole community in so far as they expressed the rights of the members of that community, for rights exist only in so far as they are acknowledged, and only to the extent that those who claim them acknowledge them in the person of others. That is, no man can claim a right which he does not recognize for others. No man can claim a right who does not at the same time affirm his own obligation to respect that right in all others. In so far, then, as legislation can be an expression of the rights of individuals, that legislation can flow from the whole community because it will take on the form of that which is universal. If men are capable of recognizing rights as well as of claiming them, then they are capable of forming a community, of establishing institutions whose authority will lie within the community itself.

The revolution gathered about the rights of man. That has been perpetuated in the Declaration of Independence and the statement that men are born free and equal. The great and outstanding illustration of such rights is property. No one can make a claim to property except as he admits it in others.

When men came to conceive the order of society as flowing from the rational character of society itself; when they came to criticize institutions from the point of view of their immediate function in preserving order, and criticized that order from the point of view of its purpose and function; when they approached the study of the state from the point of view of political science; then, of course, they found themselves in opposition to the medieval attitude which accepted its institutions as given by God to the church. The medieval monarch ruled by divine right. In England, where the Puritan government was to be a régime of sense, it was still assumed. that the form of the state was determined from without. With the revolution this form was brought within the rational power of man himself in society so that institutions could be criticized and discussed to determine what they were designed to accomplish, and to see how far they did accomplish what they set out to do.

This general attitude is rationalistic, and is expressed specifically in three accounts of government—those of Hobbes, Locke, and Rousseau. These are roughly dated about as follows: Hobbes about the time of the Puritan Revolution; Locke by that which passes in English history as the Revolution, that is, the disturbance in which the Stuarts were sent across the channel and Parliament brought over William and Mary as the sovereigns of England; and Rousseau by the French Revolution.

The work of these three men undertakes to justify these revolutions. In one sense, of course, the doctrine of Hobbes is not a justification of revolution. On the contrary, it is a criticism of it. But in criticizing it Hobbes attempted to go back to a study of human nature and to discover from that study what sort of a state ought to exist. He does not go outside of that which man's reason can compass in order to account for the institution. The result which he reached as a consequence is much like that of the medieval community. From Hobbes's point of view every human being is necessarily selfish, seeking for what he wants; and this brings to the community an inevitable conflict between all the individuals who are seeking what they want. When they seek the same thing, they are at war. This picture is given by Hobbes in his *Levia-*

than. [The conception of the state arises out of the social contract. The individual has natural rights, which spring from his own impulses and desires. But if one gathered together a group of such individuals and the desires of all were set into operation, one would find that the different people would often desire the same thing and would come to blows. A community established upon the basis of natural rights would lead to what Hobbes called "a war of all against all." It was because of this anticipated result that he advocated the absolute monarch. This was the Leviathan; it was not the absolute monarch that belonged to the catholic tradition, the tradition of Christendom, but one set up by individuals who were unable to agree with one another. The individual was, from Hobbes's point of view, too entirely individualistic for the success of any but an autocratic state. Yet you find in him, in his reason, the principle of social organization.

This seems actually to have been the result of the attempts made in the revolution to establish a state on a rational basis. Men fell out with one another; there was turmoil, internecine warfare; and the final solution was found in the Leviathan, in the form of Napoleon, who took all the power into his own hands. And that seemed to be the only solution that could be presented at the time.][1]

Going from Hobbes to Locke, we find that the latter had a different view of human nature. He assumes that property, for example, arises naturally from man's adding value to natural objects by means of his own labor. If an individual has added this value to the natural object, then it becomes his property. And Locke assumed that men will recognize this as regards the product not only of their own labor but also of the labor of others. He assumes that man is naturally social, that he has an interest in the good of others since all are found in social relationships with each other—in their families and their neighborhood. So from Locke's standpoint there is material for the building up of a society based upon human nature. What is needed

[1] Taken from student notes of the Summer Quarter of 1928.

primarily is some sort of an impartial authority, which all will recognize, to overcome the disputes which will arise over property, over the rights of individuals in their social relations. But he assumes that, if these disputes are settled from a standpoint which all recognize, this authority will also be recognized. It is the court, then, that is really central in Locke's conception of human society, a court which will settle disputes in accordance with the accepted principles that are to be found in human nature itself.

When we reach Rousseau, we have a somewhat different approach to the problem. It is an approach which was determined by the political situation in France. The authority there lay entirely with the monarch. All powers came back to him, and all the authority which the different administrators of the state exercised came from the king. He was the monarch, and everyone else was a subject of the monarch. Rousseau approached the problem from the current fiction of a social contract in order to see how a community could be established in which the authority could rest in the people themselves. The king, as the monarch in France, was proving inadequate to the task which belonged to him. For example, he maintained orders which served no function in the community and which had all the privileges of the old feudal caste. Among these privileges was that of high taxation. The king was unable to rid the state of this incubus. There were advances in the administration of the community, but it was still unsatisfactorily administered and was criticized by the active intellects of the time. This was done indirectly, for example, by Montesquieu in his *Esprit des lois*, a special study of the old Roman order and of the English order which serves as a critique of the orders which existed in France.

But could the authority be brought back to the people themselves? This idea presented the seeming paradox of people being both sovereign and subject, and this Rousseau undertook to solve. How can the people be both? The answer he presents to this is that the people may be sovereign in so far as they exercise a *volonté générale*. If they exercise this general will, each is a sovereign. On the other hand, each is a subject in so far as he obeys the laws which the general will enacts. He can be both subject and sovereign if his will is the will of the community.

This assumption, as over against Hobbes's, is that there can be such a general will, that a man as an individual in the community can act not simply as a representative of himself or for himself but for the whole community if his will is identical with the will of the other members of the community. This not only presupposes common interests, which were emphasized by Locke, but it presupposes that the very form of the will which man exercises is universal, that is, a man wills something only in so far as he puts himself in the place of everyone else in the community and in so far as he accepts the obligations which that act of will carries with it. A striking illustration of this is found in property. If one wills to possess that which is his own so that he has absolute control over it as property, he does so on the assumption that everyone else will possess his own property and exercise absolute control over it. That is, the individual wills his control over his property only in so far as he wills the same sort of control for everyone else over property.

That represents the difference between the attitude of a rational being in a society and that of the man whose strength or cunning is able to hold on to something. When the latter wills to hold on to something, he does it despite everyone else. It is his by his strong arm. He does not will that others shall maintain possession of their property. On the contrary, he is ready to take things away from everyone else. To will to hold on to what he has on the basis that might is right is to will to deprive everyone else of his property just in so far as he has the opportunity to get it. There is a fundamental difference between these two acts of volition. To will on the basis of power threatens everyone else in the community with the loss of that which he has, because the power of one person is greater than that of another. On the other hand, when a person comes forward and says, "This property is mine, I propose to maintain it as property," he can do it only in so far as he can present evidence that it is his property on bases which everyone else recognizes; it is property only in so far as everyone's possessions are property. In this sense property is something universal. The type of possession guaranteed by might is quite particular.

There can be, then, a type of volition which is not, as Hobbes conceived of it, individual in the sense of grasping for what one wants. It can be a demand simply for that which belongs to the individual in the same sense as the same sort of possession belongs to everyone else. What one wants is possession guaranteed by the community itself. He wants property; he does not want mere possession. Possession may be nine-tenths of the law, but it does not become valuable unless it is the law. One cannot call upon the community to support it, cannot depend upon the institutions of the community to back his claim, unless that possession does constitute the law, unless that sort of possession on the part of anyone else would give him property rights. A community in which the volitions of the different members would be of this universal character would, in the nature of the case, be one made up of both sovereigns and subjects. The volition of each would be the volition of all in so far as his acts were universal, not simply because they happen to agree, but because what they set up is that which is guaranteed by all. What makes property extremely valuable in the community is that it does give to each man a right which everyone else recognizes, which no one can take away. If the volitions of the members of the community take on the form of rights which are acknowledged and recognized by everyone, the community is made up of individuals who are both sovereign and subject.

Of course, there are details in the doctrine of the *Contrat social* which call for discussion. This conception of the universal will, which could be the will of the individual and yet the will of all the community, is of one which is universal not simply because of the number of people who get together and who have the same ideas but because that which is willed is willed by everyone in the community; it is because what is willed gets its value through its being the common will. In other words, this is the nature of a right as such, and it does not exist unless this is recognized. On the other hand, we see in the case of property no such thing as a right which does not carry with it necessarily certain obligations. One cannot assert his right without at the same time asserting his obligation to recognize other people's property. One cannot assert his rights to property without at the same time recognizing his duties toward that property. Otherwise it will not be property but mere possession; mere possession is not property.

Again, if one seeks for enlightenment, he seeks that for which he realizes all others must also seek. He is trying to find that which has meaning for everyone, that which has value only in so far as it is generally received, generally recognized. What are the so-called laws of nature to a community which is ignorant of them? What is the value of a great work of art in a community which is blind to it? What is the meaning of enlightenment in general? If everyone is bound down by superstition, what is the good of one's own private enlightenment if it exists for no one else? Education, which, of course, is the source of enlightenment, must be general if it is to have the value which ought to belong to it. One may, of course, exist in a class by himself to which other classes are subservient, not a part of his own community. But in so far as one has social relations with others, one's own enlightenment has value for him only to the extent that it is shared by others who have social relationships with him. If you are in the midst of a stampede of cattle, it is of no use for you to know the purpose of their stampede. They do not know it themselves. An enlightenment has no value unless it is universal. Of course, one may use the ignorance of others for one's own advantage. But enlightenment as a social affair must be universal to have any meaning.

The values which lie behind the organization of the institutions of the community must be universal values; and in so far as the will of individuals confirms these values and makes them the basis of those institutions, it is what Rousseau called a *volonté générale.* This principle does not go back to a simple rule of majorities. The rule of majorities may be the most satisfactory means we have of expressing this general will, but it will be a faulty one at best. If we seek for an expression of what we mean by this, we find it in what is called "public opinion," that is, that attitude which is itself a universal attitude, which goes to make up the character of the individual. When there is an effective public opinion, one that really expresses the attitude of everyone in the community, one recognizes it as one that has and will have authority. It may be that such a universal opinion cannot be reached. Or it may be that enlightened individuals within the community can recognize what is the meaning of the social situation, can bring it home to the consciousness of the people in the community, enlighten them, and thus give leadership. We may have to muddle along with a very inadequate expression of such a general will, but we assume that the authority of our institutions lies in the rational nature of the individuals which make up society. This point of view we have taken over from the revolution. We do not assume that the institution depends upon an outside authority. We do not assume that human beings have been trained in certain habits, like trick animals in a circus. We assume that there flow from man's own rational nature judgments and volitions which are or can be universal in character, and that it is this which makes human institutions possible; that one wills for himself what he wills for everyone; that one obeys the volitions of others because he identifies them with his own volitions. That is what lies back of what we call, in general, democratic institutions. The form of democracy is not essential to the doctrine. What is essential is the assumption that men are sufficiently enlightened to recognize that their own volitions in great social matters will be identical with those of others who are so enlightened that when one wills such things as property, enlightenment, and security, these things will be recognized as public ends which are also the ends of the individual. As a result of this, the individual will will for himself what is good for others.

Back of this point of view lay the doctrine of rights. In this sense a man's own volitions give laws for society, and only in so far as the individual's volitions do give laws for society is a society possible which does not depend upon some external authority. This is a society in which the individual is the source of the institutions. A society is possible in the sense of the old empire, the ancient world, a society established by force. Such a society is possible, but a society which springs from the citizen himself is possible only in so far as the citizen can give laws for the community; and he can give laws only to the extent that his volitions are an expression of the rights which he recognizes in others, only in so far as he expresses the volition of others because they affirm rights which the others recognize in him to the extent that he affirms them for himself.

The rights which Rousseau recognized are few in number. They are those which gather about property, about the simplest social institutions such as the family, the rights of education, and the general right of liberty, that which is embodied in our Declaration of Independence.

Liberty became the slogan for the French Revolution. It was naturally the gathering ground in the fight against arbitrary authority. It carried with it the assumption that, if men were free, their interests would be common interests. That, you see, is what is implied in the conception of rights—that the interests of men are, after all, common interests. Even such an interest as that of possession becomes a common interest when one recognizes it as property. If what one wants is not simply possession but property, then one wants something that is universal, because that which he wants involves his recognition of the possession of property by others. That is, he wants that which is recognized by everyone; and of course he can demand that of others only in so far as he recognizes their property rights. What is essential for a community is common interests. This was represented in the slogans of the French Revolution, not simply by liberty, but by the others—equality and fraternity. These all imply that the interests of men are common interests, that that which one person wants is something which other persons want and which, at the same time, he wants them to have.

Now that can be formulated, as John Stuart Mill later formulated the idea of liberty, in the assumption that one wants freedom of action on his own part in so far as it will not interfere with freedom of action on the part of other people. This is somewhat vague; it cannot be put into a clear-cut formula as is the case with property, yet it lies behind most of our judgments in our demand for freedom of action. A person is free to act providing he does not tread on someone else's toes. One wants freedom, but he should ask only for that which he is willing to grant to others. If he asks for the opportunity to express himself, he must at the same time recognize the rights of others to express themselves, and his freedom must not encroach upon the freedom of others.

One can make a general statement out of this; but the difficulty is to give it in clear-cut outlines, to make it clear just what this sort of freedom is. We can discover it in certain cases, as in the freedom of the ballot, of the vote; freedom of expression, of speech. In these cases you can make a definite statement that that which you want you must recognize in the rights of others. But if one attempts to make it the basis for the order of society, one will find that it is negative, not positive. Possession is positive. And if you ask that your possession should be the sort which you recognize in everyone else, then you can formulate it in the law of property, as it has been formulated in all communities in one way or another, and, of course, more exactly in the more highly civilized communities. But it is very difficult to start off with a conception of freedom and make it the basis for the organization of society, for the concept is in itself negative, asking simply that the individual shall be free from restraint. But you have to recognize that you cannot ask for freedom if that freedom will put you in the position of enslaving someone else, of encroaching upon his freedom of action.

Turning to the conception of equality, we have a still more difficult doctrine, but it does, at least, have positive content. Freedom taken by itself is negative. Equality is the doctrine that each person shall have at least the same political standing as every other person. It may, of course, be carried over from the political to the economic field, where we demand that every person shall have the same property as another. It can even be taken over into other fields, in which, however, it is more difficult to define. But in the field of politics one can define it in terms of the right to vote and the counting of votes so that one person shall count for one and only one. That is something that can be stated in positive fashion, in terms of democracy. Democracy is the rule of counted votes, and consequently the rule of the majority. This is a simple conception and in it, in the application of the revolutionary principles, we come back to a quality of a political character—that in which each individual counts for one and only one and which, in the exercise of the vote, the counting of a ballot, leads to government by the majority. The question then remains, of course, as to whether this conception, if it is so simple, can be made the basis for the organization of the community. The rule of the majority which this leads to is not necessarily the rule of the community. Fifty-one per cent is a majority, but it does not necessarily express the desires of the community as a whole. It is an external statement. Yet it may be the best working method that we have for getting at what does represent the will of the community.

The remaining idea, that of fraternity, is still more general. It comes back to the attitude of neighborliness, the identification of ourselves with others, a common emotional interest in others. This comes under the general term "sympathy." It is very vague, and it is only under very exceptional conditions that it becomes universal. These are just the conditions which a universal religion undertakes to establish. It can establish it only in certain ways, in certain periods, under particular conditions; but the conception is one to which all universal religions come back. In so far as all are creatures of one creator, in so far as all are children of one father, belonging, therefore, to a single family, we get this conception of fraternity. But we can see how varied and elaborate are the conditions by which it is universalized. It has been true in religion, as elsewhere, that people have to depend upon their sense of hostility to other persons in order to identify themselves with their own group. This idea has been found to be much too vague to be made the basis for the organization of the state.

CHAPTER II

KANT—THE PHILOSOPHER OF THE REVOLUTION

ROUSSEAU'S conception, which I have stated in as brief a fashion as possible, had a very great influence on Kant, in the development of his doctrine. As I have indicated, Rousseau's *Contrat social* was really the gospel of the French Revolution. It was good rhetoric and took hold on great groups of people. It was simply stated, so that the ideas could pass into untrained minds. His abstract idea that the rights of all the individuals in the community were the basis of the state, was put into common terms. If you can put the action of the state in terms of the rights of individuals, you can make the members of the state both subject and sovereign, and it is not necessary to set up a monarch in whom all rights rest. Hobbes talked about natural rights, but they were only the rights of might. Such rights would all have to be handed over to a single man if there was to be any order in the state. But rights which are acknowledged and which have value only in so far as they are acknowledged, rights which carry with them the condition of obligations, can be enacted only in a democratic community. If the people want property, then they want that which every-one recognizes, which everyone in some sense possesses, which everyone wishes to maintain. This conception, of course, can be carried over from property to other institutions in the com-munity. In that sense it can be made universal. This character of the community is something which flows from the character of human nature itself, from its rational character. Rousseau said that rights, in this sense, are universal, that is, rational. In so far as the volitions of the community are in these terms, they can be made the laws for all.

What Kant did was to go a step farther and say that all our

volitions should be of this same universal character. He generalized the position of Rousseau; he made it the basis of his moral philosophy. Rousseau indicated that the legislation of the community should have the form of the expression of rights. In so far as it did have that form, it made political structure possible. Kant went on to say that every act which a rational being carries out should take on this universal form. For him morality, as such, consists in giving a universal character to every act. In so far as an act does not have this character, it is amoral. That is, if a man seeks for something which he does not at the same time recognize as lying within the pursuit of other persons, if he seeks something simply for himself, he is, to that extent, selfish, immoral. Kant undertook to identify this doctrine with the Golden Rule. His position was that man, in his social nature, could give laws to society in so far as his own end was a universal end. What this means has been illustrated through the concept of property as over against mere possession.

Rousseau referred to those situations which gather about property, which gather about the defense of the community against the power that attacks it from the outside, about the institution of the family, about the duties and rights of enlightened education. He selected those rights which everyone recognized and insisted that in the community these ought to be universal in character. They should be universal because it is only in so far as they are universal that they have any value. An enlightenment that is confined to a single mind only, which cannot be maintained over against another person on the basis of a rationally accepted doctrine, is of no value, is not truth. A thing is true if it is in such a form that you can convince another rational person that it is true; otherwise it is not true. A family would have no meaning unless the relations of the father and mother and children were relations which were recognized by the community itself as a means of ordering the interrelations of men and women and the care of children, and unless they were the same for all members of the community.

Kant went on to say that every act which is moral should take on this universal form. He put this in the form of a categorical imperative: So act that the maxim of your action can be made a universal law. That is, act in every case as you do with reference to property. When you demand that you should have possession of your own property, you are demanding that everyone else should have possession of his own property. This should be the basis of all conduct, and on this basis Kant founded his moral theory. He undertook to show that the human being could be a lawgiver because he is rational; could be a sovereign because he is rational, because he can give a universal character to his volitions. Everyone would then be a lawgiver, but only in so far as he took account of the duties arising out of his volitions so that he would also be subject to the laws that he himself gave. Man's intellect, in proportion as it is rational, is a lawgiving intellect. It can create society by being universal in character. In this sense, because he generalized this principle of Rousseau's, Kant may be considered the philosopher of the revolution.

We have seen how Rousseau's principle was generalized by Kant into his categorical imperative, in the affirmation that the individual should make a general principle out of the maxim of his act, to use Kant's terminology. One should ask himself, when he is on the point of willing anything, whether he can also will that everyone else should will the same thing under the same conditions. Then he would discover whether or not his volition is universal. For example, if one wills to tell a lie, if he asks himself if he would will that everyone under the same conditions should tell a lie, he will see that this would lead to evident contradiction, because, if everyone should lie under those same conditions, then no one would believe anyone else and there would thus be no purpose in the lie.

What I have been trying to bring out is that the will of the community must take on some such form as that expressed in terms of property. It has to have an economic statement of some such form as that. It is that which makes the will of the individual the will of all, the *volonté générale*. If you get that sort of an expression, you have the basis for the organization of the community. And Kant, as we have seen, tried to reach this simply by making it the basis for a moral doctrine. That is, Kant said, if you could make your act formally right, it would also be right in content. And the illustration he gives is his best illustration; it is that you cannot make a lie right because you cannot make a lie universal; it contradicts itself. You have that turned around the other way in the statement of the Cretans. They had a bad reputation as to veracity in the ancient world. It was said, "All Cretans are liars." But suppose the statement that all Cretans are liars is made by a Cretan. He belongs to the group that are liars. Therefore his statement about the Cretans is a lie and the Cretans are not all liars. That is, the proposition runs into a contradiction. Kant conceived that you could use such a rule as that to determine all moral conduct. All you have to do is to try to make the maxim of your act the truth for everyone under the same conditions. The result seems to be that one should use this universality of one's act as a test of its morality. This is Kant's assumption, that if you would only make your act universal you could test it. If it involves a contradiction, it is wrong.

Kant did not succeed in that. He did not succeed even with reference to lying. There are many situations in which lying is not immoral. Sometimes it is highly moral, as in the typical case of the man who deceives an assassin trying to murder someone. We talk about morality in warfare, and, of course, warfare is a game in which you have to deceive your enemy. The general, the military strategist, succeeds by deceiving his enemy. And then we have the whole list of white lies that we always tell—cases where we feel we are justified in deceiving a person who insists on knowing something he has no right to know, where we give a reason which is good but which is not the real reason, in order to save somebody's feelings. There are all grades between the whiteness of truth and the blackness of lying. It is not possible to draw a hard and fast line between them. If everyone insisted on telling the truth all the time, society itself would perhaps become impossible. When Kant tried to work out other matters on the principle of the categorical imperative, such as the case of a man who wants to commit suicide in order to relieve himself from suffering from a disease and his friends from the care they will have to give him, or the case of the man who is too lazy to work although he has competence, I think the principle broke down pretty definitely.

What Kant was appealing to were values. He was not considering simply the universal form. He was considering also what the values are that give significance to life. These were what Kant really came back to. What the problem is, then, to come back to my former position, is to give a universal form to the interests of man in society. We can do that in the very abstract case of property in such a form that that which you possess is something which you want every other person to possess. A familiar illustration of that is the desire to have property itself widely distributed in the community. We say the person has a stake in the community. He cannot want to preserve that which he has without at the same time willing that others should preserve what they have. So the conservative who wants to keep the present order is anxious for a relatively wide distribution of property so that everyone, having a definite stake in the preservation of that order, will also want to preserve it. The interests of such a community must be universal in their character, which means that they shall be of such a form that when a person wills something for himself he is willing the same for others.

But, of course, the difficulty is in stating that specifically. It can be stated, as we have seen, in relation to property and also with reference to truth by the spreading of enlightenment. Truth is valuable only in a community where it has universal acceptance. If a thing is not recognized as true, then it does not function as true in the community. People have to recognize it if they are going to act on it. For example, we expect a person to be familiar with the laws of the community—

the essential, fundamental principles. People have to be familiar with these and recognize them as universal. We are anxious to have universal education so that everyone may recognize the operation of natural laws. We depend on other persons knowing what we know. Otherwise knowledge has no advantage. Of course, I can get special advantage by knowing something in advance of someone else as regards the stock market; but in order to get advantage from even that type of information, it must become part of the knowledge of others as well. If I shut away my knowledge, I might get a certain satisfaction out of knowing something that would be of value if others knew it; but to give it actual value it has to become a part of the knowledge of all. There is a story of Frederick the Great, who was much beset by people who wanted honors given them. One man in particular, whom Frederick did not consider worthy, requested a particularly desired post. Finally he was told, "You can have this post on one condition." The man said that he would take it under any condition, and the emperor said, "I will grant you a privy counselorship, but under the condition that you shall never tell anyone of it at any time." The value of holding an office is in its recognition by other persons. So the knowledge which you have is of value only in so far as it is universal in character—only in so far as, being affirmed, everyone will accept it. The perfect form of your knowledge is that you can put it to proof; it is that which everyone everywhere must accept. That is the ideal, although it may never be reached with reference to truth; but that is the goal toward which knowledge proceeds.

What our different states undertake to do, so far as they are democratic, is to give rights which shall be universal in their character. Our laws try to state the rights and the privileges of individuals in such a form that they are universal—not that everyone now possesses them equally, but that everyone under the same conditions would have the same rights.

But Kant took this position not only in regard to man's will in society, that is, that man gives laws to society through the extension of his will; he also affirmed that man gives laws to nature. In his *Critique of Pure Reason* he approached this principle from another angle and carried it much further. There Kant undertook to show how it is possible for us to build what he called "synthetic judgments a priori." The beginning of that is that one should be able to state that a straight line is the shortest distance between two points. There you have a proposition in which "straight line" is subject and "shortest distance between two points" is predicate. You can analyze the idea of "straight line," and you will not find in it that of the shortest distance between two points; and you can analyze "the shortest distance between two points," and this will not convey the idea of "straight line." Yet, you make the judgment that a straight line is the shortest distance between two points. This is a synthetic judgment because it puts together ideas which are not already contained in each other. When you say that man is a rational animal, you have already defined man as rational, and it is no great trick to ascribe the same predicate that you already have in the subject. That is an analytic judgment. But the synthetic goes further than the analytic. It takes two ideas, neither of which is contained in the other, and affirms that these ideas belong together.

But where do we get our intellectual authority for this assertion? How are synthetic judgments a priori possible? In the *Critique of Pure Reason* Kant contends that they are a priori because in this connection, as in the categorical imperative, he came back to a type of experience which determined in advance what the forms of things should be. This lies both in the forms of space and time and in those of the understanding, that is, the logical forms. Those which belong to the sensations he called the "aesthetic," and those which belonged to the understanding he termed the "judgment." In this division, and in the argument that flows from it, Kant was trying to meet the skepticism of Hume. He said that Hume had wakened him from his dogmatic slumber.

Hume's skepticism said that all our knowledge seems to be

simply an organization of our impressions and ideas—impressions meaning sensations, and ideas mainly images. Sensations, as such, are simply the states of our own consciousness. Locke had recognized this in regard to secondary qualities—color, sound, taste, and odor. These do not belong to the object outside; and if they convey those characters to the object, we ought to recognize that they come from us. Berkeley went a step farther and said this relation was true not only of secondary qualities but also of primary qualities—of extension, of motion, and of solidity—that is, of those qualities pertaining to the occupancy of space. When one feels of a desk, one gets a sense of its solidity, its extension, and its mobility. But this is just a feeling of the individual. It is impossible to distinguish between this sensation and that of the color of the desk, as sensations. Locke admitted that the color did not belong to the desk but was simply an impression made upon us through light that reaches us from the desk. Berkeley says its extension is just another impression of the same kind.

In other words, Berkeley, who is called a subjective idealist, went a step farther than Locke and said that the world of extension is nothing but a world of our impressions. He asked why we should assume that this spatial order, which comes to us both through vision and the sense of touch, should not be regarded as relative to our sensitivities as well. What is the space about us but the impressions made upon us of things that we will say are ordered in a certain fashion? What evidence have we that that which causes these impressions has any other character than that given in our experience? We say that a vibration of a certain amplitude is responsible for the color red. That is, red is the feeling or the experience which we have when the retina is hit by those particular vibrations. With another vibration you have the impression of violet. Well, Berkeley asked, why should we assume that that which causes in us the sensation of extension is extended, if that which causes in us a sensation of red is not itself red? If this latter is not the case, why should that which causes in us impressions of extension in three dimensions itself be extended in three dimensions? Is there any reason for giving any particular authority to the primary qualities which we deny to the secondary qualities? And being sure that the answer to that question was in the negative, he went on to seek what the cause of our impression could be and, being a bishop, found it is the Deity who produces in us sensations of extension though he himself is not extended. Berkeley was very sure that there must be such a power, for he said that there could be no effect without a cause and that our attitude toward these impressions, whether primary or secondary, is a passive attitude. Therefore, it could not be a cause. No man can create a sunset. The sunset is there. One can recall sunsets he has seen, a number of them, and picture in his imagination something that he has never seen on land or sea; but the pigments he uses are those which he has taken from past experience. Man is passive with regard to these sensuous experiences; therefore the cause of them must lie outside of him, in God, said Berkeley.

Hume pushes on and asks where Berkeley gets his evidence for causation. His only answer is that we have been in the habit of expecting things to happen in the future in the same order as they have happened in the past. The sun has risen regularly in the past, and we expect it to continue to do so. But the only result we can reach from analysis is the juxtaposition of two events, sunrise and sunset, so that if one has uniformly succeeded the other we expect this succession to continue in the future. In other words, Hume, in his turn, went one step farther than Berkeley, and asked him what evidence he had that there must be a cause. Why could not these things just happen? He analyzed the concept of causation, and what he found was that we expect those things to succeed each other which have succeeded each other in the past. That was all Hume could find in the so-called "law of causation." If things have succeeded each other in the past in a certain uniform way, then we expect this relation to continue in the future. If that is all that can be found out about the law of causation, it does not take us outside of our experience at all. Locke assumed that we could go outside of our experience of color and sound into a world of moving physical particles which cause such impressions as those of color and sound. Berkeley assumed that we could get outside of our experience of an extended matter to a God which caused in us the experience that we called an experience of extended matter. Hume showed that the law of causation, which led Locke to say that vibrations from outside produced in us a certain succession of color or sound, and that led Berkeley to assume that the sensation of extension must be produced by God, lies inside of experience and that there is no way of getting outside of that experience.

Hume also undertook to show that the so-called "self" is nothing but an association of certain groups of our impressions, our states of consciousness; that especially those which come to us from our own body, and those which are associated with certain other impressions, such as our own name, get firmly linked together. But that is nothing but another object, another thing. It is the most important thing in our experience, but it arises as any other object arises. From the standpoint of empirical philosophy this task involved nothing but the organization of a certain succession of color, of form, of feel, so organized together that when you see a color you naturally think of a certain feel. We see these in different situations, when they impress us somewhat differently, and we recall experiences that were true in the past. Our organization of these qualities is in such a permanent fashion that they become, for us, a fixed object. Hume assumed that the self arose also in this fashion. The baby has sensations—pleasure and pain, warmth. The sensations from his own body get associated together. If he moves his arms, he gets certain sensations; if he moves his arms again, he gets the same sensations. These get permanently organized together, particularly about the sensations which are pleasurable and painful. The infant finds itself addressed by certain words, certain names. Certain experiences come when it responds in a certain fashion. Out of this arises the association of a set of experiences which make another object, an object which the infant comes to call the self. He identifies it with the "I," the "me." From that standpoint there is no functional relationship between the subject and the object. The subject is simply another object. It is a central object about which the experiences of the individual develop. But there are other objects which also become central under other conditions. Over against this empirical conception Kant brought in the idea of a transcendental self which was a sort of functional unity. But the empiricist comes back to the experience of a self. And the empiricist assumes that in order that there may be an object, there must be a subject. The two involve each other. For Kant this subject-object relationship, however, is not static; it is not such a relationship as that spoken of in which certain impressions are made on the mind, in which physical things in some fashion impress a consciousness which lies inside the mind. It is not that sort of a relationship, but one in which we have one phase of a process necessarily leading to another phase, and that phase leading back to the first. This is the typical situation in a subject-object relationship.

The position which Kant took was a more or less natural development of the position reached by the English empiricists. Their result was skeptical, at least it was in Hume's statement. He undertook to show that there could be no knowledge of an object. Objects as such were broken up into sensations and images, or impressions and ideas, to use his words. He analyzed objects simply into a set of these impressions and ideas, and the connections between them were those of association. The connectivity then also belonged to experience, and, for Hume, was psychological in character. That is, there is no way of getting from these impressions and ideas over to an object which lies outside of them and is supposed to be the cause of them. He analyzed the idea of causation and carried it back to the simple expectancy that the succession of impressions and ideas that has taken place in the past shall continue in the future. He could find no ground for this except in a habit, a habit which he recognized as being so strong that we could not avoid acting upon it. But in no way could we get outside of impressions and ideas.

Kant's reaction against skepticism was against the skepticism of Hume. What Hume had pointed out was that the world which arises in experience is relative to the sensitivity of the individual. We live in a world of color, sound, taste, and odor. But the world has color and sound only if the individual has normal vision and hearing. If we had other organs of taste and smell, the world would have other tastes and odors. We can readily conceive that if the structure of the retina were different the world would have an entirely different set of colors. We can live with a person who is color-blind without discovering that fact. He refers to certain colors, which exist for us as yellows, as reds. And there is no way of detecting this except by a set of colored yarns in the psychological laboratory by which you can find out that a certain color is different for him. Our world is relative to our own sensitivities. We can go back of those particular sensitivities to what we call the physical causes of those sensations, and we can, for example, identify different colors with certain rates of vibration which are not dependent upon our sensitivity. So we can go back to something which we assume to be there in independence of this relation to our eyes and ears. We feel hot and cold, and our theory is that there is simply a movement of molecules which are imperceptible to vision or feeling except in the sense of temperature. But motion is not the warmth that we feel, and the lack of motion is not the cold that we feel. We assume, also, that there is a world of physical things that have mass, that move, that have a certain shape and form—characteristics which Locke called the "primary qualities," while the secondary qualities admittedly belong only within our experience. But the former, too, can be stated in terms of our consciousness, as sensations, and as the images of those impressions which Locke called "ideas."

The result of the Humean skepticism, which was the natural

product of this view, was to destroy the passage from a subjective world over to something outside. With this went all necessary science. Our concepts of the laws of causation, of substance and attribute, to mention only two, are found to be nothing but associations of ideas, in the Humean sense of that term. But science seems to dispute this, and Kant undertook to justify the approach of science. He insists that there is such a thing as science and such a thing as necessity. And he tries to find out how these are possible. We have, we will say, the statement of a straight line being the shortest distance between two points. Accept Euclid, and you have propositions starting off with certain axioms and reaching certain results. We accept these as necessarily true. Kant asks, How is this possible? He insists that we do accept them and that out of such propositions all our necessary sciences arise. His answer is that there are certain forms of the mind itself—for example, space with its structure, and time with its structure—so that that which takes place must occur according to the forms of that mind in which they appear. Mind, then, gives these forms and, to that extent, gives laws to nature. In this way Kant reached the same position in regard to nature at large that he reached in regard to human society, namely, that it is the mind that gives laws to nature. So we see again that he was the philosopher of revolution all the way around.

In the end the problem boils down to this: Is necessity possible within the world of experience? Hume says that causation, the supposed instance par excellence of necessity, must be considered as simply a set of relations between different experiences. Kant agrees that our world is made up of such experiences. But, from the fact that we do live in a world of experiences, Hume drew the conclusion that there could be no such things as laws of nature because the most famous of them all, that of causation, is nothing but a set of happenings, connections in our experience, in which one impression succeeds another according to our habit of expectation. That is, we say that we have always found that swans are white, and wherever we find the form of a swan we find the white color; so we lay down a law of nature that swans must be white. And then someone goes to Australia and finds black swans. All our laws of nature are nothing but certain uniform associations, certain experiences which are invariably connected with each other. There may be a succession which is contrary to that. This is what was found in a somewhat intricate sort of fashion in the case of observations recently made in regard to the position of stars during an eclipse. Light is susceptible to changes in direction. In so far as light offers such response to a change in direction, it has what the physicists call "mass." Now, mass can be measured in accordance with Newton's laws. The path of the light of a star passing the edge of the sun ought to be shifted a certain amount, depending upon the mass of the sun and the mass of the ray of light, and so forth. On the Newtonian basis, you can figure out how much it ought to be shifted. Einstein has another theory of gravitation. He says that the amount of the shift ought to be twice that predicted on the Newtonian theory. On observation, it was found that Einstein was right. The only facts that you have in this case are the position of the light of the star in its relation to the rim of the sun. By means of photography this can be measured. All facts, the so-called "data" of any subject, are nothing but certain experiences that the observer has in their relation to each other. The relation which is found at any given time on the basis of such investigations may be found to be all wrong a few generations later. In fact, we can be pretty sure this will happen. More recent theories of scientists have replaced older theories. Certain facts remain the same, but the theories have been replaced. Can there be any such thing as universality and necessity which belong to the laws of nature in a world which is a world of experience, a world of certain uniformities? You ask a scientist what a law of nature is, and he says it is nothing but a uniformity. But when you ask just where that uniformity is found, the answer is that it is found in the experience of men who observe. They have certain impressions, and they find that these are uniform. Can you have such a thing as universality and necessity under such a condition?

Hume says it is evident you cannot; your statement boils down to the fact that certain things happen and you cannot tell that others will not happen. But the fact that things have happened in a certain order forms in you and me the habit of expecting them to happen in that order. That is what the laws of nature—causation, for example—are. Now Hume described the world as a world of experience in which the so-called laws of nature are nothing but our habits of expecting things to happen in the future as they happened in the past. Berkeley accepted Locke and went him one better; Hume accepted Berkeley and went him one better; and Kant accepted Hume and went him one better, but along a little different line.

What Kant pointed out was that we have in the mathematical sciences results that are necessary and universal. Yet they belong to a world of experiences. We believe that the angles of a triangle are equal to two right angles, that a straight line is the shortest distance between two points, that seven and five make twelve. We believe these things, and, if other people did not, we should still continue to believe them; we should call the others irrational. Kant took the position that these things are necessarily true. But how can they be necessarily true? Kant's answer is that our minds give laws to nature. If there is only one mold in the pantry and you know that there will be pudding for supper, you know, a priori, that it will have a certain form. That is what Kant would call a piece of "transcendental logic." You know in advance what form the pudding must take because there is only one form available. You can give a law which will include all puddings that are to be as long as you can control the number of molds there are in the kitchen. Well, similarly, Kant said that what we call space and time are nothing but forms of our sensibilities. The experiences that we have, then, will take on the forms of space and time, and we can argue that all the experiences we can possibly have must take on those forms because they are the forms of the mind. And he also asserted that the mind—"judgment," as he called it—has certain other forms, which he called the "categories." The two most important—there were twelve altogether—are those of substance and causality. Anything that we sense in terms of space and time, because these are the forms of our sensibilities, we have to think of in terms of substance and attribute, and cause and effect. We think of them in terms of substance and causality as well as in terms of space and time because we cannot help it. The former are forms of the judgment; the latter are forms of the sensibilities.

Kant had another faculty, that of "reason," whose function was higher than either of the two mentioned. But all I am trying to do here is to point out the sense in which Kant could refer to the human mind as giving laws to nature. Just as control over the molds can give laws of the form of puddings, so the forms of the mind can give laws to any experience which man may have. These laws are necessary and universal for all possible experiences. They do not go beyond experience, but they can give laws for all possible experiences. Thus Kant finds necessity and universality within the limits of a world of experience such as Hume had set up.

Kant's affirmations in regard to these forms of space and time have been somewhat shattered by the non-Euclidean geometries. He assumed that the sum of the angles of a triangle is equal to two right angles and could not be otherwise. We know, of course, that a spherical triangle does not conform to this law. But we can say that he was not talking about a curved line triangle but of one composed of straight lines. But if the space on the surface of a sphere can be curved, why cannot all space be curved? In fact, we are living on the surface of a sphere. Our ancestors had to find out that we were not living on a plane. If a man at that time had followed the line of vision and kept on going until he came back to the point where he started, he would have been put up against it to explain it. Is there any reason why the space which is curved on the surface of the earth should not be curved throughout? One of the conceptions given by mathematicians is that of a moving collection of planes, stacked up one on top of another. Suppose all those planes were curved ones, because we know certain geometries work out this way, then the axiom that parallel lines will not meet except at infinity has to be abandoned and we have different geometries based upon the theory that you can draw more than one line parallel to another.

Kant's supposition was that he could get hold of the forms of the mind in terms of which experience must be presented, and that, if he could, then he could give universal and necessary laws to nature. So, he conceived of man's mind as giving laws to nature itself. The starting-point was that man's nature is rational; therefore it can give laws to society, provided those laws expressed man's rights. He generalized this position and conceived of man as giving laws to nature as well as to society. He accepted Hume's statement that knowledge must lie within experience. But what he insisted upon was that there are necessary objects in experience, that there is universality in it. And he undertook to show, by a transcendental solution, how these things were possible. By "transcendental" Kant meant that he could form, in advance of an experience, a judgment as to what that experience could be. It was transcendent in the sense that it transcended the experience itself. His explanation of this was, as we have seen, that the mind had certain forms into which this experience must fall, so that one could be sure in advance that our experience would be subject to the structure and laws of space and time, because these were forms of our sensibility, and subject also to the categories of substance and attribute, of cause and effect, because these are forms of the judgment. We cannot think in other terms than these. Therefore, these forms are given in advance of experience, and they are necessarily given because everything that occurs in experience must take on these forms. The result of this process is what Kant would call an "object."

In this way Kant assumed that he had rescued science as a source of universal and necessary knowledge. We have geometry because the form of space is a form of the sensibility. We have laws of arithmetic because these are involved in the very order of succession as given in time. We have the laws of the understanding, those which give us substance and attribute, cause and effect, those which give us necessity and probability. These are what give us the universal and the particular. They are all forms of the understanding, and any experience which we have must take these forms. Of course, there is a large part of our experience which is contingent for us. That is we cannot tell, in advance, what colors, sounds, tastes, and odors we will have; but we do know in advance that, whatever particular ones they are, they must occur in a world of space and time, for nothing can appear outside these forms of the sensibility. We do not know, in advance, what the substantial character of an object will be; but we know that we cannot think except in terms of substance and attribute. We have to think of a thing as having substance; and its qualities, its characters, are attributes which inhere in that substance. We cannot tell in advance what the cause of an event will be, but we know in advance that every event must have some cause. So there is given to us in the very forms of the mind the necessity and universality of laws, particularly those of mathematics and of mathematical physics. And our empirical experience, the content of our sensuous experience, will all fall into these forms. But forms do not determine what the content will be. They determine how we shall experience that content when we do experience objects, but we cannot tell in advance what particular experience we shall have. We do know in advance what form it must take, because the forms of experience are given to the world by the mind itself. In that sense Kant could legitimately speak of the mind giving laws to nature as well as to society. We have already indicated how this later is accomplished through his carrying-out of the doctrine of Rousseau.

This notion of Kant's came back to a very subtle and somewhat obscure analysis of judgment. Kant asked why objects are units, and where that unity comes from. He accepted the Humean analysis of the object into its various elements. Take such an object as a tree or a house. You can analyze it into the different experiences you have. Color, feel, extension, all the different sensations are associated with each other; but the house or tree or animal is something more than a compiling of such impressions and images. It is a unit; it has a certain unity. A heap of sand has very little, if any, unity. Of course, you can regard it as a single thing, but you are more apt to consider it as a conglomeration of separate grains of sand. A house, however, has a perfectly definite unity. All the different parts belong together; they have a definite relationship to one another, a relationship which arises from the uses to which the house is put. An animal has a definite unity. It has varied organs, but all these are organized in the unity of its life-processes. It is a living thing in which all the parts have certain functions. Any object that is a thing has a certain unity, and Kant's problem is to discover where that unity comes from. It is not a mere sticking-together of different pieces. If you break an object up into sensations and ideas and then stick them together by the law of association, you still do not get the unity of the object.

Now Kant could find only one source of unity in experience. He found this in the judgment, in the statement, "I judge that this is such and such a thing; this is a house." That is, one judges the house from the point of view of its uses. There are the dining-room, the kitchen, the bedrooms, the drawing-room, all looked at from the point of view of the processes of living. One sees house, thinks house, perceives house, in terms of the life that goes on in relation to it, just as one sees, perceives, and thinks an animal in terms of the life-processes that take place through all its organs. This unity is, as Kant insisted, something more than a mere association together of one experience after another. It is an organization, a holding-together of experiences within an experience of a certain form. We see that when we are confused by some object, when we cannot grasp what it is, cannot make any unity out of it, it is only a set of different sensations. Then suddenly we grasp its meaning and everything takes its place with reference to everything else. You can see what the organization is, what the purpose of it is, what the structure of it is. Well now, that grasping of these different elements, these different parts into a whole, as Kant conceived it, is an act of judgment. I judge this to be a table. I judge the object which I see outside the window to be a tree. I relate all the different parts of the object to each other, relate them in certain definite ways, spatially, temporally, in terms of substance and attribute, cause and effect. I organize these wholes in the process of my perceiving them. One of the experiments of the psychological laboratory is that of a dark box in which a spark is introduced so that suddenly when the spark is there you get a confused picture of something on the side of the box. Then the electric contact is made again and there is another spark, and you get a sense of structure. After a number of repetitions you see a perfectly distinct picture. You have organized what you see into the relations of a landscape, of a cathedral, or of a castle. You see it as a whole; you put it together. Our perception is just such a process as that. It is an organizing of the different elements of experience together. We get a clue to a thing; and then, as soon as we get that clue, things fall into their different relationships to each other.

Unity such as this, Kant said, is essentially that of judgment. It is found even in perception. We look at an object in the distance which is somewhat confused through the misty air, and, by putting our attention to it, we finally get an outline, such as a house; and then we can see it more clearly, grasp it for certain as a house. We are looking for the face of an acquaintance in a crowd, and we can finally identify it. There is the image which we have of that particular face. Our perception is a process of organizing different elements into a whole. It always has a certain sort of unity. And this is more than the mere sum of the parts. If you break up your perception into different elements like parts of a jig-saw puzzle and simply match them up together, you do not get a picture. You must get them organized in a certain way. Someone organizes the different notes in a melody, and we get the whole of the melody. One organizes the ideas which come, we will say, in an address which one is hearing; and they begin to take shape, they begin to have relationships to each other, and one gets the line of the argument. So, also, one gradually grasps the plot of a play he is seeing. Our knowledge is a process of relating different elements together and giving unity to them. That unity, in Kant's conception, comes back to the judgment as such.

Back of all perception, of all thought, of all conception, lies this high judge. As he did to most of his ideas, Kant gave a ponderous construction to this, calling it the "transcendental a priori unity of apperception." It is a priori because it is something which is given in advance of experience; it is transcendental because it is imposed on, and not derived from, experience—it is necessary. That is, our experience consists in judging. So far as it is an experience, it is an experience of things having a unity which does not come from the content but from the process of experiencing, as in perception and thought. It is something that is given in advance of the actual experience. We do not know what things we are going to see; but, if they are intelligible experiences, everything will have a certain unity which comes from our experiencing it. So, the transcendental unity of apperception, as Kant conceives it, is not simply the association of one sensation or image with another but the organization of them—of the appearance of a face into that of an acquaintance, of the dim outlines of an object into a house. It is more than perception, in the sense of having sensations. Our perception is a structure, and Kant called it "apperception."

Now this transcendental unity of apperception, Kant said, comes back to the fact of judgment, to an "I judge." Such an I or "ego" that judges is, as we have seen, transcendental, that is, something given in advance of perception. In Kant's earlier speculation he spoke of a transcendental self that he conceived of as being given in experience. But he was committed to finding objects only in experience. Forms of experience could be given in advance, but they do not become an object until the latter actually appears in experience. Thus, this transcendental self was for Kant just a function of experience, not something actually given. The transcendental self was not a thing. The selves of our experience are empirical. We have certain feelings. We have certain memories. We have feelings of our bodies, the images we see of ourselves in the looking-glass. We have the experience of our relationships to others, family relationships, friendships, national relationships. All these just happen to us. They are empirical. They lie within experience. These selves are like other objects that appear in experience, tables, chairs, trees, and houses. They are empirical in character.

These empirical objects are there in experience, but they have reference to something beyond themselves. Such a thing as this table before me, Kant would say, just as it is, is made up out of our sensations and our memories of experiences we have had in the past of similar wooden surfaces. It is all organized together in the forms of space and time, that is, in the forms of our sensibilities; it is organized as substance. We will say that the wood is a substance and that it has certain qualities. One type of wood has one quality, and another type of wood has another quality. The wood has certain relations, and these we organize into a table. But we always imply that there is something which lies behind this actual experience which we have of the table. We have the actual experience of a table whenever we come into the room, and it ceases when we leave the room. We remember it and expect to have the same experience when we enter the room again. We think of a something that does not get into experience, a something which is still there when we are out of the room. We think of something which transcends experience, something which Kant called a "thing-in-itself," a *ding an sich;* that something which is not in experience but which experience implies.

Our science gives us a "thing-in-itself," though not quite in the Kantian sense, of course. We think of the table as made up of molecules, of these molecules as made up of atoms, of atoms as made up of electrons and protons. We say that they are responsible for the different experiences we have. If they vibrate in a certain way, we get a certain color. Well, what about the ultimate particle itself, the electron? We go over to the physics laboratory and are shown a model of the atom, with protons and some electrons at the center. We think of atoms as little galaxies like the solar system, the sun represented by a proton at the center, and the planets by electrons revolving around the proton, little stellar groups. That is what goes to make up the atom. We think of them in terms of spatial relations and of the color which they have. But they cannot themselves have any color, for they are responsible for color. They could not be responsible for color and be colored themselves. The electron is too small to subtend a wave of light anyway. It could not be colored, and it is too small to be felt. Now, such objects could not possibly be experienced, and yet, in a certain sense they are the things which we do experience. A thing that could not possibly be experienced and yet is the thing that is experienced is what Kant called a "thing-in-itself." It is not dependent upon us for its existence. It is, rather, something upon which our experience may be thought to depend. We assume that there is a world of things-in-themselves and that they are not experienced—in fact, they are supposed to be the conditions of experience. A world of things-in-themselves is implied in experience. But Kant insists that, inasmuch as they cannot be experienced, we cannot possibly know them. If we could know them, we would experience them, that is, they would fall under the forms of our sensibility and no longer be the conditions of experience. Color is a process of experience. All our knowledge is a process of experience. One says he knows; that means he is experiencing color, feeling, locality. If we experience the particles of which the physicist and chemist speak, those ultimate electrons or matter which lie beyond objects, we have to assume something which is responsible for that experience. A "thing-in-itself," says Kant, cannot be experienced; we cannot know it. We may assume such a "thing-in-itself," but that assumption cannot be an act of knowledge.

Kant accepted that position from Hume. You can have necessary knowledge in the world of experience itself. That is, you know that our experience must always take on the forms of space and time, of substance and attribute, cause and effect. But you cannot possibly know anything beyond that experience. You may have to postulate a world of things-in-themselves, but you cannot know such a world. This is the result of Kant's *Critique of Pure Reason*. He analyzed experience, coming back to what was necessary and universal in it, that which made science possible.

But that holds only for experience. If the mind has such forms as those of which we have been speaking, then our experiences must take on these forms. Our judgments are judgments about past experiences, they are not judgments about a world which is the condition of our having experiences; we are assuming a world that we cannot possibly experience, and so one which we cannot know. We can give laws to the world of our experience, the laws of our own mind; but those laws hold only for experience, only for possible experience in the future. We can make a universal judgment that any experience we have must evidence these laws, but this judgment holds only for experience itself. We cannot know a world which lies outside of experience. Kant called this world of experience "phenomenal." It implies something beyond itself of which it is the appearance. Just as I have said, we can assume that the world has order, is the appearance of something. But of what it is the appearance we can never know. We cannot even know that there is anything there. We can postulate it, but we cannot know it.

But this postulation is something that takes us over into conduct. We are continually acting. Our experience has been of a world composed of seemingly solid matter; but we can analyze that into the space of sensibility. Our world is spatially organized; we find that organization is a form of the mind. It is a world in which there are uniformities; we find that those come back to the forms of cause and effect, and that is a law of the mind. We are postulating that experience will continue. We are putting our feet right into the future, so to speak. We are expecting that our experience will continue as it has continued. We know, or at least we assume, in advance that if experience continues it will be of a certain sort.

But will it continue? Is there a world of "things-in-themselves" that starts this experience of the world? What evidence is there for that? Kant says there is none. All our evidence holds simply for experience. We are asking for a world upon which experience depends. We will always postulate such a world; and we will always postulate that that world is intelligible, is intelligently organized, just as our experience is intelligently organized. Our conduct carries with it such a postulation as this: Our intelligent conduct will be justified by our later experience. But will we have further experiences? That is something we cannot tell, although we postulate possible experiences as having intelligent order.

What is more interesting from Kant's standpoint is that we postulate a responsibility on our own part for our own conduct. That is, we regard ourselves as responsible; and therefore we must postulate that we are free morally, that we can act as we feel we ought to act. Kant says we cannot prove that. In fact, when we look at our conduct, we always put it into terms of the law of cause and effect. We explain an act by saying that such and such motives were acting upon us. As we regard the act itself, we explain it, bring it under the law of cause and effect, and yet we continually accept the responsibility for our own conduct. And that acceptance of responsibility carries with it the postulate of freedom. If there is such freedom, it must not belong to this world of appearance, for, in it, every event is caused by a preceding event, comes under the law of cause and effect. If the self is responsible, it must be because that self is noumenal, a "thing-in-itself." Now we cannot know that. Kant says this reality belongs to a world which we cannot experience, a world which is responsible for our experience. But we are always making a postulate that we are responsible. Conduct carries with it a set of postulates which cannot be proved but which we cannot avoid. We also assume that the world of "things-in-themselves," which we cannot know, is an ordered, intelligible world. Our very conduct carries that assumption with it. We cannot help assuming that we are responsible for our conduct, that we can act freely within our experience as such. Our conduct seems to be determined by previous events. If we can act freely, it must be because there are noumenal selves not bound by this law of understanding. We are always postulating that. In conduct we postulate selves which are noumenal, not phenomenal, selves that belong to the world of "things-in-themselves." We postulate that, just as we may say that scientists postulate electrons. The scientist can never get direct evidence of these in perception but, nonetheless, he assumes that there are such things. So we assume that there is such a thing as a self which is not bound to the law of cause and effect—a self which is responsible. This postulate of the self is involved in our action, in our conduct. It is something we cannot know, for knowledge is confined to experience. Experience is always of things that are caused, as such. But our conduct constantly postulates a free self. By way of this self, then, we go over to an assumed world of "things-in-themselves."

CHAPTER III

THE REVOLUTION BREAKS DOWN;
ROMANTICISM IS BORN

WE HAVE been considering the political revolution and the rôles of Rousseau and Kant as philosophers of it. The former gave a popular vogue to its doctrines; the latter incorporated its principles into a speculative system. The undertaking of the revolution, as we have seen, was to substitute for the arbitrary authority of the old institutions one that was based upon rational principles; one which was found, as presented in the theory of Rousseau, in the rights of man. The assumption was that one could deduce from the essential rights of man the structure of political institutions to take the place of the older institutions. The rights of man were, as we have seen, universal in that the individual in asserting his own right, in the very nature of the case, recognizes and asserts the same right for others. In so far, then, as the legislation of a popular assembly is confined to the rights of men, one can reach that *volonté générale*, that general will of Rousseau in which the individuals are both subjects and sovereigns; the will which gives laws for all in the very form of the right as such; and which also recognizes that right, accepts it as that to which it must conform. The undertaking of the French Revolution was to establish a government, a state, a political society on the basis of such rights. The assumption was that it was possible to deduce the whole structure of the state from what were recognized as universal rights.

But the political revolution broke down. In France one constitution after another was undertaken without the result of a stable and secure government. Out of the insecurity arose the opportunity of Napoleon. By the exercise of military power, which he controlled for the time being, he was able to set up the imperialism which dominated France and Europe for fifteen years. The hold imperialism had on France was that, in a certain sense, Napoleon appeared as the champion of the Revolution. The opponents of France were undertaking to set up the old order again—the divine right of kings, the right of the church in its medieval claim—and Napoleon was the leader of the armies of France that defeated them one after the other. For this reason he was regarded as the champion of the Revolution. There was another sense also in which he was its champion—where the armies of France went, the old order broke down, particularly in Germany. The old medieval order had remained in the latter country more than in any other. In France, at least there had been an attempt to introduce administrative efficiency. At least the feudal power had been centered in the monarch. Although feudal privileges remained with the whole upper class, the power had passed over into the hands of the king, so that administrative efficiency became possible. In Germany, however, there was no central monarch. We must remember that Germany, more than any other country, had suffered from the conception of the Holy Roman Empire. The German monarchs of earlier centuries had tried to establish themselves as the Roman emperors; and, in doing that, their eyes were constantly fastened on the lands beyond the Alps. The interest which centered in this establishment of an empire, in the securing of the iron crown on the part of the German contestant, had detracted from the development of a national German state, so that Germany remained broken up into an indefinite number of little feudal states, with a few powerful states in the midst. And the monarchs of the little communities made the same claims for themselves that the monarchs of the larger communities—Prussia and Austria—made. Now, wherever the armies of France went, this old order crumbled and people rejoiced at the freedom that came as a result of this breakdown. This was especially true in the Rhine Valley, so that there was a strong sympathy with the movements of Napoleon and even a strong feeling of attachment to him. In that sense we can speak of Napoleon as the champion of the Revolution as over against those who undertook to set up the old order again.

But the order that he set up was imperialistic. It was an order in which he was a dictator, and it became more and more tyrannical in its character, particularly in suppressing popular institutions. It was identified with the militaristic régime. Only so long as Napoleon was fighting could it live. He could not establish himself in the sense of a French king, could not attach himself to the older traditions of the French monarch. There had to be fighting for him to maintain his place. And in the nature of the case, the régime broke down as France was worn out, as strong men were sacrificed on the battlefield.

This was the situation because of the failure of the French Revolution. And out of this failure arose the imperialism of Napoleon. To the extent that this imperialism did not go back to the old order, it regarded itself as supporting the Revolution. It went back to the acceptance of the community as such. That is, Napoleon had the support of France behind him in the form of a plebiscite. His imperial throne rested not upon the divine right of kings but on the support of the people themselves. But the constitution of his state depended upon his own will. He was the dictator. And yet, in very many respects he did carry out the Revolution. Particularly, he carried out the principles of political revolution involved in the dispossessing of the privileged classes, bringing the land back to the peasants themselves. This was the most important effect of the French Revolution and of the reformation under Louis XVIII. In that respect there is a parallelism between it and the Russian Revolution. The Russian Revolution put the land in the hands of the peasants, even though the communistic doctrine does not recognize private property. In the same way, we may say that the French Revolution put the ownership of land into the hands of the peasants; and, although the old order was reinstated, no attempt was made to change that fundamental reconstruction. Furthermore, we have seen that the imperialism of France was a military organization of France against her enemies, and one which was triumphant for fifteen years. It made France the dominating power in Europe and gave that glory to the French army and the French nation which was so sweet in the mouths of the Frenchmen of the period. But it was not an establishment of the state on the principles which were drawn from the social contract as Rousseau presented it. In that sense it was a failure; and after Napoleon finally was defeated, France went back in some sense to the old order, as did the rest of Europe.

The French had undertaken to establish a state, a political society on the bare principle of political equality, with such an ideal of universal form as that of truth or of property. As we know, they did not succeed. It is not necessary for us to follow out the history of the failures of the different constitutions which were established, or of the conflict of interests which led to the final collapse of the French Revolution in its political form. Out of it rose Napoleonism, the imperialism of France. First of all, it was a dictatorship which established order, security in the community, which was of primary importance. You can get an organization of all where you have one single lawgiver who has behind him a force to enforce the law. It is the simplest way of dealing with politically disturbed conditions. Napoleon was, first of all, able to make himself a dictator, by the somewhat ruthless use of power.

But, of course, Napoleon was also one of the world's greatest military geniuses, and France was attacked by the reactionary governments of Europe. The victories of Napoleon over these enemies, who were the enemies of the Revolution as well, were, in a certain sense, victories for the principle of revolution. Actually, there was dictatorship and tyranny as there had been before the Revolution. In some sense there was more severe political tyranny. But after all, Napoleon was fighting against the foes of the Revolution, that is, against those who wished to bring back the institution of the divine right of kings, of the old feudal order, of the ecclesiastical power. Those who wished to maintain this old order were fighting against the powers in

France which gave expression to the Revolution. Even England joined with the others, although the English government was quite liberal in character, as indicated by Burke's reflections on the French Revolution, which were very influential. And Napoleon in fighting these powers was, from the point of view of France and liberals throughout the world, the champion of the Revolution, not because he himself was interested in establishing a democracy on the contrary, but because he was an enemy of those who were determined to have the Revolution wiped out. He was the enemy, at least, of the enemies of France; and he was the victor over their armies. His power, then, was, first of all, that of a dictator who established security. And in the second place, he had the enthusiasm of victorious France behind him.

Of course, it was not simply the principle of revolution that was involved here. It was the principle of nationalism as well. Medieval Europe and the remains of medieval Europe that we find in the eighteenth century had very little place for what we term "nationalism." Take Austria, for example. It was composed of an indefinite number of different communities, different races, speaking different languages. That which was common to most of them was their religion. But the different groups were racially, linguistically, historically, different; and yet they were all organized into a single monarchy. There was an economic ground for this organization which we are recognizing in the troubles of Europe at the present time. Those within the communities bought from and sold to each other, produced and distributed in such a fashion that the organization of this Austrian empire did answer to certain very important economic demands. The process of setting up commercial treaties between the different communities and different states that have arisen out of the Austrian empire is a very difficult thing. But still there was a single state, made up out of different groups which now make up a whole set of different societies, and societies which had a vivid sense of their own entities and of their hostility to others.

The beginning of this nationalism can be found in the victories of Napoleon, in the sense of the superiority of the French armies and of the French nation. And this sense of superiority which comes with the conflict of a certain group that is united in its language, in its history—this sense of solidarity which we call "nationalism"—might be said to have had its beginning in the imperialism of Napoleon. There had been nationalism before, but no such vivid nationalism as that characterizing the history of England in the nineteenth and twentieth centuries, for example.

The breakdown of the old feudal institutions in France helped the development of this nationalistic spirit. In so far as it equalized everyone, it left everyone a Frenchman. The *émigrés*, that belonged to the old régime, felt more at home with their own class abroad than among the Frenchmen who had driven them out. People of various classes might feel more at home among the same class abroad. Just in so far as there had been a leveling process that had brought everyone to the same level, there was the opportunity for the development of nationalism. Nationalism is a leveling conception. Each one has his position simply as a member of a certain nation. We do not get the sense of nationalism in its most vivid form where castes, or classes, are present. We get the most vivid sense of it in situations where everyone can stand upon the same level. Revolution, in so far as it breaks down social castes, is favorable to the development of nationalism.

What gave Napoleon his power, then, was, first of all, his capacity for introducing order, security, into the state; in the second place, his victories over the enemies of France and the French Revolution; and, in the third place, the power that came with these victories over all the armies of Europe, the ability to stand as a dominant power on the Continent.

But the French Revolution as an undertaking had definitely broken down. If the armies of Napoleon had crushed the enemies of the Revolution, they had not established its principles in the French state. They had established another empire, the Napoleonic empire. There was a definite sense of defeat, then, as far as the Revolution was concerned. After the defeat of Napoleon the emperors of Russia and of Austria and the kings of Prussia and of England undertook to wipe out the Revolution and put things where they had been before. Of course, they could not do that; it was impossible to re-establish the old housekeeping after the breakdown of the old, moth-eaten furniture of the medieval period. But an attempt was made in that direction, going back to the old order of things.

There came a sense of defeat, after the breakdown of the Revolution, after the failure to organize a society on the basis of liberty, equality, and fraternity. And it is out of this sense of defeat that a new movement arose, a movement which in general terms passes under the title of "romanticism."

I have said it was impossible to re-establish the old order of things, passionately as many men wanted it. But that desire did lead to a very intense interest in that old order. England, of course, was unwilling to accept the power of France, the imperialism of Napoleon. Prussia, too, arose as a nation not simply to re-establish the old order but also to drive the French out of their country. Thus, owing to the revolution itself, nationalism had arisen in other communities. But they were putting down the French Revolution, for it was out of that Revolution that Napoleon had arisen. In England the sentiment for the revolution, as depicted in Dickens' *The Tale of Two Cities* and in the eloquence of Burke, was in peril. The revolution was supposed to be that which tore society down, the savageness of the Days of Terror. It was supposed to represent the actual disintegration of society, and people turned from it in terror and looked for those institutions which had been in existence before the French Revolution had arisen. So there was a turning to the old world with a certain passionate attachment. There was a revival of medievalism.

This revival was one of the aspects of romanticism. You remember that from the barbarians who came in to destroy the Roman Empire we have kept the term "vandal" as a term applying to a barbarous community which destroys everything before it. The term "Goth" had exactly the same meaning, and "Gothic" was applied disparagingly to the architecture of the medieval period from the time of the Enlightenment as such, the time of the turning-away from the obscurantism of the medieval period. But in this latter period we find a return to the medieval attitude, and the term "Gothic" took on the same meaning that it has for us—that of a certain type of architecture which we consider very beautiful. This is just an illustration of the attitude that was taken at the time. With the breakdown of the revolution came this attempt to re-establish the old order. The clock was turned back; the Holy Alliance was established between the monarchs of Austria, Russia, Prussia, and England, in an attempt to safeguard this old order.

What I want to point out is that this return to the old order was very different from the old order as it had existed before the revolutionary upheaval. Men came back to something which was regarded through different eyes than before. It was, in the first place, treasured in so far as it represented a security which had been so rudely shaken in the revolutionary upheaval. It was precious in a sense in which it had never been precious before. Previously, it had been accepted as a matter of course, as the normal status of society. The evils of it had led to the revolution itself. But now it appeared as security, as that which seemingly had been lost and now was recovered. Thus it assumed a glamor.

But there was another aspect of this reaction, that which gives it its peculiar, its romantic, flavor: this is that men came back to it from the standpoint of new individuals, new selves. Europe had been through the revolution. As an undertaking to establish things on the basis of the new political entity, the citizen, the political individual who was supposed to stand on his own feet, so to speak, this movement was felt not simply in France but in all Europe as well. It was represented by such vivid imaginations as those of the young Wordsworth and Coleridge, by a feeling for a new life, an assertion of a self that could stand on its own feet, on its rights. There was the same movement in America, of course. Here had been the reflection of the gospel of Kant, of the skepticism of Voltaire. Here too had arisen a new individual. In liberal England the revolution did not appear in the violent form in which it took place in France. In the former, as we have already seen, the revolution had, in a certain sense, taken place in the Puritan upheaval which sent the Stuarts out, brought William and Mary in, and which established a representative institution, Parliament, as the final authority. Parliament went over to the people. It might put on the throne a monarch who ruled by divine right, but it was Parliament that put him there, and he could remain there only with the support of Parliament. Thus, in a certain sense the revolution had taken place in England, but it had left an organization of different interests. It was not yet a democratic structure. In France the attempt had been made to set up a democratic structure coming back to the political man—a man with rights. The Englishman was still what he was by virtue of his social status, because of his connection with the great organizations of industry and of trade. He did not take his position as a human being who had political rights. The Americans came and presented that doctrine in England at that time. There were repercussions of the French Revolution in England, but it did not sweep over England in any such sense as it did over France. Still the sentiment was there and elsewhere in Europe —in Germany, in Italy, in Spain. And that spirit meant that the individual looked at himself as having his own rights, regarded himself as having his own feet to stand on. This gave him a certain independence which he did not have before; it gave him a certain self-consciousness that he never had before.

It is this self-consciousness that he took with him when he went back to consider again the old world to which he was returning. He came back with a different self-consciousness from that with which he had left it. He looked at it through different eyes. He did not look at it with hostile eyes; he wanted at least the order, the security, of the old order re-established. The attempt to set up a new state on a democratic basis had failed. People now wanted to get rid of that. They came back again to the old order; but they came back as different individuals, and they now looked at the old order from another point of view. They had become self-conscious in regard to it.

What the Romantic period revealed, then, was not simply a past, but a past as the point of view from which to come back at the self. One has to grow into the attitude of the other, come back at the self, to realize the self; and we are discussing the means by which this was done. Here, then, we have the makings of a new philosophy, the Romantic philosophy.

First of all, the discouraged self that had undertaken to re-build the world on the basis of rights, the self that had followed out the gospel of Rousseau in attempting to reconstruct society on the basis of what was universal in the individual, on the basis not only of that which he found in himself but which he recognized in others, found that the undertaking had failed. It was not possible to build up a new community on the abstract rights of men. Of course, in a certain sense it may be said that America succeeded in this attempt where France had failed. One finds the same abstractions in the Declaration of Independence that one finds among the doctrinaires of the French Revolution. But the American community was not built up on the Declaration of Independence. This instrument was a banner of liberty flung forth to the world; but the government that was set up was based on the liberal institutions that had been carried over from England and had gone through the fire of the long colonial period. When the Constitution was finally formulated, it was an expression of the political institutions which were an inheritance from the mother-country, institutions the technique of which was to be found in the common law. The American government was not an institution built up on abstract rights. When the French undertook to do this, they found that they did not have the material with which to work. They broke down the imperialism of Napoleon and took charge of the chaotic situation which resulted. But they had no basis upon which to undertake to build up a new state whose authority should be based upon the reason of the individual; and their plans failed. The individuals who undertook it returned from the quest in the discouraged condition that characterizes the breakdown of revolutions. This was the situation all over Europe, for, while the revolution had centered in France, the movement spread over the whole continent.

But, though the self had failed in its undertaking, it was still there with its own point of view; and it now turned to the past. Its first, almost passionate, endeavor was to get back to this past, to get rid of the horrors of the imperialism of France and of the collapse of the Revolution, to set up the old order again, and thus get back the security that came with it, get back the values that seemed to have been lost. But when these were put in place again, the house refurnished, the process was undertaken from the point of view of a sophisticated self that was aware of its own defeats, that was interested not only in getting the house refurnished but interested in the inhabitant, in itself. There is a self-consciousness about the process which distinguishes this movement from the medieval situation that it was undertaking to re-establish. There is that bitter attitude about the beginning of the Romantic period, but with it there came unexpected treasures. The old world was discovered, and it was highly interesting, exciting, as presented, for example, in Goethe, and in Schiller's *Die Räuber*. Thus we come to a new interest in a medieval world that had been thought to be nothing but dust and ashes. Once again it becomes a living affair. It is portrayed in the attitude of the pageant, of the drama, the attitude of living over the old life where one assumes now one rôle and now another.

And with this came the further discovery, not only of the old world but of the self. Men had gotten the point of view from which to look at themselves, to realize and enjoy themselves. That is, of course, the attitude which we find in the romantic individual, in the romantic phases of our own existence. We come back to the existence of our self as the primary fact. That is what we exist upon. That is what gives the standard to values. In that situation the self puts itself forward as its ultimate reality. This is characteristic of the romantic attitude in the individual and of this period.

Of course, we have many illustrations of it. For example, the Byronic poetry; that affirmation of the self in which the eye is thrown aesthetically upon the heavens, in which the self swallows everything else. In Bryon this is presented with a certain cynicism. The attitude is expressed in a Mephistophelean experience, but in it the self asserts itself; it is there over against the world, against God, against the devil; it is there as the primary thought with reference to which everything else must be oriented. That is the starting-point in such Byronic experience, the attitude which is implied in the use of the term "Byronic."

The romantic experiences to which we have referred are also presented in Scott, and in the attitude toward Gothic architecture. Those attitudes are a result of the journey of the self into the past. It is a reconstruction of the self through the self's assuming the rôles of the great figures of the past. That is what gives the peculiar flavor to romantic literature, a character that we recognize at once in contrasting the novels and poetry of Scott with Malory's *Morte d'Arthur* or his *Chronicles*. In these latter there is a simple, direct attitude, while in the hero of Scott you have a self-consciousness which is historically out of place but which gives a flavor to the whole romantic experience. There the self is used as the point of orientation in its own reconstruction. What we recognize in Scott, as over against the figures in the *Chronicles*, is self-consciousness, awareness of self, an attitude which is entirely out of place in the naïveté of those medieval knight-errants. The hero of the Scottish novel would have been perfectly at home in the period of Scott himself, had he taken his armor off. He has the consciousness, the background of a modern individual; and, largely for this reason, he was all the more picturesque when put into the garments of the medieval period. This whole thing is caricatured in Mark Twain's *A Connecticut Yankee at King Arthur's Court.*

Perhaps the most vivid and the most moving picture that we can get of this in English literature is to be found in the writings of Carlyle. He, as well as Coleridge, De Quincey, and a small group of Englishmen, came under the influence of Romanticism. His early contacts were with Goethe, who, like Schiller, was very much influenced by the Romantic philosophy. The influence which particularly moved Carlyle, though, was that of Schelling, although Fichte too had his influence, as is shown particularly in *Sartor Resartus.* If you read that, you will get a more or less emotional reflection of the Fichtean philosophy. The responsibility which is depicted as lying in man, and which makes him a creative center in the universe, which identifies the individual with the Absolute Self in the universe, is Fichtean.

Europe discovered the medieval period in the Romantic period, then; but it also discovered itself. In fact, it discovered itself first. Furthermore, it discovered the apparatus by means of which this self-discovery was possible. The self belongs to the reflexive mode. One senses the self only in so far as the self assumes the rôle of another so that it becomes both subject and object in the same experience. This is the thing of great importance in this whole historical movement. It was because people in Europe, at this time, put themselves back in the earlier attitude that they could come back upon themselves. When they had done this, they could contrast themselves with the earlier period and the selves which it brought forth. As a characteristic of the romantic attitude we find this assumption of rôles. Not only does one go out into adventure taking now this, that, or another part, living this exciting poignant experience and that, but one is constantly coming back upon himself, perhaps reflecting upon the dulness of his own existence as compared with the adventure at an earlier time which he is living over in his imagination. He has got the point of view from which he can see himself as others see him. And he has got it because he has put himself in the place of the others.

From the standpoint of the earlier period the structure of things was moth-eaten, riddled with worms. It was breaking down and people were looking for something new to take its place. When, in its turn, this new order had proved itself to be a deception, they tried to go back to the past. But when they came back, they were different individuals. They were now looking for something in the old order that was precious, something that had never been recognized in it before. And, in doing this, they were in an essentially self-conscious attitude. That is, they were aware of themselves in the whole process. Now, it is this self-conscious setting-up of the past again that constitutes the romanticism of this period. It made the past a different past. In the first place, people who had hardly been willing to accept it before were willing to accept it now, and to accept it as a pageant. It gave them an emotional experience which was novel, exciting. It created a different past from that which had been there before—a past which was discovered, into which a value had been put which did not belong there before. This value was security, the security of an old order which people thought they had lost and which they now had recovered again. But this was a value which had not been recognized there before, and it gave to the self which discovered it a content which it had not had before. That content, as I have said, was primarily an emotional one. It was the feel of the thing that men got out of this experience. And there was also the freedom that came to the self in traveling back into the past, assuming one rôle after another. I am particularly anxious to bring out this difference in the attitude of men toward the old order. They returned to it with a sense of relief because the French Revolution had meant disturbance, the most considerable war that had been waged in Europe for a long time, together with all that goes with continuous warfare. What followed it was a return to the security of the past, a setting-up of that again, so that men came back to the past with an appreciation which they did not have of it in the earlier period. Furthermore, the self that examined this past and savored it, enjoyed it, was a different self from that of the period of revolution.

We have been discussing the romantic period as a passage from the period of the revolution. The latter undertook to find in the rational nature of man the authority for institutions, as over against the arbitrary authority which belonged to the medieval conception of the institution—whether of the church, the state, the school, or the family. The revolution undertook, in its opposition to this arbitrary authority, to find an authority in the rational nature of man himself. Of course, this turned particularly about the political revolution. In this connection an attempt was made to set up a state on the basis of what were considered the rights of man; to develop rationally, from the theory of these natural rights, what the order of the state should be, to find that which was universal, which was recognized in the attitude of every member of the community. What do you find in the attitude of every member of the community which he asserts as his right and which he recognizes as the rights of others? What do you find there as the basis for the organization of the state? The answer to that question was the undertaking of the revolution, in an attempt to set up the state on the basis of universal rights. But, as we have seen, the revolution broke down and we find the Romantic period taking its place.

As representatives of this latter movement in Germany we have Schiller and Goethe, especially in their earlier productions. Their presentation of the medieval period which was so attractive, so vivid, so full of color, and, on the other hand, that sense of novelty in the self which came from the assumption of different rôles, that, I say, is what constituted the romanticism of this period.

CHAPTER IV

KANT AND THE BACKGROUND OF
PHILOSOPHIC ROMANTICISM

THE self of the Romantic movement is attached to the Kantian self with which we have already become acquainted. We have it very interestingly presented in Schiller's *Aesthetic Letters*, which is one of the early romantic developments of the Kantian doctrine. The Kantian self, as we have seen, had two aspects. One aspect is purely formal as it appeared in the transcendental unity of apperception, that unifying power which holds together, constructs our percepts, makes them different from bare sensations, and gives unity to them. But this unity was a pure function from Kant's standpoint, it was not an entity, was not a spiritual being; it was just a function of unity. The other aspect of this self, we have seen, appears in the *Critique of Practical Reason*. Kant reaches it by way of his postulates. We find ourselves accepting responsibility for our own actions. We could not lay any such responsibility upon ourselves unless we were free, unless actions were our own. From Kant's standpoint, the very fact of the acceptance of responsibility carries with it the postulation that men are free. But in the world of experience—the Kantian world of experience—everything is subject to the laws of the mind, those of the sensibilities—space and time—and those of the understanding—the categories. What takes place there takes place in accordance with the laws of cause and effect. Every effect is a necessary result of its antecedent causes. Thus, freedom cannot be found in the world of experience as we know it. Kant's assumption is that we must postulate a self which, so to speak, lies in a different realm from that of the phenomenal, namely, in the noumenal world of "things-in-themselves." He has proved to his own satisfaction that we cannot know anything of this latter world, but we find ourselves continually postulating such a world. A self, then, that belongs to the world of "things-in-themselves," the noumenal world, is the implication of the *Critique of Practical Reason*. It is a self that must be constantly postulated and that cannot be known. What took place in the Romantic period along a philosophical line was to take this transcendental unity of apperception, which was for Kant a bare logical function, together with the postulation of the self which we could not possibly know but which Kant said we could not help assuming, and compose them into the new romantic self.

Kant's nearest approach to this came not in the first two critiques but in the third, the *Critique of Judgment*. What he points out in that critique is that in life, in vital phenomena, we cannot help assuming some sort of an end which determines the nature of the process that goes on. That is, he brought up the conflict between what is known as the teleological and the mechanical interpretations of nature. Our physics and chemistry undertake to state the nature of the living process in terms of the necessary succession of cause and effect. What takes place does so because of what has occurred before. On the other hand, the biologist talks about functions, about the life-process maintaining itself. He deals with all the functions—respiration, the circulation of the blood, the assimilation of food—from the point of view of the maintenance of the species. There is an end, that is, which lies ahead. The life that is to be lived by the species is to be maintained; it exercises a control over the living process. Kant pointed out that in our perception, our judgment on living things, we are always assuming some sort of an end which determines what takes place. What he is referring to here is not any metaphysical conclusion that can be drawn from this, but that the very object as we know it, the animal or the plant, is perceived as carrying with it its future ends and purposes. We perceive a plant as something more than a mere congeries of atoms and molecules. We perceive a tree as getting moisture from the earth, constructing the starch necessary for the building of its tissues, turning it into sugar, and so forth, as processes essential to its being a tree. These processes together are what a tree is. There is something more in this than in the sort of statement, the mechanical account, that the physicist and the chemist can make.

And then Kant turned his attention to the field of aesthetics, of beauty. There our process of perception constructs that which is itself pleasing, agreeable to our aesthetic taste, and which is not the same as perception. It goes out beyond the mere physical object, the mere sensations themselves, and creates them in such a fashion that one shall get a certain sort of delighted response in connection with the object. There is a creative process that puts things together in such a fashion that we can enjoy them. And that enjoyment is a thing which is involved in our aesthetic appreciation.

The judgment, then, which is involved in the recognition of the life-process of plant and animal, the judgment in our recognition of that which is in itself beautiful, is, in a sense, something which seems to go beyond the world as it is presented in the *Critique of Pure Reason*, the world of science, with its necessity, which is a priori. It even goes beyond the mere affirmation of responsibility which we find in the *Critique of Practical Reason*. It reconstructs the world from the observation of certain ends and purposes—those involved in the very processes of living, on the one hand, and those involved in art, on the other hand.

As I have said, it was, perhaps, from these three different points that the new doctrine of Romantic idealism grew, or to which it attached itself: first was Kant's transcendental unity of apperception; second was the self, the free self which our moral attitude postulates; and third was the experience as depicted in the *Critique of Judgment* which sets up a sort of end or purpose as determining the life-process of living things, and which determines the structure of that which delights our aesthetic tastes. These were the points around which grew up the philosophy which succeeded Kant. One of the earliest expressions of it is found in Schiller's *Briefe über die asthetische Erziehung des Menschen*. These are a study of the aesthetic experience in so far as it expresses this new or romantic self. The new self, as we have seen, appears actually, in the experience of Europe, at the time when people deliberately opened their chests to regain the treasure which belonged to the past but which people now felt, for the first time, might be valuable.

In this connection it is interesting to see that here we have, perhaps for the first time, an expression of our modern historic attitude. That is, people were turning back to the past and were interested in that past as a means of appreciating present conditions. The philosophical representative of this historic phase of the movement was Herder, with his presentation of earlier conditions which were to be found among more primitive people. There was a going-back to the earlier legends and stories and myths that gather around histories, such as the Cid in Spain, and the early French heroes; a going-back to those figures which lay in the memory of the race, of the nation. This process is to be found in the early history of the Romantic movement. In England it is found in the legends of King Arthur and his Round Table.

This historical interest attaches itself to the same movement of the self back into the past. What one has is just such a transcendental unity of apperception as Kant's phrase implies. That is, the self looked back at its own past as it found it in history. It looked back at it and gave the past a new form as that out of which it itself had sprung. It put itself back into the past. It lived over again the adventures and achievements of those old heroes with an interest which children have for the lives of their parents—taking their rôles and realizing not only the past but the present itself in that process. The old stories were brought back in their archaic form. That form had the same fascination for people that old garments have for children. People turned back into the past, became interested in it, and got an interest which showed itself not simply in the pageant, in the story, in the myth, but also in getting the historical connections, seeing how the present had grown out of the past. As I have said, we have in that the beginning of our whole modern historical interest. It had not, as yet, taken on its scientific technique, it had not yet gathered together all its periods; but it was the beginning of that scientific movement.

What I want to bring out, in this connection, is that this interest arises only through the new self going back into the past. It is only because this new self had gone back into the past that such an organized past arose at all. We know, for example, the difference between the histories which are written at the present time and the old chronicles, and we marvel that people could have been willing simply to put down a set of events, the accounts of certain battles, the crowning and death of kings, a mere statement of the meetings of ecclesiastical councils, all these being bare bones without flesh. And yet we have to recognize that history does not exist except in so far as the individuals of the present in some sense put themselves back into the past. It is only in a process of memory—memory of the people, if you like—that history can be created. And such a reconstruction of the past is possible only when we have, so to speak, reached some such point that we can become aware of ourselves. Thus, all the moments which come with the development of adolescence are what make adolescence a romantic period. The child up to the age of twelve does not have a past in any such sense as a child who perhaps only two or three years later has a very definite past. There have been, of course, a succession of days, seasons, years, of periods of vacation out of school, but the past is there simply in those detached events which lie behind. When he goes through the later period—the romantic period, if you like—the child more or less suddenly discovers this past. He discovers it in his reaction against the order of things in the family, the school, and the community. He is in more or less of an attitude of opposition; and in this attitude he goes back over the past, and generally he has a set of grievances which he recognizes. This attitude which belongs to adolescence is essential if the past is to have a definite structure. Otherwise, it is just taken for granted, it is just there; but now it becomes a part of the individual himself. He creates it. Thus in the Romantic period a new self arose, an adolescent, self-conscious self. It turned back upon its past, lived it over again, took up this and that incident and presented them from its own present standpoint.

What I want to make clear is that such a past as that of which I have been speaking is always the creation of a new self, one that has attained content that it did not have before. I want to attach that romantic attitude as we find it in Europe to the attitude which we all have passed through in our own romantic eras. It is a perfectly natural development. It is that of a self that has become aware of itself and turns back upon its own past in order to hold onto that self and, so to speak, create that past as its own. This was the atmosphere of the Romantic period. It is presented vividly in the discussion of Fichte and, more particularly of Schelling, in Royce's *The Spirit of Modern Philosophy*.

The revolution had attempted to define the principles for the reconstruction of society as these are found in the rational nature of the individual. Kant generalized this and undertook to find in the mind of the individual the principles for the organization of nature itself. This position of man had been abandoned in one sense in the breakdown of the French Revolution, but the self that turned to the old order as a result of this breakdown was a very different one than existed originally under this old order. It had taken on a critical attitude. It was in that sense independent. It looked upon the old order, as it accepted it again, from the point of view of one who had rejected it but was again taking it up with more or less definite acceptance.

There is a story of the transcendental period in this country which is illustrative of this. It is a story about Margaret Fuller, one of the transcendentalists gathered about Emerson. This, of course, was the Romantic period as it found philosophical expression in America. Margaret Fuller said, "I accept the universe." To this Carlyle rejoined, "Begad, she'd better!" This represents the attitude of the Romantic period. It accepted an order of things that was there. Its acceptance was a part of the romantic attitude itself. The mind went back to the old order but in a different sense. It went back to it and found something which the mind accepted, and in this the self that accepted the old order was a very different self from that which had existed under the old order, a self which had accepted that order without questioning. It is this different self which is the important characteristic of this Romantic period.

A good illustration of it can be found in the aesthetic attitude toward religious ritual. This is the romantic return to the old religious order. The self sought for that which was aesthetic, attractive in the ritual itself; it was not interested in the dogma as such. The dogma of the church was accepted, but the interest of the individual did not lie in the dogma. It lay in the ritual, the form which united people together in the process of worship, which was expressed in the architecture of the church, in the pageantry of the ritual itself. This appealed directly to the religious response and became characteristic of the religious response during the Romantic period. This response comes back to the individual, to his aesthetic approval or disapproval. In the end, one gets to the point at which he says, "I like this or I do not like this." Of course, there is a great deal more than that in the aesthetic judgment; but at the bottom, one does reach that attitude. That is, one gets back to the direct response of the individual as a basis for judgment. There may be an objective beauty, something that is there independently of the man who appreciates it; but it exists for him only in so far as he is aware of it. Dogma, of course, directly binds man's reason in so far as he accepts it. And this acceptance, from the point of view of reason, is not based upon one's own rational comprehension of the dogma. It transcends the reason of man. It was said, "One believes because the thing believed is impossible." The Trinity, the transubstantiation, were mysteries that transcended the reason of man. Yet, man accepted the dogmas. He did not undertake to determine whether he should accept them or not by their rational character. Dogmas are given by God. They come to man through inspiration, through God's agent on earth —the church—and man accepts them because of his relation to God. Thus dogmas do not appeal directly to man for their support, do not appeal to his reason for their acceptance. But an aesthetic response, on the other hand, always depends upon the individual himself. One responds to them or one does not. And in so far as the revival of religious experience characterized the Romantic period, and in so far as its revival was one in which the aesthetic element was dominant, it inevitably emphasized the individual's response. One found within himself the emotional reason for responding to this ritual. One found in himself that which gave the basis for his acceptance of the church.

There is something of this same attitude in the response to the old political order in so far as it still continued to exist. It had a romantic flavor. Men brought back the pageantry of things. They could not reinstate the knight-errant, for the methods of fighting had driven him from the field; but still they were very much interested in him. He became the object of romance. Novels of the type written by Scott were written about the knight and about the feudal order. And it was the aesthetic response to this order that was of peculiar importance during the period. It was highly interesting, it was fascinating; and, where one went back into it, as did those who had seen the revolution fail, one was able to get a delight out of it which did not belong to the earlier period itself. In that sense the Romantic period rediscovered the Middle Ages. It discovered the aesthetic values in the past that gave the peculiar flavor to it.

Turning again to the philosophical aspects of romanticism, we find the relation of subject to object more fundamental than that of substance and attribute. The way to this lies, of course, through Kant's doctrine. Substance and attribute, cause and effect, are just categories of the mind. Kant did not speak of them as expressions of an Absolute Self, but as forms of the mind itself. The Romantic school, on the other hand, comes back to a Self that is infinite, divine, absolute—one that inevitably has a not-self as its object. That is the nature of the self, that it should have an object; and this latter as an object is a not-self. We cannot have the one without the other; there is no self without its not-self. The self must have a world within which it lives. You can set up an absolute substance in the Spinozistic sense, make everything simply a part of it, and there is nothing which is opposed to it as a not-substance. But if you make the relation between subject and object the central one, you come back to a self which is a subject. But this self cannot be thought of without a not-self, that is, without an object. Furthermore, this relation cannot be presented in static terms. If you are to have an infinite self it must be all-inclusive; you cannot set up a not-self. If you are to reach that outside, you will have to do it in terms which are not static, but dynamic in import, in terms of a process. The self must set up its own not-self. But if it does set it up as a not-self, it must eventually identify this not-self with itself.

Thus, when we come back to the self, which is the dominant conception of the Romantic period, we reach that which must have a relationship with something else beyond itself. The self does not exist except in relation to something else. The word "itself," you will recognize, belongs to the reflexive mode. It is that grammatical form which we use under conditions in which the individual is both subject and object. He addresses himself. He sees himself as others see him. The very usage of the word implies an individual who is occupying the position of both subject and object. In a mode which is not reflexive, the object is distinguished from the subject. The subject, the self, sees a tree. The latter is something that is different from himself. In the use of the term "itself," on the contrary, the subject and object are found in the same entity. This very term "itself" is one which is characteristic of a romantic phase of consciousness. Romanticism turns about a vivid self-consciousness. The romanticist sees things through the guise of his own emotions. Not only that, but he himself bulks larger in his own experience than do other things. He assesses them, evaluates them, in terms of himself. He sets himself up as the standard of values, or at least his own standard of values is that which is dominant in his calculations. That is characteristic of the romantic experience. Whether we find it in such a Romantic period as this which we are considering, or in the period gone through in our own lives, that assessing of things in terms of one's own feeling, one's assertion that a thing is valuable because it is valuable is characteristic of the Romantic period. The self sometimes becomes inordinately prominent in the experience of such an individual. We have to assure people, at that stage, that it is transient, that they will pass through it, and that things will have a different value a little later. It is a period in which the self itself and the relation of things to this self are the important factors in experience. I again want to refer to the peculiar aspect of this self, namely, that it is both subject and object. The individual under these circumstances, then, is apt to be subjectivistic, self-centered, turned in upon himself. I just used the words "turned in upon himself." That is perhaps not characteristic of the Romantic period. The romantic attitude is rather the externalizing of the self. One projects one's self into the world, sees the world through the guise, the veil, of one's own emotions. That is the essential feature of the romantic attitude. The self-centered attitude may be one which is anything but romantic. It may be a hard, selfish attitude, or, on the other hand, a very conscientious attitude. Neither of these is romantic.

The romantic attitude is the ability to project one's self upon the world, so that the world is identified in some fashion with the self. At least the world has value to the individual only in terms of himself. I have referred, in this connection, to the subject-object relationship. At least here in self-consciousness one has both the subject and the object given in the immediate experience; and, if you think of it, it is an attempt to get the subject and the object together, so to speak. That has been the goal of epistemological thought in philosophy in so far as it has attempted to solve the problem of knowledge. How can we assure ourselves of the validity of our knowledge? How can we be sure that what we see and hear is there; that the meanings of things that we grasp are really the meanings that belong to them in the universe outside? That has been the search of philosophy, to get the justification for our knowledge as it appears in experience. Philosophy, throughout its whole existence, has been fighting with the dragon or bogy of skepticism that arises out of the negative answer to this problem.

The philosophy of the Romantic period grew out of the last two critiques of Kant, the *Critique of Practical Reason* and the *Critique of Judgment*. In a sense these belong rather to the period of the revolution. They tried to define the rational nature of man as the ground for his conduct and for the order of society. Kant generalized the position involved in the theory of natural rights, which was that one could claim for himself only that which he recognized equally for others. And Kant gave a generalization of this as the basis for his moral doctrine, the categorical imperative—that every act should be of such a character that it could be made universal for everyone under the same conditions. Kant said that this judgment was one which carried with it the sense of responsibility. As a rational being, one found himself responsible for making such universal judgments; that is, one assumed the responsibility of acting as he would wish everyone else to act under the same conditions. If he should act in that way, he must have the freedom so to act; otherwise he would not be responsible for his act. The sense of responsibility in man, then, leads to the postulate that he is free. In Kant's theory of experience, however, there could be no freedom. Everything came under the law of cause and effect. If man's will is free, it must be that his will, his self—the self—embodies in itself such a responsible will; it must be that it belongs to the world of "things-in-themselves," and not to the world of our immediate, our phenomenal experience. But the order of the world as it appears in experience is a mechanical order. That is, it is an order in which the effect is the necessary result of the preceding cause—in which, therefore, the idea, the end, the purpose that a person could have, all the idea or purpose involved in life, is such that it can have no causal value. There can be no final cause in a mechanical world. And yet, as Kant pointed out, our whole understanding of that which is living, and our whole understanding of that which is beautiful, which is art, implies ends. There is a determining purpose. There is something in our comprehension of the world which transcends the order of the world as science presents it to us. And this something would have to be found in the realm of "things-in-themselves," the noumenal world.

Well now, the Romantic movement, as I have said, grew out of this phase of the Kantian doctrine. Kant thought of a mind which gives laws to nature. But these laws which the mind gives to nature are simply the forms of the mind, the molds into which experience inevitably falls. If the mind has a certain form, then its experience must take on that form. We postulate freedom on the part of the individual, but we cannot know it. We cannot know ourselves in our freedom. We cannot help postulating that we are free, but our knowledge of ourselves is always a knowledge of cause and effect. For example, if a person considers one of his acts, he inevitably explains it in terms of the reasons for his conduct, and those reasons are expressed in terms of his motives. One's explanation itself is one which seems to wipe out the freedom which he attaches to his own conduct. One feels responsible for one's acts, and yet they are explicable in terms of cause and effect. This is a paradox, one of the antinomies that Kant says we cannot avoid. One does not, then, give laws to nature in the sense that the self is the source of them. The laws are already there, embodied in the mind itself—not in the empirical self, the self which is the concern of psychology, but in the one that has to be postulated as lying back of the forms, a self which is free.

In other words, the problem that lies back of skepticism and of the empirical school, and that to which Kant gave his critical answer, was met by the romanticists by the indentification of the object of knowledge and the very process of knowledge in so far as that was found in the self. Kant had to postulate that the self must be a thing-in-itself; or, at least, he had stated that this was a postulate that conduct involved. All our conduct involves the assumption that the self is a cause, and that the conduct which results from this cause is accompanied by a sense of obligation. Obligation implies freedom, and freedom implies causation on the part of the self. But, from Kant's standpoint, this self could not enter into the field of knowledge; it could be only a postulate.

In dealing with this problem, the Romantic school went back to the experience of a self as involving itself as an object. This is the experience which corresponds to the reflexive mode to which I was referring. In that mode, you will remember, the self is present as a subject only in so far as it is present as an object, and is present as an object only in so far as it is present as a subject. There cannot be one without the other. Our self-consciousness involves both of these essential characteristics. If, now, one can make this relationship of subject and object a primary relation in experience, one more fundamental than those of substance and attribute, cause and effect, then it can be said that we have, in self-consciousness, the self presented as both subject and object.

This relationship guarantees the reality of our knowledge. It does this not simply in the sense that there are certain experiences there, certain impressions and ideas, but in the sense that there is a self there that finds an object in itself. That was the position of the romantic idealist that distinguished him from the position of Kant or of Descartes. Kant affirmed that the self was postulated as an ultimate entity. It was a reality, but it could not possibly be known. Descartes affirmed that the self must exist because we think; and because we think, we must be. But he did not posit an immediate experience of the self in this thinking. It is to the experience of the self as such that the romanticist goes back—that experience in which the self is the most real thing, the most poignant reality in experience. Then the romanticist undertakes to carry back all experience, at least all cognitive experience, to this immediate experience of the self. All other experiences flower out of this one.

Now, the romanticist, on coming back to the experience of the self, found not only the evidence of existence which Descartes has signalized in his *Cogito ergo sum*, that is, found evidence not only of the ego or self, but also found in that self an object of knowledge such as Kant affirmed could not be found through introspection. It is this which gives the peculiar character to Romantic philosophy. It comes back to an experience in which both subject and object are immediately given. In introspection—that is, in the introspection of the English empiricists, Locke, Berkeley, and Hume—one is dealing only with states of consciousness, with impressions and ideas, or sensations and images, but not directly with the self. Hume undertook to show that the empirical self is simply an association of these states of consciousness. That is, it is not primary, but secondary. It is a congeries of some importance, an importance that gathers about the significance that comes from the body. This self was analyzed by Hume into a set of relations, of associations. It was not an object of knowledge. That is, it was not given as an object of knowledge in the process of knowledge, and there was no way of reaching it, as knowledge, in that process. The states of consciousness were those out of which the self was built up; they were simply associated together into a self. The self was not given first with the states dependent upon it. The states of consciousness—that is, the impressions and ideas—were present, and they became associated with each other in a certain pattern which constituted the self. If you undertook to analyze this group of impressions and ideas, you saw that they were simply associated together as those impressions and ideas which, when brought together, go to make up a table, tree, or any other object. Kant took this same position as far as the empirical self was concerned. Such an object was simply the organization of our so-called inner experiences, although Kant said that these fall under the categories of substance and attribute, cause and effect. But these categories belong to the mind, they do not actually reveal the self as an entity, as a composition of these impressions and ideas.

The Romantic philosophers, like their predecessors, came back to the age-old problem of knowledge: How can one get any assurance that that which appears in our cognitive experience is real? The skepticism to which we have referred had shattered all the statements, all the doctrines, of the medieval philosophy. It had even torn to pieces the philosophy of the Renaissance. As we have seen, it had destroyed the substantial structure which had been presented in such a magnificent fashion by Spinoza. It had shattered the natural structure of the world which the Renaissance science had presented in such simplicity and yet such majesty, that causal structure that led Kant to say that there were two things that overwhelmed him, the starry heavens above and the moral law within. This picture of a world which was the expression of simple but universal laws had also been shattered by the skepticism of Hume, and the only antidote that Kant could present was the postulate of conduct.

This is the old problem of assuring one's self of the reality of one's cognitive experience, that our world was not such stuff as dreams were made of, that it was there as we know it, was there again for this new philosophy to try its teeth upon. And the romanticists approached it, of course, from the point of view of the self, but a self which was not simply an associative experience. The self to which they came back was the presupposition of such an experience, a self which was the most real thing in the experience of the moment. The assurance was, first of all, largely temperamental—an emotional experience. It was the assurance that the adolescent has that he is the most important element in the whole universe, an assurance which leads him to test everything from the point of view of his own judgment. It was that assurance, but it was something more too. It was an assurance that was backed up by this discovery that one can, by taking the rôle of the other, come back upon himself and secure himself as a given object of knowledge. It was this, I say, which was the center of the Romantic philosophy; and it was by using this point of view, this leverage, that the romanticists undertook to deal with the problem of knowledge.

It is interesting to contrast this philosophy with that of Spinoza, because he exerted a profound influence upon thinkers of this period who were not technically philosophers—such men as Goethe, for example. Spinoza's philosophy was like the philosophy of the Romantic school in that it was monistic. That is, it came back to the conception of a single principle, a single divine principle from which all that appears in experience must be thought of as arising, or within which all that was found in experience could be conceived of as placed and ordered, getting its reality from this fundamental principle. The Spinozistic approach was from the point of view of substance. Spinoza's *Ethics*, his principal philosophical work, starts with the definition of this divine principle as the *causa sui*, the cause of itself, that which is responsible for itself, which does not look elsewhere for the reason for its existence. This was conceived of as a fundamental substance which had an indefinite, infinite number of attributes, one of which was extension and another consciousness, or thought, as Spinoza expressed it. I have brought that out to show that the positions of subject and object are in these different respective philosophies. Spinoza's conception is, as I have said, of a divine, substantial Being which exhibits itself in the form both of extension and of thought. The world as we think it, as we are conscious of it, is the same God, under the aspect of consciousness, as is the world of extension. It is the same reality from two points of view. There is then a necessary point-for-point relationship between the two. That is the Spinozistic doctrine. Here you see the relationship between a subject that knows and an object that is known. That relationship of subject and object belongs to the attributes of the one substance. The relation between them, then, must be a one-to-one relationship. That is, everything that appears in extension must also appear in thought, and vice versa. Here is, among other things, the beginning of the parallelistic doctrine so widely used in psychologies of today. But the subject-object relationship is one that follows from the attributes of this substance. Substance and attribute have to be accepted, first of all, as the fundamental character of reality; and it follows from this that there should be a mind that knows an object, but it is the same substance expressed both in the mind and in the object.

If one wanted to make a statement to bring this out from a more concrete psychological standpoint, it would be a distinction between the sensation and that which is sensed, or what modern psychology refers to as the "sensum," and the sensation as the sensing. We can take it from either approach, either as that sensed or as the sensing. In somewhat the same fashion we may say that Spinoza conceived of this fundamental reality both as that which is extended, and as that of which we are conscious. Both are the same substance.

The romanticist comes back to a different form of experience, that which is referred to in grammatical construction, as I have pointed out above, as the reflexive mode. In this mode of experience we have both the subject and the object given in the same process. Then, seemingly at least, we have something of which we can be sure. If we know ourselves, we seem to have a case of knowledge which can be depended upon. It is going back in one sense, of course, to Descartes' syllogism or inference, "I think, therefore I am." But Descartes was simply assuring himself of the existence of himself. What the romanticist is doing is assuring himself of the existence of the object of his thought. In his thinking, Descartes started off from the knowledge that he existed; but whether that which he thought about existed was another question, and he had a long metaphysical probe before he got an answer to that question which satisfied him, and which, incidentally, has not satisfied most philosophers who have succeeded him. All the romanticist maintained was that this attitude to which I am referring is an attitude that assures him, not only that he exists in his own thinking, but also that the object of his thought exists, or that not only he exists in his consciousness but the object of his consciousness also exists. Where Descartes could assure himself simply of the existence of consciousness itself in the process of self-awareness, the Romantic philosopher assured himself of the existence of that of which he was conscious. Not only the thinker that thinks, but also that about which he thinks, exists in this reflexive mode. For Descartes, I am conscious and therefore exist; for the romanticist, I am conscious of myself and therefore this self, of which I am conscious, exists and with it the objects it knows. The object of knowledge, in this mode at least, is given as there with the same assurance that the thinker is given in the action of thought.

If one can make this reflexive situation the central position in one's philosophy, if one can come back immediately to the consciousness of self instead of to substance and attribute, one can say that this consciousness of self is at the center of the universe. In this, one has, so to speak, a test—a philosopher's stone—by means of which one can determine what is given in knowledge. It was, of course, a very sympathetic attitude for a Romantic age. That is just what a romanticist does. All values are those which he feels as a part of himself. Out of this experience, in which the mind, the soul, the individual, is both subject and object, the romanticist builds a universe. The self of this mode becomes the assured center of the universe, that out of which the world is to be built.

I have just pointed out the elements of this identification between the self and the not-self. The very unity is assumed in our experience. It is a unity which comes from the very process of experience. The latter may be composed of an indefinite number of different elements, and yet it appears as a unit, organized and related with reference to our own organism. Thus, the very unity of the object is the unity of the self. The great sphere of the heavens is a projection of the sphere of the eye; the straight line is a projection of the line of vision; our sensuous world is the structure of our very process of sensation. We cut out, so to speak, the world in which we are to act. The content of perception is taken back to the content of our own sensation; the organization and content of the object can be taken back to the self. Yet, the perception is not the sensation; the object is not the self. In fact, the self can appear in experience only in so far as there is a not-self which yet has this very content and form of the self. As I have been saying, the fundamental opposition to which these romantic idealists came back was this opposition between subject and object, with the assumption of a fundamental identity between them. The self and the not-self are opposed to each other, and yet they are identical. Whether you take it from the point of view of morality, as Fichte did, or from the point of view of the artist's intuition, with Schelling, or from that of thought, as Hegel worked it out, there is always this opposition between the self and the not-self; and yet underneath this opposition lies the assumption of their identity.

CHAPTER V

THE ROMANTIC PHILOSOPHERS—FICHTE

WE HAVE looked at the movement which we have been discussing, namely, Romantic idealism, from the point of view of its philosophic background, that is, Kant's critical philosophy. We have looked at it also from the standpoint of the political revolution, which failed in its first undertaking. The after-effect of this revolution was to emphasize the self-consciousness of the individual of the period. In the first place, Rousseau had undertaken to find in man the principles upon which he could reconstruct the state, substituting a rational form of the state for the arbitrary form which belonged to the medieval system. This, as we have seen, proved an immediate failure, and the Napoleonic imperialistic régime came in to take the place of this attempted rational state. I have said that the effect of this was to throw individuals back upon themselves. Theoretically, they undertook to go back to the old régime. And, returning to the régime from the standpoint of their own self-consciousness, they discovered in it what they had not discovered before, namely, what is called its "romantic tang." They discovered the medieval period and all the fascination of its pageantry, of the characteristic figures of the period—the knight-errant, the saint, the magician, and the learned man—and they discovered the adventure that went with it. They went back into that old pageantry with a fascination which it had never had for them before. That is the romantic phase of the movement, this return to the old world from the point of view of the new self-consciousness.

On the philosophical side, this meant the return to the old rationalistic world, especially as Kant had left it, from the point of view of the self regarded as a thing-in-itself. Just, as in some sense, this older world was reconstructed from the point of view of their romantic imagination, so a return was made to the transcendental philosophy of Kant from the point of view of Fichte's self, the self of Schelling, and that of Hegel, the romantic self which was identified with the Absolute Self, in which individuals were conceived as mere finite expressions of this larger Self. An attempt was made to deal with the problem that philosophy presented from this standpoint. And we can find that out of which this problem arose, or at least the materials it used, in Kant's antinomies.

Those antinomies represented for Kant the attempts of the mind, its reason and understanding, to go beyond experience, beyond the phenomenal world, to a noumenal world which it was necessary for Kant to postulate. Every attempt of that sort, according to Kant, meant an antinomy, a contradiction in the terms that were used. For him these antinomies served as the sign of warning that the mind had got beyond the limit of its own legitimate use. The only path, as Kant saw it, by means of which one could leave the field of experience, with its fixed forms, was through the postulates of conduct. Here one did not profess to know, in that one knew that one could not know; but, nonetheless, one postulated a world of things-in-themselves, and particularly postulated a free will, that is, a self that is free and which could, for that reason, assume obligations.

The Romantic idealist started from this postulate not as a postulate but as something which is directly given in experience —not only given in the sense of obligation, which Kant recognized, but given also in conduct, in the experience of freedom. Romanticism also recognized antinomies, that is, it recognized that the passage from the conduct of the self, this free self, over into the field of experience took place over contradictions or oppositions.

There are three attempts to deal with the problems to which this situation gives rise—those of Fichte, Schelling, and Hegel. In a certain sense these represent a progression, a development.

That of Fichte is an attempt to solve the problem of the self and its object in terms of moral experience; Schelling deals with it from the point of view of aesthetic or artistic experience; and, most fundamental of all, Hegel deals with it in terms of logical experience, the experience of thought.

In a certain sense, there is an advance in these three undertakings. The common problem is that of bringing the world which seems to be independent of the self into the experience of the self. It is quite true that in any self-experience we have both subject and object. But it does not follow that the experience that one has of one's self is veritable. One is often deceived in regard to himself. This is especially true in a romantic mood. But at least the self is there as an object in experience. One senses himself as there, and he is there in the attitude which he has at the time. The object is there, and the subject is there. The two are brought together. But now the problem arises, can that mode be used to bring over into the self the world which is seemingly not the self? Can the world which is independent of the self be brought into its self-experience? The experience which we depend upon for the direction of our conduct, that which we call "objective," has to do with things that are not ourselves. We have to find out about them. They are in some sense foreign to us. We have to learn their ways; learn what nature is, what its laws are. Can this world of reality outside of us, the world with which we have become acquainted, be brought into this relation of subject and object which we have in self-consciousness? This, I say, was the problem of the romanticists. This was the problem, the adventure which called these thinkers. Given a subject and an object of knowledge in the self-experience itself, can one go out to the great universe that dominates the self, that precedes and antedates it, that outlasts it, that is so independent of it, and capture that universe and make it a part of one's own self-experience?

The Romantic idealists came back to the process of the self. We have seen the background of this. The self was looked at not as a static affair; it was not conceived of in the medieval sense as a soul that was born into the world with the body and changed the body, a self that was endowed by a divine fiat. Rather, the self was looked upon as a certain process, something that is going on.

The first characteristic of this process which Fichte laid stress upon was that it involved a not-self. The very existence of the self implies a not-self; it implies a not-self which can be identified with the self. You have seen that the term "self" is a reflexive affair. It involves an attitude of separation of the self from itself. Both subject and object are involved in the self in order that it may exist. The self must be identified, in some sense, with the not-self. It must be able to come back at itself from outside. The process, then, as involved in the self is the subject-object process, a process within which both of these phases of experience lie, a process in which these different phases can be identified with each other—not necessarily as the same phase but at least as expressions of the same process. This, you see, makes a different thing out of knowledge than does the copy theory.

The copy theory of knowledge goes back to ancient thought. It assumes that the object impresses its form on the mind. A favorite analogy, of course, is from vision. In some way the form of the object impresses itself on the retina, and from the retina on the mind itself. The camera obscura of the eye has served unwittingly on the part of philosophy as determining knowledge from the impressions of experience. As Aristotle thought of it, the form of the thing in some way floated through the eye into the mind. It impressed itself there on the mind. Sometimes the mind was spoken of as a wax tablet on which the form was impressed. This is an analogy of which the empiricist made use. It is a static theory of knowledge. Knowledge is simply the reception of a certain form impressed upon the mind. The object in this case does not necessarily involve the subject. It involves the mind as something on which it can be impressed. As far as the doctrine is concerned, that mind might be subject or not.

The first attack made upon the problem, the one made by

Fichte, was through the development of the Kantian principles into the philosophy of romanticism. Specifically, he utilized the moral experience which was the center of the Kantian metaphysics. In this moral experience, as we have seen, the individual identifies himself with his duty. In this philosophy Fichte took a step beyond Kant. Kant never got beyond the formal character of conduct. Our conduct is moral, he says, in so far as it is universal. We test it by seeing whether or not we can make a universal law out of the maxim of our act. The Fichtean position is one that goes beyond this and identifies the self with the task to be performed. This Fichte presents as the reality of the moral experience—that one finds before him something to be done and then, in the doing, finds himself identified with it. It is not only a task: it is his task. He is involved in it. And the accomplishment of the task, the doing of the duty, realizes the individual. It is just in so far as one does what he has to do that he becomes really moral. It is only in so far as he identifies himself with an undertaking that he achieves himself. We speak of this process as the "development of character," and we speak of "character" as the core of one's personality. Now, character is attained only in so far as one does identify himself with the situation which presents itself before the moral vision. Selfhood is attained in a process in which the individual identifies himself with his task. The individual realizes himself in that process.

This is the point of approach in Fichte's philosophy. For the individual the world is always a task to be accomplished. It is not simply there by chance, as something that just happens. It is there because one realizes it as a field for one's endeavors. It is not a world simply in so far as there are sensations, in so far as there is the movement of masses of bodies. It is a world, a real thing, just to the extent that one constructs it, that one organizes it for one's action. The objects about one are means of conduct. They take on meaning in proportion as one uses them as means. The ground is something to tread upon. The objects about one are all implements. The universe is a field of action. It is organized only in so far as one acts in it. Its meaning lies in the conduct of the individual; and when one has built up his world as such a field of action, then he realizes himself as the individual who carried out that action. That is the only way in which he can achieve a self. One does not get at himself simply by turning upon himself the eye of introspection. One realizes himself in what he does, in the ends which he sets up, and in the means he takes to accomplish those ends. He gets the rational organization out of it, sees a relationship between means and ends, puts it all together as a plan; and then he realizes that the plan of action presented in this situation is an expression of his own reason, of himself. And it is not until one has such a field of action that he does secure himself. This process, according to Fichte, is what is continually taking place. The self throws up the world as a field within which action must take place; and, in setting up the world as a field of action, it realizes itself.

This is, of course, just putting into philosophical form the rediscovery of the medieval period as that in which the self could imaginatively act and then come back upon itself. In this the process is carried out in a dramatic fashion, under an aesthetic mood. Fichte raises it to a process within a moral world in which the individual organizes the world into a field in which he must act.

However, the problem is not yet solved. It is true that the meaning which our world has does lie in what we are going to do with it. The meaning of the world is not to be found in its atoms and molecules, in its electrons. Their framework, whether they shall take on the form of trees or of men, depends upon the experience of those who inhabit the world. You can look on it as just a congeries of electrons, but that does not make the universe that we inhabit. All the meaning of life is something that depends upon living beings, upon conscious beings, beings with eyes that paint the world in its colors, with ears that give it its resonances. It is this world that arises out of the individuals that live in it. And yet, this world of physical things is there, and it is there seemingly before the self comes into existence in it. In fact, it seems to be a condition for the existence of the self. Fichte simply assumed that the Absolute Self, which is the organization of all selves, built up such a world, set it up as the field of endeavor, that it might realize itself. But there is an independence about this world. It is the scene of endeavor, but still it is a scene that has to be given before endeavor, in order that the latter can take place. Our scientific picture of the world is independent of the individual who inhabits it. He comes into it, and it may be the scene of his endeavor. It may take on his values, the values of society, but still it is there in advance of him. It does not seem to be dependent upon him in any way.

This was the period in which evolutionary thought first appeared. It was presented first in the hypothesis of Lamarck, later in that of Darwin. Thus, the conception was before men; and that conception holds that man and all that man means— his self-consciousness, his values—are dependent upon the prior development of a physical universe—the appearance of continental masses which kept the earth from being completely immersed. It is quite possible, quite conceivable, of course, that the water might have covered everything. There is enough water to cover the whole of the earth if the continents should be plunged into the depths of the sea. Had this been the case, man, of course, would not have appeared. What life there would have been would be the vertebrates in the ocean, and perhaps not even these. There might have been only unicellular forms that float upon the surface of water. It would seem to be simply by chance, then, that the world developed such a species as man. After all, it is our scientific knowledge—the most clear knowledge that we have—that presents man as an accident and not as an essential product of the nature of the universe.

Of course, it is true that on the moral side man is the center of the universe. The moral world is there because of man, for, if there was no self-consciousness, there would be no morality, no claim that one could make upon another, no society with its contentions, customs, and laws. Morality is dependent upon man; and as long as Fichte remained within his moral philosophy, he could conceive of the self as responsible for the world. But when he attempted to make the development of the world itself simply a phase of the moral experience of man, he found himself in a clash with the surest knowledge that we have. The attempt to build up science, knowledge, out of this moral experience was not successful on Fichte's part.

Of course, Fichte had attempted this on the basis of the development of a dialectical argument which goes a step beyond what Kant called his "transcendental logic." Kant, you remember, said that there was an analytic logic that simply breaks up an idea into its different parts and then affirms one of those parts of the conception—for example, the conception of man as having essentially an animal nature, and of that animal nature as being, in its very essence, mortal. You cannot think of an animal or of man without also thinking of mortality as a part of them. That, says Kant, is the pure analytic process, a process in which you are merely confirming an idea of an object which already belongs to it in the very conception of the object itself. If you say, "Socrates is a man," you already state, in the conception of Socrates as a man, the idea of mortality. But, Kant contends, when we come to the sort of judgment with which he started, that is, the judgments that we find in the axioms of Euclid, we come upon judgments that are of a different type. Kant's illustration was of a straight line being the shortest distance between two points. You can analyze the idea of a straight line as much as you want and you will not find in it the idea of the shortest distance between two points. This latter is something added to the former idea; and Kant asked how such judgments, which he called "synthetic judgments a priori," could be formed. It is easy enough, he said, to see how we can form empirical judgments involving something new. You find out something about your friends, you add to your ideas about them through experience; but that is not the process of synthetic judgments a priori but of synthetic judgments a posteriori. That is, they are empirical judgments, in which we find something that we did not find before, but something that has been given through experience. But judgments such as the Euclidian axioms are judgments that stand at the beginning of your science. You have them as postulates with which you can start. Kant's explanation of this is in the forms of the mind which determine the nature of our experiences. They are, so to speak, the capital with which our science operates. These forms are given in advance of experience and make such synthetic judgments a priori possible. Now this sort of logic Kant distinguishes from the other analytic type by calling it transcendental. Thus we can affirm everything of our experience which belongs to the structure of the forms of the sensibility and of the understanding. At least, Kant thought so. He was quite sure that he had the whole structure of our possible experience, that he had anatomized the whole of our experience and could show just what its form was and must continue to be. But this description is static. According to it, the forms are all there and nothing is added to them. They do not require any process of development.

Fichte's world was not one of static forms. It was a world in which there was opposition between the self and a not-self which took the form of a task that had to be done, an obstacle that had to be overcome. He undertook particularly to show that moral conduct consists in the assimilation of the not-self to the self. He assumed that the self set up, posited, a world that was a not-self and that this not-self had to become the self. That is the antimony which Fichte says has to be overcome in moral conduct. This is the central point in his position. The very thing that we feel we must do is the thing that seems foreign to us. It represents interests which we do not recognize, which are not our own. And yet we feel the moral necessity of making them our own. Effort that has to be expended is effort not simply in doing something but effort expended in making something one's own interest which at first is not an interest. And yet one recognizes that this interest which is not one's own ought to be a part of one's self. One has certain obligations to the group to which he belongs. These are duties which really make him a part of the community. They cannot be divorced from the person. He is a free member of the community, but on the condition that he exercises the rights and the duties of citizenship. It is this that makes him a free member of the community. There could not be any community unless the individual did do his duties, and yet he finds them to be a nuisance. He does not want to take the trouble to vote, to enter into a campaign. He wants to do other things that he feels are identified with himself, things which he is interested in doing. And yet he wants to be a member of a democratic community, and he wants to have the rights of citizenship, with all that citizenship means. That is something which is not the self and yet which is essential to the self. That is the attitude which we all recognize as appearing in our moral life. Moral conduct consists in so assimilating this obligation that it becomes a real interest of the individual and not just a disagreeable duty. It is to that phase of the moral life that Fichte comes back in endeavoring to present this view of his in regard to the nature of the self, namely, that it constantly transcends the not-self which is to be made part of the self.

The antinomical contradiction is there, but it is in a different form from the Kantian one which indicates the limits beyond which knowledge cannot go. Fichte says the contradiction represents an actual step in the development of reality, of the self. The self grows by overcoming those obstacles, by making them its own interests. That assumption that reality is a process of development, the development of the self, is the first step in the idealistic dialectic. This is what reality is. And this development takes place over obstacles or contradictions.

Fichte can, of course, point to other phases besides that moral phase to which I have just referred, but this is the one that is central to his position. He can point particularly to the very nature of the self. The self is a type of experience which we attain only by becoming, in a certain sense, not-selves. That is, we cannot get the experience of ourselves as selves except in so far as we take the attitude of another and regard ourselves from that point of view. There may be the experience of pleasure, of pain; there may be the presence of colors and sounds about us; and yet these do not become ours in the sense that we recognize them as ours unless we can in some sense distinguish ourselves from other selves. We have to realize ourselves by taking the rôle of another, playing the part of another, taking the attitude of the community toward ourselves, continually seeing ourselves as others see us, regarding ourselves from the standpoint of those about us. This is not the self-consciousness that goes with awkwardness and uneasiness. It is the assured recognition of one's own position, one's social relations, that comes from being able to take the attitude of others toward ourselves. We cannot recognize our rights in demanding them of others without being ourselves in their place and recognizing their rights. We have to put ourselves in place of the other to recognize the self. Here again Fichte can come back to a character of the self which involves a not-self. There must be a not-self in order that the self may exist.

Fichte's idealism, like that of others of this Romantic idealistic school, is what is called "Absolute Idealism." That is, it assumes that there is an Absolute Self of which our selves are mere finite expressions. We have seen that, for Kant, the conceptions of the infinite and the finite represent one of the antinomies or group of antinomies that indicate the limits of our possible knowledge. For Fichte it represents the relationship between the finite self and the Absolute Self. He said that the self could not posit itself as a finite self without at the same time positing an infinite, unconditioned, and Absolute Self. To posit one's self as finite involves identifying one's self with the Absolute. As Fichte expressed it in a picturesque way, "I create God every day." It is the very experience of realizing one's self as a finite self that involves the assurance of the identity or centering of the self in the Absolute Self.

Fichte lived during the early part of the nineteenth century, when Germany was under the domination of Napoleon. The

French were in control, and naturally there arose among the Germans a national sense of opposition to this invasion of the outsider within their borders; and there arose among them the national movement which finally, in conjunction with the movements in other countries, drove the French out of Germany and led to the defeat of Napoleon. It was a great national and moral movement in Germany, and Fichte was one of its spokesmen. In Berlin, where he had been appointed professor of philosophy, he delivered a series of addresses to the German people, in which he summoned them to their task. They were very stirring addresses, and called out echoes throughout the whole of Germany. They emphasized a new type of national life, one that was not expressed in the relation of the Hohenzollerns to their subjects.

Frederick the Great was the man who had, up to this time, administered Prussia from the top down. He was a monarch who recognized himself not simply as monarch of the state but also as the state. His control was absolute. He took his subjects with him into various wars in which they had no immediate interest and which were of doubtful moral character—those wars in which Poland was defeated, in which Prussia seized Silesia from Austria, wars of the Austrian Succession, wars in which Frederick was fighting for the aggrandizement of his house and of his kingdom, but wars which were not an expression of a popular movement. They were not wars that grew out of an expression of a demand of the people for an interest with which they identified themselves. The immediate successors of Frederick did not have his genius or his power; but, nonetheless, there grew up under the conditions of the new period an ideal of a national life that could defend itself against the invader and establish itself again on its own, new national basis. It was out of this movement that the nation at arms arose. The army of Frederick the Great was an army which he chose from among the people for the purposes of his military undertakings. This new movement was the one in which universal military service, with the nation as such in arms, appeared for the first time.

Furthermore, there was behind this movement a recognition that there must be intelligence, a popular intelligence, one that did not come simply from the populace up or from the top down, but which permeated the nation as a whole. With this military service went popular education; and for a few intensive years there grew up in Prussia a national life which made an entirely different power out of it, one that was able to cope with the genius of Napoleon and with his armies.

The immediate political and social background of Fichte, then, was the war in which the western and eastern states drove Napoleon out of Germany and Austria. With this background, Fichte appealed very vividly to the national sense of the Prussians, presenting this task to them as one which the people themselves had to undertake. He pictured a German nation which had certain definite duties before it which it must meet, but meet with intelligence, comprehension, with a recognition that morality rests upon intelligence. It was distinctly a historical situation in which the people had to create their own approach, and create it in terms of a task which they had to fulfil. They had to realize themselves in that task. It is, of course, in such a movement of defensive warfare that, in the past, a nation has come most completely to consciousness of itself, has achieved a national self-consciousness in fulfilling such a duty as that of meeting an enemy already within its borders, an enemy already breaking down the organization of its own state. Here, then, is a task which has to be accomplished, something that has to be done, in the face of danger and suffering of every sort. And in that there is attained national self-consciousness which does not exist under ordinary conditions. Under the latter, we buy and sell, we carry out our usual social processes. In a vague sort of way we all know that we are members of the same community, but we are not conscious of it. We find ourselves in more or less hostile relations with our competitors, and we do not identify ourselves with the community as a whole. But in other moments, such as this of which I have been speaking, when the community has to defend itself against an ènemy that has already taken possession, people get together in a common undertaking, identify themselves with each other, and get that larger self-consciousness to which Fichte was appealing. This occurs in just that sort of a situation which I have expressed metaphysically as the self realizing itself in the not-self, finding its not-self in the duty which it has to perform, and in doing that duty, in making it its own, reaching a higher self-consciousness than it had before. Warfare is not the only way in which that has been achieved in the past, but it is one of the most common ways. It seems to be the easiest way in which people can recognize themselves as belonging to the same community, the same group. This they achieve in that attitude of defense against a common enemy. And it was just such a situation that lay behind Fichte and which he put into his form of the Romantic philosophy.

This situation he conceived to be not only the very process of national consciousness but also that of the universe itself. This very not-self, this separation, so to speak, of the task from the person who has accomplished it, is what Fichte comes back to, to explain the world as something that is there over against the self and which the self cannot control, or at least for which the self does not seem to be responsible. The moral situation to which I have referred is one in which, to a certain extent, we do create our own field in so far as we assume a certain task. But the world itself is a world of physical things, is one which is not the self. It is a not-self in a different fashion. The task which one does not want to assume is a not-self. But that it is a task at all is due to the fact that we accept it as a task. We accept the universe. The moral universe, like the physical, is there because we do accept it. If we did not have a moral attitude toward it, it would not be there. But, seemingly, the physical world is there anyway, and that was the problem that Fichte had to work out philosophically.

How could he take this moral point of view over into the situation in which the individual does not set up a not-self as a task and then overcome it? How was he to identify this subject-object relation with that of our cognitive experience, with that of the world we are aware of about us? Can these two be brought together? That was his problem. How could he take our awareness of a world there independently of us and identify it with this moral attitude in which the individual does set up a task which, for the time being, lies outside himself but with which he later identifies himself? That, as I say, was the task of Romantic philosophy as Fichte presented it, or as it presented itself to Fichte. He must make the subject-object relation as it appears in our moral experience a relation of the knower to the known, a relation between that which we sense and the organism which senses it, a relation between that which we think and the mind that thinks it. Can one identify this relation with the moral relation? Fichte undertakes to do this, and it is an undertaking in which he was only partially successful. The picture he presents of the world is that of a task, a picture of a not-self which in a certain sense is foreign to the individual. It is something that has to be overcome, and, being overcome, is made a part of the self. If, now, Fichte could conceive of the world in a moral sense, he could conceive of it in some sense as the creation of that self.

Remember how Kant left this problem? For Kant there was a world of science, of knowledge. Of course, science is nothing but exact knowledge. The world is determined by the very characters which the mind has stamped on it. The mind gives these laws not by choice but because they reflect its structure. They are parts of its own structure; they are molds, so to speak, in which experience falls when it comes to the mind. But the mind does not give itself those laws in the same sense in which a man regards himself as giving the character to his act. Here he feels his own responsibility, for he recognizes the act as coming from his own initiative. Thus he is responsible for his act in a way in which he is not responsible for the laws of nature which are given in the forms of his sensibility and of his understanding.

But Fichte conceived of the world as being essentially moral, not simply as something that is known. It has moral significance, for it presents itself as a task, as an accomplishment that must be carried out. If the self could be free, if it could have initiative in its moral conduct, then, if the world was a moral world, it could be the creation of the self. The self could be free in giving its task, just as it is free in doing or not doing its task. And yet the world is, of course, independent of any one finite individual's self. That is, in some sense we find the world given. We are born into it; we die, and it remains behind us. How is it possible to conceive of the self as creating such a world? From the moral standpoint one does, in a certain sense, create his immediate world. That is, one makes it his own task. One finds himself in the midst of an immediate environment, something that is there; but he organizes it from the point of view of his own responsibility. That responsibility may be infinitesimal as compared to the whole universe, but still that universe exists for one as that for which he is in some sense responsible. He has to get his day's work done. He has to select out and organize this world about him in such a way that he can carry out his task. The ground on which he treads, the means of transportation which he selects, the building he enters, and the apparatus that he uses are all organized by him with reference to his particular function. It is only in so far as it is there, organized in this way that he can act on it, that he can do his duty. One is always organizing one's world with reference to one's duty, with regard to the function which he has to carry out. He looks at the world from the standpoint of the means which he can make use of to carry out his function. That may be a small part of the world, but for him it is the ground upon which he can tread. Everything is, in his mind, organized with reference to carrying out the act which is his own.

So much for the world so far as the particular individual is concerned. If we extend this response and take in all the individuals in society, we can see that they can all, in some sense, create the world in which that society lives, calling out the ideas that belong to that society. All men are, in some sense, organized in so far as they belong to a single society; and as that society clears its land, sows its crops, builds its buildings, it creates a world in which it can definitely live, and each man has his part in that society as a whole.

Now what the philosophical imagination of Fichte did was to go beyond this conception which united man with society, and to conceive of the man as an integral part of the universal Self, that Self which created the universe. We are all of us, as St. Paul says, parts of one another. That is true. We all of us have content which belongs to us only in so far as we share the selfhood of others. We see ourselves as others see us. The society that we belong to gives us our peculiar selves. We belong to that society. We are what we are because we belong to that society, and yet that society is nothing but an organization of selves. Now, what Fichte did was to conceive of an Absolute Self which is just such an organization of *all* selves; an infinite Self which is the organization of all finite selves. Then, just as society sets its tasks in terms of the act of all its members, so this infinite and Absolute Self sets the task for itself in terms of all the functions of all the finite selves that go to make it up. The universe as such is, then, the creation of this Absolute Self in the same sense as cultivated areas and great metropolitan areas are created by the society that lives in them. This Self creates its own world, and it creates it as a set of things to be done. Fields are cultivated to be reaped, to grow the grain that can be harvested. The means of transportation, the tasks that have to be carried out on the part of the personnel, everything of this sort, is an expression of the function of some member of society. Now then, enlarge this conception so that you can conceive of an Absolute Self that is made up out of an infinite number of different selves, and the universe as the expression of that Self, as a casting-up, so to speak, of a place in which that Self can act, as the expression of the task which that Self has to carry out, and you get Fichte's conception of an Absolute Self of which all individuals are merely separate parts. In this view we are all parts of God. We each have a finite part in an infinite creative power.

Organized in the one Self we, together with an infinite number of other selves, create the universe. And for Fichte this creation is moral, for he conceives of the world as an obligation, as a task which the Absolute Self has to carry out, has to fulfil.

This, then, is the point of view from which Fichte built his philosophy. And we have seen that it goes back to a point in Kant's philosophy. Fichte assumed that the self is causal, productive, creative. It is, however, in the moral realm that these characteristics apply to it. Accepting Kant's two postulates, that in the moral realm we determine our conduct and that the mind, through its forms, determines the character of nature, Fichte turned to the moral world and found it to be the field of action. It is what it is in order that the self may act. And, without going back to the metaphysics of it, we do find that situation in our own experience to a very considerable degree. When we make a moral decision, we have more or less definitely determined the character of the situation. If a man, for example, assumes that he is under obligation to undertake a certain duty in the community—that, for example, he should go and be a watcher at the polls—he places this over against each of the other of his different obligations. He has to relate them all to one another. If he carries out this duty, he may place himself in considerable danger. He has to consider what that danger would mean. He has to relate it to his other obligations. He has to consider, on the other hand, what his duties as a citizen are. In doing all this he constructs a certain definite field which has the form which in some sense he gives to it. That is, those values as related to each other are values which express the man. What he does will be an expression of the man himself. If he is of a timid nature, he tends to avoid obligations that come to him from outside, and prefers to let somebody else carry on the public functions of the community; and the chances are that he will construct the sort of situation in which his own immediate interests will bulk larger than any others, while those of the public will be given an insignificant character. The sort of a world in which he will live will be very different from that of a man who recognizes his public duties, who comes forward even under conditions of considerable risk, standing on his own legs refusing to be jolted, taking the duties that come with the occasion, and playing the part of a good citizen. His world will be a different world from that of the other. The comparative values which they give will make out of their actions and out of the objects upon which they act two very different sorts of situations. Each creates a definite field of action by the attitude that he takes.

Now this is true, of course, in another sense in regard to our sense perception. Our vision, our attitude, our contact experiences, do determine in some sense the sort of world in which we live; but over this we have no control. If we have eyes, we live in a world of colors. If we are colorblind, these colors are perhaps limited to only two. If we have islands of deafness, there are certain parts of the sounding world that are shut off from us. In the other case, the moral case, the man also determines the *sort* of world he lives in. He builds up the world in terms of his duties, his obligations, and thus makes it of one sort or another.

It is to this sort of constructive character of the world that Fichte comes back. And here, I can say in passing, his philosophy branches off from Kant's, which was entirely formal in character. Fichte recognizes this constructive character, as was shown in the illustration above. A man builds up a world in which the self-government of the community can take place, in which the political rights of the individual are respected. There are certain values which are identified with himself, and his conduct tends to build up such a world as that. In this sense his conduct is creative. What the situation is depends upon ourselves. We may have the souls of rabbits and retire from everything that involves risk, live in a little world which is secure from danger; or we may have a sense of moral adventure and go out to live in a broader, wider world. It depends upon the individual as to what kind of a world he lives in. Fichte, in going back to Kant's self as a creative power, identified that creative power with the moral impulse, the impulse to map out a world which constitutes one's duty.

And here Fichte comes back to that moral self that I have already referred to by way of illustration. The duty that arises before a man at the time of an election is distinctly a not-self. He does not want to take the time, run the risks, go to all the inconvenience which the occasion requires. This is something that distinctly lies outside of himself at the time. He is interested in his immediate environment, in an immediate occupation, and here is something which presents itself from outside. For the time being, it is distinctly, definitely, not the self that the man is up to that time. If he accepts this as a duty, builds up this world in which he feels he ought to act, he is definitely, perhaps, for the time being, unwillingly, identifying himself with it. What it comes back to in the end is that a man cannot keep his self-respect and not accept these obligations. He cannot let somebody else do what he ought to do. He feels that he has to identify himself with this particular situation. He has to make it his own. This is definitely what takes place in such a situation. First of all the task appears as a not-self, as something outside of himself. He has to come to terms with it. It is disagreeable, foreign to his own immediate interests; but it is just through recognizing it as, for the time being, foreign to his own interests that he can get an idea of himself, that he can come to a higher self-consciousness than he had before. He comes to see himself as a person shirking his duties in the community, as a person "letting George do it," refusing to take over the tasks that belong to him. He sees himself in this situation from the point of view of this not-self which he created when he set up this particular task before him; and by identifying himself with the not-self, he definitely becomes a larger, a more effective self than he was before.

It is in that sort of a process that the individual recognizes a not-self, and from the point of view of that not-self that he recognizes the self that answers to it. Then, through the actual doing of the duty, through the accomplishment of his task, the individual becomes a larger self. Fichte assumed that that process, a subject-object process, was the fundamental one in the universe. Therefore, he was not concerned with the relation of substance and attribute. This dynamic process, which is opposed to Kant's static account of the problem, Fichte found in the moral experience of the individual. If a self is to be a self, it must achieve this in the identification of itself with the not-self, thus overcoming any opposition between the self and that which lies outside of it. This is the fundamental process of the universe from Fichte's point of view. In its duty the self recognizes itself as a not-self, then it identifies itself with the not-self and so becomes a larger and more effective self. Thus, from Fichte's standpoint, the relation of the subject and the object, in the moral sense, is the fundamental relation in the universe.

Of course, the basic metaphysical relation is that of subject and object. Fichte wanted to distinguish the philosophy of the Romantic school from that of the philosophy which, in some sense, largely influenced this movement, namely, that of Spinoza. He found the distinction between these two in this: for Spinoza, as has already been said, the fundamental relation was that of substance and attribute, while for the Romantic school the fundamental metaphysical conception is that of subject and object. Spinoza said that there could be but one substance. He defined substance as that which is the cause of itself. From this definition there could be only one such substance. Fichte's philosophy too, like that of the other romanticists, centers in the conception of one Ultimate Being; but in this case it is described as an Absolute Self in which all finite selves center. Fichte insisted that the self is created in its moral conduct. But what reference has this to the universe? The latter exists about us seemingly not as the result of our own experience, of our creation. It is there in advance of us and will be there when we are gone. It has an infinite extent, and we are finite and ephemeral creatures. In what sense, then, can we be its creators?

The three different attempts made to answer that question are those of Fichte, Schelling, and Hegel. The first attempt was a severely moral one. It does not, perhaps, present itself in the guise of adventure, the romantic attitude. The justification which Fichte gave for this attitude is that which I have been presenting. We are under obligation to identify ourselves with this world which is there before us. That is, the world exists as a field of moral endeavor. The reason that it seems to be so independent of us is that it is a duty, something that has to be done, in a certain sense an obstacle to be overcome. But when the duty has been done, then that which was foreign has been identified with the self. I have described this process in regard to the duties of citizenship. The process is, of course, from Fichte's point of view, a moral self-experience, that of meeting a world which is not the self and making it the self. The duty which is done ceases to be the not-self and becomes the self. And not only is this true, but it is only from the point of view of what was the not-self that one is able to realize the self. First of all, one may regard one's self from the standpoint of disapprobation. He sees the thing he ought to do and does not want to do. He sees that he ought to love, but actually he hates. This is that division which St. Paul presents so poignantly. The "other man" has to be overcome in some sense. One looks at himself from the standpoint of duty. And then there comes approbation from the standpoint of the achieved self, the quiet conscience which indicates that the individual, the self, is at peace with himself. Thus it is revealed that it is only from the point of view of the not-self that the individual can reach himself. It is not simply that one grasps the world in making it himself, in doing his duty, but that one grasps himself in identifying himself with that duty. He gets a standard from which to judge himself when he identifies himself with the duty he ought to do. Then he can pass judgment on himself. When the duty is done, he can be at peace. He has in this way identified himself with the object.

It is not only an adventure in capturing the universe, so to speak, and bringing it within the range of a self-experience, but it is also an adventure in discovering one's self, a mutual experience both for the world and for the self. That is an experience which we go through with unaffected by the sense of duty. It is a step beyond the position of Kant. You remember, Kant sets up a categorical imperative. One must make the maxim for one's act a universal law, and one must act solely from his sense of respect for law, not from inclination. For Kant, immorality is only that conduct which is motivated without this respect for law, this sense of duty. We must do what we are to do from a sense of duty. From Kant's standpoint, if an act is done from inclination it is not moral. It is not necessarily immoral, but it is non-moral. Epigrammatically, Schiller put it thus, "How can I be sure if I am right in loving and assisting my friends? If I do it from affection, I am doing it from inclination and may be wrong. If I am to be sure, I must hate them. Then, at least, I will know that when I assist them I do so from a sense of duty." But the Romantic moralist goes a step beyond Kant. His doctrine is: So succeed in identifying yourself with your duty that it becomes your inclination. Your friends are yourself, and you can assist them with the real affection that goes with friendship. It is true that, at least in moral experiences in which there is a problem involved, we go through exactly such an experience as this to which Fichte comes back, the experience, that is, in which the world takes the form of a task to be performed. If it is to be done, then everything takes its relationship to that task. The whole thing is simply a field within which the task is to be carried out. The world as it was, and as it is to be, is there as the field in which this very disagreeable thing has to be gone through with. It is a field of moral undertaking and endeavor. Now, after the task has been performed and we have come to realize it in terms of our own self, then this attitude of separation, of division, is overcome and we do identify ourselves with the very interests that we have gone into.

Take the situation, let us say, which is represented in the experience of Father Damien, a Catholic missionary who went to the leper settlement on the Hawaiian Islands and lived among them, identified himself with them. It is a picture, at least to the outside world, of a person who is acting the part of a martyr. He gave himself up to the case of those who had a loathsome disease and shut himself up there practically for life. In fact, eventually he died of the disease. This is a striking illustration of a sensational sort of the way in which duty may appear to a man as something which is utterly foreign to all his inclinations. He is called upon to identify himself with that from which he instinctively withdraws. Duty is that which is outside of everything identified with the individual himself. In the medieval period one of the ways of laying up treasure in heaven was to wash the feet of a leper. That is the sort of situation in which, seemingly, the duty is something which is just a task, which is not a part of the individual self.

Take another picture; that of the scientist who is intensely interested in the study of leprosy. He is interested in identifying the microörganism responsible for it. He welcomes the opportunity to go and work, and to live among the lepers, to carry out this task of his. He is dealing with a disease to be overcome. He carries with him the modern weapons by means of which this dread villain can be overcome, and he goes joyously to the battle. It is not a task which is put upon him that is not himself. It is a task he has sought. He has asked for the opportunity to go out there and live among the lepers. It is true that part of his panoply is defensive. He takes the proper aseptic precautions against the disease; but, nevertheless, here is the task of caring expressed in a much more profound way than Father Damien could. The enthusiastic research man is completely absorbed in his duty, in the thing he has to do.

Put the two figures together, so to speak. First of all, here is something that has been done that is not one's self, and yet one can enthusiastically identify one's self with it. It is that experience which is at first something outside of one's self but which can become identified with one's self—such an experience as that which Father Damien seized upon, which accomplishes the goal of the Romantic philosophy. It is the experience of bringing the world within the range of the experience of self-consciousness, that experience in which the object of consciousness has the position of the self of which consciousness is aware, the position in which both subject and object are one. To the extent that this can be attained, the romanticist can put the subject-object relationship in place of that of substance and attribute.

This is the sort of situation that could be presented at the time of Fichte because Germany, in its fight with Napoleonic imperialism, was going through the throes of coming to national self-consciousness. The people as a whole were getting self-conscious. They were learning their history, the history of the political situation in which they lived, learning it in terms of a nation which was subject, which had lost sovereignty over itself, which was a vassal of Napoleon. They came to realize the duty that the nation owed to herself—to free herself from these bonds. That duty had to come in terms of a national self-consciousness, of seeing the situation in terms of being German. And Fichte's addresses to the German people were calling them to become aware of themselves in this way. He presented it as their duty to do so. Fichte had a very vivid sense of that mission which the German people have so definitely carried on. And he called on them to have that sort of clear, objective consciousness which belongs to science, but to reach it through a sense of national self-consciousness. How far those two can be brought together is another question, but Fichte undertook to arouse that national self-consciousness in terms of intelligence, of scientific endeavor, as well as to arouse the people to a sense of moral obligation. There was, of course, even at this time, more popular education in Germany than elsewhere in the world and more satisfactory apparatus for bringing about popular training intelligence. Germany's political history had been one in which she had been deprived of the national self-consciousness which had come much earlier to the French, the English, and the Spanish. The Germans, having been deprived of it, found this the time, at a somewhat belated period, for the development of national self-consciousness. And they got it at the moment of meeting the enemy, of throwing the enemy out of their borders. It was at a proper time, then, that Fichte presented this task of Romantic philosophy to the German people.

CHAPTER VI

THE ROMANTIC PHILOSOPHERS—SCHELLING

I HAVE been presenting the philosophical problem of Romantic idealism. It was an attempt to state the world of knowledge, the world as known, in terms of a subject-object relation as that appears in the experience of the self. The statement that Fichte gave of this was that of the moralist. The view we are about to consider, that of Schelling, was given from the point of view of the artist. In each case the self is in some sense responsible for its object. In each you can show the self realizing itself in the not-self. And the relation of the self and the not-self can be identified with the realization of the self in the not-self. One can identify that with the subject-object relationship. That is, the self as the subject is responsible, and the attitude for which it is responsible appears definitely as the not-self, as the object. It is something that for the time being is foreign to the self. In each case it is a task that has to be performed. But when the task has been completed, it has been made a part of the self. In the moral situation, which Fichte emphasized, this relationship of subject and object is one in which, first of all, the self realizes itself from the point of view of a moral attitude, from the point of view of its obligations. The subject-object relation, however, is one in which the task, in being accomplished, becomes essentially a part of the self. That is, the duty one does identifies that experience with the self; the self has made it its own.

In the case of the artist, the attitude which Schelling emphasized, the stress lies in the recognition that the self discovers its ideas, its meanings in the world, in its object. The artist finds himself in the object. In this he finds the meaning of the world; and, of course, at the same time he finds his own meaning. As an artist he is creative. He constructs his objects, his world, and yet that which he works on in this construction is the not-self. But it is constructed in terms of the idea, of the meaning, of the artist. He stands over against his material. It is that in which his meaning is to be found; he has to find his meaning, his own ideas, in the material with which he has to work. Thus the object is his own idea; it is his own construction. It is this attitude which Schelling presented, with the constant insistence that this meaning, this idea, is identical with the nature of the self.

Before we can get a background for Schelling's approach to this problem, we have to come back to another phase of the Kantian doctrine and the romantic development of it. Kant, you remember, assumed that our knowledge, in so far as it is reliable, belonged only to the field of experience. He assumed that we can make certain judgments which are necessary and universal, but only for experience, and that we can know nothing of that which lies outside of experience. But, if, as he assumed, it is true, that there must be certain forms of the mind into which our experience must enter, then we can make certain judgments for all possible experiences. Just because the forms are there which every experience must take, we can say in advance that any experience whatsoever will have these forms. So our necessary and universal judgments are judgments for experience only; they do not hold for what lies beyond experience. In particular, they do not hold for the noumenal world which we assume but of which we can get no knowledge. Kant said that if we try to go beyond the field of possible experience we are made aware of that fact by falling into contradictions, antinomies. If we transcend the field of possible experience, we find ourselves caught at once in these traps, traps which seem to be there to keep the unwary phenomenalist from treading upon noumenalistic ground.

For example, if one tries to get back to a cause which shall be the cause of everything—a first cause—he finds that he reaches contradictions. When we extend our line of causation, as we do in experience, we always find an antecedent cause for every effect and we are always justified in assuming a prior cause *ad infinitum*. That is as far as we choose to carry it. Every event that appears in the field of experience is the result of some previous event or group of events. Well now, if we say there must be some cause that is the cause of this experience but which lies outside of it, some primal cause, we force ourselves by this same logic to set up some antecedent cause, because we have brought the system within the field of causality. We set up a first cause, and yet we have to postulate another cause as the cause of the first cause. Thus we find ourselves entrapped in one of Kant's antinomies.

Or, suppose we try to get behind our experiences to the matter which is the ground of those experiences. As far as experience is concerned, we get hold of this matter and we crumble it in our fingers, and then we take particles so small we can hardly see them and bring them under the microscope. Finally, we get to the limit of ultra-microscopic vision and the imagination comes into play, and we imaginatively subdivide these particles, and so on. We are moving toward a limit which shall be the final element. That is, the world is made up of particles; at least, that is the way we experience it. If it is anything, it must be made up out of ultimate elements because what we have in the universe as a whole is not a sum of nothings but a sum of somethings. So, the final element that we reach must be something; but if we come to the final element by way of our crumblings, we can always continue the process of subdivision indefinitely. To Kant, this shows the impossibility of getting beyond the field of possible experience. We can imagine ourselves getting at smaller and smaller units, continually subdividing matter with which we are dealing; and yet the assumption of our experience is that things are made up of particles that have some extension. Thus we find another antinomy which results from the continued subdivision. We move toward the limit of the indivisibly small; and yet we cannot imagine a particle so small but what it could still be divided.

And, if we undertake to move in the other direction to the farthest limits of the stellar system, we find nebulae which, according to our present system of measurements, are millions of light-years away. And we will say that that represents the horizon of our stellar world. But when we reach that boundary, we find more space beyond. There is not any limit there, and yet our movement is always toward a limit. But the limits which we tentatively set up can always be transcended. And so we reach another antinomy.

Then Kant finds still another antinomy involved in moral conduct, namely, that all our conduct is explicable in terms of cause and effect, that we express every one of our actions in terms of the motives from which they spring, and yet we carry a sense of responsibility for our conduct which implies that it is not caused by these preceding events but through the volition of a free self. So we have the impossibility, the antinomy, that is due to the causal determination of our acts by preceding events and at the same time the assurance of our own obligation, of the causal relation between ourselves and our acts. Again, we assume that the world in which we are living is intelligible and ordered, and that this order which we find is due to some plan or purpose. That assumption is deeply ingrained and finds its expression in our views of nature. Since it is an ordered affair, it must have been ordered by some intelligent being. We set up the assumption of a deity, an intelligent being, who is responsible for the world having the order, the symmetry that it has. But when we try to come back to any mind that itself has ordered such a world, we find that we have put it outside of the very field of experience within which we had located it. In order to understand such a being, we have to locate it within the field of experience. But if we bring it into this field, we have made God a part of experience and then we must find a cause for God, since everything in experience falls under the idea of causation.

Kant's general theory of these antinomies is that we are trying to explain experience by getting outside of experience, and yet every attempt to do that is an attempt lying within the field of experience. We cannot be both inside and outside of experience at the same time. That attempt is, says Kant, the basis for these antinomies. The moment we become involved in such a fundamental contradiction we can be sure that we are trying to know something that it is impossible for us to know, something that lies outside the limits of our possible knowledge. When we reach such a point, we have to turn to faith rather than to knowledge. And this faith, in Kant's sense, is the acceptance of the postulates of our conduct.

We find ourselves acting, and inevitably our action does present a transcendence of our immediate experience. The latter stops at the moment in which it is taking place. The next moment that is added to it does not lie in experience, and the reasons for it do not lie in experience. We have to get outside of our experience in order to reach the moment into which we are always entering. We are always putting our foot out into a world which is as yet not experienced. Now what is the world that continually lies just beyond, just over the threshold of experience and knowledge? The only thing that we can set up in regard to it is the postulate of our continually acting within it. The human being cannot see ahead. He cannot see what is going to happen. The only thing he can do is to look back and then into the future. Then he can say something of what the future is going to be, for, if it is experience—that is, if he is going to know it as a part of the field of experience—it will take on the forms of his own mind. But what the actual content of it is going to be he can never tell. Our insurance companies try to make a guess at it, and they can do it within sufficiently determinable limits to put it on a business basis. Also, prudent people can determine what, in general, their lives are going to be. But our attitude toward the future is always of the statistical sort. That is, it is highly probable that things that have happened in the past—like the rising and setting of the sun, the experience of colors, sounds, and so forth—will happen in the future. We think these are probable future occurrences, but we have no evidence of it outside of this statistical estimate. When things have happened, we can turn back on them and analyze them; but what is going to happen is something of which we can never get hold. There is always some sort of novelty about what happens in the most commonplace sort of an experience and the most ordinary sort of an action, always a tang of novelty about whatever takes place. That novelty is something which cannot possibly be predicted. We can predict something that is going to be strange and novel, but its very strangeness indicates that there are some features about it which depend upon its entering into experience before they can be known. Even what can be predicted—that you are going to meet your friend at the station, that you are going to read a book—always carries with it something which is different from what could possibly have been anticipated. Novelty is always present. There is something in respect to the future in regard to which we can only make postulates. We assume that it will be of an ordered, intelligible sort; and yet with every breath we are stepping into a world that has a novel element in it.

And that novelty, I should say, extends with regard not only to what we call the future, it also extends to the past. We speak of the past as irrevocable. What has happened has happened; what has been spoken has been spoken. But when we come to historians, whose work it is to discover what actually was spoken, what actually did happen, we find we get different accounts. This is particularly true when we look at what took place in the past from the point of view of two succeeding generations. We find that each generation has a different history, that it is a part of the apparatus of each generation to reconstruct its history. A different Caesar crosses the Rubicon not only with each author but with each generation. That is, as we look back over the past, it is a different past. The experience is something like that of a person climbing a mountain. As he looks back over the terrain he has covered, it presents a continually different picture. So the past is continually changing as we look at it from the point of view of different authors, different generations. It is not simply the future which is novel, then; the past also is novel. The world is continually changing in ways in which we cannot predict. Of course, we may be able to predict that it will change, but we cannot tell what sort of world it is going to become. For example, it would have been impossible, on the basis of the Newtonian theory, to have predicted the doctrine of Einstein. It would have been impossible, on the basis of the old biologies, to have predicted the Darwinian hypothesis. No one could have predicted the Copernican universe on the basis of the system set up by Ptolemy. The world is continually blossoming out into a new universe, and in this generation we have had fundamental conceptions brought forward that entirely change the character of the physical universe. Take such experiences as those represented in the quantum theory, a theory in accordance with which reality has to be regarded as both continuous and discontinuous. You are brought up against something that in the nature of the case you cannot predict. But we go right on without any disturbance from that front. We are pleased to have these revolutions take place in our theories, gratified to have our universe fall down so that it is replaced by a new one. We erect institutions called universities and invite research professors at high salaries who wreck our universities and substitute others in their place. And it appears to us to be perfectly right and natural.

It seems as if the world which lies beyond our actual experience will continue to be just the sort of ordered world we live in, and we hope a better one. These are the postulates of our conduct. We are always postulating something about what is going to happen, something which determines our own conduct. That is the attitude which Kant says we have to take in regard to the world of reality. We cannot know things as they are in themselves. The moment we reach the edge of our own knowledge, we find ourselves caught in an antinomy. But if we go ahead as we should go ahead, as, indeed, we must go ahead, and act on the basis of the assumption that the universe is going to continue to be rational and that we have our part to play in it by being moral individuals, then we should take these postulates which we make, but which we cannot prove, and make them the basis of our action. This is, of course, the principle of Kant's *Critique of Practical Reason*.

Now, Kant said there are certain postulates that go with this assumption of our moral conduct. The first two I have indicated already. First, we are responsible, moral beings and we have to accept responsibility for our acts. Second, the world has a rational character that transcends our experience. As I have said, we take the world and set it in that rational order; and yet we expect that someone in this generation or the next will set it in an entirely different way. That is, there is some sort of an order that transcends any statement that we can make of our experience, that goes beyond it. We find ourselves in an ordered world, a world which requires an ordering intelligence. These two postulates come from our conduct: our freedom of will, together with our moral responsibility, and the intelligent God that directs the world in accordance with reason, knowledge. When we take this point of view, we always find that the new world becomes rational. It is irrational from the point of view from which we have taken it, outside of the field of experience, but it is more rational than the other.

Kant's third postulate is rather curious. He said that, since we are rational beings, our conduct must always be rational. You remember the form which he gives to his categorical imperative: So act that you can make a universal law out of the maxim of your act. This categorical imperative is practically the only one that Kant can set up, but there are some others that can be drawn from it. The test in question is, you see, that we should make our conduct perfectly universal. If we are to make it universal, it must not depend upon our inclinations. We must not act for our own interest or for our own pleasure. We must not act for our own immediate, particular ends, for our conduct must always be universal and the motive for it must be respect for law. Universality is the very core of Kant's morality. But our inclinations, unfortunately, are not universal; they are very particular affairs. We may say to ourselves that when we are hungry we should eat; but Kant's reason for it must be that it is good hygiene, not because we particularly want a beefsteak at the moment, not in order to get rid of a gnawing sensation, not for the sake of pleasure or for the avoidance of pain, but because it is our duty to eat. This is the only reason why we should ever act on anything.

Well, here we seem to have two parallel lines. One must always act with reference to a universal, while one's inclinations are always with reference to some particular. But, says Kant, what we look forward to is moral perfection; and that can be achieved only in situations in which the individual's own nature seeks what his conscience tells him he ought to seek. Our nature is made up of inclinations for particular things, and our conscience tells us always to act in a universal fashion and from respect for law. Now how and where are we going to bring these parallel lines together? Only in infinity. Therefore our conduct requires the postulate that we have an eternity within which to reach that perfection. The very break in our nature between the particularity of our inclinations and the universality of our conscience, of our reason, seemingly presents to us an immortality of the self, of the soul, because only in eternity can we possibly bring together two such divergent tendencies as an inclination for particular satisfactions and a conscience that demands that we should act only from respect for law. These postulates, then, lead to freedom of the will, the existence of God, and the immortality of the soul. But you see Kant's philosophy reaches these not by deduction but by postulation. He says these postulates are involved in intelligent conduct. Thus, it is only by postulation that we can get beyond experience. In this way we can get beyond it, but this is not by knowledge. If we try to reach this end through knowledge, we find ourselves involved in an antinomy.

The contradiction that Fichte set up was that of the opposition of duty to inclination, the very opposition which Kant made the ground for his doctrine of immortality. The thing that we have to do, that we ought to do, is the thing that we do not want to do. It involves an effort. From the point of view of Kant we can never be sure that we are moral unless, as others pointed out, we are doing something we do not want to do. The moment you do something you want to do, you had better look out. The chances are you are being immoral. Essentially, the opposition seems to lie between what you have to do and what you ought to do at times of great stress, at strenuous moments in life. That is the characteristic of our duty. Not that everything we do not want to do we ought to do, but that what we ought to do is something that we do not want to do. We have to overcome the obstacle before us if we are to accomplish what we ought to accomplish. But, says Fichte, when we have done that, it becomes a part of our own nature. We have attained the knowledge we ought to attain. We have the education, the training, that we have forced ourselves to get; and, if we have made it a part of ourselves, it is what we really want. That is, it is when we look back at it. That is the dialectical process by means of which the self is constantly creating the world. There is a contradiction between what one wants and what one ought; but if the contradiction is overcome, then the individual advances to a new world.

Thus, the antinomy took on another character in the Romantic philosophy than that which it had for Kant, just as his noumenal world took on a new character. Kant said we have to postulate the self as noumenal, and the romanticists said that that is exactly what we are. We are at the center of reality. The self is the creative element of the universe. The finite self is one phase of the Absolute Self, of God himself. The antinomies which Kant set up as indications that we are going beyond the range of possible knowledge become, for the romanticist, the very process of creation. The antinomy in knowledge, instead of being the indication that we are trying to know something that we cannot know, is the very process by means of which knowledge itself arises. The antinomy is a stage in the process of knowledge.

This process is called after the term which was used in the old Greek speculation—"the dialectic." Of course, what "the dialectic" means is a process of discussion, conversation in which the ancient Sophist sought to entrap his opponent in a contradiction. That was the "outdoor sport" of the Athenian, discussing some question with the first person he met, and trying to catch him in a contradiction in his statement. And the Sophists were those who could play the game to the best advantage. Socrates was the supreme Sophist because he could catch the professional Sophists at their own tricks. But for Socrates the process was not simply a game; it was a means for getting back to certain fundamental realities. For example, he would ask a man what justice is; and when the man undertook to define "justice," he would point out contradictions in his statements. This little game is presented to us in the opening sections of Plato's *Republic*. The absolute definition of "justice" is rendering to a man what belongs to him. This is a good workaday conception. Socrates then asks, "Well, suppose somebody had given you his sword. It would be justice to give it back? Certainly. But, suppose the person had developed a suicidal mania and was intent on killing himself, would it then be just to return the sword?" And his opponent has to admit that it would not be just under that condition. In other words, his definition breaks down. And so on. What Socrates undertook to show was that, if you are criticizing definitions of "justice," you must be criticizing them from some standpoint. There must be such a thing as justice; otherwise you could not criticize definitions of it. You may not be able to define this thing, but evidently you have some idea of a perfect justice which is the basis for your very criticism. That is what Socrates undertook to show was the case. He tried to show that there must be "ideas"—in the Greek sense—of these moral perfections or we would not be able to point to them as being such. The very conflicts involved in these definitions indicate some perfect definition. And then Socrates, in ironical fashion, said that he did not know what this perfect justice was, but that evidently the person he was talking with knew, because he was criticizing every definition brought up. Thus, in asking the person for the basis for his criticism, he caught the Sophist at his own game.

What I want to point out is that here we have the dialectic as a means of advancing from contradictions to a truth. That is what the old process was, at least as Socrates worked it. The Sophist used it continually. He undertook to tear it down by means of the contradiction that he introduced. For example, what is the reason for obeying laws? They are nothing but enactments of the people in power. If one man becomes dominant, he will make laws to suit himself. If the majority of the people make the laws, they make them in the interest of the majority, to the disadvantage of the minority. The laws are always to the advantage of those in power, then why obey them? To avoid a penalty, of course. There is no such thing, then, as justice as such. That is the way the Sophist proceeded. Socrates took their method but utilized the contradictions as a means of reaching the truth.

As Kant left the antinomies, they were simply the indications of the mind's attempts to push its knowledge beyond the field of experience. Wherever it did that, it got caught in an antinomy. What the romanticist endeavors to show is that these antinomies are really steps by which we are going beyond experience. Of course, we do go beyond experience very day, every minute. We go into the past; and, as we look at the past from the point of view of the present minute, it is a different past from that which we viewed from the standpoint of the previous minute. The world is continually developing, says the Romantic idealist, by a process which he calls a "dialectic," a process which involves these contradictions, but a process which overcomes them in a continual synthesis.

Let us take, then, the steps which led from Fichte to Schelling and Hegel. Is there a phase of self-consciousness which can be responsible for the world as an object? This is the question which all the romanticists asked. The answer that Fichte gives is found in the moral nature in so far as the world is the scene of the duty of man. But the world is there before man; it is prior to his duty. The moral aspect may be the most important aspect of it after man appears. One may even conceive of it as being the purpose for which the world exists. But you have to presume the existence of the world before the moral self appears. Can the romantic attitude present the world as an object which appears to us when we are not in the moral attitude? Can the world be presented as an object for other than the moral phases of our nature? That is, can you find that it has the same many faceted existence that we have? This is the question that the romanticists asked when it was found that the answer that Fichte gave was inadequate.

The first answer to this further question was given by Schelling. He takes the point of view of the artist rather than that of the moralist. The artist discovers himself in his ideas, in the material with which he works. For the function of the artist—or rather, I should say, the process of the artist—is not simply that of taking dead material and fashioning his idea in it. He discovers the idea in the material itself. He finds the form in the clay which he is molding, and it is only as he molds that he finds out what the form is in his own mind. He may have worked that out in imagination before coming to the material, before getting his hands on the clay; but, as a rule, it is the process of working with the material that brings to the artist's mind what it is he is trying to present. The artistic procedure, the experience of the artist, is a discovery of his own ideas.

What Fichte was not able to do with the moral conception was to present the world as known. He could present it as a field of duty; but when he tried to state that in terms of knowledge, his statement was inadequate. He was faced with the problem of finding the content of knowledge, or the object of knowledge in the object of duty, starting with the Kantian assumption that the self is causal in its conduct and that it belongs, in that sense, to the world of things-in-themselves. He found the essence of duty to lie in the presentation of the task or obstacle that had to be overcome, and he identified this not only with the moral act but also with the process of self-consciousness, of being conscious of one's self. In this process lay the possibility of realizing one's self. But what has this to do with the problem of knowledge? Is the object of knowledge something that presents itself as a task, as an obstacle? On the face of it, this does not seem to be the case. Our objects of knowledge are about us; they are there as the world in which we live, move, and have our being. As such, they are not there seemingly as obstacles. There are, of course, tasks to be undertaken, duties to be done in which we have to recognize the nature of things; and some of our tasks, including that of gaining knowledge, are severe and difficult undertakings. But is knowledge, as such, of the nature of a duty that has to be done, of a task that has to be accomplished? That does not seem to be the nature of it.

Schelling recognized this and so he approaches the general problem from another angle. For him the world, as over against the Absolute, was that in which the artist found his idea, realized himself. He took the artistic attitude, that of artistic intuition, as Fichte has taken the moralist's attitude. According to Schelling, the point of departure is the attitude of the artist, that experience in which the artist discovers himself, discovers his own idea in the materials with which he is working. The artist gives himself to nature and finds in it the very ideas which he himself is trying to bring to consciousness. He turns to the society about him; he finds in social relations and in the history of the past those ideas which he is seeking to express. So Schelling conceived of the Absolute Self turning to nature or finding in nature an objective expression, an external expression of the self.

What Fichte insisted upon was that this world as known is identical with the self that knows. And he carried out some very subtle and profound analyses to establish his point. Of course, some of this work had been done in the empirical analysis of the English school. They had discovered in the ideas of Locke, in his philosophy of sensations and ideas, the very stuff of the world. For them, however, the self was a mere organization of such experiences. To some of them the self was a mere bundle of impressions, particularly those centering about the body and about our social relations. Certain groups of these impressions and ideas which remained relatively permanent became the self in experience.

But the Romantic philosophy pointed out that the self, while it arises in the social experience, also carried with it the very unity that makes society possible, which makes the world possible. At least from their point of view, it is impossible to reduce the self to the world, for the very unity of the world comes from the self. It is our thinking, our perception of the world, that gives it its unity. In our experience there is great diversity and multiplicity of sensations and experiences, but in our cognition these are all organized. That organization, according to the Romantic idealists, taking their cue from Kant, comes from the self. It is the self which organizes this world; but when it has organized it, it has really organized that which is identical with itself, it has organized its own experiences. It has, in one phase of its nature, discovered what it is in another phase.

Here, as I have said, Schelling turns back to the artist's experience for his analogy. The artist finds himself before a landscape, we will say, and in this he finds all the multiplicity of color, of form, of moving and stationary objects, and these take on a certain definite shape. The whole thing gets balance. The different parts of the landscape become arranged with reference to each other. But it is the mind of the artist that has organized it into this whole. He has discovered in it that unity and organization which belong to himself. He has discovered in it the sensations which are his own. He has discovered not only the landscape but himself as well. What he has hold of is his own experience, the expression of himself.

Now, it is upon this identity of the object, that we grasp in our process of knowledge, that is, in our intuition, with the self that grasps it, that Schelling laid his whole stress. It is there to start with, but the process of knowledge identifies the content with the self. His position went under the name of *Identitätsphilosophie*, "the philosophy of identity"; and his whole undertaking was that of showing the identity of the object of knowledge with the self that knows. Nature, for Fichte, was the process of the self coming to consciousness of itself. The same subject-object relation is present in Schelling's philosophy, but for Fichte's moral statement he substitutes the analogy of the process of the artist. The assertion of identity on the part of Schelling came back to the reality of the artist's intuition, his seeing nature through his own idea, through that which gives the unity and meaning to it.

CHAPTER VII

THE ROMANTIC PHILOSOPHERS—HEGEL

IN HIS criticism of this use of the artist's intuition, Hegel insisted that Schelling had left out of his philosophy an account of the process by means of which this identification of the self with its object takes place; he left out of his philosophy a statement of the process by means of which the identification of the self and the object could be effected. Hegel's criticism of Schelling's philosophy is that it is a bare assertion of identity instead of being an actual presentation of the process by means of which the self and the object can be identified.

You will remember that I mentioned earlier that romanticism is a philosophy of evolution, of process. It was the background for the development of the theory of evolution. Back of this latter conception lies the assumption of a living process which takes on successively different forms. The assumption of all evolutionary thought is that life, as a physiological process, is the same whether in a complex or in a simple form, in plant or in animal. It is a single living process as such. And this process takes on a multitude of different forms. This is the background for Schelling's philosophy of identity; the living form persists and is identical, although it appears in different forms.

But what Schelling did was to assert this identity of the process and its expression of the self and its object without working out the detail of it. In another field Lamarck—and, with even more success, Darwin—presented a picture in terms of which the detail of the process could be worked out. Darwin showed a life-process appearing in different forms; and he showed these differences as expressing the life-process now in this environment, now in that. Then he was able to show how, through variations, a new form might conceivably arise which would be better fitted to meet the exigencies of a new environment. Take such a situation as that which appeared during the glacial epoch, when a great ice sheet came down over Europe and America. It brought with it a different climate, different living conditions; and the forms that survived had to change their characters. The woolly elephant, the hairy hippopotamus —forms of the sort of which we find the remains—were adjustments to a new environment. In that gradually changing climate, those forms survived which were able to grow such coats of hair as would enable them to withstand the cold. For some reason forms that could live on certain foods survived over those that could not. Forms which belonged to marshy areas gave way as the swamps dried out, and those forms which could migrate over greater distances took the place of those which could not. Such a picture is presented by Professor Marsh in his statement of the development of the horse here in America from a five-toed animal which gradually gave way to one with a single toe in the form of a hard hoof which enabled it to travel farther so that it could live on more sparsely scattered grass, and thus had a decided advantage over other forms. Back of all these pictures lies the assumption of a life-process going on in different environments in which it takes on first one form and then another, wherein it has to become a different object in its relationship to the world within which it lives. The world and the form have, then, an identical content. The adjustment of the one to the other gives rise to the appearance of the different forms.

What Hegel insisted upon was that here is a process going on, a subject-object process, and that this process must exhibit the differences which we find in the world as we know it. We cannot simply come back to the assertion that the world is identical with the self that knows it. We must be able to show in the process of knowledge itself the identity which is known to exist between the subject and its object, between the form and the world in which it has to live. Hegel, then, lays greater stress upon the dialectic than did Fichte and Schelling. He takes over, so to speak, the antinomies of Kant, those seeming contradictions into which thought was plunged when it tried to transcend the phenomenal world and get over to the standpoint of things-in-themselves. The antinomies from the point of view of these Romantic philosophers were not simply a warning that the mind had gotten beyond the limits of its knowledge; they were the actual process by means of which the object itself arose in the subject-object process. That is, the fundamental contradiction, or antinomy, for this school was that of the subject and object; and they were looking for the process by means of which they could pass over from the one to the other and achieve a larger self than that with which they started as a result.

Fichte had attempted to solve the contradiction by reference to the nature of the experience of the moral self, by pointing out what is involved in doing one's duty. Schelling attempted the same thing through reference to the intuition of the artist. What Hegel undertook to do was to show how this opposition between subject and object could be overcome, in some sense, by means of the recognition of the nature of the process of thought itself. In biological evolution we overcome the opposition between the identity of the life-process in all forms and the diversity of the living forms themselves by studying the process as it is taking place. We examine unicellular forms floating on the surface of the sea; we find other bits like these become colony forms living on the bottoms and in shallow water holes. Out of these have arisen bilateral forms which move toward their food with bilateral symmetry. We see how these have come out of the water to live on land; how plants and animals adjust themselves, especially in regard to their chemical needs, to one another, taking on successively different forms during the process. Now, Hegel attempted to set up a picture similar to this as it applied to the thought processes, to the process of knowing, and possibly of all sensing, perceiving, and thinking. He set out to follow this through as an identical process having different expressions. In this process we have another instance of the contradiction between subject and object, but at the same time we see an identity of the two.

As illustrative of this fact, take Hegel's statement in his *Phänomenologie des Geistes*, which is one of his earliest philosophical works, in which he said that under the simplest situations a person simply identifies something as here. There is a house here, and there is a tree over there. That is the only thing one can say: "Here is the house; there is the tree." But, if one shifts his position, he finds himself saying, "The tree is here and the house is there." The only statement that one can make under the new condition leads to the contradiction of the statement made before. One says the time now is such and such o'clock, and writes this down as 10:30 o'clock. Later one looks at the clock and finds that it is not 10:30 but 3:30, and the assertion made about the time now contradicts itself. Evidently, in our perception the here and the now are determined by the position of the observer. What was here is there, and what was there is here. What was now is then, and what was then is now. This shift depends simply upon the location of the self. You have a process in which you have to distinguish between yourself which is here and the object which is there. But you cannot maintain that position, that distinction, because you shift your own position. It is only in so far as you get back to the fundamental process of your experience that you can get some sort of an expression of the identity of these opposing positions. You have to bring back all these experiences, the experiences of this point and of that, of this moment and of that, to a self-process which is continually going on, taking on now this form, now that. When we pass from one situation over into another, we are denying any statements that we made before in the previous situation. We are putting ourselves at this moment in opposition to ourselves of a moment before. But we overcome the opposition of this fact by realizing that there is an identical subject-object relation which persists throughout. The stuff of the process is the same in both cases;

but now it takes on this form, now that, just as biological evolutionists find this animal a living form and this other animal another living form. They are diverse, and yet each exhibits the same living process.

Hegel took the identity revealed in the subject-object relationship and sought to show that this identity persists in all the different forms of thought. This always brings him back to a contradiction. But what he shows is that this contradiction, instead of leading to a simple destruction of thought itself, leads to a higher level on which the opposing phases are overcome. That is, in the total process he discovers what he calls a "thesis," an "antithesis," and a "synthesis." In other words, he adds a third, a unifying, step to Kant's twofold antinomies. The most abstract expression of this is that which Hegel presents with respect to the very bare idea of Being itself. There can be no more abstract conception than that of Being. We cannot say that it has any sort of being. We cannot describe it. It has no particular quality or quantity. We can say nothing of it but that it is. We have to empty out everything that could be put into Being in order that we may get back to just Being itself. But that, said Hegel, is not a definition of Being, but one of Not-Being. If you have given up every possible qualification which you can give to the idea of Being, you simply have a statement of Not-Being. The very idea of Being, taking simply the bare idea, brings with it the conception of Not-Being, of Nothing. Being and Nothing are identical, and yet in sharp contradiction to each other.

But this opposition does not, from the Hegelian standpoint, lead simply to the destruction of these ideas. Being and Not-Being are simply the two phases of Becoming. What becomes is Being, but what was before the Becoming is Not-Being. As I say, then, if you try to define Being from the Hegelian point of view, you find a situation which is practically a description of Not-Being and seems to contradict and destroy Being itself. But, if you can get hold of these as moments in a process instead of thinking of them as the same, you find that you have a conception which harmonizes with what was previously a pure contradiction. In and of themselves, Being and Not-Being are contradictory; taken as moments in a process, they represent Becoming. Here we get a synthesis. It is in this process of bringing together subject and object that Hegel finds contradictions, but finds them as phases which lead to a synthesis or a higher expression of the self.

Hegel undertakes to carry out in detail the process by means of which the object appears both as the construction of the self and also as the not-self. He undertakes to carry this out in detail, and he calls it "logic." If we want to get an illustrative instance of this point of view of Hegel's, we can find it in the attitude of the research scientist. As I shall point out, Hegel does not do entire justice to this position; but still, it is the position which he is trying to present.

Let us take, for example, the discovery of the typhoid-fever germ. Before it was isolated, typhoid fever was known simply as a contagious disease. That is, it was spread through contact. A person who had the disease carried it to someone who did not have it. That was the theory of it. It was not known just what the nature of this contagion was, but it was assumed that where the disease spread there had always been contact between the person who had the disease and the person who became infected. Now let us suppose that a sporadic case of fever appears, that is, a case in which there has been no contact. No one else in the community has it, and this individual is a person who lives in the community, has not come in from the outside. He has had no contact with an infected person, and yet he comes down with typhoid fever. There you have, we will say, a contradiction between the actual experience of the physician or the health officer and the theory which is current with regard to the spread of typhoid fever.

There is a conflict there. The scientist under such circumstances sets out to find out what the meaning of this contradiction is. He gathers other instances, in so far as he can find them. He finds sporadic cases not only in his own community but elsewhere. As other cases come up, he plots them on a map. He puts a pin on the map at the location of every house in which the disease appears. Then, let us say, he finds these pins all run along the line of a water course, or a milk route, or along the paths of persons who go to a certain market. That suggests to him that there is some sort of cause for the disease which is not necessarily given by contact but may be carried in the water, the milk, or the food from the market. And we assume that investigation is carried on until the microörganism which is the carrier of the disease, the cause of it, is finally identified. That is, the research scientist starts from a conflict, a contradiction. The contradiction in this case is that between the accepted theory in regard to the transfer of a contagious disease and the facts of the disease as it appears. There is a contagious disease, and yet no contact. This involves a conflict, for we are dealing with a disease which is both contagious and not contagious. You see, the procedure of the scientist is one in which he goes from what we may call the thesis and the antithesis to a synthesis in which both the others are taken up. It may be true that the disease is directly conveyed from one person to another. The microörganism may be transmitted directly. It is also possible that the disease may be considered contagious in the sense that may be conveyed by the organism through a stream of water or through milk, that is, by means of a carrier where no direct contact is made between the person who has the disease and the person who becomes infected. The conception of the microörganism is, you see, one which synthesizes these occurrences of typhoid fever so that the conflict which we first come to is overcome. In the former instance the appearance of a sporadic case was in direct conflict with the theory of contagious disease. If, now, we assume or can prove that the disease is conveyed by a microörganism, we can bring out and explain all the cases that have been explained by contact and also the sporadic cases that have seemed to be in conflict with the theory. A synthesis is constructed which takes up the opposing situations—the thesis and the antithesis—and unifies them.

The abstract statement of this is the one I have given above in the first movement of the Hegelian logic. In this Hegel attempted to present Being, showing that the definition which he gave of it also, and inevitably, presented the definition of Not-Being. Being and Not-Being seem to be in conflict with each other. Yet, if you take bare Being by itself, you give it no content; and what you have defined as Being is also Not-Being. But the conception of Becoming is definitely one in which both Being and Not-Being appear. That which arises, which has arisen, is Not-Being as over against that which exists, which is Being. Thus a synthesis of the two opposites is established. This is a highly abstract statement of the type of problem which I have just given.

The definition, the thesis, in the case of contagious diseases is one which does not take into account the sporadic case. If you try to bring the latter into the statement, you have a carrying of disease without contact. In other words, you find yourself in a contradiction. Well, now, the passage from one of these to the other through the conception of the microörganism enables you to state both the contact experience, where the disease is actually transferred from the one who has it to another who has not, and also the sporadic case, in which no direct contact between persons is made. The difference between Hegel's abstract statement and the illustration I have used is that Hegel assumes that the statement which is made of Being carries with it the opposing statement of Not-Being. That is, he assumes that his universal will always have in it the opposite of itself. The opposition which is found in the case of the illustration I have used is not between two universals; it is not between the theory of contagion, that is, the carrying of the disease by actual contact, and the very opposite of that. That is not the conflict. It lies rather between the theory of contagion and the actual incident in experience, the sporadic case. That is, the conflict lies between the universal and an exception to that universal. That is where the problems in science always arise. They do not arise between the theory expressed in a law, for example, and the very opposite of that law. The conflict arises between the theory of the law and some particular observation, some particular so-called "fact" which is in conflict with that law. It is a conflict, then, not between universals but between the universal and the particular. If we put it into the terminology of logic, it is a conflict between a universal affirmative and a particular negative proposition. The sporadic case is an instance of getting a disease without contact, but you do not set up a universal proposition which says that no cases of disease are conveyed by contact. What you show is that, while there may be some cases in which it is conveyed by contact, there are at least some in which it is not. The scientific problem appears, then, in the form of an exception to an accepted law. And the conflict which the scientist, the research man, undertakes to solve is that between the exception and the law—not that between one law and another, one universal and another.

The general criticism of this point is, as I have already indicated, that Hegel assumed that our development, including the development of science, takes place through the conflict of universals, of ideas with each other. Actually, it takes place through the conflict of universals, or laws, and some particular event, some exception. If we make this reservation in regard to the Hegelian doctrine, we may still say that Hegel is correct in the assumption that the development of our knowledge takes place through conflict. It takes place through the appearance of problems and the solution of these problems. You have a thesis and an antithesis, and then you advance to a synthesis. Reflection is a process of solving problems. What we call our "reflective intelligence" is brought out in regard to some exception to what we have been in the habit of believing. We put all our views, our ideas, our methods of conduct, into universal form. We recognize that these universals are likely to be subject to exceptions, but we are in the habit of acting in that way. We expect things to happen in a universal fashion. But when an exception arises to that, then we are presented with a problem; we have something which we have to think out reflectively. And that thinking involves the presentation of a hypothesis.

The illustration which we used before made use of the conception of a microörganism in water, milk, or food stuffs. These can be ingested by a person together with the organism and so convey the disease. Another highly interesting, sensational illustration of this situation is the case of yellow fever. In this case the disease is conveyed from one person to another through the intermediation of the mosquito. The person having the disease takes the organism into his own body, and there this microörganism runs a certain portion of its life-cycle. Then it is conveyed to some other victim at a later stage. The assumption was that yellow fever was a filth disease. That is, if you clean up a district, you can keep it free from yellow fever. Senator Wood went to Havana and cleaned up the city. He cleaned up the houses, the streets, the sewers—everything. But yellow fever continued. It was already known that the mosquito was a carrier of malarial fever. Therefore, the hypothesis was presented that this might be true of yellow fever, and it was tested out and found to be the case.

The Hegelian synthesis, in these cases, is the hypothesis which will reconstruct the older theory, harmonize it with the facts. The hypothesis is a construct in the mind of the scientist. He does not spin it, so to speak, out of himself, as a spider spins his web. He takes facts that are there, meanings that are assured; and then he finds some suggestion that will give him new hypotheses, new ways of looking at the situation in question, in such a fashion that it will take up both the facts belonging to the older law and these new exceptions. Out of these two the new hypothesis is made. In this sense, then, Hegel is correct in his assumption that our knowledge grows through the giving of problems—problems which arise out of contradictions in our knowledge. But, as I have said, he was not correct in assuming that this conflict is one between universals. It is not that. It comes when there is an exception that conflicts with a law and leads to the appearance in the mind of the scientist of a hypothesis which will solve his problem. And the hypothesis does arise out of the mind of the thinker, the scientist. It is a creation of the self. And when it has been created, it carries with it a new world.

Thus the world has been rebuilt over and over again. Since the period of the Renaissance entirely new conceptions of matter and of motion have come to take the places of the older conceptions given in the Aristotelian doctrine. We have changed the world from a Ptolemaic to a Copernican one. The sphere of the heavens has changed from a most limited universe to an indefinitely great universe. During the last half-century we have been busy at the task of reconstructing the universe all the way down in terms of space and time. We are continually reconstructing the world. That reconstruction is something that comes out of men's minds, out of their heads. It comes from the process of thinking. It involves the thought of Copernicus, of Kepler, of Newton, of Einstein, to give us these new views of the world, these new worlds. We did not stumble upon them. These men were not simply more open-eyed than others. The process of advance consists in thinking out some hypothesis that will solve a given problem. When this hypothesis has been thought out, it has to be tested, of course. I do not mean that the scientist can sit back in his chair to create a new world to take the place of the old. He can create a new idea of the world, and then he can take that idea out and see if it corresponds with the facts of experience; and, if it does agree with the facts of experience, it becomes the world as we live it. When we say the sun does not move about the earth, we accept this contradiction of the senses because of the thinking of such men as Pythagoras, Aristarchus, Copernicus. They had to think things out before the world which revolves on its own axis could take its place in our experience as a great sphere in heaven revolving about the sun. Which it is, the one or the other, depends upon the actual thinking of scientists. Then they take this thought of theirs and bring it into the field of experience and see if it agrees with the facts. But the idea is theirs, their creation, the product of their creative intelligence.

All this is what Hegel really comes back to. The world of our experience is a world which we are continually creating in our thought. The astonishing thing is that such rapid reconstructions have taken place in recent times, such rapid reconstructions of fundamental ideas, such as those of matter and motion. These changes go on without our being disturbed about them. We naturally think of matter simply as subdivided stuff such as we can get between our thumb and finger. We break it up as far as we can under the microscope and with the imagination, but we always come out with something that we might get between our thumb and fingers if they were only small enough. But now we have come to conceive of matter in terms of energy. Mass itself has to be stated in terms of electromagnetism. We conceive of motion as that which goes on with certain velocities. Motion has been recognized for some time as relative; but now we find that motion itself varies in terms of distance covered and time passed in reference to the observer, and it also depends upon whether or not the observer is himself moving. The very distance covered is greater in one consentient state than in another. Such fundamental contradictions as that go into the very structure of the most primordial things in the world. This reconstruction is going on all the time. We expect it. We build our science on the theory of research. We assume that the world we know today will not be the world of our grandchildren. If it is, our descendants will have been poor scientists; if they cannot prove that we are wrong, they will be poor progeny. The business of science is to continually reconstruct its world. Science is a research procedure. Research does grow out of problems. Problems are exceptions to laws, rules—exceptions to the theory of the universe that we have accepted in the past. And the solution of these problems and the new worlds that come with them have to come out of the minds of men.

In the philosophy of Hegel the development of mind is the

same thing as the development of the world. Fundamentally, it is the position of absolute idealism that this relation between the mind and nature constitutes things, that all relations, as such, are essentially aspects of that relation. It is thinking that relates things. This is a statement of absolute idealism, of course, because the world ultimately goes back to the Absolute Self which constructs and continually maintains the world through a process of thinking it. That is the metaphysical principle of this idealism—the world is the expression of the thought of the Absolute.

As an object, then, the world answers to the subject, which is the self. And the relationship between the object and the subject, as it appears in these relations, is just that of the subject to the object; and this is a process. Just as thought itself is a process, so the world to the Absolute is essentially a process that is going on; and that process is the mind of the Absolute. It is a process that constitutes things, and the process is one with the Absolute Self.

The romantic phase of this idealism, as we have seen, places emphasis upon the self, and especially upon the emotional expressions that belong to the self as such. Of course, there have been idealisms prior to that of the Romantic school. There has been the idealism of Plato, of the Neo-Platonists, of Leibnitz; but in the idealism of none of these was the center of reality the self, although for them, too, the relations of things were the relations of thought. It is the self-process, the realization of the self through the not-self, and the construction of the latter by the former which gives the peculiar romantic character to the idealism of which I am speaking.

The world, then, is a creation of thought; it arises out of the process of thinking. That is the subject-object relation as Hegel presented it. It is a relationship in which the self finds conflicts in its world and then reconstructs this world through a synthesis, through a hypothesis, and finally advances to a new conflict. This is a statement of what goes on in science, in the process of the evolution of thought. It parallels the process of organic evolution. In the latter we have forms, animals, and plants that have certain habits, certain ways of living in the world. And then something happens, some geologic change occurs so that the animal can no longer get hold of the object that it eats as food. It meets a problem in obtaining nourishment; it meets a new enemy, a parasite, a microörganism. Something happens in its world which makes it run counter to the world in which it has been living. If we can conceive of a sufficiently successful mutation, we can perhaps find the solution of this problem within a single generation. What seems most often actually to take place are gradual changes, but the result of these changes is that there arises a new type of animal or plant which is adjusted to these changed surroundings. But with this arises a new world, for the animal or plant determines its world, its environment, in terms of its life-process. If an animal has eyes, it has an environment that has color; if it has ears, it lives in a world of sounds; if it has taste, its environment is sapid; if nostrils, its world is odorous. Change the animal and you change the environment, the world in which that animal lives. Give the animal a different digestive tract, and you have a new food. You may say the object is there before the animal, but it is not there as food. The animal comes with a stomach that can digest only certain things, and so determines its own world. Its own sensitiveness, its own methods of reaction, its own fashion of dealing with the world make a new world out of it. Thus we see that evolutionary advance means the solving of problems. The problem is put up to the individuals, to plant or animal, in terms of life and death; and the solution has to come in the appearance of some new form, a variant that springs from the older form. And with the new form comes another environment, an environment that is dependent upon the new form itself.

This is an opposition which appears in another manner in our thinking. It appears, for example, in the modern theory of relativity. The world within which the individual finds himself is a world in which he finds himself at rest while objects about him are in motion. Those objects which are at rest belong to the same consentient frame as the self. To a man on Mars the planet Mars would be at rest instead of in motion. The earth would be moving about the sun and spinning on its own axis. To a man on the sun, the sun would be at rest and all the planets and suns would be whirling about it. And it could not be said that any one of these structures is the correct one. If you say that the position of a hypothetical man on the sun is the correct position, then you have to ask as to the movement of the sun itself, for the sun is moving. Then you say, well, we will take the co-ordinates of the fixed stars and set them up as a fixed frame of reference while everything else moves within that frame. Then you soon find that the stars are not fixed and that you cannot get any object at rest which can be made a co-ordinate within which all motion can take place. Absolute motion is gone; absolute rest is gone. Motion and rest are to be stated from the point of view of the observer. That, in some sense, determines what the world in perspective shall be.

I bring up this modern situation simply to indicate what lay back of the Romantic philosophy. It is a statement of the world from the point of view of the individual, varying as it appears in the experience of different groups of individuals. Yet, the fundamental assumption is that the world is the same world for all. The world that we see is the same world that a man on Mars may see if there is a man there, the same world that would be seen by a man on the sun. And yet all these worlds are dependent upon those different individuals and their positions. The process of perception, of thought, of organization, determines what the world shall be; and yet these different worlds, from these different standpoints, are in some sense identical. You can see that the problem remains the same.

The problem remains the same, but it is differently approached. We have left behind the Romantic philosophers' solution to it. The problem with which they were dealing now appears in a different form. There are different worlds in the experience of different individuals, and these different worlds are determined by the very process of sensing, of thinking, in the individuals. It is our thought, our perception, which determines the world in which we live, so that the world of each is in some sense different from that of the others, and yet it is identical. It is the same world; it must be the same world. There would be no meaning to our conversation, no coherence in our own thought in regard to the world about which we are all of us conversing, if it were not the same. If that in the perception of the individual which gives different persons different worlds were not, in some sense, organized into a single process, there would be no meaning. The opposition, then, between the world as it appears as an absolute object, if there is such a thing, and the self that knows it, is a real problem, a problem differently stated from the point of view of different philosophers at the present time. Einstein, for example, gives one type of statement, which is followed by Eddington; Whitehead gives another sort of statement. The problem is stated differently at different times in an attempt at its solution. The general problem now is presented in the form of an Einsteinian statement. We find the assumption that each sentient individual puts a certain frame of reference on the world so that the world has that particular form, just as if one looked through a curved glass. Then the world is subject to the curvature of the glass. If we look through plain glass, the world is another world. The world itself is dependent upon the perception of the individual. Yet the assumption remains that these worlds are all identical.

There we see the fundamental problem which was present for the Romantic philosophers in the opposition between the subject and the object. As I said before, what they were doing was to give a philosophy of evolution, because such a philosophy assumes that the development of the world is a process of meeting problems. We carry the conception of evolution over into life and even into inorganic processes. We speak of the evolution of a star out of a nebula. First it is a whirling mass; then it breaks into a double star; finally the stellar body passes from its neighborhood and branches out into spiral form. Each one of these steps is the solution of a problem presented to this particular form. Evolution is the process of meeting and solving problems. What the Romantic idealist attempted to do was to take this idea over into the field of thought. He recognized that what the human intelligence does is to meet problems and solve them, and that in doing this the individual mind is constantly recreating its world. Thus, what gives the peculiar character to this Romantic philosophy is the assumption that each mind is only a phase of an Absolute Self, so that our thinking is just a phase of the thinking of the Absolute Self. The process, however, that is, the important part of it, at least, is one in which conflict arises. In the philosophy of Hegel this appeared as the conflict between the thesis and antithesis, which is overcome in a synthesis. As he worked it out, Hegel's dialectic is a very abstruse, a very complicated, theory. But it is one which can be applied to every phase of life, and not only to the theory of knowledge. It can be applied to the theory of the state, the theory of law, to history, to theology, and, of course, as we have been showing, to science. It is a grandiose statement that had astonishing success for a time, during which it seemed to be the last word in philosophy.

There was, however, a surprising lapse of interest in this Hegelian dialectic. I have pointed out that this dialectic failed to agree with the scientific method. Hegel undertook to show that advance took place through conflicts between universals, whereas scientific procedure is the result of conflicts between universals and exceptions to them. Hegel undertook to show what the development of science must be, but he made himself ridiculous as a result of certain rash assumptions which he made as to what the development of science must be. The Hegelian dialectic did not devise a statement of scientific method. His method was one worked out in science itself, that is, the method of the scientist was worked out in science itself—that of the appearance of the exception and the statement of this in terms of the definite problem, the working-out of some hypothesis, and then the testing of that. That is the scientific method, and it cannot be stated in terms of the Hegelian dialectic. After all, the world is essentially a scientific world; and any philosophy which fails to express, to make use of scientific method, is a philosophy that is out of place. And the Hegelian doctrine, notwithstanding its astonishing success for the moment, lapsed simply because there was no real use for it.

However, there was one field of endeavor in which it did obtain a more lasting success, and that was in the theory of the state. Hegel's assumption was that we are all parts of the Absolute Self. Any view that the individual has is, however, finite, limited, incomplete, and consequently untrue when taken by itself. It would have to be supplemented by those of all the other selves organized in the Absolute Self. Hegel assumed that the community was a closer approach to the Absolute than was the individual. The highest form of the Absolute on earth was, in his mind, the state, so that the state represented a high form of intelligence, higher than that which the individual possessed. On this basis it was the duty of the individual to subject himself to the state. Hegel's doctrine was well received by the Prussian court, which agreed with its absolutistic attitude, with the absolutistic philosophy which lay behind it. It was a statement which expressed some of the organization and discipline of the Prussian community—a government of the individual, an intelligence higher than that of the individual himself, a government from above down. The Hegelian statement did fit in very well with the theories of the Prussian state, for the Prussian state was very highly organized from the point of view of its trained intelligence. It was a bureaucracy. It had a monarch. As Hegel said, a monarch was just as necessary as the dotting of the "i." The real state was the organization of the bureaucracy itself with the trained intelligence that was behind it. This was worked out pretty definitely in the Prussian state by Frederick the Great. It was not autocratic but bureaucratic, having in its bureaus highly trained servants of the state itself, so that the state came to represent in the minds of the members of the community a higher type of intelligence than that found in the individual. And there was a devotion on the part of the individual to the state, a willingness to subject himself just because the state itself seemed to represent this higher type of intelligence. This, you see, was quite in accord with the Hegelian conception of the Absolute Self, and of the state as a higher expression of that Self than was found in the individual.

The Hegelian doctrine was successful, and exercised considerable influence in another field also. This other field was history, especially the philosophy of history. This whole Romantic movement was a very vivid stimulus to historical research and interest. It started off with a romantic interest and led on into an interpretation of present conditions in terms of past changes, and a correlative interpretation of past changes in terms of present conditions. This new historical interest in a process that had been going on leading up to present conditions, this backward look over the process from the point of view of present conditions, was what gave a peculiar interest and vividness to the historical sciences in all fields. It had back of it, of course, the evolutionary theories to which we have already referred. I have stated that the Hegelian dialectic was essentially an evolutionary theory, a recognition, that is, that new forms arise out of conflicts of old forms. In order to explain present forms, it is necessary to recognize the function of the old form and to discover the point at which it broke down, so to speak. This breakdown opened the door to the appearance of new forms. The Darwinian doctrine of evolution afforded an excellent hypothesis for the statement of this in concrete biological processes. The history of institutions could be explained similarly. On the basis of this doctrine you could find what the function of the old feudal institutions was, what the function of the organization of primitive society was. You could identify their functions in all the different forms of these institutions, and then you could show how the institution in one form broke down and a new form arose out of it. For example, you have the blood revenge as a method of control in the interrelationship of clans within a tribe, then the repression of the attack of one individual upon another through blood revenge, and the recognition that this very revenge is one that attacks the life of the tribe itself, for it sets up a vicious circle in which the punishment of one murder leads to another—the shedding of blood had itself to be again avenged. Out of this arose a method of rude justice, the court, with the taking-over of the administration of justice, of its own assessment of the crime and a penalty that should attach to it. There you have a conflict of interests, and yet you can trace the same function through them all. And then you have arising out of this the next form, which takes up the interest which lay back of the avenger's mind and the interest, later, of the community in the life of all its members and of fusing them into a body of law, with courts and their functionaries that should enforce that law.

I have pointed out that Hegel starts in his logic with the conception of Being and Not-Being, with the advance from this to Becoming. We find the same dialectical process in the development of his own thought and in the history of the race. There is an advance from quality to quantity, from quantity to measure, from measure to the physical thing, and so on up to the "idea" in the Hegelian sense. You have in the individual the development of one idea into another. That is the process of the history of philosophy. You also find the development of one cultural movement into another. That is the process of the philosophy of history. In other words, we find the same process in the history of man that we find in Hegel's logic.

This conception of the philosophy of history and of the history of philosophy is important in Hegel's philosophy. His assumption in this connection is that the development of human society follows the same set of categories as those which appear in logic. Reality develops, as we have seen, through Being, quality, quantity, measure, physical things, and so on up to the "idea." When we come to analyze the object of knowledge, we find that it passes through these different stages. In other words, the categories develop themselves. To return, for a moment, to Kant, you remember he conceived of the categories as forms of the mind given in advance of experience. Hegel assumes that the categories are forms which themselves arise through an inevitable process which shows their implication from one to another. This is, of course, the most general statement that could be given to evolutionary principles, and in this sense we can refer to one philosophy of the Romantic movement, that is, Hegel's, as definitely a philosophy of evolution. He traced the development of our ideas as they appeared in human history, following out the appearance of Being, as he conceived it, in the Milesian school of Greek philosophy, and followed it all out in detail from then on. He had to force matters a bit to get the historical development into the framework of his own logic, but he succeeded fairly well. He not only undertook to do this for the development of ideas in Greek philosophy and in the Greek community but was able also to give a statement for all the essential Christian dogmas as these appeared both in history and in logic.

I have tried to trace the historical background of this position. It reflects the importance that the self had reached after the French Revolution, when men were thrown back upon themselves, after the warfare of the French Revolution, and their return, perhaps with the sense of defeat but still with a heightened sense of themselves, to the old world which they had left behind, and to a rediscovery of this world when they revisited it in this character of the self. That is what constitutes the romantic character of this period, the emphasis upon the self, making the self the center of reality, conceiving the world as that which the self sets up, and sets up, so to speak, for the purpose of realizing itself, of putting itself into the not-self in order to realize itself.

In a very definite sense we can speak of this philosophy also not only as an evolutionary one but as one which is social in its character. Its most important result is to be found in the interest taken in human institutions, especially in the evolution of these institutions. Remember that these institutions had been thought of in the medieval period as given by God. They were there as forms of social organization which were, in some sense, given in advance of man, in the mind of God. They were fixed, just as Kant's categories were fixed. This latter important effect of the Hegelian doctrine was one not so evidently dialectical in its character. It found its expression in the study of social institutions; it laid emphasis upon history as that within which the forms of society have arisen, upon the study of ancient history not simply for the recording of bare political events, not simply as the scene for the appearance of great historical characters, but as that process within which the very forms of later society had arisen through a really evolutionary process. This approach to history was very much stimulated by the Hegelian doctrine; and although the Hegelian character was largely lost, the impetus which it gave was of very great importance.

What Hegel undertook to do, and in a great measure did do, was to show that institutions, as such, arose in the social process. It is in this process itself that institutions come into being. Of course, this gave a new standpoint from which to interpret, to understand, to criticize, these institutions. You can go back to the history of them, see how they have arisen out of particular conditions, see that they represent ideas that take on different forms in different situations. Then you are in a position to consider the form which the institution has at present, to see how far that form may be changed. One can study the institutions as he can study animal and vegetable forms. One can realize that the form of the institution is an expression of the period, and that, as each period demands change, that change can be brought about in the institution itself.

There was a very vivid interest in the study of human institutions. I have pointed out the vivid interest in history as such. It was carried over to the study of institutions. The Roman law, which was the background for the whole legal practice on the Continent, was presented from this standpoint; the ancient city was studied from this standpoint. And the laws of institutions, the family, the various governmental forms, the schools, were all looked at from the point of view of such a process of evolution; they were all looked at from the standpoint of structures which arose in a process, and which simply expressed that process at a certain moment. They were structures which carried within themselves contradictions, problems which must lead to further reconstructions.

This, of course, was carrying over revolution into evolution. What the political movement had undertaken was a revolution which should sweep away the old forms and substitute rational structures for them. Its leaders sought a state built absolutely upon the principles of reason, upon the rights of man. What such a philosophy as the one we are now examining presented was a long history of institutions which were adjusting themselves to the changes which were constantly taking place. If one could get into the structure, the movement, the current of the process, so to speak, then not only could one recognize in that a very gradual change but one could become a part of that change. One could recognize what the change must be, and set out to bring it about.

Thus evolution was brought in as a conception which was very important from the point of view of the institution. Another very important development which we will consider later in greater detail was that of the economic structure of society. There we have to go back to the so-called Industrial Revolution. In the period of Hegel that revolution had, in a measure, taken place; and Karl Marx undertook to interpret it from the point of view of what we call "socialistic propaganda." We will come back to that later. This was, however, one of the phases of the Hegelian dialectic which lasted after Hegel.

The two most important expressions of the Hegelian philosophy were to be found, then, in the interpretations of human institutions, and, more particularly, in this Marxian theory of the state which was both socialistic and communistic. The latter found its expression in the *Communist Manifesto* of 1847. These are the two fields within which the Hegelian dialectic did maintain itself. One was that of economic doctrine, the economic interpretation of history, as expressed in Marxian socialism, the dialectical materialism which has had added impulse of life through the control which the Communists, the Bolsheviki, have obtained in Russia. On the other hand, a new lease on life was given the Hegelian dialectic in England, not in the labor group, which answered relatively late to such a movement, but in the universities. Among them there grew up a definite Neo-Hegelian school that found in the dialectic something of a program which was not only philosophical but also social. T. H. Green is the representative of this latter phase of it. The religious field also came to be regarded as a possible field for the development of the dialectic. The interpretation which Hegel had given of ecclesiastical and doctrinal history appealed to the liberal theologian in England, especially to those within the established church. Anything can be explained by this dialectic. Not only that, but a great deal could also be explained away while still seeming to keep the meaning of that which could be regarded as having one form in one age and another form in another age. The dialectic opened the way toward a comparative history of dogma, of ecclesiastical institutions. It opened the way to the history of religion, with the interpretation of earlier religious forms and beliefs in terms of their function in the life of the community.

That sort of interpretation of history, then, in which there is found a continuance of function in organic process with the continual appearance of new forms, was a recognition which came very naturally through the Hegelian dialectic. It was carried over, as I said, in English thought in these two interests—one, a study of old institutions on the ecclesiastical and doctrinal side, the setting-out of the function of the doctrine, as over against its form, the interpretation of the particular form that doctrine took under particular conditions; and, on the other hand, it opened up a new world through a new approach to the social problem, the relation of the individual to the community, which was expressed particularly in the Neo-Hegelian philosophy of Green at Oxford. Here we have the identification of the individual with the community made a process not so much for the subordination of the individual to the state, as it was in the political philosophy of Hegel, but as an identity of the individual with the community, with a sort of inspiration for individual endeavor toward social ends. This identification of the individual with the community was very characteristic of the philosophy which was used in the political philosophy of Hegel for its statement of the subordination of the individual to the state. One could turn this the other way, recognize that the individual was what he was through his relation to the community. He owed himself to the community itself; he had a devotion to the community. And not only that, but one could recognize that in the reaction of the individual in the community arose those situations out of which changes took place. The individual could become the social reformer, one who could stand out in inadequate situations and point the way to higher syntheses. It is possible to take either attitude in the identification of the individual with the community—either the subordination of the individual to the state or the recognition that the individual is the means by which advance takes place.

There was, then, a very considerable revival of interest in England along these two lines; and the Hegelian school not only became, for the time being, the dominant school in English philosophy but it remains a very strong influence up to the present time, though more recently, of course, it has been displaced by the Realistic movement.

What I wanted to point out with reference to the labor movement and with reference to this history of institutions in society, particularly its development in England, was a continued life of Hegelian doctrine. After it left the philosophical chairs in Germany, it lapsed quite suddenly in German universities; but it had new life in England and in America. Royce, for example, is one of those Neo-Hegelians to whom we have referred. Dewey, in his early development, was another. The Romantic school was represented by the Concord school, by

Emerson and others of that group. They were parallel, really, with the interest reflected in England, first of all in Coleridge and then in Carlyle. However, the real Neo-Hegelian movement belonged to a somewhat later date than these last-mentioned men, when it came as a sort of transplanting of the Hegelian doctrine from German soil to the Anglo-Saxon community.

CHAPTER VIII

EVOLUTION BECOMES A GENERAL IDEA

PASSING as we have from Kant over to the Romantic idealists, we proceed from a conception of static forms which are originally given, and which serve as the whole basis of Kant's transcendental philosophy, to an idea of the development of the forms through a process, an evolutionary process. Kant conceived of the basic forms of the world as being given in the character of the mind itself. The forms of space and time—given in the sensibility, the forms of the understanding—given in the categories, and the forms of the reason, all there are in advance of experience. If the object, as such, arises under Kant's doctrine, it is because of certain contents of the sensibility passing into these forms. That is what makes it an object. It is not an object for our cognitive experience unless it has these forms that give it its reality. Sensuous experience itself, unless it takes on some form, has no meaning, no reality; it cannot be known except in so far as the experiences have some form. And in the Kantian doctrine, the form is given in advance. This is what Kant expressed in terms of the "transcendental logic," the term "transcendental" meaning the logical pre-existence of the form to the object. This concept, you see, belongs to pre-evolutionary days. The logical pre-existence of the form to the object cannot be stated in terms of process; therefore it falls outside of evolutionary ideas. In order that there might be an object there, Kant, as over against the empiricists, said that the form must be there originally, in advance. The latter undertook to show how an object might arise out of the mere association of different states of consciousness. Kant insisted that, in order for there to be an object, the form must be there first.

But the Romantic idealists changed all that. For them, the forms arose in the very process of experience, in the process of overcoming antinomies, overcoming obstacles. We are responsible for the forms. In other words, we have, in experience, not a pouring of the characters of our sensibility—colors, sounds, tastes, odors—into certain fixed forms, but a process of experience in which these very forms arise. Logic, as the romanticists conceived of it, was a dynamic, not a static, affair—not a simple mapping-out of judgments which we can make because of the forms which the mind possesses, but a process in which these very forms themselves arise.

The process of experience, according to these idealists, creates its own forms. Now this has a very abstruse sound, of course; but what I want to call your attention to is that it is nothing but an abstract statement of the principle of evolution. These Romantic idealists were undertaking in the field of philosophical speculation what Darwin and Lamarck were undertaking in the field of organic phenomena at the same period. What the Romantic idealists, and Hegel in particular, were saying, was that the world evolves, that reality itself is in a process of evolution.

This was a different point of view from that which characterized the Renaissance science of which I have previously spoken. This Renaissance science started off with just as simple elements as it could. It started with mass and motion. And Newton defined "mass" first as a quantity of matter; but, as that involved a conception of density and there was no way of telling just how dense your matter was, he had to get another definition. And he found it in terms of inertia, that is, the response which a body offers to a change of state in either its rest or its motion. If you want to measure the mass of a body, you measure its inertia. You see how much force is necessary to set it going, and so forth. And in that way you measure its mass, so that mass is really measured in terms of accelerations, that is, accelerations that you add to motions of a body. We come back to these simple conceptions of mass and motion; but we really define our mass in terms of certain sorts of motion, that is, velocities, accelerations. With these very simple conceptions the physicist undertook to build up a theory of the world. Newton gave the simple laws of mass and motion, and then, on the basis of mathematics, worked out an entire mechanics, which up to within a very short time has been the classical theory of the physical world. On the basis of this physical theory, there is just so much motion; there is just so much mass; there is just so much energy in the universe. When the system was more fully worked out, as it was in the nineteenth century, the principles of the conservation of energy were added to those of Newton, although they were implied in his system anyway.

Now, such a world as this is made up simply of physical particles in ceaseless motion. That is all there is to it. We speak of the different objects about us—trees, houses, rivers, mountains —all varied, all part of the infinite variety of nature—but what this science does is to break them up into ultimate physical particles, molecules, atoms, electrons, and protons. The object is nothing but a congeries of these; and, as already stated, the relationship between the particles in one object and in another object are just as real and just as important as the relations found between the particles within any single object itself. For you, the tree is something that exists by itself. When it has been cut down, it is so much lumber. The stump continues to exist as a thing by itself. And yet, from the point of view of mechanical science, the relationship between atoms and electrons in the stump of the tree with those in the star Sirius is just as real as the relations existing between the electrons in the trunk of the tree. The trunk is not an object there because of the physical definition that you give to it. Every field of force that surrounds every electron is related to every other field of force in the whole universe. We cut our objects out of this world. The mechanical world reduces to a mass of physical particles in ceaseless motion. So far as such a world can be said to have any process of its own, it is that which is represented in the term "entropy."

With the appearance of steam engines, people tried to work out the theory of them. And a Frenchman, Sadi Carnot, had the happy idea of thinking of the heat which was responsible for the formation of steam as flowing down hill through different degrees of temperature. When the steam was hot, its expansive power was great; and then, as it lost heat, it lost its power to expand. As it flowed down the hill of temperature, it lost its power. Of course, energy is not lost in the universe. It is just dispatched into surrounding objects. Thus, Carnot was able to work out a theory of steam engines which hinged upon this knowledge of energy flowing down a temperature hill. You put your piston rod into this stream and it will work the engine; but when it is at the bottom of the hill, it can do no more work. The mill cannot be turned by water that has passed. Well, now, this presented a picture of the whole universe as just a congeries of atoms in the sort of motion that was called "heat." If you set any sort of motion going, you know that you use up energy by friction in some way or other—that you produce heat. The whole universe seems to be running down toward a condition in which this motion will be evenly distributed through the entire universe. All manifestations of energy are due to the fact that they are on high levels, so to speak; but, given time enough, in the course of millions of years, everything will get evened out and all the particles will be in a fairly quiescent condition, with a slight, even motion of a Brownian sort distributed throughout the whole universe. That is the conception of entropy. That is the goal of the universe, if it has one, in which there will be some kind of energy evenly distributed throughout. We can be very thankful that we do not exist at that time. Of course, we could not exist then in any meaningful sense. That mechanical conception which science presents has no future—or a very dark one, at best. Not dark in the sense of catastrophies, for those are always exciting; but dark in the very monotony of the picture. The conception of entropy is anything but exciting. Such a universe would answer only to an infinite sense of ennui.

The scientific conception, the mechanical conception, of the world did not seem to be one that gave any explanation to the form of things. As I have said, science does not justify us in taking a tree, a plant, an animal, a house, as separate objects by themselves. As we know, from the scientific standpoint there is no difference between life and death—simply a shifting of energies. From the scientific standpoint, the forms of things have no real significance. Of course, if you start off with a certain thing, given a certain form, you can use scientific technique to analyze it; but your abstract mechanical science, that to which Newton gave form, does not account for any object, does not account for the acceptance of one object rather than another.

It was Kant who took the first step toward a theory of the heavenly bodies. He was very devoted to the mechanical science of his period; but his imagination carried him a step farther, and he tried to conceive how the present form of the heavens might have arisen out of earlier forms. His statement was one that really got its scientific formulation in Laplace's conception of the solar system as a great nebula, intensely hot to begin with, and which gradually cooled down. Kant had to assume a whirling nebula which cooled down and resulted in a series of rings moving about the center as it condensed, gradually developing into a system of bodies of unspecific form. The velocity of the bodies on the outside of the system would keep them from moving in toward the center, and out of these rings the planets would arise. That is the suggestion which Laplace took from Kant and made into an explanation of the way in which the solar system arose. This was the first step toward a theory of the evolution of the heavens.

But what I now want to present is something different from this picture which mechanical science gives of the universe. It is an attempt to state an object in a certain form, and to show how that form might arise. If you think of it, that is the title of Darwin's book, *The Origin of Species*, "species" being nothing but the Latin word for form. What is the origin of these forms of things? Mechanical science does not offer any explanation of them. Anyway, from the point of view of mechanical science, the form has no meaning. All that this science says about a particular form is that in referring to a certain object you are isolating a certain group of physical particles, taking them off by themselves. Really, they are related to all physical particles. But the universe that we know is more than particles. It is a world of forms. Now, the question is, where do these forms come from? Certain of the principal forms, Kant said, come from the very structure of our own minds. The theology of the period said the forms of animals and plants go back to a creative fiat of God. He gave the earth its form and all the stellar bodies their forms and their motions, as well as those of the plants and animals on them. And that, of course, was the point from which the descriptive sciences of the time—biology, botany, and zoölogy—started. They assumed species of plants and animals which had been created by God when he made the earth.

What Darwin undertook to show was that some of these forms must conceivably have arisen through natural processes. But how could the forms as such have arisen? Mechanical science could not explain them, because, from the point of view of mechanical science, form does not exist. There are only two objects—one the world as a whole, and the other the ultimate physical particles out of which it is made. All the other so-called "objects" are objects that our perception cuts out. That is, we distinguish the chair from the table and ignore the relations between them because we want to move them about, we want to sit on the one and write on the other. For our purposes, then, we distinguish them as separate objects. Actually, they attract each other as physical particles, parts of a single, all inclusive electromagnetic field. The forms are not explained by the mechanical science of the period. The biological and other sciences —such as cosmology, astronomy—all explained certain forms which they found, in so far as they did account for them, by saying that they were there to begin with. And even Kant assumes that the forms of the mind are there to begin with.

Now the movement to which I am referring, under the term

"theory of evolution," is one which undertakes to explain how the forms of things may arise. Mechanical science cannot explain that. It can break up forms, analyze them into physical particles; but it cannot do more than that. Biological science and astronomical science both start with certain forms as given. For example, Laplace's conception is of rapidly revolving, hot nebular bodies which were present to start with. Biological science started with certain living forms; geology, with definite types and forms of rocks. These sciences classify things in accordance with the forms that are found. But they do not generally undertake to show how the forms arise. There is, of course, the science of the growing form, embryology. But this is a recent science. It accounts for the way in which the adult arises out of the embryo. The older theory of biology assumed the form already there; it even conceived of a complete man as given in the very cells from which the form of the embryo developed. The assumption was that the form was there as a precondition of what one finds. This is Aristotelian science. It is also essentially Kantian. We have seen how we conceived of the forms of the mind as given as the precondition of our experience.

Now, Lamarckian and Darwinian evolution undertook to show how, by a certain process, forms themselves might come into being, might arise. Starting with the relatively formless, how could one account for the appearance of forms? Lamarck started with the hypothesis that every activity of the form altered the form itself, and the form then handed on the change to the next generation. As a picturesque example, assume that the progenitors of the giraffe wanted, or had, to feed off the leaves of trees, and so stretched their necks. They handed this stretched neck on to their longer-necked offspring. The inheritance of so-called "acquired characteristics" was Lamarck's suggestion to account for the appearance of forms. He assumed, as did Darwin, that you start with relatively formless protoplasm, and he went on to show the process by means of which forms might arise from that which was relatively formless.

In the previous chapter we were discussing Romantic idealism, and we pointed out that it was a development or an expression of the spirit of evolution, of the definite entrance of the idea of evolution into Western thought. Indeed, we spoke of Hegel's philosophy as a "philosophy of evolution." This highly abstruse speculative movement is simply a part of this general movement toward the discovery of the way in which the forms of things arise, of origins. As a scientific undertaking, it was not helped out by the physical science of the time. It had to make its own way, and this it did to an amazing extent. In later generations it became a guiding idea in practically all investigations.

I mentioned earlier the distinction between the conception of evolution that belonged to the older, the ancient thought, that which got its classical expression in the Aristotelian doctrine, and the evolutionary theory of this period. The Aristotelian evolution was the development of the so-called "form," the nature of the thing which was already present. It presupposed the existence of the form as something that was there. In this conception a metaphysical entity was thought of which existed in and directed the development of the form. The species—which is the Latin word for the Greek term "form"—was actually conceived of as a certain nature that supervised the development of the seed of the embryo into the normal adult form. Under the conception of Christian theology this form was thought of as existing first in the mind of God, then as appearing in the plants and animals and various other objects that he created, and finally as arising in our minds as concepts. The form, however, was not thought of exactly in the Aristotelian sense as existing in advance, as being an entelechy, the nature of the object existing in advance of the actual animal or plant.

The difference between that conception of evolution and the modern conception is given, as I have already pointed out, in the very title of Darwin's book, *The Origin of Species*, that is, the origin of forms. It is an evolution of the form, of the nature, and not an evolution of the particular animal or plant. What this theory is interested in is the evolution of the nature of the object, of the form, in a metaphysical sense. It is this which distinguishes the later theory of evolution from the former, namely, that the actual character of the object, the form or the nature itself, should arise instead of being given.

As you may remember, Darwin got the suggestion for his hypothesis from Malthus' doctrine of population. This was an attempt to show the relationship which exists between population and the food supply, and what effect this relationship may have on the future of the race. Of course, Malthus' statement was greatly disturbed by the introduction of machine production; this upset many of his calculations, if not the theory as a whole. Yet, it is interesting as an attempt to state in definite ways what the experience of the race will be in the light of a single factor in its environment, that is, the food supply.

Darwin became very much interested in this problem, and it led him to undertake to explain certain variations which take place in forms as being due to the pressure of population. In nature there are always more forms born into the world, more plants and animals, than can possibly survive. There is a constant pressure which would lead to the selection of those variants which are better adapted to the conditions under which they must live. This process of the culling-out of these better-adapted forms would, in time, lead to the appearance of new forms. What lies back of this conception is the idea of a process, a life-process, that may take now one, and now another, form. The thing of importance is that there is a distinction made between this life-process and the form that it takes. This was not true of the earlier conception. In it, the life-process was thought of as expressed in the form; the form had to be there in order that there might be life.

The idea of which I have just spoken I have referred to as Darwinian. The same idea lies back of the conception of Lamarck. He assumes a life-process which may appear in one form or another, but which is the same process whatever form it takes on. The particular form which it does assume depends upon the conditions within which this life-process is run. Thus we find the same fundamental life-process in plants and in animals—in the amoeba, in man, and in every form between. It is a process that starts in the separation of carbon and oxygen. These two, in the form of carbon dioxide, exhaled by animals as a by-product of the assimilation of food, are found in water solution in plants as carbonic acid. Through the mediation of the action of chlorophyl cells and light this eventually becomes food, in the form of various sugars and starches. These starches are then carried to tissues that expend energy, that burn up and set free energy in the life of plant or animal, get rid of waste products, set up the means of reproduction, and so pass on from one plant or animal to another, from one generation to another. The essentials of that life-process are the same in all living forms. We find it in unicellular forms, in multicellular forms. The only difference is that in the case of the latter we find a differentiation of tissues to carry out various functions; we find different groups of cells that take up one of the phases of the life-process and specialize in that—the lungs take in air, oxygen; another group of cells becomes the means of the circulation of the blood; others take over the functions of ingestion, of locomotion, of secreting fluids that make digestion and reproduction possible. In other words, separate groups of cells carry on different parts of the life-process. The whole process, however, is the same as that which goes on in unicellular forms. That, you see, is involved in this conception of evolution—a life-process that flows through different forms, taking on now this form, now that. The cell, as a single entity in the whole, remains fundamentally what it was in the unicellular form. All living cells bathe in some fluid medium; those cells on the outside of us are dead. Living cells are those which are bathed in the fluids of the body, such as the blood or lymph. They are the only ones which are alive, and they carry over into the body some of the original sea from which our original unicellular existence migrated. These cells went from the surface to the bottom, and there multicellular forms arose. From the bottom of the sea to man, they had to bring this precious fluid in which alone cells can live.

This was first found in plants. And animals then came and lived upon the plants; but the life-process has flowed through all, and remains the same life-process.

Given such a conception as this, it is possible to conceive of the form of the plant or the animal as arising in the existence of the life-process itself. It is very important that we should get the conception of evolution that is involved in it and distinguish it from the earlier conception, especially if we are to understand the appearance of this conception in its philosophic form. We are concerned with a theory which involves a process as its fundamental fact, and then with this process as appearing in different forms.

Now, the Romantic idealists, who first developed a philosophy of evolution, came back, of course, to our experience of ourselves—that reflexive experience in which the individual realizes himself in so far as, in some sense, he sees himself, hears himself. He looks in the glass and sees himself; he speaks and hears himself. It is the sort of situation in which the individual is both subject and object. But in order to be both subject and object, he has to pass from one phase to another. The self involves a process that is going on, that takes on now one form and now another—a subject-object relationship which is dynamic, not static; a subject-object relationship which has a process behind it, one which can appear now in this phase, now in that.

To get the feeling for this Romantic idealism, one must be able to put himself in the position of the process as determining the form. And it is for this reason that I have said what I have in regard to evolution. That does not get us as deep into our experience as the subject-object relationship does. Logically, it is of the same character, namely, a process in this case, a life-process, going on that takes now one form and now another. The process can be distinguished from the form; yet it takes place within the different forms. The same apparatus for digestion has to be there; the same apparatus for expiration, for circulation, for the expenditure of energy, have to be there for the life-process to go on; and yet this life-process may appear now with this particular apparatus and now with that. In your thought you can distinguish the process from the form. And yet you can see that there must be forms if the process is to take place. We have spoken of the unicellular animal as having no form in that sense. That statement is not entirely correct. We know that there is a high degree of organization of molecular structure in the cell itself. We can follow it out in a vague sort of way. There is also structure there. You cannot have a process without some sort of a structure; and yet the structure is simply something that expresses this process as it takes place now in one animal and now in another, or in plants as over against animals. That life-process that starts off with carbon dioxide, with water and carbonic gas, goes on through plant and animal life and ends up as carbon dioxide, in the carbonic acid gas and water that we breathe out. That process is something we can isolate from the different organs in which it takes place, and yet it could not take place without some sort of organ. We can separate the process from particular organs by recognizing them in one or another animal, in one or another plant. But we could not have the process if there were not some structure given, some particular form in which it expresses itself.

If, then, one is to make a philosophy out of this evolutionary movement, one must recognize some sort of process within which the particular form arises. In the biological world this process is a life-process, and it can be definitely isolated as the same process in all living forms, because in the scientific development of physics and chemistry, as well as of physiology, we are able to find out what this life-process is, that is, to think of the life-process apart from the particular form in which it goes on—to separate, in other words, such a function as the digestive process from the digestive tract itself; to be able to realize that the ferments essential to digestion, the breaking-down of starches and proteins through these ferments, and the organization, the synthesis, of these into organic products which the animal can assimilate, goes on in the amoeba, which has no digestive tract at all. The importance of the digestive tract is dependent upon the life of the particular group of cells that go to make up an animal. The problem presented to the animal form is the conversion of edible protoplasm, which is found in plants, into an assimilable form. The plant had to protect its fluid by cellulose. In order to get at the fluid, the animal has to be able to digest away the cellulose. Such an animal as the ox has to have a very complicated apparatus within itself; it sets up a whole series of bacteriological laboratories and brings into them microörganisms that set up ferments to get rid of the cellulose that surrounds the edible protoplasm in its food. The digestive tract of the animal is, then, an adaptation to the sort of food which these living cells feed upon. The animal has to have a structure which will enable it to get at the edible protoplasm itself. On the other hand, the tiger, which lives on the ox, has a rather simple assimilative problem on his hands. The ox has done the work, and the tiger can feed on his flesh. Of course, we are in the position of the tiger, except that we take the ox from the stockyards! The point is that our digestive system, like that of the tiger, can be much more simple than the ox's. Our whole life-process is not devoted to digesting away cellulose that surrounds food.

This indicates the way in which the form arises, so to speak, within the life-process itself. The form is dependent upon the conditions under which the life-process goes on. It is the same process, but it meets all sorts of difficulties. It has to have a particular apparatus in order that it may meet each of these up-cropping difficulties. Such a life-process as this, which is the same in all these forms, was entirely unknown to the ancient physiologist. He could look at the animal only from the outside. He could see what were the function of the mouth and the feet, of the various limbs and external organs; but he could not get inside the animal and discover this process that was flowing on, that was taking on these different outer forms as the plant or animal needed a certain apparatus to enable it to live under certain conditions. It is essential to science and to the philosophy of evolution that it should recognize as basic to all a certain process that takes place, and then that it should undertake to show the way in which the forms of things arise in the operation of this process.

The question as to whether a Darwinian or Lamarckian hypothesis is to be accepted is not really of such great importance. The important thing about the doctrine of evolution is the recognition that the process takes now one form and now another, according to the conditions under which it is going on. That is the essential thing. One must be able to distinguish the process from the structure of the particular form, to regard the latter as being simply the organ within which a certain function takes place. If the conditions call for a certain type of organ, that organ must arise if the form is to survive. If conditions call for an organ of another sort, that other sort of organ must arise. That is what is involved in the evolutionary doctrine. The acceptance of the Darwinian hypothesis is simply the acceptance of Darwin's view that selection under the struggle for existence would pick out the organ which is necessary for survival. The heart of the problem of evolution is the recognition that the process will determine the form according to the conditions within which it goes on. If you look at the life-process as something which is essential in all forms, you can see that the outer structure which it takes on will depend upon the conditions under which this life-process runs on.

Now, if you generalize this, make a philosophic doctrine out of it, you come back to some central process which takes place under different conditions; and the Romantic idealists undertook to identify this process, first of all, with the self–not-self process in experience, and then to identify this self–not-self process with the subject-object process. They undertook to make these one and the same. The subject-object relationship is, from the philosophical standpoint, and especially from the epistemological standpoint, the more fundamental one. But the self looms up very importantly here, as you can see, for it is a self that is a subject. As I pointed out above, the object was in some sense explained by the empiricist. If you are to put the object into the subject-object process, you have to find a subject that is involved in the presence of the object. The old doctrine assumed that the world was there and that human beings later came into it. In other words, according to this view, the object was there before the subject. The appearance of the subject seems to have been purely accidental, incidental. The object might just as well be there without the subject being there. But, what the Romantic idealists insisted upon is that you cannot have an object without a subject. You can see very well that you cannot have a subject without an object, that you cannot have a consciousness of things unless there are things there of which to be conscious. You cannot have bare consciousness which is not consciousness of something. Our experience of the self is one which is an experience of a world, of an object. The subject does involve the object in order that we may have consciousness. But we do not as inevitably recognize that the subject is essential to there being an object present. According to our scientific conception, the world has arisen through millions of years, only in the last moments of which have there been any living forms; and only in the last second of these moments have there been any human forms. The world was there long before the subjects appeared. What the Romantic idealist does is to assume that for these objects to be present there must be a subject. In one sense this might be said to be reflecting the philosophical dogma that the world could not be present unless created by a conscious being. But this problem is something more profound than a philosophical dogma. It is the assumption that the very existence of an object, as such, involves the existence of a subject to which it is an object.

Well, if we are to find an instance of that in which the object involves a subject, as well as the subject involving an object, we can come back to the self. The self can exist as a self only in so far as it is a subject. And significant objects can exist only as objects for a subject. We can see that the self-process of the Romantic idealists—this fusion of the two phases of experience, the self-experience on the one hand and the subject-object experience on the other hand—was one which enabled them to insist not only that the subject involved an object but also that the object involved a subject. This, then, was the central process for them: the self, the not-self, are expressions of a single process, and in this also is found the subject-object relationship in which both terms are always mutually involved. Just as there can be no self without a not-self, so there can be no subject without an object, and vice versa.

One more word about evolution. We have a statement of the human animal as having reached a situation in which he gets control over his environment. Now, it is not the human animal as an individual that reaches any such climax as that; it is society. This point is cogently insisted upon by Hegel, the last of the Romantic idealists. The human animal as an individual could never have attained control over the environment. It is a control which has arisen through social organization. The very speech he uses, the very mechanism of thought which is given, are social products. His own self is attained only through his taking the attitude of the social group to which he belongs. He must become socialized to become himself. So when you speak of this evolution, of its having reached a certain climax in human form, you must realize that it reaches that point only in so far as the human form is recognized as an organic part of the social whole. Now, there is nothing so social as science, nothing so universal. Nothing so rigorously oversteps the points that separate man from man and groups from groups as does science. There cannot be any narrow provincialism or patriotism in science. Scientific method makes that impossible. Science is inevitably a universal discipline which takes in all who think. It speaks with the voice of all rational beings. It must be true everywhere; otherwise it is not scientific. But science is evolutionary. Here, too, there is a continuous process which is taking on successively different forms. It is this evolutionary aspect of science which is important in the philosophy of the contemporary French philosopher, Henri Bergson, whose work we will consider later.

CHAPTER IX

THE INDUSTRIAL REVOLUTION—THE
QUEST FOR MARKETS

I HAVE pointed out, in a general way, the great changes that took place in France during the Revolution. The soil passed over from the feudal lord to the peasant who worked the soil. In England this process had never taken place on any such scale. On the contrary, the development of agriculture in England tended to bring more and more of the allotments of land into the hands of single farmers, single landowners. The lands could be worked more profitably that way. The processes of agriculture which were being introduced in England could be worked more profitably on large holdings than on the little holdings that the tenant had been able to work. The older, medieval production had been intensive rather than extensive. It was built up by old feudal conditions and had no relationship to farming proper. If this was to be changed, it was necessary to bring the scattered holdings together under a single head. The result of this was that more and more of the tenants became farm laborers, and the direction of farming passed from the hands of the peasant into the hands of the larger farmers. Where in France he worked them himself, in England the allotments that belonged to the peasant passed under the control of the landowner or the large farmer, and the farmer was taken out of that direct control over the process of agriculture which was characteristic of conditions in France. Under proper methods of farming there was no need for the number of hands that were required under the older method. The land could be more profitably operated by a smaller number of men. Thus there grew up a surplus of population upon the land. This is one of the conditions that favorably prepared the ground in England for the rapid development of what is called the Industrial Revolution.

We find a very varied background out of which this economic change took place. First of all, there are the markets, the growing-up of voluntary organizations for the distribution of goods, which were able to adjust themselves to new demands. We have the development of the credit system, which had grown up under other conditions and for other purposes, being carried over into business. We have a change in the religious attitude, which brings a certain discipline of mind into the process of business. And then we have the flowering of the so-called Industrial Revolution, in which production is taken away from the home and is carried over into more favored situations in the factory, in which the artisan's occupation is taken to pieces, broken up into a whole series of different tasks, and these tasks given over, as far as possible, to machines driven by water power, steam power, and, later, electricity, so that the man in occupation becomes a part of a vast machine production. This is the process which was taking place and of which the shifts in population connected with the Industrial Revolution are only parts.

The shift of population, of course, followed the factory. With the older textile industry, the spinning and weaving went on in the homes. The capitalist sent his employees about, carrying certain of the raw materials which they brought back as finished products. With the factory, the different looms were brought to a single place where they could be driven by power. The population inevitably followed the loom to the factory, and in the great industrial centers we have the building of the factory city. This took the individual definitely away from the soil. All feudal privilege, all feudal organization, all feudal administration, gathered about the relation of the individual to the soil. The feudal lord was one who was lord over his land. He held it, perhaps, under another, and he under another, until they came to the highest; but the individual belonged to the soil. The social organization was determined by this relationship to the soil.

The breakdown of this feudal system and the concentration of large units of population around the new factories are the features of the Industrial Revolution which are spoken of most often. Back of this, however, lay the development of the larger market, a market which required production on a larger scale. Various social structures answered to this demand. What I want to point out in this connection is that such a larger market means, of course, a more highly organized society; it means bringing people into closer relationship with each other in terms of economic needs, supplies, and so making out of groups which had been isolated from each other, partially unified groups. That is the social organizing process that goes on in economics. It needs to be emphasized because in the economic process itself we are apt to abstract from the total picture everything except that which is involved directly in the process. For example, when we are buying and selling, we consider only the prices, their advantage or disadvantage. We put economic men over against us, and we regard ourselves simply as economic men. In business, religion is supposed to be abandoned. The dictum of *caveat emptor* is one that lies back of this attitude. It answers to what we term the "materialistic" view of life. And yet all the advances which have taken place in the modern world have been dependent on this bringing people together in terms of their needs, wants, and supplies as these are met in an economic fashion. And this very abstraction of the economic from the other social processes has been of great importance and of great value. It is possible for people to buy and sell with each other who refuse to have anything to do with each other otherwise. That is, it is possible to hold people together inside of an economic whole who would be at war otherwise. Economic organization is of importance in holding together parts of a society which might, without it, be distinctly and mutually at variance. If you will take it, you will find this view of society from the perspective of economic development very interesting.

I shall refer to it again when we come to the development of socialism.

For our immediate purpose it is important that we have in mind an outline of the conditions under which the Industrial Revolution sprang up. It is a period in which an expansion of an economic character was taking place with the development of larger markets and the gradual development of methods of production which would meet this larger demand.

This involved changes in social conditions which are to be noted, in a general way, as characteristics of the Western world. Among these is the appearance of arbitrary organizations of all types in the midst of fixed institutions. Out of this arose in large degree the medieval city, with its groups of individuals not immediately connected with the soil. Under the old feudal conditions, of course, the population was allotted to the soil, belonged to it. The city, growing up first as the fortress, the center for a garrison, and as a place in which the ecclesiastical powers centered, tended to become more and more a trading center; and there grew up guilds which supplied the immediate needs of the community and, besides that, carried on the trading which connected these communities with the wider economic world. The growth of these different voluntary organizations played a large part in the development of the industry of the modern world and invited those mechanisms which responded to the demand. What was essential was the larger demand and then a sort of a social mechanism that could answer to this.

We find in the middle of the eighteenth century a very considerable increase in population, which it is rather difficult to explain. Unquestionably, the beginning of this lay in the earlier part of the century and, of course, affected conditions, bringing with it the larger markets at home and abroad of which I have already spoken. I think no one has adequately pointed out just what the conditions were that brought this about. Probably to a large extent it represented improved conditions of health. In other words, the death-rate probably decreased; and, with the dropping of the death-rate, with a larger number of children, as well as adults, surviving, the population as a whole commenced to increase steadily. With this increase came an increased demand for occupation on the part of the populations, together with an increase in the demand for goods. Altogether it is a very complex problem, but in general we can bring it back to the development of larger markets and of institutions which were sufficiently elastic and responsive to meet the needs of this market.

I have already pointed out what the characteristics of this development were. The factory was the center at which production was carried on under better economic conditions than those found in the home. The most important of these changed conditions was the subdivision of production into a number of tasks. These could be carried on more rapidly by separate individuals, and so the process of creation was simplified. And, as it was simplified, the way was opened for the machine; and with this came the stimulus to invention. With this stimulus to invention came also the demand for power with which to drive the machines. I will insist that this is not simply a question of the unusual development of inventive power. We assume that, by and large, each generation carries with it as much inventive genius as any other, and that it belongs to one community as much as to any other. The difference lies in the demand, a demand that goes back to such a situation as this which I have just presented, one in which production itself is analyzed, broken up into a series of separate tasks which are made sufficiently simple so that a good many of them can be carried on by machines. The result is that the laborer tends to become more and more a machine-tender, a person who keeps the machine going. He becomes a part of the machine activity. The demand implies a difference between the new condition and the old; it implies that the means of production which had been used were not adequate. It implies a general shift in the economic situation. Of course, it also implies that there are those able to make use of such apparatus; that there is available labor which can be utilized, can be put into new vocations. This,

I say, is possible only where you can get power to drive the machine which is greater than mere man power. Water power, the development of the steam engine with the demand for fuel such as that provided by coal, the consequent development of the coal industry—this whole process can be traced back to its beginnings in the sixteenth and seventeenth centuries, and that not only in terms of a process but also in terms of the attitude of mind, in terms of the industrial discipline of the community. There are, of course, other changes which, perhaps, are made too central, such as the development of iron and coal. Machinery was essential to the development of the factory to its full productivity. Machinery meant iron. The power to drive the machine meant coal. And there in England, at that time, close to the surface, was the ore and the coal. Conditions, then, were very favorable to the flowering-out of this rapid productivity, with all the changes that it carried with it. But this was a result, not a cause of the wider movement.

Of particular importance was the shift in the population, and with this the breakdown of the feudal conditions which still persisted, on the social side, in England. Most of the population had been governed by the squire and the curate, whose positions were those determined by the whole feudal situation. The individual peasant or farmer worked the soil belonging to another person. He held it as a tenant. His position in the community was determined by his relationship to the soil. While in France there had developed a centralized government which took over more and more of the control of production, in England there grew up the squirarchy, a form of legal government through the squire, that is, through the justice of the peace. This had an astonishingly large part in the government of England. It was carried out by men, relatively untrained in matters of law and administration. The squire and curate were central figures of this period, and the peasant occupied a position of subjection. The central power of the government expressed itself through the squire. He was an aristocrat. He had, of course, higher courts above him; and when serious issues arose, he might be brought into a position in which his power would be questioned; but under ordinary conditions the squire represented the government. It was a modern feudal condition, a feudal condition, however, in which the feudal lord was himself definitely interested in what was still the greatest form of production, agriculture. The feudal lord was a great landowner and one who introduced better methods of production. He was interested not only in this production but also in the stability of things, in the maintenance of peace. In this he was the representative in his own district, representing the local government as over against the central government. But his power was very great, greater perhaps socially than it was in terms of administration, than it was in legal terms, so that the average individual felt himself definitely under his superiors, and what he produced came to him under conditions which were dictated more or less by the social order of which the squire was the head.

The changes to which we have referred shifted this relation by moving the population, or portions of it, from the soil to the city; and in the city the individual was under no feudal lord. Here his task was one which he himself elected, or at least that was what seemed to be the situation. He came as a day laborer. As a day laborer he needed no skill. The skill which he had as a weaver, for example, was of no service to him in working power-driven machines. He came in, then, as a day laborer in return for a wage, and the wage belonged to him not in terms of the product of the soil but of his own effort. He got money in return for his services instead of for the products of the soil, and he got it under no feudal conditions at all. This freed him, in a certain sense. The wage was all too often a starvation wage, but it was his own. It separated him from the soil.

There is one characteristic of the city as it appears in the modern world as distinct from the city of the earlier Graeco-Roman world—that is the appearance of voluntary organizations in the Western world. At first, the cities grew largely out of fortified places, and these fortifications or garrisons led to the appearance of groups of warriors who entered into voluntary agreements with each other for various purposes which they had in common. They could shift from one place to another. Then there also appeared in the church various voluntary organizations, among the ecclesiastical representatives. These were succeeded by the organizations out of which the guilds arose, that is, those occupied in production; and they had their own organization with something of their own control. In all the groups—the warrior groups, church groups, industrial groups, in the so-called university or school groups—we find, in the Western community, voluntary organization.

I suppose we may explain these in part by the comparatively chaotic conditions. The new communities grew up in the decay of the old ones. The mechanism for the control of the community rotted out. New methods of control had to be built up gradually. And they were built up, first of all, over against an ideal situation. That is, Europe conceived of itself as belonging, above all else, to the Holy Roman church. And, back of that, lay the assumption of a political organization under the church, the Holy Roman Empire. Each of these organizations carried with it an assumption of an order of society which was not realized. The church presupposed a community, a blessed community, in which the interest of one was the interest of all. In it were devout worshipers of God, persons carrying out his behests, utterly unselfish, having the nature of the so-called "saint" of the period. This was the ideal which the church presented, an ideal which was anything but satisfied with the actual order of things. During the so-called Dark Ages, Europe was in a state of constant warfare between very little groups. It was a period in the Western world in which there was such chaos, such continuous, unmitigated hostility between little groups as there has not been since. And yet, Europe had accepted the conception of the church. It was assumed that the new world would exist in the New Jerusalem, in the world to come. In this present world men were under probation. There was an ideal of society, then, not yet realized, but one which remained in men's minds. And the same situation existed in the political organization. There was one political head; and all those under him, the various feudal lords, were subject to the Roman emperor. The actual subjugation was largely fictitious, but this assumption lay in men's minds. Europe was a community in which there were ideals of social organization which were not actually realized.

But the fact that they were not realized was an essential part of the life of the time. The world was supposed to have been created by God that men might realize their ideals; and God knowing that they would not realize them, that they would sin, fall from grace, appointed such institutions as the church and state that were to carry on, so to speak, until the day of the Last Judgment. The world was not conceived of as being the sort of place in which such a society as men conceived could actually exist. But it was there as an ideal which ought to exist; and because it did not exist, men were in a state of sin. The institutions of the time were built up definitely with reference to man's being in such a state of sin. That is, the ideal, in one form or another, was a definite part of the life of the community, an ideal which was not realized. It is that situation, and the comparative chaos of the period which lent itself to the appearance of these voluntary organizations, of which we have been speaking.

Perhaps the form of this with which we are most familiar is the appearance of the different religious groups, of the so-called "heresies" which were constantly arising. Men conceived of themselves as having received inspiration from God. They undertook to interpret the monuments of the church in a different fashion than the church itself, and gathered together those who agreed with the new interpretation. Thus, there arose new religious bodies. These were continually springing up throughout the whole medieval period. For example, during the Reformation, we have the appearance of the Protestants. This was nothing but another expression of the breaking-up of the community into voluntary organizations. The same thing took place on the political side, particularly with the appearance of the free cities

—cities that worked themselves out from under the control of overlords, bought their privileges for themselves, bought the opportunity to pay their own way. And out of this arose cities that were relatively free, which had their own peculiar place within the Holy Roman Empire. And they grew up largely about industrial conditions.

What I want to point out with reference to these various voluntary organizations—political, economic, military, or among the students of the different universities who gathered together in national groups according to the different countries from which they came or in accordance with their interests—is that they came to play a part in the actual control of society. The most striking example of such a process in our setting is the political party, the party that has no recognized place in the constitution of the state and yet which is an essential part in the government of the community. That is one characteristic of the whole Western life, of the whole Western community— the appearance of voluntary organizations gathering about the ideals which lay back of the various institutions but which were not definitely incorporated and expressed in them—the ideals of the state, of the church, of the university. In all these there were voluntary organizations which grew up and came to play a part in the actual control of the community, of the church, of the school or university. One finds this in the Western community; one cannot find it in the Eastern.

The phase of this process in which we are interested at present is the economic. The guilds as such were voluntary organizations in which the artisans got together to control their markets, their prices, and then got a more or less recognized position, came into relationship with the feudal overlords or with cities, won rights and privileges. With the peasants themselves it was relatively easy for new types of organizations to arise. First of all, there were organizations of the sort of which we have been speaking, that is, of weavers, spinners, persons having a common interest in their occupation, who formed groups in order to try to get hold of certain markets, to get their goods bought for better prices, to establish certain monopolies.

But, relatively early, there arose within these organizations the capitalist, who brought in a different type of economic structure. The form which appeared in the guild was a social structure in which men got together with common interests, protecting each other, trying to get the best prices they could, trying to control their markets, get better distribution for their goods. But with the capitalist another situation arises, namely, that of a person who has some accumulated wealth and who can use it for purposes of increased production and distribution. With the increase in the amount and the expense of apparatus, with the advantage which could be obtained by holding the product so that it could be sold at a profitable time, ready capital was found to be of great value. And with this accumulation of wealth there arose the capitalist, who brought about the new structure.

Now, this is the process which we think of as having developed late in the eighteenth and early in the nineteenth centuries. We can, however, trace it out very much earlier. There was a gradual development of the capitalistic type of industry, owing to changes in the social situation, owing to advantages that would come to those who could gain control over wealth for the production of apparatus and for the holding of goods that were to be put on the market in order to get better prices and in order to be able to get the goods to larger markets and to markets at more distant points. For capitalistic enterprises we need only to go back to the commercial voyages of Drake, during the reign of Queen Elizabeth. Queen Elizabeth had a large proportion of the stock in the undertaking. Capitalistic undertakings were going on, then, as early as this; the method of operation was developing, waiting simply for the situation that would further its increase.

That situation was, as I have said, the development of larger markets, especially for such goods as textiles, which could be created in much greater quantities as the demand increased. The sort of market that one gets in a closed community is fixed.

Only a certain number of shoes can be worn, only a certain amount of clothing is needed. The guild represented a group that could answer to that particular demand. Standards could be fixed. But there was no opportunity in such a situation for the development of industry on any large scale. But when it became possible to ship English cloth to Europe, to send it off into Russia, down into Portugal, the markets naturally became larger. When the market in England and Europe itself increased, there was a tendency to develop this on a still larger scale. The market was continually growing. There was also the opening-up of the New World, with its treasure brought in in the form of precious metal, and the beginning of a community that demanded things also. This constant expansion of the market and the increased number of things that could be purchased on a large scale was dependent on apparatus for their production. But the apparatus which was there was largely that utilized for the markets belonging to these closed communities, so that we have just the situation in which there would be a growing stimulus to the inventor for the production of apparatus that should lead to the production of goods on a large scale.

There was also growing up the capitalistic organization, banking institutions that appeared largely in response to a demand for national dynastic loans which monarchs had to put through to carry on wars, which the church put through to support its manifold activities. Banking came to be regarded as a legitimate form of usury. This contrasted with the previous attitude. In general, the whole of the medieval world was under the influence of the doctrine of the church that usury was not legitimate, that interest was illegitimate. If you borrowed something, it was your duty to return it in as good condition as received; but beyond that no claim could be made. Charging interest was an outlawed practice. It was a curious thing, though, that just at this time church officials themselves, as well as monarchs, were borrowing on a large scale. That was recognized as fairly necessary. But it was still not considered legitimate for ordinary business. Here, again, you come back to the idea of a closed market, a situation in which there was no call for capitalistic industry. The growth of this capitalistic industry was one which corresponds to the process to which I have been referring, one which had been taking place gradually from the time of the Renaissance.

It is rather interesting to see that the Protestants, especially the Calvinistic Protestants, were those who adjusted themselves most rapidly to this economic change. Luther's doctrine was one that spread among the peasants. It was one which he carried into the moral atmosphere which belonged to that phase of the Reformation. It had been an attitude of the church; but it was also retained as an attitude of the reformed dogma, which came back, of course, to faith as over against works, to the soul's immediate approach to God. But Lutheranism was largely a peasant movement. It was not one that had any particular sympathy with the making-up of the modern city. On the other hand, the Calvinistic movement is a city movement. Of course, Calvin belongs to Geneva. What the Calvinists recognized was that men were put on earth, as we have seen, to carry out their problem under the conditions that God set for them. And Calvinists recognized business as part of these conditions. Being strenuous in business meant serving the Lord. As part of the dictum taken over by Calvin, it was recognized that one could not carry on business, especially in the city, without capital. As a result, Calvin was led to recognize the legitimacy of interest. And, interestingly, he took over something of the discipline of the church itself into business. There was no difference between it in the two cases. The discipline that belonged to the artisan was the determination of standards of goods and produce. But there had not been any discipline in the business which centered about money as such. This was introduced into the picture by capitalism. The form of business which we speak of as capitalistic grew up, in its earliest form, in close connection with the doctrine of the Calvinists. It belongs to the Protestant groups, especially to the Calvinists, and in the various new sects, as in England, which opposed themselves to the established church.

In order that the various processes of the new capitalistic setup might be carried out, capital had to be provided. That is, men had to find the means of production, and wealth had to be paid into the hands of the producer in advance of the actual returns. The credit system had to be worked out. The whole banking process was carried over into industry, and it came to be recognized as necessary that money which had been held in the form of wealth should be utilized for production and that such a mechanism as this had to be paid for just as much as the machine had to be paid for. The result was that capital was accumulated and put into the hands of the producer so as to enable him to produce on a larger scale. The capitalist must pay for the money that is put at his disposal. Calvinism, which was the city form of the Reformation, recognized these needs of business, and thus recognized the legitimacy of interest as against usury. It is important to note that change, for it represents our economic development from the medieval situation over into the modern situation.

One of the striking illustrations which we have of this is in Shakespeare's play, *The Merchant of Venice*, a picture of the old order against the new, Shylock representing a figure who was objected to and yet recognized, in some sense, as a person fitting into the needs of the community, but also as one in a position to take advantage of his opportunity. There was a struggle going on between the old order and the new. And it was the Calvinistic group which recognized the change as it was taking place and who came to regard the business process as one which was instituted by God, one in which man was called upon to carry out with vigor—it was his duty, laid upon him by God. Man was to be strenuous in business, serving the Lord. This was the motto of the Calvinist, and with it was carried over into business the discipline of the religious life. Men were to put into the former the same determination, the same conscientiousness, as had marked their attitude toward the latter. To a very considerable extent this discipline of the modern economic type, that which pursues the success of business and which pursues it with determination and intelligence, was carried over by the Calvinistic régime from its religious side into the economic process. It is of very great interest to recognize this passage. We do not find it in the Lutheran community, in the older Catholic, ecclesiastical, Church of England group. At first it was limited to the Calvinistic group, where the application of their religious discipline taught that the individual in all his tasks, even the most minute and the most materialistic, could still be serving God if he carried out his duty conscientiously. It was a combination that played its part, not only in England, but in American life in Puritanism, a combination of conscientiousness and economic thrift, with the assumption that the two go together, that man is put here to be economically successful. The Puritans turned back to the Old Testament and profited greatly by the Proverbs, under this new interpretation.

So we see clearly that the great changes taking place were not those that appeared upon the surface. They pass in history under the term of the Industrial Revolution, which is supposed to have taken place during the end of the eighteenth century and the beginning of the nineteenth. The study of economic history has made it evident that this process had already started both on the Continent and in England much earlier. It goes back to that period in which the agricultural industry of England changed from the raising of grain to the raising of sheep and the weaving of cloth. The development of the population there turned its attention to the development of wool and of the woolen industry. This naturally gave rise to the cloth industry, to the spinning and the weaving of the wool, which were processes that could be carried on in those days in the houses of tenants on the land. The wholesale industry was one of men who provided the wool, took it about to these different houses, and then gathered it up afterward. There was considerable capital involved in this; and out of this combination we have the development of capitalism, as we use the term, together with the shift in industry itself from that of the soil to that of the spinning and weaving of textiles. Of course, the development of other industries came along at the same time. The mining industries were quickened; the beginning of the use of coal was appearing; and with the development of new machines at both ends of the process came the stimulus to invention. Invention is dependent, of course, in one sense on the endowment of the inventor; but that sort of endowment is, presumably, always present in approximately the same degree in different periods. The question whether it gets expression or not depends upon the demand for differences in apparatus.

If you look back over the ancient world, you see a society which for a thousand years or more had used practically the same sort of tools, had used the same mechanisms of warfare, of farming, of producing practical needs. Of course, we find a gradual perfection in these. They vary all the way from the crudities of a semi-barbarous period up to the highly organized mechanisms of the factories of the period of Roman civilization. And yet, actually, the tools used were essentially of the same sort. We cannot find through the whole period of the ancient world—we will say stretching through the whole Graeco-Roman period—an invention which changed the process of life, not even in the field of warfare. There, of course, stimulus was the greatest. They had found out different modes of warfare. But these different methods belonged to different nations. The Persians, for example, used vast armies with chariots in front and with more mobile forces in the wings. The power of the army was in its mass; it simply rolled over its opponents, crushing them out. The strength of the Greek army, on the other hand, lay in the phalanx, in the close organization of the men. It was smaller, could drive with lances right through the clumsy Persian army, and then come back at it from the rear. The Roman legion was a still more mobile organization. It was organized in small units called "maniples." Men were armed with javelins as missiles, and with short swords. They could penetrate into the Greek phalanx and break it up. The Roman legion, when broken, could come together again, because it was made up of separate units. And the Roman legion was triumphant. It was the most flexible, the most effective, structure among the armies of the ancient world. We find the same formation used throughout the period of the Persian Empire, among the Greeks, among the Romans. We find it perfected as we read the history of it, but this is simply the perfection of an accepted order. Of course, all the armies used some missile; but the missile was not the important weapon. And there was no invention of new types of missiles. It is a curious thing to pick up a book which presents the antiquities of the medieval world and compare it with the history of the armed forces of Europe from the beginning of the world up to the later periods. We think of the medieval world as rather static in character; and yet the armed forces of Europe were changing radically throughout the whole period in their methods of fighting, in the laying out of their campaigns. In a comparatively short time they advanced from the soldier who was lightly armed to the heavily armed knight, who, when he fell from his horse, had to be helped on again. Then we have the archer coming in and unhorsing the knight.

In such a book of antiquities we find very rapid changes not only in the fashion of fighting but also in the fashion of dress. And we find not only changes in fighting and dress but also in arrangements for housing people. The ancient house was most perfectly presented in the house of the god, the temple, which reached perfection in the Greek architecture; but it was not a different sort of house from that used for other purposes, for living. The house of the feudal lord was the castle; it represents changes from a mere hovel to a structure forty feet thick which dominated the whole area. The change in the fashion of housing is shown not only in these but also in the churches. The Greek temple was the home of the god, a perfected house. The home of the god of the medieval religion was a house into which the god entered because it shut out the rest of the world. It was built to shut the world out. The light of the world without was brought in through many-colored windows. The whole movement within was a movement upward. The effect on the worshiping people was to exclude the outside world. The Greek god was simply the first citizen in the community; he invited others to come into his house. Medieval Gothic architecture shut the rest of the world out and tried to invite the population within; the church was the house of a god against whom they had sinned and from whom they must get mercy. In the expression of these ideas we have a structure which is changing from generation to generation.

If we turn back to the feudal world, to the castle, we find it expressing an idea. The feudal lord was not simply a man who was in immediate political and military control over a certain district, including the peasants or serfs, the tenants who belonged to the soil. He was also the representative of the Holy Roman Empire. And it is interesting to see what hold this ideal of the Holy Roman Empire had upon the whole population of Europe. It was true then, as always, that it was "neither Holy, nor Roman, nor an Empire"; and yet it had a romantic hold upon the imagination of the people of Europe. They believed they belonged to it. They recognized it as a political order that had to exist just as the community pictured in the gospels of Jesus was a community that had to exist. It existed in man's mind, even though unconsciously; and the feudal overlords were the representatives of this empire. They were housed as they were and defended as they were because they represented it. That is the point I want to bring out—the structure of the medieval world expressed ideas. Of course, any house can express an idea, that of living in it, of protection from the climate, of providing means of getting food, of bringing about social life; but we do not think of a house as an idea, but simply as a house within which these activities of various sorts have to go on. And the same thing could be said of the religious life as it took place in the Greek temple. One did not think of the temple as expressing the ideas behind Greek religion. It was a place where men met the gods, so to speak. A man merely met the god in his temple. The power of the god was manifested there. But the church, as such, expressed an idea, an idea which was not religion. It ought to have found expression in religion, but it did not; so it was expressed in stone and mortar, through the architecture. Just as did the castle, so the church expressed the idea of the Holy Roman Empire.

As an illustration of this take Goethe's *Götz von Berlichingen*, and you will see the hold which these ideas had on medieval Europe. The dominance of ideas which have to be expressed and the expression of the ideas varies from generation to generation, from artisan and artist of one period to another. Where the idea is actually embodied in the apparatus itself, we do not think about the idea as distinct from the structure; but in the medieval world the idea was expressed as an idea.

All this is a part of the whole series of very interesting conditions leading up to the appearance of the Industrial Revolution. What I want to warn you against is the assumption that it suddenly appeared at the end of the eighteenth and the beginning of the nineteenth century. You can trace it all way back to the period of the Reformation and beyond. It grew out of the gradual change in situation which led, first of all, to a larger market that could utilize the voluntary organization of which I spoke earlier, which could make use of the apparatus already present—such as the growing presence of capital in connection with the obligations of the church and state.

What is of particular interest in connection with this is the assumption of a sort of economic community that lies behind that whole economic process. Europe, of course, recognized itself as belonging to a single spiritual community, Christendom; but that was largely broken up under feudal conditions, and then there appeared national states, particularly those of Spain, France, and England. Germany lagged behind. The larger community was broken up, and warfare was a very large part of the interrelation of these communities with each other. The economic community, on the other hand, was a community that looked for peaceful conditions. The individual might profit by war, but economic procedure looked for peaceful conditions. Also, it brought together people who were separated nationally, in language, in customs. The economic community brought them together on a common basis. It was more universal in one respect than the church. One could carry on economic processes with the infidel, with the man who was an outcast from religious or political communities. One could carry on economic processes with the savages. It was the most universal aspect of the life of this period—more universal than the church itself, so far as intercourse between peoples, between communities, was concerned. It was, therefore, a process that abstracted very largely from the fixed standards of the community.

We must keep clearly in mind the point which I presented in the last chapter, because it had a very definite bearing upon the appearance of Adam Smith's *An Enquiry into the Nature and Causes of the Wealth of Nations* and the development of the economic school of which Adam Smith was the great representative. Hume belonged to the same period, and Smith carried over some of the former's thought in his own discussion of finance. A development of this point of view also took place in France in the appearance of the physiocrats as over against the mercantilists. In this doctrine we have the development of a point of view which recognizes a form of community that lies back of political and ecclesiastical organization. The very title which Adam Smith gave to his work is illustrative of this point of view—the wealth of nations, a wealth that belonged to nations, as if they constituted one community. It is a reaction against what is called the "old mercantilist political economy." This economy was directed toward getting just as much of the precious metals as possible. It was a political economy of the man who was the direct servant of a dynast, of a monarch who had to finance a court and an army. Such a minister looked toward the gathering of precious metals into the realm. And any form of industry was fostered which would bring precious metals in and hold them in the country where tax-gatherers could get hold of them, the latter being presumably, a desirable phase of the situation. The mercantilist looked upon wealth in terms of precious metals and undertook to control industry and commerce so as to bring them into the realm. Mercantilism did not go very deeply into conditions of production and wealth themselves. What it was interested in was a by-product of wealth. Under such conditions the monarch might set up all sorts of monopolies and charge for them exorbitantly. But in the end, this would only decrease the wealth of the community. We have the political power endeavoring to extract, as far as it could, what money could be got from the economic processes of the community, endeavoring to control production and commerce to bring in wealth. The physiocrat, on the other hand, was one who at least carried his analysis further. He went so far as to ask what the source of the wealth was. And, as far as he could see, it came out of the ground. It came out in the form of agriculture or in the form of the results of mining. In one way or another the soil, or what lay under it, was the source of all wealth. And it was of importance, if one wished to gather the coin itself as a symbol of wealth, that one should control the source from which that wealth came. That, at least, was an advance upon this superficial character of the mercantilist doctrine which dealt with wealth simply in terms of money and which tried to control industry and commerce so as to produce the greatest amount of money. At least the physiocrats recognized that governmental procedure which increased the produce of the community was of more importance than that which simply brought in gold and silver.

The conception which lies behind Adam Smith's *An Enquiry into the Nature and Causes of the Wealth of Nations* is not that of immediate sources of production of articles which become wealth, but rather the process of exchange. It is the market that lies behind the political economy of Adam Smith. And not only the market in the particular community but the world-market. The mercantilist thought of the money that could be extracted by tax-gatherers. The physiocrats thought of the soil as that out of which valuable articles which could be bought and sold arose. Adam Smith thought of wealth in connection with a market within which exchange takes place. Of course, there must be something to exchange. And this exchange must be profitable. The assumption of the mercantilists, and the physiocrats, too, for that matter, had been that every bargain was a battle of wits, that somebody was victorious and someone else was defeated; that the nature of a bargain was that between horse-traders. Someone got the best of the bargain and got the better of his opponent. Adam Smith looked further than that. He said a bargain, to be worth while, ought to be good for both parties. He presented a picture of communities that produced more than they could use, and, in so far as they did produce more, they took the surplus into the world and traded it for the surpluses of other nations. They took their own surpluses, articles not valuable at home, into the world-market where persons wanted them and where they bought up this surplus, the articles over and above those which were wanted in their own homes. Persons came together under those conditions who could both profitably carry out a bargain. One has something that he has produced beyond his own demand; another has something which he has produced beyond his demand. They want to make an exchange. After this is accomplished, both are better off. That conception is what lay at the bottom of the political economy of Adam Smith. It makes all sorts of assumptions, of course, but it is a step beyond mere production with reference to a fixed community such as the guild. It is a step beyond the political economy that simply looks to returns in the form of dollars and cents. It is also a step beyond the doctrine of the physiocrats that simply looked to the general source of wealth in a community. It came back to the actual demand as it appears in the market—a demand which implies production beyond the demand of the community that produces, and a production that is brought to the central market directly or indirectly, to be exchanged with the surplus of another community. Adam Smith brought out this conception with its various implications in *An Enquiry into the Nature and Causes of the Wealth of Nations.*

What was back of this conception was the possibility of production on a large scale. In order to make profitable the sort of bargaining that Smith presented, one must produce something which one does not want in order that it may be exchanged for something that someone else produces that one does want; and one must produce in wholesale fashion, beyond one's own demand. This led to the establishment of the factory. And when you have the factory, when persons can begin producing for a market which goes beyond the needs of a single community, the demand then comes for a division of labor. One man can do one thing more rapidly than he can do several things. An artisan carries his article through from the raw material to the finished product. He cannot do all the necessary things as rapidly as a man could carry out a single process. Divide a process up into its various steps and then you get production at a greater rate. Of course, as you subdivide the process, you invite the machine. And, with the coming of the demand for the machine, there comes the stimulus to the inventor. You may have a complicated process, such as that of making an entire shoe, which, of course, it is not possible to do with the machine, at least not at first; but if you can make the process simple, the sewing of simple seams and so on, the machine can perhaps do it better than man and does not tire as easily. The stimulus to the production of machinery, then, comes with the demand for production on a large scale, from the breaking-up of the process into simple parts\which a machine can do rapidly and better than a man. First of all, one must have the means and such a market as that which Adam Smith contemplated, where the surplus of one community could be brought into exchange against the surpluses of other communities; one must have the factory in which production can take place on a large scale. When you have these, there is a constant demand for apparatus which will accomplish what man cannot accomplish. One must have division of labor. One must divide a single process up into a set of processes which can be brought within the range of the machine process. That is what lies back of the problem of production.

Back of the whole thing lies the market, the economic situation with the gradual building-up of a mechanism for it, with the possible developments of the independent organizations such as lie in the very genius of our Western institutions, and with the building-up of all the financial apparatus lying behind the freeing of capital. That process which is traced back to, which is summed up in, what we call the Industrial Revolution, is of interest. But the final conception—perhaps not final, but that which has been of dominant interest until recent days—is that of the market which makes possible the exchange of surpluses.

Thus we get a conception of wealth which makes possible a world-economy process. We can see how the devout economist of this period, such as John Bright, could be a pacifist who could look toward the development of free trade and to the elimination of warfare because he had behind him a community which took in all warring nations and whose activity was one which meant production and not destruction. It is possible, of course, to turn even such political economy over to hostile purposes, but the first conception of it was of the development of a peaceful economic process in which there would be a continued development of wealth throughout the whole, that is, the international economic community. As I have said, in this conception of the market in which one trades what one does not want with someone else who brings in what he does not want, each wants what the other does not want, and ideally each party profits in the exchange.

That conception of the bargain and that stimulus to production were on a large scale; and out of that the factory, the division of labor, the demand for apparatus, machinery, to produce on a large scale, all arose. And back of that lies the demand for power. You cannot drive machinery with hand power, and so we find a growing demand for steam. That is the way in which the matter ought to lie in our minds. You cannot think of the economic revolution as having arisen out of the production of steam. If you do that, you take the very last element of the process and set it up as the first. To deal with this process, you have to go back to the type of community, to the development of the market, and then to the development of apparatus.

In our discussion of the Industrial Revolution we have treated the two theories which were used in the interpretation of it. That of the orthodox Manchester school, whose three important figures were Adam Smith, Ricardo, and Malthus, was a social philosophy, especially as developed by the Mills, who interpreted the economic doctrine of these men and undertook to make a social philosophy, a utilitarian philosophy, of it. The doctrine was one which undertook to deal with the economic processes from the point of view of the market, the determination of prices by the market in which the producers exchanged their surpluses with each other and thus established the prices of goods in more or less universal world markets, and found in these prices the stimulus for production. The process was one which led to the factory system, the intensive production of those goods whose prices stimulated this production. Thus we have a situation of supply and demand; and perhaps in the end the demand is more important than the supply, because the supply springs up in response to the demand. As there is a demand, the different means of production arise. Especially in the invention of machinery this demand brings the production of machines by means of which to answer this demand. This implies a social process going on in a community in which the need of the community stimulates production, and the determination of the prices is a way of registering this need.

The process of production is one that calls for a reduction in expense, because what one is seeking, of course, is profit over and above the cost of production, and the prices you can get in the market determine this profit. Successful production is that which leaves a margin, which will permit the accumulation of wealth. The two phases of the process are the cost of production, on the one side, and the price which can be obtained for the article, on the other. The economic process is one determined by the relation of supply and demand in the market so adjusted that profit results to the producer. Well now, if any producer can bring down the cost of production, his profit will be greater and the accumulation of wealth greater; and then he can produce on a larger scale. So he tries to get down the cost of production in all sorts of ways. If there is a surplus of the means of production, of course, the price of these means will go down. If there is plenty of ore, of coal, of raw material, the price of the metal, of the coal, of the material, will go down. One of the very large elements in the cost of production is labor; and, of course, if there is a surplus of labor, the price of labor will go down. What the producer seeks as far as he can is a surplus of those articles which he is to use in his production, for there lies the possibility of getting a lower cost and hence a larger profit. Inevitably, the producer must seek to reduce his cost of production. The cost of production will depend, of course, on the surplus of the article. If there is a surplus over and above the demand, then the price of that commodity will drop. All this applies just as logically to labor as to anything else.

It is here that the Malthusian doctrine comes in. What Malthus thought he had discovered was that population always increased at a greater rate than the means of sustenance. In any community the increase in population will be greater than the increase in food supply. I noted the fact that sometime about the middle of the eighteenth century there was a notable increase in population in England and Europe, presumably because of a decrease in the death-rate. Malthus did not take into account the relationship of the death-rate to the birth-rate. However, he gathered figures which, as far as they went, seemed to support his contention that the population, itself, by and large, would always be greater than the supply of food and that there must be a continual holding-down of the population by the process of starvation. More children are born into the world and more survive than can continue to survive with the food supply available. Taken in terms of the birth-rate, the latter will always be too large in proportion to the food supply.

Well, this offers to the manufacturer, to the producer, just the situation he wants, that is, a surplus of labor, one of the main items in the cost of production. If you can get a surplus of coal, iron, anything that enters into the cost, then the price of that will sink and will reduce the price of production. Of course, in the same fashion, if there are more laborers than there are jobs, the price of the laborer will sink proportionately. What Malthus' doctrine implied was a surplus of labor which would keep the price of labor at the level of a starvation wage, for, after all, that would be the limit to which the price of labor could sink. Otherwise the laborer would starve to death. If there is a surplus of labor in the market, people would continue to work under those conditions as well as they could, getting just enough to keep alive. A starvation wage would be the limit below which the price of labor could not sink, and the limit toward which a Malthusian doctrine would inevitably carry it.

Here we have, then, the essential element of this doctrine, which, you see, is more than an economic doctrine. It is a theory of society in so far as society is bound to a method of production which is constantly stimulated by demand. The means of production, that is wealth, arise in proportion as there is a difference between the cost of production and the prices of the articles produced. If it costs you less to produce an article than the price at which you sell it, you have accumulated wealth; and then you can go on with the process of production. There will be a constant tendency, then, to bring the price and the cost of production closer and closer together. All the means by which the cost of production can be reduced will serve to bring about profit.

Freedom of exchange is that which will establish the world-market, in which the prices of things will be definitely determined. If there is freedom for exchange, we will have, presumably, the most helpful economic situation, for then those articles will be produced which are least expensive. Consequently, the price of them can be brought down until it is a price in which capital, as such, tends to pass into the hands of those who can most intelligently utilize it. The price is being continually forced down by a free market. The cost of production must be brought down if a profit is to be made possible. It is in a large concern, where manufacturing is on a wholesale basis, where the factory system can be carried through to its logical conclusion, where division of labor can take place to the limit, that you get the lowest cost of production. As I have said, one of the very large elements of the cost of production is the price of labor. And, according to the Malthusian doctrine, this will continually gravitate toward a starvation level. This is not a cheerful view for society. It leads to that capitalistic class into whose hands the capital itself will naturally gravitate, for they are the ones who can most successfully utilize it in production. The latter has to be carried on on a large scale, with expert managers and engineers; and investments have to be made in an expert fashion if capital is to be successfully utilized. The tendency will be, then, for capital to gravitate into the hands of those who can invest it most successfully, and then it remains in the hands of those who can most successfully utilize it in production by constantly keeping the cost of production down to its lowest level. The so-called "iron laws" of nature, as exhibited in economic conditions, then, seem to lead toward a picture of the community in which its capitalistic class would inevitably gain more and more of the wealth while the rest of the community would get closer and closer to a starvation wage, which is rendered inevitable by the natural law which Malthus is supposed to have discovered, namely, that reproduction in the community will always be greater than the food supply.

It is interesting that Darwin's theory of the survival of the fittest came to him from reading the brochures of Malthus. The latter's statement quite agreed with what the former had seen in nature, namely, that among both plants and animals there is always a larger number of young forms arising than can survive. Something that inevitably follows, and about which Darwin asked himself, was whether in the competition of these young forms for a living there could be found any force which would select particular forms rather than others; and the idea of the survival of the fittest occurred to him. He himself has related how this took place. It is one of the most fruitful and important ideas that has come to man, and it occurred to Darwin through his reading of Malthus' doctrine. Of course, Malthus did not present him with the idea, but with a situation out of which the idea could spring. If there is such a competition of young forms, then, presumably only those forms will survive which are particularly adapted to the environment in which they find themselves. If, as some biologists have computed, there is a death-rate of 99.9 per cent among cutworms, you can see that those that survive will be particularly adapted to the surroundings in which they live. There is an enormous overproduction, with the consequent survival of a relatively few.

That is the situation that this economic doctrine presented; and it is interesting to see how one passes from a highly optimistic view of human nature and society, as Adam Smith presented it, to a very sorry view which logically follows the working-out of his view by Ricardo and the addition of the Malthusian theory in regard to population. As we have seen, Adam Smith recognized a community in which a bargain of intellects was always a good bargain and demanded that the hands of government, in the form of restrictions on trade, should be taken off so that such good bargains might take place. It was a doctrine directed against governmental interference, against monopolies, against the international life of the time, at least as that existed in the form of actual and potential wars. Free production on every side would bring people together under conditions in which they could presumably most profitably exchange their goods, enabling those who could produce surpluses of one sort to exchange them elsewhere for surpluses of another sort. In order to reach this desirable result, all you had to do was to let trade and the economic process alone. Do not interfere with it. Do not allow monopolies to arise. Let people produce under those conditions in which they can most successfully do so, and these will be most favorable to trade and society itself.

Now, carry out the doctrine of Adam Smith with its intense production, figure in the cost of capital, and bring these two sides of the shears together—on the one hand the cost of production, on the other hand the price which will be continually going down with resultant curtailment of profit—and then add to that Malthus' doctrine which provides society with a surplus of population that has to be kept down continually by starvation, and the capitalistic picture so optimistic from Adam Smith's point of view becomes very dark.

CHAPTER X

THE SOCIAL RENAISSANCE—UTILITARIANISM

AS WE have seen, the orthodox economic doctrine was very simple—take away all restrictions, and that production will take place in any community which is most economical, which is most productive. Each community will produce that which it can produce better than others can. If it undertakes to produce that which others can produce better, it will destroy its own industries. The theory comes down to this: simply remove all restrictions, and trade will follow the most helpful channels. But in the actual processes of the various countries themselves, it was found gradually to be a more complex problem than it had been thought to be. The economic doctrine, as such, in its simplicity broke down. It could not be said that any other definite, clear-cut theory took its place. This was one of those times when people were feeling their way. The assumedly fixed situation that grew out of the Manchester doctrine was seen not to be in accord with the facts. As a result, it was practically abandoned.

It is in such a situation that opportunism arises. This is true even in the most rigid form of the socialist doctrine, which, with utilitarianism, we are about to consider. Just because people could not tell what the so-called "fixed laws" of economic and social processes were, they wanted to go ahead and bring about results which they could see were really advantageous. They wished to improve the conditions of the working man, to see that he lived under proper conditions, to get rid of the slums. They initiated movements toward minimum wages, toward dealing, through insurance systems, with those conditions with which the laborer himself could not deal. These are all movements which go with the pressure of labor itself in its organization. The result was that, if you look over the statistics of the nineteenth century, you will find a gradual increase in wage, an actually effective wage which does not answer to the economic doctrine at all. You find also in various countries a falling-off in actual increase of population, and a tendency toward a decrease in the proportionate increase in population which seemed to answer to the intelligence of the community itself.

That is the situation, then, which really led to a feeling of the way in socialistic and other economic views toward improvement at various points, with an attempt to set up a program of what the order of society ought to be. There was, in other words, a sense of progress without a definite conception of an ideal order. People felt that they did not know where they were going; but they were sure they were on their way; and that changes which were advantageous could be brought about.

An economic law was presented by the Manchester school which called for free trade as that which was most satisfactory for economic production. But England was practically the only country that adopted it. England, of course, was in a very favorable position for the operation of free trade. She had the raw materials for building factories, she had coal and iron. But she was in great need of other raw materials for the manufacture of articles that she needed. She also needed, as she found very soon, more food than could be produced in England. There had to be, then, large importations, and, of course, large exportations. But England not only exported goods. With the increase in capital, she exported capital itself as well. She needed to have the channels open so that there should be freedom of movement within and without. The other countries in Europe and America adopted tariff laws of various types, and there were very varied influences and motives behind these laws. Of course, they all had to do with industries which they were supposed to protect. They all protected the price of goods, but the reasons for this protection varied. The customs union, for example, was very important in bringing about the national organization of

Germany. It brought together the different German countries under a customs arrangement and opened the door to the political union that took place later. An organization of its industries with reference to the various policies of the government which could in a manner control the direction of production and of trade was made possible through the tariff laws. That is, the government in the manipulation of its tariff laws could open up doors in various directions and close them in others. Particularly within the country itself, it could give remissions from certain types of tariff taxation. The control which a government exercises over its railroads, for example, enables it to help the development of its industries. In Germany there gradually grew up a governmentally controlled industry which was organized with reference to its foreign trade and which became a definite part of the foreign policy of the government itself. And, for this a tariff system was necessary. In other countries there were, of course, different interests which gathered about the different trades that were affected by the tariff. In our own country there was a real tariff policy which undertook, in the mind of the greater part of the community, to protect the laborer against the starvation wages of Europe. It gave the industries that were so protected the advantage of higher prices. Under these conditions there grew up, however, in America itself a type of organization of trade not directed by government but arising simply out of the economic situation, the building-up of prices. I will not go into a discussion of this except to point out that the tariff situation proved to be far more complex than it was then presented in the orthodox economic doctrine.

Along with socialism we find the beginning of another social theory which had as its objective the control of the social situations which were arising as a result of the complex changes that followed from various economic practices, particularly as these affected the living conditions of the great mass of workers. Bentham was the originator of this latter movement. He was a man who approached the needs of English society from the standpoint of administrative reform, particularly of criminal reform.

What he wanted in a philosophy was such a statement of the motives and ends of men as could be easily used in terms of government and also in other processes with which government had to do. He found such a statement in utilitarianism, a position which was already extant in the philosophy of Hume, and which goes over, in one way or another, to Bishop Butler, at least in connection with his theory of desire. These men found the motive of all conduct in a desire for pleasure and the avoidance of pain. That was the statement that Bentham took up.

You can see how that fitted into a program for the reform of criminal law. The sanction of the law is punishment; the motive which operates is presumably the suffering which punishment brings, or the relief from the fear of punishment which comes from avoiding crime. Those motives are the sort to which this type of philosophy would naturally turn. The suffering inflicted upon the criminal was to be in proportion to the crime. The more heinous the crime, the greater the suffering. And in so far as punishment is supposed to be a preventive, the more heavy the punishment the less likely the individual is to commit crime. If you can state motives in terms of pains and penalties, you seem to have hold of the springs of human conduct. It is an overly simple, a superficial statement of human conduct; but it is one which fits in perfectly well with a program of criminal reform.

I would not imply that this is the only interest which Bentham had in his utilitarian doctrine. He regarded it as a means of presenting the whole field of human nature. In its simplest form it was a way of getting over from those interests which were the dominant characteristics in earlier societies back into what became a more democratic society. That is, what was demanded in an English society was the preservation of the old order, with the values which the old order conserved. But, however much one may recognize the importance of keeping these old values, one realizes also that they cannot all be kept and that some have to change. Then the question arises as to which of these values ought to be kept and which ones changed. How much change can one actually bring into the fixed order of society?

To illustrate this, let me mention the problem of the importance which the preservation of game took in men's minds. In itself seemingly a trivial matter, it carried with it a sense of prestige as well as of the enjoyment of sport on the part of the privileged, the landed, classes. On the other hand, along with the desire for satisfaction of a certain sort of sport, there was the desire for getting food on the part of the poacher. This does not seem to be anything that strikes very deep; and yet you find it standing as a symbol for the old order and having, therefore, a value way beyond anything that seems to be socially assessable.

In the face of such a conflict, what was the community to do? It wants to preserve what is valuable in the old social order. Here is a practice that the upper classes cling to, especially those who have rights over the preservation of game. They demand it as fiercely as anything else. Now the problem is to determine what these values are, so that it can be seen which of them are important and which are of less importance. What system of evaluation can be introduced into a community which has to change, to shift, to reform, many of its old practices, to abandon many of its old institutions? That was the need which the most intelligent in the community felt. They wanted some way of assessing these values to find out what was worth while.

The simplest statement that could well be made, however inadequate it was, was the utilitarian. When it came to such an illustration as that which I have just given of poaching, they would say that you must consider the relative values simply in terms of the pleasure that those who exercise the sport get out of it as over against the pains and penalties involved in poaching. On this basis it can be said that one has greater value than the other. Furthermore, you can go ahead on this basis and set up a system, a quantitative system, which is the easiest sort of a system to manage. When you put colors over against each other in a color scheme, you find it very difficult to assess directly. You can say that red and yellow have movement and life, while blue and violet are cold, and green is calm. But it is very difficult to arrange these qualities so that they have a different, a definite, meaning in a scale. You can get a vague scale, if you like, all the way from the vividness of red and yellow around through the calmness of green to the deadness of blue. But there is no such satisfactory basis for a schematism as can be found in a statement of colors in terms of waves. Then you find that colors are represented by waves of different lengths and that there are long waves at one end of the spectrum and short waves at the other end and that all the different colors can be arranged in terms of amplitude of waves.

Now, in the same way, when you come to a statement of certain experiences as over against each other, some seem intensely important, others trifling, and you try to arrange them with reference to each other—some fine, some vulgar. But what is the way in which these experiences should be—may be—assessed? If you take them in qualitative form, you find that it is difficult, if not impossible, to arrange them on any satisfactory scale. But, supposing you say we will consider simply the amount of pain and pleasure a person gets out of each. Then you have something that, at least on the face of it, can be quantitatively ordered. One gives a greater amount of pleasure than the other. Then you can add them up, make an algebraic sum of the pleasures and pains—the pleasure positive, the pain negative—and determine what the action ought to be. And, more important, you can go into the community at large and say: "Here is the experience of a single individual, but it is one of great importance to him. What does it mean to the community?" For that purpose the thing you want to get at is the pleasure this man gets as over against the privation of the whole community. Here is a man who holds rights for the shooting of game. It means everything to him—his prestige in the community, his connection with an old line. It is of enormous importance to him. What is that compared to need in the community, perhaps starvation? What right is there in taking the amount of pleasure of this man and saying that it is more important than the suffering of the rest of the community? If stated in terms of pleasure and pain, you have a way of assessing situations, especially of dealing with old privileges such as those which, in some sense, marked the structure of English society of that time but which needed to be reconstructed.

From that standpoint the utilitarian doctrine that stated every case in terms of pleasure and pain was a very valuable doctrine. The greatest good of the greatest number could be set up over and against the good of the individual, and the greatest good could be stated in terms of satisfactions and of discomforts and pains. You see that, from that standpoint, we also have a leveling doctrine. The advantage that the landlord gets out of his position is something that belongs to him as a privilege from the community. Is his enjoyment of more value than that of others? How can we find this out? He is a privileged person and should have certain satisfactions. Well, why should he have them rather than somebody else, no matter how low on the social scale the other may be? The hedonistic statement is a leveling statement. Each man counts for one and only one. One man enjoys a picture; another, a game of football. How determine which is more valuable? It is the pleasure that the person gets out of it that counts. The only thing to consider is the pleasure of the one and the pleasure of the other. As Bentham stated it, the pleasures of poetry and of pushpin, as pleasures, are on the same level, even though pushpin is on the same level as tiddlywinks. It is pleasure that is of importance.

Such a doctrine was a theory of great value in enabling people to approach a situation which called for the reconstruction of an old order. In this you can put Bentham and his followers over against Carlyle. Carlyle wanted to keep the privileges of the old order; he wanted to keep the values that attached to the old order, to keep the old interests. But he recognized that in order to do this he must substitute, for the old feudal captain, the new captain of industry. He tried to deal with the situation as though it were a new feudalism, and he failed in this attempt. He felt the same problem as the utilitarians, that of the necessity of reconstructing society. What both of them needed was some sort of theory on the basis of which such reconstructing could take place. But the utilitarians certainly offered the more workable theory. They set up a way of assessing the ends, the values of life which could be satisfactorily used in a program of reform.

I have already referred to Carlyle as giving in England a reflection of the German Romantic movement, the philosophical movement which we have already discussed. Carlyle's own attitude was a feudal attitude. The value of that order was staring him in the face. What he tried to bring to the attention of England was that conditions had so changed that, if the older order were to be preserved, it had to be in the form of a new type of feudalism. A phrase was introduced that Carlyle made current, a phrase which has a very different significance now—the "captain of industry." He was a leader; one who led his laborers; one who was the head of the new economic community as the squire was the head of the feudal community. Carlyle looked for such a change to take place, for such leadership to be set up. What he did not realize was that the economic situation was one which had shaken loose the feudal figure, for the individual laborer, no longer connected with the soil, could not be made to have the same dependence upon an economic overlord that the peasant had felt under his feudal overlord on the soil. The same sort of personal relationship between the so-called "captain of industry" and the laborer as had existed in the earlier order could not be set up in the new situation.

While Carlyle was reactionary in the sense of wanting a new feudal order, he was responsive and sympathetic to the condition of the laborer. When labor was brought into the factory centers, there sprang up great cities in which men and women lived in almost impossible conditions. And there sprang up factories built around the machine in which men, women, and children worked under ever so hideous conditions. This was not because people were heartless. It was due to the fact that conditions changed so rapidly, because the factories had come into

existence so quickly, because the machine brought its own social conditions with it; and men did not anticipate all this. They
could not foresee its meaning. The community regarded industry as that which provided the morale of a laborer community.
It was assumed that no greater blessing could be given to the
child than to have this work. The important thing was to get
the child started in the right habits and to maintain him in
them. To give the child a job as early as possible and to keep
him at it as long as possible was an act of kindness to the child.
He was getting habits of industry which would make him a successful laborer. So the captain of industry would go into an or-
phan asylum and place children from there in slavery in the
factory, drive them to work with whips, keep them at it until
the children could not keep their eyes open. Women and children were taken into industry under abominable conditions,
dragging as beasts of burden, the cars that carried the ore and
coal. The machine itself was allowed to determine the human
conditions of labor. I said this was done not because men were
heartless but because they had no idea of what this situation,
this industrial development, would mean—because they carried over the standards of an entirely different economic situation into the new one.

Well, these conditions of an inadequate wage and wretched
living conditions were reflected in Carlyle's writings. He responded to them; he saw something of what they meant. He
recognized that there was springing up an organization among
the laborers themselves. He wanted that organization headed
by the new feudal economic lord who took the place of the
feudal lord of the past. I have already referred to the characteristic in our Western society of voluntary organization which
played so large a rôle in the development of the Western community. We meet it again in this industrial situation. The labor
union was organized and composed of laborers themselves in
their effort to protect themselves economically in any way they
could under these new conditions. Help did not come to them
from the more enlightened part of the community, the com-

munity that could be so sympathetic toward the tenant. The great people, those that gathered about the manor and about the curate's house, and about the vicar, could care for the sick among those on the land, and those in distressed condition; they felt the responsibility for the tenantry. But in the city there were no persons to take their place, and the community itself did not respond to the conditions. It was left to the laborer to assert himself, and he did so through voluntary organization as in the past. The labor union sprang up. It expressed itself as an organization of that type which appears when it is more or less necessary to fight with violence. And it called forth the most rigorous legislation which tried to crush it out. But the Western world never succeeded in crushing it out. It grew in strength; and finally England, through its Parliament, consented to consider what these conditions were which sprang up about the factory town. Then came that group of highly intelligent men who gathered about Jeremy Bentham. The two most forceful figures of this group were James Mill and John Stuart Mill, father and son.

To see what these men were working against, it is necessary to go back to conditions such as those indicated by the so-called Industrial Revolution, in which children were taken into factories, driven to work, forced to remain at work twelve and fourteen hours a day, under most unhealthful conditions and with low wages. You have to go back to such conditions and to the utter ignorance of the masses, and even beyond that to conditions that existed in these great industrial centers. If you want a vivid picture of the life in these centers, take the group of books by Arnold Bennett, in which he tells the tales of *The Five Towns*, in which he gives an account of his grandfather's life as a child, the way in which he had worked. There is the most vivid statement I know of in literature of the suffering of a child in industry in such a period, and you can multiply that many thousand times and get a realization of the amount of misery there was.

The champion of feudalism, Carlyle, could do nothing but attack utilitarianism, terming it a scheme to take a world of knaves and make a world of men out of them by an appeal to their worst motives. But he himself realized the conditions in industry and assessed past and present and presented a picture of conditions which must be changed. It is that sort of a picture that we must get in our minds—a need for reconstruction on the political side. We know all about the rotten boroughs, the system of parliamentary representation that could not be considered representative by any stretch of the imagination, in which the monarch and the ministers bid for the vote of each member of Parliament by emoluments they had to offer. You have a seemingly utterly rotten system which had been held too long in its place by the fears of the French Revolution, sanctified by the rhetoric of Burke. The reformation was long overdue in this situation.

But how was this needed reform to be carried out? How could people determine what was to be kept and what scrapped? These are problems to which utilitarianism certainly offered the best answer at the time. As I said, it set up the individual as its final element. It was, in that sense, democratic in character. And it found a statement, "the greatest number," which was very satisfactory for dealing with the evils and misery of society. On the other hand, when it tried to state the great experiences of life in terms of pleasure, it failed. The ends which we pursue are not subjective ends. The great things of life are objective. We may have a most vivid, most private inner experience; but the things that are worth while are not pleasures and pains that we have suffered. The greatest things are those for which we sacrifice ourselves and thus realize ourselves. That phase of human endeavor the utilitarians could not present. For them the end was always the pleasure that one got out of what he did. It was not food one wanted, it was the pleasure one got from eating it; it was not music from great artists one enjoys, but the pleasure that one got out of music; it was not friends, not children, not the person to whom one surrendered one's self, not the issue to which one gave himself, that was the end of effort, but the satisfaction that one got out of working for others, out of giving himself to a cause, out of devoting one's self to one's home and children. It was the pleasure they got out of these things which was the end for the utilitarians. This is a poor picture of human nature; it is an unjust one. On the credit side of the balance the utilitarian presents an utterly inadequate statement of the ends of human endeavor. But if you turn to the debit side, and see the miseries there, you realize that to appreciate them you have to add them up. One must put himself into an actual sympathetic suffering of the pains of others. It is pain itself that we must get rid of. After all, all great religions gather about the mitigation of suffering, and what the utilitarian doctrine gave was a vivid statement of the amount of suffering going on that ought to be got rid of. Over against that it presented the peaceful sum of pleasure of the few privileged individuals. The doctrine was, however, individualistic in England. It came back to the pleasure and pain of the individual.

James Mill, Bentham's immediate successor, was a Scotchman with great force of character and an enormous capacity for work. He came to England as many Scotchmen did at the end of the eighteenth and beginning of the nineteenth centuries to make his way. He had had training in Scottish religion, and he became attached to Jeremy Bentham. Bentham was a peculiar character; himself a squire, an owner of considerable property, he was, nonetheless, a person who had a very vivid interest in the change which was taking place in England, the change from the feudal order over to the new order which we have been discussing. His immediate interest gathered about the administrative changes, especially those taking place in criminal law. Criminal law, of course, had been administered first of all by the feudal lord, and in feudal fashion. It had been inadequately generalized for each community from the Renaissance on. What Bentham saw was that it did not meet its own purpose. He saw the repression that went with its application, and that this repression did not succeed in keeping down crime, that the penalty was out of proportion to the crime. It was assumed that a heavy penalty stopped crime. Bentham saw rather that this frequently increased crime. The whole situation called loudly for some intelligent study, and Jeremy Bentham turned his attention to these old feudal conditions. If you want a picture of the criminal conditions of England at that time, take Meredith's *Egoist*, which was written at the peak of his career. Here is a picture of the squire in his autocratic situation, and of the radical under these new economic situations. What you realize is that the whole governmental control in any district was lodged in the squire. He was the one who exercised all police power, who in a certain sense represented national government at that point; and, not only that, but he was father of his people about him. He had both positions. For him, at that time, game laws seemed more important than any others. They were important not at all because he was interested in his hunting and fishing but because they represented his position from the time of the beginnings of the feudal order. The right to hunt, to preserve game, was the sign of the man who was in power, and so it remained, so that the poacher was a person who was undermining the order of society. It seems to be a very trifling affair, but it was magnified because it represented an attack on the center, on the power of the administrator, upon the police power in the community. The part which fox-hunting played in that period is brought out here, and in Trollope's novels, as well as in Bentham's career. What we find difficult to realize is the symbolism of this simple sport. It represented a right, a sort of social right around which the meaning of the order of society gathered.

The political and social revolution was in a certain sense directed against the feudal lord, most of whose rights and powers gathered about the social situation. It is for this reason that Carlyle became so interesting as an interpreter of the situation. He wanted to preserve this feudal order. As I have already said, in that sense he was a conservative. He wanted the social arrangement adjusted so that the old order could pass over into the economic situation. His book *Heroes and Hero Worship* gives a picture of his social philosophy. The mass of the community were to follow their leader, and there must be leaders there. And the fierce gospel that Carlyle preached to England was a gospel that was to call out these leaders who were to realize their responsibility, who were to carry over into industry that sense of responsibility for laborers that the feudal lords had felt for their tenantry. But the laborer himself was still to be in the hands of this economic overlord. He must be recognized, his rights recognized, his hates and fears listened to; but he himself was to continue to be in the feudal situation of the older world. For this, of course, it was necessary that strong and sympathetic men should be brought up to undertake this sort of work in the community. And Carlyle, in true romantic fashion, went to history to find his appeal. His *Heroes and Hero Worship* was followed by *The Life and Letters of Cromwell*, by his *History of Frederick the Great* and other studies, in which he was looking for strong men who should be leaders in the community and who should carry over the order of things from the earlier situation into this later situation.

In this hurried fashion I have again gone over the different features of the Industrial Revolution. I have done this in order to show how the utilitarian doctrine—and particularly that of Jeremy Bentham—played such a large part in it. The interest in this philosophy was part of the shift from the feudal to the industrial order. We have seen how this same interest is found in Carlyle, who was also an important factor in England at this time. Carlyle and John Stuart Mill, the third significant member of the Utilitarian school, may be set over against each other as two characteristic figures of this period, at least up to the middle of the nineteenth century.

The best, rather the simplest, statement of the utilitarian doctrine is one many of you are familiar with—Mill's *Utilitarianism*. It is a short statement but very desirable in its way. What it does not reveal is the enthusiasm this doctrine aroused. As Mill states it, it is more or less convincing. But you cannot really think of the youth of the community being inspired by it. In order to realize the inspiration that it gathered about it, we have to realize that it did present a workable doctrine in social reform, that it was democratic in its implications, that it allowed one man to count for one and only one, and, particularly, that it set up a very simple statement of what the end of all social institutions should be—the good of the community. And when one asked what the good of the community is, it could be said that it is an algebraic sum of pleasures and pains of the community which should show how much pleasure there is, and particularly how much misery there is. When you come to set this doctrine over in terms of pleasures, it loses its effectiveness. As someone said, it seemed to express the idea of the Englishman waking up in the morning and smacking his lips over a breakfast of ham and eggs. That seems to present a pretty ignoble end for society to seek. But on the other side—that of the getting rid of misery—it becomes a doctrine which can have behind it all the enthusiasm of social reform. The starving of children, the suffering of men and women in factories under trying conditions, could be brought out and simply stated by it. They were sufferings which were not to be glossed over because they belonged to lower orders, because the world was such that there had to be suffering in it, because all would be right in the world to come. You could not push things aside for such reasons when distress could be stated in terms of the actual summing-up of the amount of suffering that people endured in the midst of long periods of strikes, of penury, of business depressions. If this is brought out and added to all the suffering together, you have something which would appeal to what was finest in human nature at that time. So, while utilitarianism put its stress on getting rid of pain, it could be an idealistic doctrine, if it tried to.

What John Stuart Mill does is to present as highest those pleasures which we commonly regard as most admirable, especially those connected with social ways of life—friendship, organization of family life, and particularly the pleasures that come from the enjoyment of literature, of science, of satisfaction of all our multiform curiosities. Mill assumed that we have an indefinite appetite for these. He was, of course, of a highly intellectual nature himself. And he recognized in the beginning of popular education in England the possibility of changing the attitude and interests of men. He had been, one might say, a victim of a theory of education on the part of his father. He was taught Greek almost before he was taught English. He studied ancient languages as a very little child. He was trained by his father, who was a very effective pedagogue. His father hit on the scheme, since John Stuart was the oldest in the family, of giving him lessons and then having him give the same lessons to his younger brothers and sisters. He would then examine the younger brothers and sisters to see how well Mill knew the lesson. It was a time-saving and very effective method. There was a system of education in England at that time which made use of very much this same principle. When England faced the possibility of popular education, people were frightened by the bill which would be presented. It did not seem possible to hire enough teachers and to pay for them to give a common-school education to every child, so that the first systems of education were such systems as this. A certain number of children were taught, and then they were allowed to teach so many more. It was a system which at least aroused a demand for public education, although it was thoroughly poor in its results.

CHAPTER XI

THE SOCIAL RENAISSANCE—KARL MARX
AND SOCIALISM

THERE was another reaction to the Industrial Revolution besides that of the reform measures that grew out of the group of utilitarians. They carried through a series of reform measures which made English industry very different from what it had been in the earlier period. The other important social movement is that which was represented at that time, and still is, by the name of Karl Marx, namely, socialism.

His doctrine is a fusion of the political economy of the orthodox Manchester school—the three leading exponents of which are Adam Smith, Ricardo, and Malthus—with the dialectic of the Hegelian philosophy—a strange marriage of minds. England especially, in the feverish industrialism of this period, and Germany, at least as represented by the romanticists, seemed about as far removed from each other as any two types of human experience could be. You remember that romanticism represented, in a certain sense, Europe's seeking for the recovery of an old world, a return to the past from the standpoint of a defeated self that gave itself up to subtle speculation, satisfied itself for its defeat by taking the whole universe into itself, by identifying reality with the ego, with the self. On the other hand, in the industrialism of England, in the sudden expansion, the development of wealth, with the enormous increase in numbers in the community itself, you have the introduction of entirely new interests which expressed themselves in the importance that came to England. With this came changes of a fundamental type in the whole community, that swept over the country like an external affair, like a force, a conquering movement that caught people unaware. To bring together the economic philosophy that lies behind this movement and the philosophy that lies behind the Romantic school is what did take place in the theory of Karl Marx. Of course, he was a refugee in London because its liberalism, of which he had little theoretical appreciation, gave him refuge from the government at home. He and Lassalle are the first great figures in the espousal of the socialistic doctrine in Prussia, and he was driven out.

Perhaps the first thing we ought to realize in trying to understand socialism is something that I have referred to already, and that is the larger society which this statement of political economy brings with it. Not only all those who want to trade, merely economic men, all standing for the time being upon the same level, but the industries themselves, lost that national character which belongs to them in the theory of the mercantilist and the physiocrat. The point of view of these political economists, you remember, was that the real interest in the process lies in the money, the wealth, which could be secured, largely by governments for their own purpose, and in the uses to which the governments were going to put the money. But that presumed an industry which did not have inelastic boundaries, one which had to be conducted from the point of view of world-markets. It was a theory of industry built up on the doctrine that, by the very nature of the process, every bargain had to be a good bargain. The markets were places where the surpluses of one community could be exchanged with the surpluses of other communities. Now, there is another side to this internationalism which this doctrine carried with it, but which it neither stressed nor clearly anticipated; that was the International, the internationalism of labor.

The conditions under which people worked in factories were not national conditions. The conditions under which the English tenant, the peasant, had woven cloth in the sixteenth century and in the seventeenth century were conditions that were peculiarly English. They could not be put against conditions that were found in other countries. They were determined by conditions there. But the factory is largely international in its character. We discover that, of course, in the development of America. We brought in people from everywhere, under a free immigration law, and successfully took them into the factory, and set them at work even before they could speak English. There are no national boundaries in the factory. And it was the factory that was the center of the economic doctrine of Adam Smith. Laborers everywhere had the same essential conditions. Prices might differ; but from the point of view of the price of labor, as presented in the theory of Adam Smith, those differences inevitably disappeared. The price for labor, as for anything else, is got by haggling in the market. The price of labor is determined by supply and demand, as is the price of everything else; and, if there is a greater demand elsewhere, the population flows there and the price of labor comes down. That was part of the doctrine. So you see that labor—the man, just as an economic unit—was much the same wherever you found it. The laborer was the same everywhere.

Here we have something of the situation to which I have just referred in discussing the utilitarian doctrine. If this theory is allowed to work without interference, the labor situation would very soon become a wretched one. And misery is the same the world over. If you take the privileged classes that secured the votes in England, that is, the capitalist classes which could buy their way into great landholdings and into peerages, you get a different expenditure of money in one class than in another. But if you come down to conditions under which people are working under supervision, you find in one country or another that that sort of industry levels things down tremendously. The international character of the factory is what we must have in mind to understand socialism.

We have to recognize these conditions in order to see the stimulus out of which the doctrine of Karl Marx and Lassalle arose. John Stuart Mill wrote a political thesis which brought the doctrines of the orthodox school up to date in his own time.

The text is a logical presentation of the doctrine; but it had a whole series of footnotes, and very many of these are what would be called "socialistic literature." That is, John Stuart Mill recognized the inevitable effects of this process to which I have referred, and particularly recognized that there has to be a control over distribution and wealth in some fashion if society is to be kept from the conclusion toward which it seemed to be moving, that is, a conclusion in which the price of the market of the article, and the cost of production, could be brought just as close together as possible, with the greater masses of people living at a starvation wage as laborers, while, on the other hand, all the capital would tend to drift into the hands of those who could most effectively utilize it for production. John Stuart Mill felt that there had to be some sort of control over the distribution of wealth if this result was not to be reached. It is the logical result of the theory itself.

The theory of Karl Marx was perhaps somewhat more heroic than anything suggested in the footnotes of John Stuart Mill's *Political Economy*. And it is logical. It portrays a process of production: the cost of production, on the one side, and the price, on the other, in a process in which these two sides of the shears are being brought closer and closer together. It is evident that it is in the method of production that the key to the situation is to be found. If you get this productive process into the hands of the community, so that it could be utilized in the interest of the community and not in the interests of those who are producing for the sake of profit, then you can avoid this inevitable result. That is, you can if you lay aside the Malthusian doctrine for the time being. If you could control your production, not with reference to the getting of profits simply, but from the point of view of the welfare of the community itself, that is, from the standpoint of the consumption of goods to the best advantage of the community, rather than for the production of wealth as such, then you could have a situation which would be relieved of the blackest side of the picture which the Manchester school presented.

In this connection we find two different suggestions: one with regard to the distribution of wealth in some fashion, and the other with regard to the production of wealth; one which might, for example, shut down the limit of the size of fortunes, take steps toward such a distribution as would be more even so far as wealth itself is concerned, and the other, which is more radical, which would undertake to determine in whose hands wealth itself, wealth used for production, that is, capital, is to lie. If you can put it into the hands of the government which simply represents the interests of the community and not the interests of any particular class, not the interests of production which seeks the lowest rate in order to pile up profit which comes back to the hands of the capitalist, but production for the sake of the community as a whole—if you can get all the capital into the hands of the community in this fashion—then you could have a possible solution of the difficulty, and that is the socialistic suggestion. Capital must be controlled by the representatives of the community, that is, by the government; it must not be owned by the individual, but by the representatives of the people as a whole. There must be no private ownership of the means of production, because production is to lie in the hands of the community itself.

In the theory of Karl Marx the world was pictured as inevitably moving toward such a solution of the economic problem. Marx presented a very logical—indeed, the only logical—solution. Conditions would continue to get worse until this scheme was set up; the poor would get poorer, and the rich, richer. The rich were a mere handful; and the poor, the great mass in the community. The clash between these must come sooner or later. Of course, the rich have all the advantages of the institutions of the community (they can maintain themselves in spite of being a minority), but conflict must inevitably come in the end if the community is increasing in numbers and if the community gives a wage which is inevitably pushed by laws of economics down to a starvation level. If the community is in such a situation, the few in whose hands lie the means of production would utilize them simply for more and more production in which the cost of labor would be kept down just as much as possible in order that it might be lower than the prices in the world-market. Such a situation is one which cannot last forever in an intelligent community. It must be turned back from this process which is grinding life out of the great mass of the community, and take control over it; and if it takes control over it, a simple method will be to get hold of these means of production and see that they are not used for the sake of profits, but for the sake of consumption.

Of course, what Adam Smith recognized was that you get a production of those things that people want to consume, and you get it in the cheapest and readiest form if you allow the process to run itself. In the end this would simply ruin society. The machine was to be allowed to go by itself awhile and then could be brought, in some fashion, under the control of the community by simply having capital left in the hands of the community itself, that is, in the hands of its agent, the government.

The world, then, was moving toward such a revolution as Karl Marx pointed out in his *Communist Manifesto* in 1847, a revolution in which the community must turn about and get control of the means of production. Marx accepted the political economy of the Manchester school. He emphasized it; indeed, he overemphasized the results to which I have referred. He assumed that what was taking place was caused by iron laws until the social intelligence of the community should come in to correct these evils. But he had back of his doctrine not simply the logical analysis of what the current political economy implied. A Hegelian dialectic lay back of it too. And the socialism of the period is, for this reason, called "dialectical materialism."

Of course, this procedure toward a revolution which, as I have indicated, carried with it the implication of a reorganization, at once suggests the Hegelian dialectic, the conflict of Being and Not-Being and the rising out of that of the process of Becoming. You have the inevitable conflict; then, undoubtedly, with the crash that comes will come revolution; and then another order of things will appear. Marx had his training in the Hegelian school, and he found, in this process which is going on, an instance of just this dialectic. Hegel himself had turned to society for the highest expression of the spirit—a higher expression, you remember, than that to be found in the individual. From his point of view, government was an expression of the will of the community and of an intelligence that was greater than the intelligence of the separate individuals. The government, or the state, we will say, was a higher expression of the intelligence or spirit than was the individual himself. There was a demand, then, on the part of the Hegelian dialectic science that the individual should subordinate himself to the state, for the state represented a higher range of intelligence than could be found in the individual. That which took place through the state is something that could not take place through the action of the individual in so far as he isolated himself from the state. Bring people together in society, let them operate through the state, and they produce something that is higher than that which the individuals by themselves could possibly produce. Thus the Hegelian philosophy called for the domination of the individual by the state, not by the monarch, who was, from the Hegelian standpoint, merely "the dotting of the 'i,'" an inevitable symbol in the community, but by a power that was centered in Prussia at that time in an efficient bureaucracy. Here one found that to which the individual could subject himself because of its greater degree of intelligence, its higher expression of the Absolute Spirit.

What Karl Marx puts in place of this political development, or this expression of faith in the human spirit, is an economic process. In other words, we have here the economic interpretation of history, which was the last word in the socialistic doctrine. The process which Adam Smith, Ricardo, and Malthus had presented was a process which, of course, can be followed out in history. It was not only taking place immediately about them but had been taking place in the past. It was due to the development of the times that matters went ahead as rapidly as they did throughout the whole of the Western world, and particularly in England. Production was advancing by leaps and bounds; it was going on in an intense fashion and had been going on in an intense fashion from the beginning. The schools attempted to establish the laws by which all economic processes must take place. From an economic standpoint, the world had always been subject to these same laws. Men had only relatively recently discovered them, just as men had only at the time of the Renaissance discovered the laws of physical nature. And, as men could look back to the period before the Renaissance and see how these laws had always operated, although at that time men had not known them, so they could look back from this period at the beginning of the nineteenth century and see how these economic laws had always been in operation, and one could interpret history from the standpoint of these economic processes. Now, however, they could not only look back into the past but they could look into the future, toward this greater end—a revolution in which the community should take possession, gain control of the means of production, and thus allow the community to express itself, through the proper form of consumption. This was the picture which Marx undertook to provide.

Hegel had gone back to the history of thought and had undertaken to show what the various categories were that had arisen in human history. He started with Greek philosophy and followed his theory through to the Western world. He took the different concepts that had arisen in men's minds, extracted ideas, logical conceptions, and showed how they represented steps in the Hegelian dialectic. He interpreted history from the point of view of the development of logic—that is, of Hegelian logic.

We have already mentioned the Hegelian development in the socialism of Karl Marx, the so-called "economic interpretation" of history. At that time I contrasted it with the Hegelian interpretation of history, using the term "logic" in the Hegelian sense. While Hegel stopped to find in the great movements of the Western world the development of the fundamental categories of thought, Marx undertook to find the development of an economic process in which revolutions succeed each other. He undertook to interpret history in terms of such economic revolutions, to interpret thus the political changes that had taken place in the world, to bring back every fundamental political change to an economic cause, and to place all in the framework of the economic theory which he had taken over from the Manchester school.

That economic theory, you remember, was one which assumed an economic process in which the individual laborer's wage, that which he got out of the process of production, was inevitably forced down to a starvation limit, while the element of profit, the difference between price and cost of production, the accumulated wealth of the community, inevitably passed into the hands of the relatively few who controlled industry. The movement of this process was toward an ultimate revolution in which the community would take control of the processes of production in the interests of the community as a whole. There was, as in the Hegelian process, a dialectic in which there was an inevitable conflict between the interests of the community and the process by means of which those interests were carried out. This led, as in the Hegelian dialectic, to a contradiction, with a synthesis upon a higher level. Finally, you remember, the Hegelian process reaches the *Idee*, in which the content and the process become one. So in Marx's development one reaches the theory in which the community's interest becomes identified with the economic process itself. That would be the socialistic state toward which the political program of the Socialist party worked.

Thus, we have a picture of the development of the Hegelian doctrine—partly Hegelian and partly of the orthodox economic doctrine—as this appeared in the 1850's, in its formulation by

Karl Marx and the part which it played in the organization of labor in Europe. Its importance is due partly to the success with which the labor group had been definitely organized by the Manchester theory.

What Karl Marx did was to take history and interpret it from the point of view of the development of the economic rather than of the logical process. Just as Hegel had centered his account of history about the various logical categories, so the Marxian historian centered it about the appearance of economic laws. He undertook to explain all that had taken place as forms of conflict, of revolutions which were expressions of the economic situation which is moving toward a final revolution in which the community should come, so to speak, to consciousness of itself as an organization which controls every means of production and thus becomes a really intelligent community, not simply existing at the mercy of these laws, but controlling the situation through the knowledge of their operation. Of course, it is true of the laws of political economies, as it is of the laws of nature, that you can control them only by obeying them; but if you can obey them intelligently, you can control them. Well, this is a picture which Marxian socialism presented as over against the very optimistic picture which Adam Smith gave, and the very much more shaded and doubtful account that John Stuart Mill gave. It is only fair to say that the latter, an orthodox member of the Manchester school of economists, recognized, as definitely as Marx did, that there had to be some sort of control over the system as then presented. The interpretation of the latter looked toward revolution. It favored the bringing of matters to this conclusion. Let the poor get poorer and the rich richer. Let the extremes emphasize themselves in the community, and we will get nearer to revolution and so get over the situation the sooner. Things must get worse before they can get better. This was Marx's inevitable assumption.

I have pointed out that the socialist doctrine carried with it an internationalism which was implied in Adam Smith's position, but which got a more definite statement in the doctrine of socialism. The latter stressed the condition of labor as a result of the process of production rather than the process itself. The laborer's condition as painted by Marx was one which was, of course, the same wherever economic conditions were at work. Men might differ in language and social institutions and traditions; but, just in so far as social laws were operative, men found themselves facing the same difficulties. The same conflict between price, on the one hand, and cost of production, on the other, would inevitably tend to force down the cost of production and the price of labor. These conditions must everywhere operate in the same fashion; and labor always, therefore, must be in the same condition and must have a common interest. There must be a solidarity on the part of labor just in so far as it came to consciousness of this situation.

It was in Germany that this program of the Marxian socialism was first put into a political form. The Sozialdemokratische Arbeiterpartei was organized there, and gradually increased in numbers partly because of the appeal of the program itself and partly because the government undertook to suppress it. It increased to something like four million voters at one time. It was a party which was, like other parties in the Reichstag, a protest party. It did not accept the way of things. Its members stood for a situation in which the present order should give way and a new order appear with the social revolution. And, of course, this socialistic party was to be found not only in Germany but in all industrial countries. France at that time was not so industrial as at present, so the socialistic party had no such part in France then as it did in Germany and Austria. But through the organization of the labor group an international organization was made possible in Europe on the basis of development of the Marxian program. It exercised a very important influence.

It was assumed at the time that this international organization of labor was so strong that it would make war impossible, that the laborers of one country would be unwilling to pit themselves against the laborers of another country. That theory was dashed in 1914, however, when the socialistic party in Germany organized itself with the government and, indeed, worked out an adaptation of the governmental theory of the superiority of Germany to all other countries, made itself essentially a part of all the propaganda of the governmental dynast in Germany. The international organization was not equal to the task of dragging down the nationalistic sense in the separate communities, and the laborers found themselves in arms against each other in a war which was more destructive of life than any other war in history. And yet, since the war the re-establishment of the International has been going on. It is not, of course, what it was before the war. That is, labor's sense of solidarity is not, as yet, as strong as it was before the war. Labor is now feeling its way in the same way as other groups in the community are feeling their way without having a clear program before them.

The international organization of labor as such was one of the great—perhaps the greatest—movements that took place in Europe in the last half of the nineteenth century. There was no other great movement that swept all over Europe, taking hold of the masses of the community as this movement did, passing over national boundaries, over differences of speech, getting together the representatives of those who were economically the lowest in the social scale, but who represented the great bulk of the community, and organizing them in the interest of the program which was essentially idealistic, one in which the members did not expect to have immediate advantages for themselves. They were looking toward a revolution that was to take place in the future. Especially in the early days, it was thought that it would be about a hundred or a hundred and fifty years before this would occur, and yet people were sacrificing immediate interests in support of this program. It was a great idealistic movement which was essentially religious in its character. It is difficult to overestimate the importance of such a movement as this in bringing about, for the time being, at least, a sense of solidarity on the part of the members of the different communities of Europe, particularly in bringing to light problems which the community had to face.

That is the other side of the movement that I want to emphasize. On the one side we have this sense of solidarity among the great masses of the laboring population throughout industrial Europe; and on the other side, a definite presentation of the problem which government has had to meet. The project which a Marxian socialism set up was one which governments were quite unwilling to undertake, and one practically abandoned in socialistic communities in Europe. The project of control over industry in the interest of the community itself, the recognition that business could not be regarded simply as existing for profit, that the other functions of business—in other words, what we call "public services"—have to be recognized, and that this recognition is one which must be enforced, if not by public opinion, then by political institution, has everywhere faced stubborn resistance. Such an institution as the Interstate Commerce Commission of this country is an illustration of the response of the community to the sort of problem that has been set up by the development of industry and so emphasized by socialistic groups. They formulated a sharp outline of the problem, so that the government was forced to approach it from a point of view that it had been unwilling to take before.

The great change as to the insurance of the labor group against those conditions in which the laborer would be unable to meet the demands which society and life put upon him is bound up with the same movement. Take the condition in which the laborer is out of work, falls sick, gets beyond the period in which he is economically productive. The older community left him to himself or to charity. The system of insurance instituted in Germany recognizes that it is the task, the duty, of a community to care for those who are willing, but unable, to labor, whatever the cause of the inability. It also recognizes that the care given in the form of charity of one sort or another was not only inadequate so far as the individual was concerned but expensive so far as the community was concerned. It was far less expensive to institute such insurance as in Germany than it was to leave the laborer under those conditions in which he had found himself previously, where he was dependent on either public or private charity. That situation, of course, was recognized not only in Germany and in other countries which introduced such insurance but finally in England. The Asquith and Lloyd George governments carried through insurance policies, now represented inaccurately by critics in England as the "dole," as a means of dealing with unemployment. It was recognized, then, that the community itself must definitely face the problems that its industry places upon it, and face them not simply in the interest of labor but in the interest of a community made up of laborers as such.

That this type of problem has been forced upon the community, forced into government programs, is in no small degree due to the development of labor parties; and this was made possible by the idealism of Karl Marx and those who followed him. I call it "idealism." The philosophy, of course, is ordinarily termed "materialism." It makes the industrial process essential in the community. But the movement is fundamentally an idealistic movement, for it is one that has looked toward the reorganization of society, toward a reorganization lying in the future. Such a movement is exactly what we term "idealistic," and this movement certainly was of that sort. It is one of the outgrowths of the Hegelian movement which we ought to recognize particularly. I have run over its history up to the present time so that you can put it in its relationship to this theory.

I now wish to emphasize again, from a different aspect, the international character of the labor movement. Finance and production, especially as these were reflected in commerce, were inevitably international. But that internationalism did not lead to any sense of solidarity on the part of the financiers, on the part of those involved in the financial process. Financiers in England and those controlling capital in Germany, France, and

America each retained a sense of his own national character; and, while involved in an international financial activity, each identified himself with the community to which he belonged. The labor process was one, however, in which there grew up a very considerable sense of solidarity of interests among the laborers themselves. The position, of course, of the laborer as represented both by Marxian socialism and the Manchester school was one of necessary misery; and misery, as we know, loves company. The laborer in the face of the threat of a starvation wage felt himself supported by others in the same situation in other countries. The movement toward a revolution which would change this order of things was, then, an international movement in which there was a sense of solidarity on the part of the laborers themselves. How deep or superficial this sense of solidarity was can be found at the time of the World War, but it was far deeper than any sense of identity or of solidarity of interest on the part of the financial groups as such. The financial groups in Germany and England were in very vivid competition with each other. They were seeking world-markets and seeking to oust each other in these world-markets, although they both used the machinery of international finance. The laborers as such had no sense of competition with each other. This is true in regard to Europe pretty generally.

In the tariff program of American politics, on the other hand, there was a very definite undertaking which had a considerable success in aligning the interests of the American laborer over against labor in the European countries. The higher American wage was presented as protected by tariffs, and the laborer was taught to regard himself as in a favorable position. The whole situation in America was one which did not lead to the development of socialistic consciousness on the part of the labor group. It has not done so up to the present time. In England also it developed comparatively late.

While they say that the Labor party in England at the present time has a definite socialistic program, it is one of the Fabian sort, which does not undertake to map out just what steps are to be taken in later periods. That is, it does not present revolution as something that must take place as a result of inevitable conflict. The changes can take place by gradual legislation, and the exact form of these changes its program does not attempt to work out. It may be called a socialistic program, but one which differs at least from that of the Marxian group. The difference to which I have just referred between the programs of the English Labor party and that of the Marxian group is also reflected in socialistic thought in a later period. Marx, of course, invented a definite program. This was worked out in the program of the Sozialdemokratische Arbeiterpartei in Germany, and it remained the dogma of that party for a number of years. Gradually, however, there arose an opportunistic group in the Socialistic party, a group that sought to bring about changes or an amelioration of conditions of laboring groups, an amelioration not only in the fields of industry but also in the social conditions of labor. There grew up groups of socialists very much interested in municipal organization, who sought to improve the housing conditions, the health conditions of the labor group. In order to do that, they had to ally themselves with governing groups in the community. As I stated before, the logical position of the Social-Democratic party was that of a protest party which refuses to work with the active political parties of the countries. They always registered their protest. But if they were undertaking to carry out any program, they had to work with the dominant parties. In spite of itself, as the opportunistic group grew in power, the date of the future revolution, and the form that it should take, became less and less definite in the minds of the socialists themselves. That is, to use a current phrase, there was a tendency to substitute evolution for revolution. It was assumed that a gradual process was taking place which would lead to some such result as that which Marx had had in mind, but it did not necessarily have to take place by means of a catastrophic overturning of things. Especially it became more and more difficult to state just what the future situation should be in the control of industry, a change which was mirrored in such a type of socialism as guild socialism.

There was an uneasy feeling that even a bureaucracy as efficient as that of Germany was in some way not adequate to the task of working industry, that there was something in individual initiative, in the trying-out of possible methods of improvements in trade, which led to individual profit—something that provided a motive that could not be obtained under a bureaucratic direction of industry. While the German railroad industry under its bureaucracy proved itself an efficient and sound institution, it was realized that this was a very different economic undertaking from that of the production of articles that had to find markets and had to be produced at continually reduced prices. That is, it was realized that bureaucratic methods were fixed methods, or tended to fix themselves. There was no such stimulus to scrap the old and introduce new methods for the old as was found in private industry. The bureaucrat does not like to scrap his apparatus. There was this general feeling that, when it came to the control of industry, the government as such had not as yet, at least, proved itself competent.

Interest shifted to the question of the control within different industries or groups of industries which might be exercised by labor itself, a communistic movement which regarded labor as the whole owner of industry. Could industry be brought into relationship with labor itself? Could labor actually exercise control? Would it be possible to get hold of different types of industries which answered in a certain sense to the old medieval guilds, in which there should be representation of the labor interest? You get a shift of interest, you see, from the control of the government over industry to a more immediate and direct control by labor itself, or the possibility of it. These were changes which went on and are going on at the present time in the program of labor groups—a change which answers to the breakdown of the old Hegelian dialectic even in the field of political economy.

Coming back to the Marxian development, we must conceive of it as having two roots: one the political economy, the industrial development which the Manchester school interpreted, and the other the Hegelian dialectic. The statement which it took from the Manchester school was of a process in which, through supply and demand, through the keeping-down of costs in the interest of the production of wealth, the price of labor would inevitably be brought down to a starvation wage, if, as it generally was, the Malthusian hypothesis was accepted. It was assumed that under favorable conditions there would always be a surplus of laborers, as well as a surplus of other articles essential for production, so that expansion could take place as industry demanded it. There should be the opportunity for expansion. In order that there might be this opportunity, there should be a surplus which could be taken up as the demand developed. A surplus of labor meant, of course, persons out of jobs, who were therefore on the verge of starvation. The ideal situation from the point of view of this political economy, then, was one in which there was a line of men before the factory seeking for jobs, many of whom could not obtain any. The Malthusian doctrine, of course, fitted into this economic demand. There would always be a surplus of population beyond the means of sustenance, so that there always would be those who were seeking for a wage even if it was at the starvation level.

As we have seen, this interpretation, plus that of the gradual passage of capital into the hands of those who were not successful in the use of it, led to the assumption on the part of this Marxian doctrine that the rich would continually grow richer and the poor would keep on growing poorer up to the point at which the community would cease to recognize this form of production and industry would pass over into the hands of the state. It was the demand of Marxian socialism that all capital should be owned by the community in the form of the state. All production should be directed by the state. It did not abrogate private ownership; it was only a question of what should be owned. No capital, no means of production, should be owned by the individual except his wage. That which came to him in his function as laborer should be his own, and the amount which that would be would presumably be determined by the state in its function as producer. And production, then, would take place not in the interest of laying aside more capital, not in the interest of profit as such, but definitely in the interest of the community itself.

The assumption of this doctrine is that the whole of history had been moving toward a revolution and that back of the great political movements of the past always lay an economic motive. The development which was taking place was traced by the socialists back to the gradual development of capital out of more primitive conditions, and then out of this capitalism it was assumed revolution itself would spring. There was always the contest between those who were producing and the masses of the community; and this had expressed itself in continued opposition, contradictions. And what the dialectical materialism, as it was termed, attempted to say was that this process was one in which there had been conflicts of opposites with the appearance of a synthesis in which, for the time being, these opposites were harmonized, and such that the final conflict, so to speak, from the economic standpoint would take place in a shift of emphasis in which capitalism as such would be abrogated and state control come in.

One can, of course, point to the seeming failures of the Marxian state in Russia at the present time. There has been great difficulty there in keeping economic processes going. The Russians seem to have made enormous concessions to private capital in order to keep their industries going. As I stated, the Marxian doctrine, which is very definitely economic dogma pushed into the Hegelian dialectic, gradually lost its hold throughout Europe and in our two great industrial communities, Germany and England. In Germany there was the Sozialdemokratische Arbeiterpartei that was inspired by the Marxian doctrine; and under the leadership of Bebel and those who followed him it still maintained the Marxian doctrine and looked forward to revolution; it still played the part of the protest party, one that refused to accept the operation of the government under then present conditions, one that was waiting for a socialistic government. As I have already pointed out, this devotion to the Marxian dogma waned in the later history of socialism in Germany. There grew up an opportunistic movement, gathering pretty largely about the force of the socialist party, to bring about various changes, reforms in the immediate conditions. As you know, Bismarck tried to undermine socialism by introducing state insurance for those who fell sick, for those who reached the old-age limit—insurance which would protect the laborer under conditions in which he was not able to protect himself. Then, as I said, the socialistic part, especially in the municipalities, wished to bring about better conditions for labor. They could only do that, of course, in so far as they worked with other parties. This gradually became the dominant element in the socialistic party. When, after the war, the opportunity came to the Socialists, who were the majority party in the Reichstag, of carrying out a program which they had produced in the past, namely, that of bringing about revolution, they became a relatively conservative party, unwilling to put control of industry into the hands of the bureaucratic state.

In English history socialism had been of a different character. The Marxian doctrine, although formulated in England itself, never took hold of the English laborer in the early days. In fact, in one sense it has not in the present day. Labor in England never looked forward to revolution as such. In England the laborer fought for better conditions and better wages, but his weapon has been the trade-union and not a socialistic party looking toward the reconstruction of the state itself. The conditions preceding the war, and those following it, increased the representatives of the Labor party in Parliament, so that it became the second largest party. The Liberal party lost largely to the Labor party and to the Conservative party, so that the two parties that stood over against each other were the Conservative and the Labor parties. This development of the Labor party centered about a program which was worked out really by the Fabian socialists, the Webbs. Sidney and Beatrice Webb were the ones who very largely drew it up, but there were others involved in it. It was a program that looked toward the various socialistic types of industries, those in which competition is eliminated by the nature of the industry itself. A public utility is successful only in so far as it has no competitors. You cannot have several telephone systems competing with each other and still have successful operation. And the same is true, of course, of other so-called "utilities." Competition—the breath of life from the point of view of the orthodox system—has no place there. It is necessary, in the case of such social industries, that there should be public control; and it is perfectly possible to have public management in these cases. It is possible, conceivably at least, for a state to pick out a good manager. It may be a question whether it can select a successful entrepreneur, a person who can take capital and build up an industry; but it ought to be possible for an intelligent government to select a good manager, and we have various illustrations of this in government-directed business—notably the post-office, and in Germany in the operation of the railroads as successfully carried on by the government. Where you eliminate competition, where the process of operation is one which has already been well standardized, there it must be possible to introduce public operation and a gradual control, through the development of the income tax, through the distribution of wealth in the community.

Speaking of the change which took place in the socialistic doctrine and the orthodox economic conceptions, I have indicated that it was a change from a program to opportunism. The term "opportunistic" does not do entire justice to the shift in attitude. It was not simply an attitude on the part of the thinkers of various types to reach out for any chance advantage that might be gained. There was always behind it the assumption that there was some sort of method or social process that could be found out, and therefore some sort of method that might be adopted so that these human institutions could be adjusted to this process; that is, that there might be laws which, if discovered, could be used to control social events. The first assumption of the economic doctrine had been that certain so-called "iron laws" of nature had been discovered which are involved in the economic process, and that the only thing one could do was to accept them and act in accordance with them; that if one undertook to contravene them he got himself into difficulties. It was like refusing to obey the law of gravitation. One must obey in order to control.

What generally came out of the struggle, however, was a gradual recognition that these laws did not have the form which an earlier economic doctrine had given to them. That doctrine led logically to the conclusions which Karl Marx drew from them. That is, if one were to accept not only the laws of supply and demand, those which control the price of things in the markets of the world, but accept also the process of competition, and the Malthusian law, the results which Marx drew from them were logical. However, out of the labor-union movement in England and in this country, out of the processes which were responsible for these movements, it was found that the price of labor could be influenced by other considerations than those of supply and demand, that it was possible to increase the price of labor above a subsistence level. What had been overlooked in the Marxian assumption was the greater productivity of labor. It had also overlooked the various social conditions that determine the fixing of the wage. Taking the laws of these first, it was found that in the struggle between the labor unions and the employers, in the discussion of the conditions under which labor operated, there could grow up a public sentiment that was effective in determining the price of labor, or at least that had an influential part in determining the price of labor. Also, it was slowly discovered that a wage which made possible mere subsistence and which kept the laborers on the verge of starvation was not a wage which produced the highest results; it was not an economic wage.

The abstract doctrine we have been speaking of assumed that man was like a machine: he could be bought and then he would operate; but he could operate only on the basis of a subsistence which he obtained in exchange for his labor, and which, if inadequate, would render his performance inadequate also. There were evidences of a social sort, of a physiological sort, which entered into the determination of the wage which were not presented in the first formulation of the economic doctrine in question.

Then, too, there gradually grew up a recognition that Malthus' law itself had not the necessary operation which was supposed to belong to it. In the first place, there was evidence which was to be found in France that population could be held down, that, actually, increase did not take place in accordance with the Malthusian law; and gradually in England itself there grew up evidence that there was what has later come to be called "birth control," which determines to considerable degree the increase of population. That is, the human race does not necessarily oversupply the world as forms lower than it do. Its method for the control of population was of a different sort than that which exists in lower forms. Man himself could determine the actual increase. In other words, it was found that the so-called "iron laws" did not have uniformity which belongs to a so-called "law of nature," and men went back to the study of human conditions, to study the process of production and distribution, the economic process; and, as this investigation was undertaken, it was found that the situations were very complex.

One result of this was the discovery of something of the same assumption that belonged to the Hegelian doctrine, namely, that the state had a higher intelligence than the individual. Indeed, something of this sort was more or less implied. Why should one assume that a bureaucratic state would be more successful in the process of production than individual entrepreneurs? One found, of course, in industry that a large number of capitalistic undertakings failed where very few succeeded. It was computed that something like ninety-odd per cent of capitalistic undertakings were not successful. It was this, of course, which led to the assumption that capital would flow into the hands of those who were successful. Why should it be assumed that the state in a bureaucratic fashion would be able to draft ability which would enable it to carry on these industries successfully? Great industries have to work on a very narrow margin if they work in accordance with economic laws, and the Marxian doctrine was orthodox in its acceptance of these laws. Something like a 5 per cent margin is what separates a great industry from success or failure. It is always, so to speak, near the edge—always has to maintain itself by a careful consideration of its conditions and the situation within which it operates, and on the basis of which it can succeed. As I said, the assumption that the state could take over such a difficult undertaking as the management of great industries and make them successful, is an assumption that implies that the state is going to control powers and capacities which it is very difficult to secure under private management. The person who succeeds is one who is selected out by a sort of process of competition, and it is very difficult to determine from consideration of the individual whether he will succeed or not. There is something of an implication that the state as such has a higher intelligence than the individual, if we assume that this industrial state is going to be economically successful in its processes.

This type of program was, as I have suggested, socialistic in character, but evolutionary rather than revolutionary. It was the sort of program which the Labor party put up. It became socialistic in the sense that it looked to the state to take over production, but has never been socialistic in the sense of making socialism a religion. The Marxian doctrine was essentially a religion, had been in Germany and elsewhere in Europe, as it is at present among the communists in Russia. That is, it was conceived of essentially as an expression of the intelligence of the community. What this socialistic doctrine has implied is that the economic process is the dominant process of the community, and that this dominant process of the community is controlled by the intelligence of the community, that if this process is developed to the proper level the community will naturally take control over it. The religious life is essentially a life of the individual in that of the whole group to which he belongs, that is, in which the individual is subordinated to the group, in which the individual realizes himself in the life of the community. The socialist doctrine, then, was in this sense a religious doctrine. It conceived of the life of the community as essentially an economic process. The individual was realized in this great social process through the Industrial Revolution. The control of the process was to pass into the hands of the community, in which the individual was the essential part. That is, the individual through the part which he played in the various labor organizations, industrial organizations, was the fundamental element in the state. And the individual, realizing himself in the life of the community, had definitely a religious attitude toward the process itself. In other words, you can find a parallelism between the statement of religion and the Hegelian state, the state being nearer to God than the individual in the community, the individual subordinating himself to the state as a higher expression of spirit. This attitude, being of a religious character, was, on the socialist side, expressed as an economic process which is the essential life of the community, and it is in so far as the individual, in his relationship to this economic organization, subordinates himself to its highest expression in the state that he gets a realization of himself in the group to which he belongs. That is, he gets essentially a religious attitude.

Now this attitude is one which you do not find in the English Labor party, socialistic as it has in some sense become. Fabian socialism is not a religious movement. It is one which looks toward the meeting of all sorts of evils found in the industrial communities by governmental action of different sorts. It feels free to use the government in industrial situations as much as it is used in political situations, and in policing situations that arise. The government can be utilized by the community to meet economic conditions and to better these conditions. But it does not assume that the economic process is the process in which the intelligence of the community as such expressed itself necessarily. The development of socialism in England is, in a certain sense, parallel with the development which took place in Germany in the passage of dogmatic socialism into opportunistic socialism—one willing and desirous of utilizing the powers of the state to bring about better conditions for labor without endeavoring to state just what the organization of society was going to be. The earlier socialists proceeded as if they had had a vision on the Mount which showed them what the order of society should be. They felt they could work out deductively what the order should be. It was that which they held before themselves, waiting to bring about this great change which, when the evolution of conditions had reached the proper point, could be carried through. In place of this we have in England a type of socialism which felt itself free to utilize the state in a fashion it assumed to be legitimate.

The old doctrine called off the hand of the state from industry. Adam Smith called for the abandonment of monopolies which the state had allowed to grow up, the giving-way of tariff, the opening of doors, the taking-off of political control of industry, allowing industry to proceed with its own laws. That is still the doctrine in the orthodox school. As over against this you have the sort of development which has been taking place not only in industrial Europe but also in America. Our Interstate Commerce Commission, for example, as I have already mentioned in passing, is an expression of government in which the control of industrial conditions, specifically the determination of rates, of the conditions under which transportation is to take place, is in the hands of the state. We have established other bureaus along the same lines, although they have not developed to the same extent or had the importance which the Interstate Commerce Commission has. We have been behind

England in the development of governmental control over public utilities. We proceed very slowly in this country as compared with England and Germany, the reason presumably being found in the fact that our local governments are more corrupt than local governments in England have been, so that the community has been wary of introducing an opportunity for the government control of great public utilities. For example, in Chicago there was a time during which public sentiment in the community as a whole was, by and large, for public ownership of the transit system. At the present time sentiment is active on quite the other side. The lack of confidence in our municipal institutions as they are organized and conducted by our present politicians is such as to make the community hesitate to turn over operations of great public utilities to them, and so this type of development of public control has advanced very much more slowly in this country that it has in Europe.

The movement, however, is one whose general lines I have sketched. We have at this time the somewhat sensational undertaking in Russia to actually carry out the Marxian program, the setting-up of a Marxian system as final, or an attempt to carry it through in its detail, with, of course, as I have said, very unsatisfactory results from the industrial standpoint, at least up to the present time. Of course, there is a certain absurdity in undertaking to carry out Marx's doctrine in Russia. Such a doctrine gathers about the proletariat composed mainly of factory laborers. Socialism has never been able to get hold of agricultural labor, and 90 per cent of the laborers in Russia are peasants, those living upon the soil. The Communist-Socialist government has had to give way before the peasantry and turn over control of the soil to the person who is, to all intents and purposes, the owner of the soil which he cultivates. The place in which to undertake an experiment such as is being carried out in Russia would be in Germany or in England, great industrial communities in which you have a large and relatively highly intelligent proletariat in a socialistic sense, men who have had training of a political sort such as the socialists have had in the

Social-Democratic party in Germany, and such as the English laborers are getting. But what was clearly evident after the war, when socialism had things in its own hands in Germany, was an entire unwillingness to undertake any such experiment; and, of course, the same thing is true in England. Laborers as such were quite unwilling to undertake any revolutionary process, any turning-over of the industry of the community to control by the state, with the consequence that there has been a serious slowing-up, if not actual discounting, of the effectiveness of such a program.

CHAPTER XII

INDUSTRY A BOON TO SCIENCE—MECHANISM THE HANDMAID OF FINALITY

THE economic organization of society which we have been discussing in the so-called Industrial Revolution has been the source out of which some of the most important of our scientific conceptions and hypotheses have arisen. The conception of energy is illustrative of this. This conception was definitely revolutionary in modern science because it brought together fields which could not be stated in terms of a mechanical science. Newton's statement was taken from the heavens and, of course, was a generalization of Galileo's law of the falling body fused with the observations of Kepler and others. Newton gave a statement of the solar system in terms of attraction, that is, of the movement of masses with reference to each other; and he gave the laws for this solar system. Then this system was carried to earth again and was made the basis for the study of the phenomena that take place about us. It was very fruitful in a field in which you could locate actual masses, but people tried to carry over the conception into fields in which they could not actually locate the different masses on account of the minuteness of the bodies. What they wanted to do was to apply the simple law of Newton's statement to other physical processes.

For example, take such a process as heat, that is, of molecular bodies moving at great velocities with reference to one another. They are beyond the range of our observation. You cannot take that problem and carry it over into the phenomena, because you cannot get a statement of the positions of the bodies that will enable you to work the law out. There were various uniformities which science could locate. Again, take the phenomenon of electricity. Here also are uniformities which could be determined. How were these different phenomena to be brought into relationship with each other? They could not be stated simply in terms of the movement of masses with reference to each other as Newton could state the movement of planetary bodies, and yet they must be made into a necessary idea. That is, you can say how much work will be done, how much work is involved in doing this or that thing, and yet not know how the atoms or particular masses are moving with reference to others. All we can determine is just how much work is done in one situation and how much is done in another. Then we have a basis for determining proportionate amounts of energy. We can look at the whole process from the standpoint of energies, from the standpoint of the amount of work done, and not try to determine just what the positions of all the physical particles are in their movements in relation to one another. Such an undertaking goes beyond our vision. But you can still say that energy is expended; you can still say how much work is involved in bringing about a certain situation, and how much can be developed.

The economist turns to the scientist and wants a theory for his new servant, the steam engine. He says, "I want to know how much work it can do." So the scientist takes the unit of work and discovers the amount of energy. That is, he finds that the machine can be depended upon for a certain number of units of work done. Thus, in the physical world you can say that energy is a bookkeeping conception. It takes electricity and light, coal, expansive steam, and the revolving dynamo, and sets up a certain unit by means of which it is able to put them all into the same class, just as the economist takes all sorts of different objects—the machinery, the soil, the plant, the workers—and sets them all together, states them in terms of the amount of labor necessary to get a given commodity. Work or energy, then, is a bookkeeping conception taken over from the economic doctrine, just as I have said the conception of the survival of the fittest in the competition for existence is taken over by Darwin from the economic situation presented by Ricardo and

Malthus and generalized in the form of the hypothesis of evolution. It is very interesting to see the sources from which importantly constructive ideas have arisen, to see what an organic thing society is; how ideas that you find in one phase of it appear in some different form in another phase, but come back to common sources.

The conception of energy, then, comes from the demand for a theory of the steam engine. The thing about the steam engine that interested people was exactly the amount of work that it would do. The steam engine took the place of human arms. It was more effective and more reliable. It did the work that laborers had done, and enabled the entrepreneur to make the work of the laborer still more productive. Work in the form of labor, of course, was an essential part of the economic doctrine. The cost of production, which was essential to the conclusions of the Manchester school, always came back to labor. The price of anything could be given in terms of labor, in terms of the amount of work necessary to produce it. Labor became a universal element in this equation. Labor was generalized in the economic equation as that in terms of which the cost of any particular article could be assessed. Of course, the success of economic production was dependent on making this cost less than the price. But in order to make your business a paying one, you have to make a statement of the actual cost of your production. And the ultimate element you come back to is stated in terms of labor. That played a very large part in the doctrine of political economy at that time. What was wanted was a statement in terms of labor of everything that was being done. The unit of labor really comes out of the economic doctrine. It is a bookkeeping term. You have to set up an equation in regard to the process as a whole; you have to make your cost of production no greater than the price you can get for your article; and you have to state the cost of production in terms of labor. Well now, if you are introducing machinery, you must be able to state what the machine does in terms of the amount of work accomplished. The unit was presented to science by political economy, and the conception of labor had the same transferability that the conception of work had. Take any object that is to be estimated in terms of manufacture and you can state the whole cost of it in terms of labor. For example, if you want to know the value of food, it comes back to the labor that has to be expended on the ground. You can put the value into terms of the amount of work done, the unit of which arises out of the economic situation.

This conception led to the setting-up of a certain metaphysics, to a theory of energy which Ostwald, a German chemist, proposed, in which energy was regarded as being the ultimate element. He tried to get rid of the conception of atomic particles. With this in mind he wrote an elementary chemistry in which he did do away with atoms entirely. Instead of talking about the union of two portions of hydrogen with one of oxygen, instead of talking about a certain number of atoms to be brought into relation with each other in chemical combinations, he simply stated the amounts in such terms as, "Take twice as much of one as of the other," and up to a certain point he was able to work out an adequate statement on these terms which got rid of atoms. He simply stated the amounts in terms of quantities. But he could not get beyond that point. In fact, the so-called "carbon chemistry," which sets up the idea of molecules in which the different relative positions of identical atoms within the molecules give rise to different organic substances, made this undertaking impossible. What this German chemist was trying to do was to set up a certain metaphysical entity of energy and say this is the ultimate substance in the universe. That in itself broke down; but the history of it, which I have briefly given, shows a very interesting development of such a scientific concept and the interrelationship of such a conception with the social structure and social theory of the period.

Let us now bring up the other side of the life of Europe, which we have in some sense neglected, and get a point of view from which to interpret a good deal of what we have said by turning back to its science. Throughout the whole of the nineteenth century Europe was essentially scientific in its knowledge achievements. The philosophies of the period which we have studied, and which we will study in what follows, no longer had the dogmatic attitude which belonged to earlier philosophies. These earlier philosophies had been, in some sense, interpreted along intellectual lines of the dogma of the church, of its philosophy of life; and where the church was the dominant element in the life of the community, philosophy had a corresponding position. The importance of the church as the interpreter of the world, the interpreter of the lives of individuals in accordance with the church as giving means of life to the individual, as a philosophy of life to the man in the street, shifted; and another form of interpretation, the scientific, appeared and became more and more dominant. It is true that in some sense in the back of the mind of these generations lies a plan of salvation presented in such form as that of Milton's *Samson Agonistes*. That remains as a sort of pattern for the interpretation of the world, that is, the idea that there is some sort of moral purpose which underlies the whole order of the universe, and that this great moral purpose finds particular expression in the life of man and in the history of man, and that, while it may be impossible, as it was earlier assumed, to take the history of that process as given in the chapters of Genesis and throughout the Bible as the single strand upon which everything is to be strung, it is still true that the moral purpose presented in the doctrine of the church itself is still, in some sense, regarded as identical with the purpose of the universe and that, if one is right with God, he is in line with the natural development of things about him. Some such feeling of the moral identity of human history with that of the universe is a conception which has come over from the ecclesiastical and doctrinal statements of the church, and it still plays an important part in our view of the world. In the form in which it was given by the church, the literal statement of that was relatively simple: man sinned; he came under the condemnation of God; he was saved by the sacrifice of Christ.

In the past there has been the otherworldliness of the great religions. It has been in relationship to the world to come, that is, in relationship to social ideals that could not be achieved in this world, that men have been able to get together. The gospel of Jesus presents a picture of a society in which the interests of one are the interests of all, in which all regard themselves as members of a single family. It is an ideal which has never, of course, been realized on the face of the earth, and which never can be, things remaining what they have been in the past. Single groups living on that basis during the medieval period had to be organized into cloisters. Men gave up property, family life, to reach a situation in which there should be that sort of identity of interest in this world. Such a society belongs in a New Jerusalem. But men still kept this ideal, although they might differ in all sorts of other things—even though they might constantly be at war with one another. The salvation of the individual soul was wrapped up in the good of the whole community, and this idea was inevitably that of another world.

Such a statement as this is, however, quite inconsistent with the one which science gives. Nevertheless, for years the two statements went along without coming into necessary conflict. I have already indicated the independent position of science in the modern world. In a certain sense the Renaissance scientist took up the study of matter and motion as a field which led outside the immediate social interests and ecclesiastic interests of the community. From the point of view of the church God had created the world out of nothing to serve as the field in which would be enacted the drama of man's fall and salvation. Science could make its investigation without coming into conflict with the doctrine of the church. It was to be assumed that an infinitely wise God would work by means of uniform laws; that he would have the ability and the interest of a supreme mathematician. Thus science might find the way in which God operates in the world without finding out his purposes. When, however, the science which dealt with matter, the science of Galileo, and especially his dynamics, which said that matter is nothing but inertia—mass as revealed in inertia—when this science went on into the fields of biology, for example, the going became more difficult. It was difficult because biology is a science which is infinitely more complex than mechanics. If biology is to be reduced to mechanics, it is necessary to carry one's view into very complex situations. Still it is possible to conceive of plants, of animals, and of a physiological mind as mechanical, and thus they could be understood, in terms of what Aristotle would have called an "efficient cause," as over against a final cause, a form of understanding which had proved itself of immense importance. Aristotle never realized that by obeying nature one might control it by discovering uniform laws. From the time of the Renaissance on, the Western world was controlling nature and using its forces by very competent investigation of its laws and a complete willingness to obey those laws in carrying out its own purposes, so that a nature that seemed to be outside the ends and the purposes of the creator of the world became more and more important to society. A science which seemed to have abandoned and to have carefully kept itself from theological inquiry in regard to the meaning of the world was coming in by the back door, and, by studying the mechanical order of things, was getting more control of nature and bringing about tremendous changes and becoming more and more important in man's mind. It continually rendered this type of explanation more and more attractive—an explanation from the statement of the efficient cause, from cause and effect and the uniform laws of nature, as over against an explanation from the point of view of final cause, of end, of purpose. Which form of explanation shall we take? Why is the world here? Why are we here? Why should we suffer, be restricted here and there? What is the end that explains all? That earlier, teleological form of explanation was set over against another form which undertakes to show how things have happened, and why, because certain things have happened in a given way, other things must necessarily follow. That is a science of physical necessity, but one which did not carry with it necessity in so far as the conduct of man was concerned. I have said that one gets control over nature by obeying it. You find out how things must happen, and then you can use things that happen in a necessary way to bring about your results. This very separation of mass, of the mechanical process from other processes, psychological and social among others, left people, in some sense, free to utilize these very social purposes.

What I want to bring out is that, while there had been a sort of theological inquiry that is still perhaps present in man's mind as to whether men are free or not, and questions of freedom of the will may still be discussed under sophomoric conditions, the necessity which science presents had not, as yet, carried with it control over human initiative. The more necessary the statement of natural sciences can be made, the greater freedom man has in reconstructing, in bringing about changes in, his environment.

This paradox is of very great importance in our understanding of the position of science in the Western world. Of course, if, with Laplace, you say that everything that takes place is simply a shift of physical particles moving in accordance with absolute law, then you can conceivably have an equation in which you have only to introduce the variables, including time, and you can determine the position of the moon with reference to the earth and sun, and so determine eclipses. You can conceivably get equations which can determine the whole solar and stellar system. Increase its generality, and all you have to do is to introduce the variable time and you can tell just where every physical particle will be at any possible moment in the future as well as in the past. Seemingly, the whole world would be absolutely fixed and determined. That is a conceivable statement of this mechanical science. But what I am pointing out is that the science which gave this sort of a view of the world is the science which was enabling human initiative to reconstruct its world entirely and, through the reconstruction of his environment, enabling man to make an entirely different society. You get this paradox: a statement of the mechanical nature of everything, one which seems to include man also, which, at the same time, gives man greater control over his environment, greater freedom of action, and allows him to set up social objectives.

Man is a physical and biological organism. What he is is the sum of all the physical particles that go to make him up. According to the statement we are now considering, if you can determine where those particles are, you can determine just what he will say and think. Such a doctrine gives you absolute necessity in everything; and yet, in working out as complete a mechanical statement as is possible, you get one which gives man a more complete freedom than he ever had in the past. The best statement that you can get of the development of science throughout this period, but especially during the early part, is to be found in Merz's *History of European Thought in the Nineteenth Century*.

The Newtonian doctrine presented a picture of an orderly, mechanical universe, one governed by mechanical laws, a universe of masses in motion. The laws of these motions in their simplest forms could be given. The changes that took place, if in a sufficiently simple situation, could also be traced out. The method of analysis which grew out of the work of Leibnitz and Newton—that of an infinitesimal calculus—sought always to take as simple a situation as possible; and, if a sufficiently simple situation could be found, it was discovered that the laws of change could be determined. The picture, then, which was presented of the physical universe was of one which was in motion, and in motion in accordance with simple laws, and that which moved was mass. There were, of course, many features of the physical universe which could not be brought under terms of mass; but it was assumed, or at least hoped, that something of this kind could be worked out, that such a mechanical statement of things could be made universal. The picture which Laplace presented was of an equation which could determine where all the physical particles of the universe would be at any one moment if you simply introduced the variable of time. Such a picture was what men had before them. So far as they could get into the intricate movements of things, the molecular movements of things, the laws seemed to hold. It was, then, to be assumed that such physical laws as these operated throughout nature, and that the whole of nature could be regarded in terms simply of masses in motion and could be brought under as rigorous laws as those which science had already discovered.

There was, however, the biological field which seemed to offer resistance to the entrance of physical law. The importance of the Darwinian hypothesis was that it seemed to open the door to a natural law in the development of physical forms. If such a hypothesis could be accepted, the changes that took place in animate nature would be due to causes operating from behind, causes which were a posteriori. That is, you would not have to assume a certain nature in plant or animal which determined its growth, but that causes were operating, or rather had been operating, which brought about results here as in inorganic nature. Of course, men had discovered many parts of the process of life which could be stated in physical and mechanical terms. Certain of the so-called "organic products" had been produced artificially in the laboratory. It was perfectly conceivable that changes which took place in living forms were simply physical and mechanical changes, that men and animals and plants were, as Descartes had guessed, nothing but machines so far as the life-processes were concerned.

Now Darwin's hypothesis came in to indicate how particular forms might arise. All it asked for was indefinite variation on the part of young forms, that every young form should vary in some respect from the parent form. Then it asked that there should be competition for life which should be sufficiently strenuous that only the form best adapted to survive would survive. What Darwin pointed out was what had been suggested in Malthus' doctrine, namely, that there were always more young forms arising in nature than could possibly survive. There must then be competition between these forms, and those among them which were less fitted to survive under the conditions in which they found themselves would inevitably disappear. Given this indefinite variation, one could fairly assume that when the difference in the form answered to changes in the environment a new form would arise which, under this competition, would maintain itself while all other forms would disappear. In this way Darwin undertook to explain the appearance of species. Back of it, as I have pointed out, was the recognition of a more or less identical life-process in all forms. The biological form of the plant or animal was the adjustment of this life-process to a particular environment. Suppose, now, that this environment changes; there must be a corresponding change on the part of the animal form if it is to survive. If we grant these indefinite variations, we may assume that through them some forms will be better able to adjust themselves to new conditions, and so new forms may arise.

Here, you see, you have simply variations from behind, indefinite variations due to the very processes of reproduction. Given the changes which are taking place in the environment as a result of geologic and climatic influences, it is possible to account for the development of plant and animal forms in mechanical terms. One could, in this way, get a picture of a mechanical universe which was governed by absolute laws which determined where all physical particles would be and therefore what all the physical things would be and everything that they would be doing, and, finally, every change that took place. It was a picture of such a complete universe as this, with its fixed laws, that is, in a certain sense, a counterpart of the picture of a fixed order of society which grew out of the Manchester doctrine and was formulated by Karl Marx as the basis for his socialist doctrine. Both of them belonged to their period.

The physical doctrine went somewhat the way of the economic doctrine. In the first place, there were, as I have already indicated, fields of experience, of nature, which could not be brought under the terms of masses in motion. Light, for example, presented serious difficulties. It was recognized as answering to some sort of wave process. The corpuscular theory, which Newton accepted, had been abandoned for the time being (though it now seems to be coming back in one form in the quantum theory); and some sort of a wave theory was found to be best to account for the various phenomena of light. Well, if light is a wave, it must presumably be a wave of something. Sound could be resolved if we noted waves of air. One could follow the waves on the ocean, in the water; and, in fact, the theories of light made use of the laws of wave motion as they could be investigated in liquids and gases. The assumption naturally was, then, that there was something in motion, something answering to these so-called "waves" of light. It was called "ether." The term is one which goes back to old Greek speculation, though it had a different meaning there. This ether did not exhibit itself in any other phenomenon so far as known at that time. It was a substance that science set up *ad hoc* for a particular purpose. The waves were not discovered in the moving ether, but the mathematics of wave motion was one which best answered to the phenomenon of light. So ether was set up as something within which the waves might occur.

When it was set up, however, it had to be fitted into the physical doctrine of the time. If it was a substance, it itself presumably moved. If all the planetary bodies were moving through it and the stars as well, it ought to respond to their motion. If you set up a body moving through water, you not only cause waves but affect the motion of the body itself. This is true of all known liquids and gases. But no measurements made have ever indicated any retardation of the motion of the heavenly bodies on account of the friction of the ether. There was no evidence which could be found of this ether being dragged along except, perhaps, in one instance. In studying the velocity of light passing through a moving liquid, it was found that its velocity was somewhat reduced; and at that time the first assumption that could be made for the reduction was that the ether was being swept along with the moving water to some degree. But apart from that, no evidence was found that ether was carried along with the earth which was supposed to be passing through it. Of course, if it were, it would affect the line of light coming from the stars and should lead to a displacement of their visual position. But no such displacement could be found, so it was very difficult to place ether in the mechanical theory of the universe. It was thought of as a something that moved; but if it was a something, it ought to have inertia and ought to exhibit itself in responses which it offered to bodies moving through it, responses in the form of resistance. And it did not do that. It could not very well be defined. When men came to define the waves which arose in, or traveled through, this suppositious ether, they found that they had to define the ether itself; and they got some very strange definitions. It was perfectly elastic, and yet how could you have such a body as that and fit it into any of the physical theories of the time? Thus it is seen that ether presented a very serious difficulty in the field of the physical sciences.

Then came the phenomenon of electromagnetism. Of course electricity, in one form or another, had been known for an indefinite period. But it was only to some degree in the seventeenth, mainly in the eighteenth century, and in the nineteenth that any scientific study of it was made. This study revealed a phenomenon that approached light in its form. Maxwell proceeded to deal with ether itself in terms which brought light and electricity into the same field. Hertz carried these speculations through and put them to experimental tests and showed that the electrical wave was of a type similar to the light wave. Then, of course, the field of electricity became one of the most exciting fields of scientific investigation. There were, however, various anomalies in it too: first, one in regard to ether, and a further one, in that the element to which one could reduce electricity under certain conditions was atomic in character. In further investigations men came back to ultimate elements, those out of which the electron has arisen. That is, you have a statement of electricity in terms of waves and also in terms of ultimate particles, bits of electrical jelly of some sort which act like physical particles under some conditions. Men found themselves driven to these different statements of electricity to account for various aspects of the total behavior of electrical phenomena. I have said later investigation has carried this same opposition within light itself. Certain phases of light, brought out by the quantum theory, are dealt with from the standpoint of ultimate elements; others, from the point of view of the wave theory.

In other words, within physical theory itself, apart from animate life, the rigid doctrine was breaking down. The laws of Newton within the world of mass and motion were invariable. They could be applied under all conditions, so far as they could be stated. The laws which Maxwell worked out for light and electromagnetism were found not to be invariable. Problems and difficulties of a serious character arose, then, in pushing the scientific theory into this new field. There was a field in which there seemed to be an operation of fixed laws, those of masses in motion. But a part of this field was that which had to do with the phenomena of light, electromagnetism, and electrons; and these were not amenable to those laws. What a few scientists undertook to do was to work out what changes would have to be made in the formulas of science if this variability of Maxwell's laws was to be maintained, and they reached rather astonishing results. One result was that the elements of time and space, the unit of measurement, would have to be changed as the velocity of the moving body changed. It was not advanced as a physical theory. It was simply the bringing-out of a mathematical theory which did apply to the measurement and investigation of electromagnetic and light phenomena. If these mathematical statements were worked out, a point was finally reached where the units of space and time had to be changed. From the point of view of a certain moving object, the units of length and of time would have different values from what they would have with respect to some other object at rest, or moving with a different velocity.

I want to call your attention especially to this. It was something that grew up, in a certain sense, earlier than the doctrine of relativity itself. It grew out of the necessity of giving a mathematical statement to phenomena discovered in the fields of light and electromagnetism. In order to give a satisfactory mathematical statement to this, the scientists found themselves giving a different value to the units of space and time in accordance with the velocity with which the body was moving. The Michelson and Morley experiment had been before the world for some time. What Michelson and his colleague had undertaken to do was to show evidence of an ether through which the earth was moving. They undertook this by means of a relatively simple experiment. Of course, if light is moving along through an ether, you can also conceive of the ether as moving in the other direction from that of the light swimming through it. Now, set one beam of light moving through it in the direction of flow and another beam of light moving at right angles to that direction, as in the situation of one man rowing upstream against the current and another man rowing across the stream. Take the distance each would cover in a given time. The man rowing upstream could not row as far as the man rowing across. Thus, in the Michelson-Morley experiment it was expected that this same difference would be found; but it was not, and this negative result disturbed people. Fitzgerald made the suggestion that this result would be met if we could conceive of the earth as shortened in the diameter which was in the same direction as that of the motion. That is, if the earth is moving in a certain direction, we can conceive of the diameter of the earth which lies in the direction of this motion as being shortened. If we found the diameter was eight inches shorter in that direction, then this Michelson-Morley experiment would be exactly accounted for. As you can see, the required changes are very minute. And the thing is, perhaps, not so inconceivable if you think of matter itself as being electromagnetic in character. What Fitzgerald did was simply to figure out what the shortening of the earth would be in the direction of the motion of the body itself, and he found that this shortening would be very minute. Then came the discovery that the mathematical statement which had been given to these so-called "measurements" of space and time fitted exactly into this shortening of the body in the direction of its motion. The two exactly agreed. And that was the statement which gave the basis for Einstein's statement of relativity.

What I have tried to do has been to point out that we have lines of development here which had been going on inside of the physical theory itself. Relativity is a statement that has grown up in the midst of it, not something that has been put down upon a physical doctrine from the outside. It is a natural development within the theory itself. It has been changing. Here, again, we have a parallelism between the physical theory and the economic theory. You start off with the assumption of certain fixed laws which operate in nature, or in production and distribution. Then you undertake to build up a theory of the universe or of society on the basis of these, and you find that there are various things that happen that do not fit in, and you have to reconstruct your theory to deal with these situations. The same thing, in a sense, happened in physical theory that happened in economic theory.

Back of this development of science lies the vast difference between a research science and any dogmatic statement of the world. If you say within any science, "This is the way the world is to be explained, and inside these limits you can carry on your investigations, but you must not carry your problem-seeking beyond them," the scientist is up in arms at once. He insists that science can find its problems anywhere. He insists that he can set up any postulate which will enable him to solve his problems, and that that is the only test that can be brought in, the only criticism that can be made. Science is tested by the success of its postulates. It brings its hypotheses to the test of experience itself; and if this test is met, then the doctrine is one to be accepted until some flaw can be found in it, until some new problem arises within it. There is, then, an inevitable conflict between a view of the world which is dogmatic and the method used by science. Any dogmatic theory of the world is found to be in conflict with the scientific method. On the other hand, we must not assume that because science makes postulates it is itself dogmatic. Of course, that is the charge very frequently and very unjustly made against science. Because science sets up such a postulate as that of the possible mechanical statement of what goes on in the world, it is accused of setting up a dogma. But it simply says that, if we start off with the mechanical process in explaining digestion, for example, we will try to carry it through in this fashion. If we cannot do this, we will try to find another explanation. But until we fail, we are justified in setting up such a postulate. The postulates of science are not dogmas; and as long as science can pursue the solution of its problems in this fashion, it is entirely justified in setting up such postulates. It is very important that we should realize the difference between a dogmatic science and a research science, between dogma and postulate. We should realize what is meant by the demand for scientific freedom: that every problem that arises may be freely attacked by the scientist; that he is justified in setting up any postulate which will enable him to solve that problem; and that the only test which shall be made is the success of his solution as determined by actual experience itself.

Now, science, with its demand for freedom, is the outstanding fact not simply of the nineteenth century but of all thought since the Renaissance, for modern science brought in the Renaissance itself. A definite method was introduced at that time. Galileo in his study of falling bodies gives a classic illustration of what is meant by "research science," and that has been the method which has been applied in a wider and wider field; and, just so far as it is brought in in any field, it has found itself in conflict with fixed dogma. And, so far, science has always been successful in its conflict with dogma. But we must not assume that in this conflict science is putting up its own dogma for the purpose of ruling out that with which it is in conflict. Science is simply setting up postulates, and it is justified in setting them up until someone can show they are not tenable; and then it is perfectly ready to abandon them and to adopt any other which will lead to the solution of the problem in connection with which the difficulty is presented.

The mechanical doctrine which was dominant in the scientific world of the nineteenth century was that of Newton, with its conception of a mechanical process which could be determined by laws of nature which presumably were inevitable and invariable. It took account only of the position of physical particles in their relationship to each other as a whole. It did not deal with the values which objects directly have in our experience—those of sensation, for example, color, sound, taste, and odor. But even as important, and perhaps more important, it did not deal with the characters which belong to living organisms. It simply stated the relative position of all physical particles in their relationship to each other. In this doctrine there was no reason for cutting out certain groups of these particles and dealing with them as separate objects and finding in them a content, a meaning which belonged to them themselves such as is found in all living forms. What this science did do, however, and it is well always to keep this in mind, was to state certain fixed conditions under which these phenomena could appear. Take the phenomenon of life, for example. The physical and chemical sciences could state what the conditions are under which life as we feel it, see it, know it about us, can arise. In so far, of course, it gives us control over the process of life. It is a statement of a mechanical, as over against a teleological, view of the world. It reduces the world simply to a congeries of physical particles, atoms, and electrons; it takes all the meaning out of it. That would be an unjust account of reality, for the development of science has always gone hand in hand with the determination of the conditions under which other characters could appear. We never could have had the advances which we have had in hygiene and medicine but for the mechanical statements which are given in physics and chemistry. We never could have got as close as we have to the life-process as a whole if it had not been for this physical and mechanical statement. From the time of Bacon on, the slogan of science has been, "Knowledge is power." That is, what we learn about nature enables us to control nature. Or, to use another of those expressions that belong to that period, "We can control nature only by obeying nature." Thus, while the mechanical science seems to have presented a world the meaning of which was all emptied out, with nothing but physical particles and their movements remaining, it has actually enabled us to get far greater control than we ever had before over the conditions under which men live as biological, psychological, and social creatures. Thus, it helped to make the ends of social activity much clearer. It is that point to which I wish to draw your attention especially, a point which we must continually keep in mind. Really the mechanical science of this period has not mechanized human conduct. Rather, it has given freedom. Humanity was never before so free in dealing with its own environment as it has been since the triumphs of mechanical science. The ability to look at the world in terms of congeries of physical particles actually has enabled men to determine their environment.

A simple review of the conditions with reference to health, to disease, shows what has been accomplished in these directions by means of scientific method. As I have already said, the food environment is one of the greatest factors in changes which have taken place in the evolution of living forms. Man has reached the point where he can conceivably control his food environment. He is, of course, the only living form that has reached that stage. Curiously enough, we find small beginnings of it in the society of the ants—the beginnings of cultivation, the planting of mushrooms and other plants in their galleries, the importing and conserving of certain insects which supply them with glucose. This seems like the beginnings of human agriculture. But human society has actually, or may actually, determine what vegetation may grow about it. We cannot change the climate, but we can move about. We can get the products that come from the various climates. We are in a position such as no animal form has been, namely, that of controlling specifically the environment in which we live. From the point of view of a Darwinian evolution the various forms have arisen very largely through the changes that have taken place in the environment, climatic and biologic changes, the conflicts that have arisen among vegetable forms; and all these changes have given rise to new species. There we have the species more or less under the control of the environment. But when we reach the human form, we have one which determines what the environment shall be. It cannot, of course, plant wheat in the Sahara Desert; but it can determine what quantity of wheat shall be produced and where it can be grown most successfully. It can measurably control the flow of its streams. It can, to an amazing degree, determine what are the conditions under which life shall take place. There we reach a certain culmination in the evolutionary process. Other forms are more or less under the control of their environments. But the human form turns about and gets control over its environment.

What has given it that control in the great degree in which it has been accomplished in these last three centuries has been the scientific method, which has found its greatest expression in the so-called "mechanical science." It is the scientific method by which the human form has turned around upon its environment and got control over it, and thus, as I have said, presented a new set of ends which control human conduct, ends which are more universal than those which have previously guided the conduct of the individual and of mankind as a whole —the ends, for example, and the policy of the government, of a group of governments, conceivably of the whole human race. The human race can determine where it will live, what plants and trees shall grow there. It can determine its own population. It can set up a definite ideal as to what human stock shall be bred, what the production shall be. It can definitely set about making its own habitat and living in that habitat in accordance with ends which it can itself work out. That has been the result of the application of scientific method. It does, in a very marked degree, you see, alter the outlook of society. It has tended to make a universal science.

This carrying-over of the conceptions of the physical and mathematical sciences into biology, the working-out of some of the most important phases of the life-process in mechanical terms, the statement of that process from its beginning in the transformation of carbonic acid gas into starch all the way through the plant and animal forms up to its final appearance in dioxides, is a most important part of the scientific period we have been discussing. This statement implied, as we have seen, that the whole process could be stated in mechanical terms or in terms of mechanical science. The process is very intricate; and it is not actually possible, at least it has not been up to the present time, to follow its phases out in detail. But, beginning with a process which could be stated mechanically, and terminating in the same, it was fair to assume that the whole process could be so stated. Furthermore, we have seen that Darwin's hypothesis made it possible to deal with the formation of species in terms of natural causation. All that was needed for this was the hypothesis which Darwin assumed, namely, the indefinite variation of young forms, the presence of far more forms than could actually subsist, a condition which brought about competition for existence. This seemed to be all that was necessary in order to account for the formation of the species themselves. Agriculture and the breeding of farm animals and of sport animals had indicated the very great pliability of the forms under the influence of selection. Nature seemed to provide such a selection in the competition for existence. The importance of these points of view, as I wanted to bring out, is that of the carrying-over of the mechanical sciences into the field of biology. Of course, it left vast stretches which could not be worked out; but it made such an assumption a perfectly legitimate hypothesis for the purposes of research.

CHAPTER XIII

MODERN SCIENCE IS RESEARCH SCIENCE

I T IS, of course, the research attitude which distinguishes our modern science. It has flourished more intensively in the last century and a half than ever before. There is one phase of it that I wish particularly to point out in this connection. Research science approaches certain problems. It does not undertake to give a systematic account of the world as a whole in any specific field. In the earlier period the function of science seemed to be that of presenting a systematic account of the universe, including all living forms; and great interest was centered in the mere statement of classes, families, genera, and species. Interest centered in the picking-out of the proper types, the selection of those characteristics which were best adapted for classification. But the interest in science shifted from that over to research work. Here we are thinking of biological science in particular. This is, however, true of all modern science. The research scientist starts from a specific problem that he finds as an exception to what has been regarded as a law. Given such an exception, he undertakes to present a hypothesis which will lead to the solution of the problem. His work, then, starts with the problem and ends with its solution. Now, what is involved in the solution is that the exception itself shall be accounted for, that a new statement shall be given which will overcome the opposition which the problem suggests.

The illustration of this process that I have often used is that of the sporadic appearance of a contagious disease. Before we knew about the microörganisms that carried the disease, it was assumed that the disease was carried by actual contact. A sporadic case is an exception to the rule. Where no person has the disease there can be no contact. The sporadic case, then, is an exception. Now, the scientist starts off with a given point of view, a given theory, a given technique; he finds an exception to this; then he sets about forming a hypothesis which, on the basis of facts which he gathers together, will enable him to connect this exception with the other facts which are recognized and which can be established. Such a hypothesis was that of a microörganism which can bring disease, which itself is carried by a stream of water or in milk, or in some such fashion. This is a satisfactory illustration of the research method. It starts from an exception and undertakes to fashion a hypothesis which will bring these conflicting causes into relationship with each other.

The research scientist does not guarantee the conceptions with which he starts. He has worked on the theory that an infectious disease of some sort goes from one person to another. The common theory had been that there must be actual contact between the man who has the disease and the person who catches it. The scientist accepts this theory for the time being, but only as a postulate. He does not accept it as something to be taken in a dogmatic fashion. He accepts the clinical account of the disease, the history of it, the way in which it presents itself—accepts it from the point of view of the science of the time but not in a dogmatic fashion. He is perfectly ready to find problems in all phases of his theory. In fact, the research scientist is looking for problems, and he feels happiest when he finds new ones. He does not cherish laws and the form in which they are given as something which must be maintained, something that must not be touched. On the contrary, he is anxious to find some exception to the statement of laws which has been given.

Science starts with certain postulates, but does not assume that they are not to be touched. There is no phase of the world as we know it in which a problem may not arise, and the scientist is anxious to find such a problem. He is interested not merely in giving a systematic view of the world from a science already established but in working out problems that arise. This is the attitude of research science. What I particularly want to point out is that the assumptions which lie behind this science are only postulates. We assume, indeed, that the world is ordered in accordance with law, that processes in it are uniform. Otherwise, of course, the world would not be knowable, at least not in the sense in which science knows it. We know the world in terms of laws, but we do not assume any certain laws to be the final formulation. We expect these laws to be continually changed. We would think any science barren which did not in one generation give a different view than that held by the generation before. And, if that difference is a fundamental one, we think science just that much more productive.

The distinction between the scientific postulate and the dogma is the distinction between research science and the science of Aristotle. Aristotle stated that it was the nature of a heavy body to tend toward the center of the earth. He set that up as a dogma, as his particular definition of a heavy body. From that he could deduce any logical conclusion—for example, that the heavier the body the greater the tendency toward the center of the earth. If that is the case, then the velocity of the falling body must be proportionate to its weight. There you have a solution of a problem in a dogmatic fashion, deduced from a dogma.

The scientific method is aptly illustrated by the procedure of Galileo. Questioning in his mind, from instances he had seen, whether or not this conclusion of Aristotle was true he took bodies of different weights to the top of the leaning tower of Pisa, dropped them, and found that their rate of fall was not in proportion to their weight. Then he set up apparatus to discover whether or not he could find a law in accordance with which they did fall. He did not start off from a given theory which stated what the nature of the falling body was and then undertake to deduce from that what its velocity must be. Rather, he undertook to find out just what the velocity was, to see if it agreed with this law or not; and, when it did not, he set up a hypothesis that the velocities of falling bodies vary with the time of their fall. With as accurate an apparatus as he could produce, he found that his results accorded with that hypothesis. It became, then, a theory, if you like, to take the place of the older Aristotelian dogma.

From the point of view of the scientist, Galileo's theory is a postulate. He does not set it up as a statement of the nature of the body, as Aristotle did. Galileo set it up as his postulate because it agreed with the facts. If, however, later observations should show that it did not agree, then any scientist would be only too glad to change the doctrine. All universals used by scientists are postulates of this sort which are accepted as long as they are in agreement with the facts. When they differ from the facts of observation, they have to be reconstructed. We can say, then, that science deals with hypothetical universals. Its conclusions are hypothetical propositions. If such and such a law holds, such and such a result must follow. But scientific research does not attempt to establish the law as something absolutely given.

Of course, the old medieval attitude had been that of a giveis form or statement of causation, a science inherited from Arntotle. And when Galileo suggested that bodies fall with velocities not in proportion to their weight, he was regarded as a heretic. From this you can see that the change in attitude which research science involved was very profound. While it starts off with certain assumptions, these are regarded only as postulates, and nothing more. They have no inherent virtue, no inherent authority.

One of the basic postulates of the scientific view which I have been presenting was the mechanical character of the universe, the assumption that we can, for example, state the whole life-process in mechanical terms. Such an assumption is a postulate which the scientist makes, but it is only that in his eyes. He is entirely justified in using it in that capacity until he can hold to it no longer. The conflict, so far as there is one, is between a mechanical and a teleological view of the world. This conflict has become peculiarly acute in biology.

If you are dealing with the force of a stream of water, you look at it from a mechanical point of view—so much energy at this point, the water falls so far, and so much energy is developed below. That is an account which is a posteriori, from behind. However, if you undertake to deal with such phenomena as the digestion and the assimilation of food, you start off with the assumption of a certain function to be carried out. This function is what would be called, in terms of an Aristotelian science, a "final cause." All this apparatus is there to accomplish a certain purpose. If food is taken in, it must be digested before it can be assimilated. The apparatus is there, then, for this function. We set up the end as something which is there to be carried out in order that a certain result may be reached. In biology we proceed with mechanical causes, but we have to have final causes in our interpretation of these. If we try to go into the actual digestive process, we have to have recourse to the chemical laboratory. We assume that the sort of organism in question has to perform a certain function; but when we come to state the operation of this function, we do not state it in terms of final causes, but in mechanical terms. We want to show that, if we have certain chemical substances present in certain combinations and we add other substances, a certain change must occur which will lead to such and such a result. That is, you explain the process from behind. You do not say, "This must be digested, therefore it must be changed in such and such a way." You say that this food is brought into contact with certain substances and that therefore it must change. You get an explanation that lies behind instead of in front. That is, you have a mechanical, instead of a teleological, explanation.

Another illustration of the difference between a teleological and a mechanical explanation is found when you set about to account for a certain murder and you say that the man who had an interest in the death of the murdered man was the cause of it. It is the end which the man had in view. That is the explanation of what takes place. If, however, the physician who is called to account for the murder does so, he says a bullet entered the body in a certain way and led to a given result. There you get the mechanical statement, a statement in terms of cause and effect. This effect is caused by another effect, and so on. You have a set of causes and effects which follow one another. If, on the other hand, you are interested in the case as district attorney, you look to ends, rather than to causes and effects—ends which the murderer had in view. The latter wanted the person's life insurance or his property. That end, the attorney says, explains the murder. That is, he gives a teleological explanation, while the doctor who performs the autopsy gives a mechanical explanation.

In biological science you bring in both these points of view. We say that, in order for the plant or animal to live, it must digest food that it takes in. This is an end that it must accomplish. Then you try to show how this takes place; and to do so, you make use of a mechanical explanation. Well, the two points that I brought out, that of the possible statement of life-processes in mechanical terms and an account of the origins of species, seem to take away the necessity of a teleological explanation. If you could make a complete statement in mechanical terms, you would not need to bring in the teleological explanation at all. If you can show just what the position of all the physical particles is, what changes they must go through, what motions will take place, what reconstructions will occur, you finally get a statement which you can understand, and one which does not involve ends. The teleological statement, on the other hand, in a certain sense, sets up your problem for you. The animal has to digest his food. How does he do it? The manner is stated in mechanical terms, but the problem is teleological. Now, supposing you could carry out the whole process of living in mechanical terms, you would not have to bring in a teleological statement at all.

That is the basis of the objections which have been offered to the so-called "mechanical sciences"; they take the meaning out of life, take out its end or purpose. And this objection, of course, was made all the more vivid in the contention over the idea of evolution. Here, seemingly, you have a mechanical explanation for the appearance of species and of their different organs. All you ask for is a set of indefinite variations, a competition for existences, a changing environment. All these can be explained mechanically. Presumably, you can show, or at least Darwin assumed that you can show, that every form must vary in some way from its present form, and also that variations could be handed on to the next generation. Of course, this assumption has been questioned. But it is the assumption which Darwin's doctrine carried with it. It was necessary to recognize the fact which every biologist did recognize, namely, that more young forms are born than can possibly live. Consequently, there must be a resultant competition for existence. You have to recognize this competition that biology, together with geology, points out, namely, that the environment is constantly changing, so that the adaptation of a form to one environment does not adjust it to another. There you can explain the origin of new forms by means of causes which lie behind. You do not have to say that there is a creator having an idea of a form and then fashioning it after that idea of his in order to carry out some purpose which he has in mind. You can simply show that causes operating in a certain way will lead to the appearance of new forms, and so you can explain the latter mechanically.

It was that which led to the very vivid fight over evolution, a fight which still continues in some parts of the world. Now, what I am emphasizing is that such an appeal to a mechanical explanation is a postulate that science makes. Its fundamental postulate is that the world is knowable, and, if so, there must be a reason for everything, and this reason will have a universal form. Of course, science has to make that assumption, for it is its business to know. Therefore, it must postulate that things are knowable. And knowing is finding uniformities, finding rules, laws. But we do not assume that the laws we have discovered are the statements which persons are going to accept later. We expect to have these laws changed. Now, one of the assumptions that the biological sciences make is that they can give a mechanical explanation to what goes on in the life-process. Perhaps they may be mistaken about this. If they are, they will be just as ready to recognize that as they are to recognize any other exception. But it is a natural and a perfectly legitimate postulate. We must go on assuming that we can give physical and mechanical statements for everything that takes place inside of us until we cannot accept these statements any longer. We must make that postulate, but we must make it a postulate and not set it up as a dogma. As long as we accept such a statement as a postulate, we are entirely justified in it. For it has been supported by the successes, the achievements, of science. It opens a door to the understanding of the world.

There is, then, no real conflict between a mechanical and a teleological account of the world or of the facts of life. The scientist who approaches the problem of digestion inevitably undertakes to make a chemical statement of what goes on. He still takes the attitude that starches are digested so that the life of the form may be maintained. That is, he states the process in teleological terms. Of course, if he carries evolutionary theory still further, he can say that this so-called purpose is nothing but a mechanical process of the survival of one form over another. But the particular form in which his problem arises is teleological. How does the digestive process go on that does enable life to continue? Take the question of the secretion of the various glands of the body. What we assume is that the various processes that are taking place there have to result in a nice adaptation to the conditions of the life-process, and that the stimulation that comes particularly from the ductless glands is essential to carry this out. We see that certain of the secretions, such as that coming from the pancreas, enable the blood to carry more sugar and to carry it in a form in which it can be most readily turned into energy. The animal must expend energy rapidly. The sugar in the blood enables him to do that most readily. But in order for it to be there, for it to be available, the system has to be tolerant of sugar. Therefore you have to have the pancreatic secretion. You see, you set the process up in teleological terms and then explain it by finding actual chemical processes that take place. You get a statement which starts off in teleological form, and then you give a mechanical account of it.

Science does not feel any conflict in such a statement. The scientist is perfectly willing to accept the problem, and he looks forward to as complete a mechanical statement of it as is possible. And he is perfectly justified in setting up this point of view until it breaks down. He can say that, theoretically at least, a mechanical statement can be made of the whole world. But he does not necessarily assume that that will be an adequate statement. The complete mechanical statement would not take account of the end, of the purpose, to which we have referred. And that seems to be necessary to our comprehension of the world. Yet there is no conflict between that teleological statement of it, on the one hand, and the mechanical, on the other. Science does not feel any conflict there. Therefore it has welcomed every advance in mechanical science because it enables it to give a statement, an explanation, of that which is taking place. The more complete you can make your mechanical statement, the more satisfactory you can make your explanation. You must postulate that such a mechanical statement of the universe can be made. And then, if you find that it is not satisfactory, you can throw it over. But you must make an assumption that such a mechanical statement can be made.

That is the attitude of our modern science. If science were dogmatic, that is, of the Aristotelian type, then to postulate a mechanical account of things would mean to abandon definitely all final causes, all ends. We would have to set up a theory, a philosophy, a theology, which would be of a mechanical sort. That is the difference between the mechanical statement that is suggested in the ancient world of Democritus and that of research science of the present time. The scientist's use of the mechanical explanation does not carry any dogma with it. He is entirely justified in making a postulate that he can give such a statement without being involved in assuming that there is no meaning in the world beyond this mechanical statement of it. His attitude does not carry that assumption. It leaves the whole question open. All the scientist assumes is that he can make such a mechanical statement, and he gives evidence to show that he can carry it out. The result is that research science has been able to take over a mechanical theory of the world and postulate such a theory without committing itself to any philosophy based upon it.

You can find scientists who do admit such a mechanical philosophy. In the middle of the seventeenth century a perfectly definite materialism undertook to abandon everything except the mechanical view of the world, not in terms of a postulate, but in terms of a dogma. It assumed that consciousness, so-called, was nothing but a secretion, in some sense, of the brain, just as bile is a secretion of the liver, and that you could treat it as any other physiological process. It assumed that there was no end or purpose in the world, nothing but mechanical procedure. What I am distinguishing between is the postulate on the part of the scientist that he can find some statement, some explanation, some solution, of his problem and such a dogma as this that there is nothing but a mechanics of physical particles in the universe. One does not imply the other. And our science is free because it is able to make use of such a postulate without being committed to it as a dogma. What people found was that such a statement of materialistic science, when taken to be the end, did not mean anything. But, of course, it exercised a very considerable influence as late as the middle of the nineteenth century. Darwin seemed to make such a dogma all the more practicable and plausible, and you find certain so-called "evolutionists" taking such a view of the universe. For a time the question of evolution seemed to be the question as to whether, as Disraeli said, you were on the side of the monkeys or that of the angels. As for him, he was on the side of the angels! That is a silly way of presenting the situation. If you get a mechanical statement which will account for the origin of species, so much the better. The mechanical statement is a postulate you set up, and you must carry it out just as far as you can, up to the point where it breaks down. And nobody is happier than the scientist if it breaks down, for then he will have another problem. He can make a postulate without setting up a dogma. And a postulate of the mechanical account of the world is that which science sets up, but not a dogma that answers to that. In science itself, there is no attempt to set up a materialistic philosophy.

The development of science, then, during the last century, the carrying-over of the statements of physics and chemistry to everything that is going on, gave tremendous push to our understanding of the world. It also had this definite effect, to show that science could tolerate no dogmatic statement. Science does not attempt to set up a dogma, as I have already insisted; and, of course, science cannot tolerate any other person's setting up a dogma. If your theological account becomes a dogmatic account, then science cannot accept it. If you say that the world was created in six days, and that creation started at some period between four and five thousand years before Christ, as stated in Bishop Ussher's calculations, you set up dogmatic statements with which science is in inevitable conflict. Science will at once turn about and ask for a justification of Bishop Ussher's calculations, will look up documents, ask what they are, where they came from, who wrote them, and pull the dogma all to pieces. If you set up a dogma of that sort, science inevitably undertakes to find a problem in it.

The field of biblical dates is, of course, one in which we find one of the most striking applications of scientific method during the nineteenth century. It passes under the name of "higher criticism." In the form in which it appeared, it started not with the Bible but with Homer. There had been more or less discussion of the Homeric texts way back in Alexandrian days. The German schools set themselves to work on these texts and found all sorts of problems. The solution which one clever Oxford fellow gave was that the *Iliad* and the *Odyssey* were written not by Homer but by another man of the same name! But what they were at work upon was to disprove the theory that these texts were written by any one man. They showed how the works had arisen and how they became woven into the form in which we have them at the present time. And that same sort of interest was turned loose on the books of the Bible; and these fell to pieces in exactly the same way, and the authors ascribed to them were shown, many of them, to have been mythical. So the dogmatic structure of the church, its theological structure, inevitably came into conflict with science.

Thus we see that science has gotten away from metaphysical dogma as to what the nature of things is, and goes back to the ordering of events which it observes. It states its laws in terms of uniformities, but it is always ready to change any statement it has made.

The acceptance of the scientific method is the most important phase of the intellectual and spiritual life of the Renaissance. I have been indicating what follows from that acceptance of the scientific method, the method of research science. It is not possible to set up any fixed statements of the laws of nature which must hold under all conditions. All that can be said is that up to the present time we have observed such and such uniformities. We postulate that those uniformities will continue. If they do not, then we will restate the laws. Of course, a still wider generalization, namely, that there are uniformities in nature, lies back of this. In the form in which science uses this postulate it seems to have come into the Western mind by way of religious doctrine. The fundamental belief had been that the world was created by an infinitely wise and omnipotent being who must have worked in an intelligent and intelligible fashion so that everything could be explained if one were only able to get back to the fundamental situation. There was a reason for everything. That is not, for example, the assumption of an Aristotelian science, which admitted certain accidents in nature that could never be explained. There were uniformities, but there were also exceptions which were just there as brute facts. The fundamental assumption that the world is explicable is also an assumption that the world is intelligible, that is, that we can know it. Knowledge is never a mere contact of our organisms with other objects. It always takes on a universal character. If we know a thing, explain it, we always put it into a texture of uniformities. There must be some reason for it, some law expressed in it. That is the fundamental assumption of science.

The scientific statement of causation is an excellent illustration of this uniformity. Science, in its more dogmatic phase, set up a universal law of cause and effect. Every effect must have a cause; every cause, a like effect. The scientist found, however, that an attempt to define causes was most difficult—finally impossible, in the sense in which these terms had been used. What could one consider to be the cause of any particular event? Let us take again the illustration which I used before, that of the assassin killing his victim. What is the cause of the latter's death? From the point of view of the prosecuting attorney, it would be the action of the assassin himself. From the point of view of the social psychologist, it would be the influences which had led to the murderer's taking such a step as that. From the point of view of the physician, it would be the actual entrance of the bullet into the victim's body, or the breaking of a blood vessel. There are different causes; and when you attempt to define causation as such, you are in great difficulties. What science has done has been to substitute for the idea of cause as a force simply a uniformity which has been discovered in nature and which we may expect to continue. What we come back to, then, is a theory of probabilities. The different causes to which I have referred in this particular illustration are causes that are determined by different interests. The prosecuting attorney has one interest, that of convicting the guilty person. The social psychologist has an interest in determining the conditions out of which such a crime arises. The physician has still another interest in determining just what the situation within the body of the victim is, what particular vital spot has been reached by the bullet. You have sets of different interests, and each interested person selects one phase or another of the situation and labels that the cause. What lies back of all these different views is a set of uniformities: those which led, for example, to the officer's detecting and arresting the criminal; those which led the social psychologist to form his judgment as to the effect of social conditions on persons; those which led the physician to identify certain conditions of the tissues with certain results. What the cause is in each case depends upon the selection of some particular one of those conditions which is of interest to the particular individual. And we call these the "causes of the event." Generally, it is some condition which can be changed in order to bring out a different result; but you can see that, as the interests vary, the causation, in our ordinary use of the term, will vary. Well, science in its general statements is not interested in these changes which are to be brought about, but it is interested in giving the uniformities which lie back of what we term the cause, so that the so-called laws of nature are the uniformities of nature. Any particular cause is some one element, some one fact, some one event, in such a uniform series. We expect that, if that or a like event occurs, the corresponding event will follow upon it; and we fall back upon our judgment of probabilities for justifying us in that judgment.

But even that assumption of uniformity is a postulate. Science has no absolute evidence that the world is explicable. It has only discovered a minute number of the so-called laws of nature. And yet, we go on the assumption that the whole of nature is intelligible. It is a postulate upon which we act and upon which science will undoubtedly continue to act, but no absolute proof can ever be presented for it. Not even an inductive proof can be given of it. It is impossible to say that, because we have found so many instances in which the operation of nature is uniform, therefore it is probable that the whole of nature is uniform. You cannot set that up, for you are assuming the uniformity to start with. That is your major premise.

THOUGHT IN THE NINETEENTH CENTURY

You can never prove that nature is uniform by means of an inductive syllogism. But nonetheless, science sets up this postulate and will continue to set it up. Not to accept it would be to surrender the results and undertakings of science, at least in certain fields. The fact that science may not be successful in certain fields does not disprove those postulates. No one can ever really disprove this postulate of the uniformities of nature, because it may be that we have not gone far enough. We could always still recognize the possibility that there might be a reason which we had not found yet. Science in its attempt to know will always carry with it the assumption that the world is knowable. However—and I must insist on this point—it remains only a postulate, inevitable, if you like, but one for which no absolute proof can be offered.

One of the results of the freedom which this gives science is the introduction of new concepts, concepts which are recommended because of their usefulness. I have already pointed out to you the important part the steam engine played not simply in the development of industrial production but also in the development of physical theory. The theory of the steam engine was first successfully attacked by Carnot, who, you remember, conceived of the steam engine as doing work in a manner analogous to that of the water wheel. It does work because the heat may be conceived as running down from higher to lower levels. As heat "runs down hill," it performs work just as water does as it runs to lower levels. After heat has reached the lowest level, it can do no more work. Having got down below the level at which it can expand, its ability to perform work ceases. You see here that the development of this theory was introducing a new scientific conception, new at least in the form in which it was presented—a concept of work done. Carnot, bringing together the process of the water wheel and the steam engine, set up this conception of the amount of work done as that which could be used for computing these two methods of operation. Of course, a unit had to be worked out, and the foot-pound was proposed. This idea is of the amount of work done in raising a pound weight through a distance of one foot. You could do that by means of the water wheel or by means of the steam engine. Then, answering to that unit, Carnot set up the idea of energy. Here is a certain amount of work done—done, of course, in very different ways in the two mechanisms—but a common result is achieved. As a means of computing the results of these two operations, Carnot, and those who carried out his theory, set up this conception of a unit of the amount of work done, and then they set up a supposititious energy that answers to this. There must be a certain amount of energy responsible for doing this amount of work, no matter what the type of mechanism used. It is a very interesting illustration of the introduction of a new concept answering to a new scientific situation.

Of course, back of this new concept lay the ideas of force. If you go back to Newton's mechanics and ask what a force is, you are told that it is a cause of motion. If you try to state that cause, you have to state it in terms of other motions; and a force remains outside the field of your actual observations. Of course, you can observe all the various motions. But energy, you see, is something that is set up answering not simply to a motion but to this conception of work done. This conception was really introduced in an effort to work out a theory of the steam engine. And one of the most important phases of the doctrine lies in this very conception out of which the situation arose, that of bringing together the water wheel and the steam engine as accomplishing the same thing, as having, therefore, the same energy, that is, as responsible for the same amount of work done. You think, then, of a steam engine as developing a certain amount of energy, of the water wheel as developing a certain amount of energy, the amount of energy being the same in both cases. Energy is simply something stated in terms of what it brings out, a certain amount of work. It is, then, something that can be located in one situation and in another; and it cannot only be located but it can be transferred from one to another and another and another situation. Suppose you want to produce electric light. You take the energy that is found in coal and transfer it to the revolution of your dynamo, thus changing it into the energy of an electric current, and so finally into the glowing filament. Thus, you have carried your energy from one form to another. Having set up this unit of work, having defined it in terms of energy, you can now go back and discover the energy that is responsible for a given amount of work now in this form, now in that, now in another. It is a very good illustration of the way in which scientific concepts arise. It is not simply the idea of a cause of motion which really has to be pushed outside of the doctrine of physical theory; it is a conception of something that can be regarded as responsible for a particular sort of result, that is, of a particular sort of work that is done. And then, when you have set up this relationship, wherever you can get that amount of work done, you can say you have just so much energy.

From this conception of energy which could be transformed and found now in this form and now in that arose that great generalization of the nineteenth century, the conservation of energy—that there is always just so much energy only it takes different forms. If you can find this energy now in one form, now in another, then all that has happened is that it has been transformed. In a sense this law of the conservation of energy was proved. If you make this postulate, you can show in any particular system which you set up that the same amount of energy is present throughout the whole process. That is, a number of instances are given of a certain system in operation, and it can be shown that the amount of energy in that system is constant no matter what different forms it may take. I want to point out this instance and put it in your minds along with the other great generalization of the century—the hypothesis of evolution.

What I have been saying about the scientific method applies also to the social situation, and makes it possible for the whole community to grasp the ends of the community as a whole and to make those ends the interest of the individual. That is conceivable and, as we shall see later, is the basis not only of social relations but of the appearance of selves. This community of ends is often achieved. For example, in the matter of hygiene, let the whole attention of the trained staff of the community be turned toward the care of the health of the individual and you reach the health of the community. And you can only reach the health of the individual adequately by reaching the health of the whole community. Save the individual, and you cherish the good of the community. And you can accomplish the latter only by saving the individual. This is the ideal of Christianity, only in this case it must be the salvation not of the soul but of the body.

The result of such a movement as that which we are considering is to get away from the abstractions which are involved in this separation of soul and body, of mind and body, of the spiritual and the physical. It is a phase of the influence of the scientific method that I want to emphasize as over against the seeming mechanical character of science. On the face of it, as I say, it presents absolute necessity, a law which determines where every physical particle should be at any moment throughout the whole history of the universe. While this seems to be a prison house for any intelligent effort, what it actually serves to do is to present the apparatus for the control over the environment and for bringing larger and larger ends and ideals within the vision of humanity. It is that side of it I wish to bring out before I leave this seemingly mechanical science.

I now want to turn briefly to a discussion of the general philosophical effect of this development of science. What I was emphasizing was the scientific method and its import. In the first place, that brought men back to observation. You remember that the scientific problem is one that arises out of the exceptional event, something that is contrary to laws as they have been accepted, so that attention is directed toward observation and toward a statement of the so-called "fact" in terms of the problem that arises. It is well to recognize that observation is not simply an opening of one's eyes and seeing what there is about, or opening one's ears and listening to what may occur. It is always directed by some sort of a problem which lies back in one's mind; it always expresses an interest of some sort. We are looking for something that is relatively novel. What we are trying to find are facts which are of the same sort as those which have been noted. Now these facts always represent possible or implicit problems with which science deals. We speak of them as "hard facts," because they have been hard enough to break down some law, some accepted idea.

For example, take the situation underlying the problem of perception. You recognize an acquaintance on the street, start to speak to him, and then find he is not the right man, after which you know there are differences that you did not note at first. Now those differences represent the problem to you, the problem of why you should have mistaken this man for your friend. They are hard facts, they defeat the anticipated conversation which you are going to have. They defeat the meeting with the friend. You have run up against an obstacle. When you recognize an acquaintance, you pay no more attention to the actual features than is necessary for the recognition of the person, that is, for allowing your conversation to go on. There is no purpose in giving attention to more than that. You just want enough to assure yourself that he is the person you think he is. But, when you have started to speak to him and find he is somebody else, then the differences stand out and you remember how your friend really looks, and you wonder why you should have made such a mistake. Or you recognize certain likenesses.

That is the character of the so-called "hard fact." And the scientist is continually noting that which departs from the accepted view, the given laws. With him it is not a disappointment but an achievement, a new problem to work on. He approaches it with interest and excitement. It is a discovery of something that is an exception to the view that has been held; it is the getting of something novel. These facts, then, arouse interest and observation. And they not only do that, but they lead to the formation of a technique of observation. I have said that scientific observation is not simply the opening of one's eyes and seeing things as the images happen to fall on the retina. What it is, is the recognition of the relationship of those things which you see to the customary view. And you have to examine facts from that standpoint. That is, you have to state them in the form of a definite problem. In the case I have just given from perception, you note that which makes you certain the person you meet is not your friend. You have to make that definite and clear. It might be an acquaintance who had had a long illness, so that you hardly recognize him. You have to assure yourself whether it is or is not the friend. You bring the images, the facts, into relationship with your customary intercourse. And then you may go to see what the likenesses were that led you to make the mistake. Now, when you come to the scientific situation, you have the so-called facts before you in terms of their exceptional characters. And you have very carefully to define in what that exceptional character consists.

The illustration of the sporadic case of the infectious disease, to which I have referred, shows this. You have believed, up to the appearance of this problem, that disease was conveyed by contact with someone who had it. Now you have a case in which there is no contact. Your observation forces you, under these circumstances, to make absolutely certain that there was no such contact. You have to comb the neighborhood. You have to make sure that the person who has now come down with the disease was not a stranger who brought it from elsewhere. You have to determine very accurately that this is an exception to the law. You have to state the case in terms of the law and show that it is an exception to it. And then, when you have that stated, the first thing you do is to look around for other instances. Now you have a way of defining your facts in terms of this law, and you look for other sporadic cases and put these down. This means that as a part of scientific method you must observe that which runs counter to the currently accepted laws.

To do this you give a very careful definition of the exceptional instances in terms of the law, so that your observation is of certain particular characters. And given these, you are able to gather all other similar instances. This enables you not only to state your problem exactly but also to insert, so to speak, the negative form of your hypothesis. It states your problem for you: How does this sporadic case, or rather these cases, mapped before me, arise in a district in which there were no other instances of the disease? The reason for it, presumably, will have something to do with the distribution of the cases, for these persons have contracted the disease in some unknown manner. There must be a common cause. You have no hypothesis, as yet, as to what the cause is; but it must be a cause which can operate in this series of instances. Therefore, you must have a hypothesis which fits in with the facts.

This is what the scientific method of observation consists in: it is the observing of that which runs counter to accepted opinion, current laws; it is the statement of the so-called facts in terms of their exceptional character; and then a gathering of all other facts that you can get hold of which are of the same sort and which will show you something of the nature of the hypothesis that may possibly meet that situation. You find that the cases of a disease are all located along a river. Then you can say that the infection is very likely one which has traveled along a water course. There you get the form of your hypothesis. If you can find some infective microörganism that can travel in water, you can test out your hypothesis. There is just as much accurate technique in observation as there is in experimentation. What experiment does is to take the hypothesis that you have formed and see if it will fit in with the facts which you have before you and other facts which you can gather. Your experiment is especially constructed so as to determine whether the hypothesis will agree with the facts. You assume that something is to be found in water. You actually isolate a microörganism; you try it on a dog to see if that particular microörganism will give rise to that particular disease in the dog. Then, having got that into the dog, you recover the microörganism from the dog itself and try it on another dog. You examine those animals which have not the disease, and prove to your self-satisfaction that they have not the organisms in their systems. So you prove positively and negatively that, where the organism is present, the disease is present, and, where not, the disease is not. But your original observation has to be as accurate as possible. You must define your facts in terms of the accepted law in order to see in what way they are exceptional. That is what we term the "scientific method."

What I was pointing out with reference to what is of particular importance from the general philosophical standpoint is that these laws which are overthrown by the facts are laws which had been accepted and have now disappeared as laws. You are undertaking to set up another law in place of the one which has been overthrown. The new law is tentatively set up as a hypothesis. You test it. When you have tested it, it becomes a working hypothesis. And if others test it and it works, it becomes an accepted theory. But, although it is an accepted theory, it is still subject to some other chance exception. That is, it still remains hypothetical. What I want to point out is that the necessary conclusions that science draws are always in the form of a hypothetical syllogism. You say this must be true—science has proved it. But if you get back to a statement by a good scientist, you will find that he is careful to say that, if these laws which have been tested by experience continue to hold, if no new exceptions appear, then such and such a result must follow. The necessity in this case is hypothetical. There are no laws of nature which are given in such a fashion that they can be made dogmas. That is, you cannot say that any law is absolute and fixed. The laws of nature, as used by science, are always hypothetical. If some exception appears, then they will have to be remade. That is the form in which all our so-called laws of nature exist in the minds of the most careful scientists. They are there as hypotheses; or, to use the expression I have used before, they are postulates. We postulate these laws; we reach certain results; we act on these results; we get the satisfaction we expected to; and we accomplish what we set out to accomplish. But new facts may arise which may make it necessary to reconstruct the postulates. We have always the private faith that any law may have to be reconstructed. Indeed, the law may disappear; but another law will be found to take its place. The law is dead; long live the law! There is always some possible reconstruction that can take the place of it. No statement that science makes is final.

We have had a striking illustration of this in the last few years in the appearance of the idea of evolution and in the modification of the fundamental laws of the Newtonian world. In both cases laws were found to be incorrectly or inadequately stated. They have had to be restated from the point of view of new experiences. We advance, then, by the use of postulates which have worked. And we continue to use them as long as they work. We can recognize that these postulates may have to be abandoned; but we also recognize that, if they are abandoned, we shall put up others in the place of them. That is the scientific method which came in and ousted the older technique, the dogmatic attitude toward the world.

There is one phase of this development to which I wish to return for a moment, that of the idea of energy. By means of it I wish to illustrate the different sources from which science gets its exceptions, or perhaps I should say the different points at which problems arise. As we have seen, in this case the problem arose out of the steam engine, which had become a very important factor in the life of the time and which made it necessary to work out a mechanical theory of it so that it could be controlled. The steam engine worked by forces which people did not understand. But what they were sure of was that there was a certain amount of accomplishment, of work done. They set up the idea of a something which was there, which could be found in coal, in the revolving wheels of the machine, in the electric current—a something there that answered to this work done. And they called it "energy." As I have said, they assumed on the analogy of the water wheel that the steam, as it flowed from higher to lower levels of temperature, did this work. Work was proportionate to the fall. The work which could be done was in some fashion proportionate to the amount of heat. So the laws of thermodynamics were worked out.

This led to the conception of entropy, the assumption that there exists throughout the whole of the universe a certain amount of energy which is in different degrees of excitement. Temperature was recognized as answering to the movement of things, of molecules, the sort of movement which we cannot see, which we cannot feel with our fingers, but which reveals itself to us in terms of temperature. Wherever there is energy, it is assumed that it is an instance of that sort of motion. Now, according to the laws of energy, this motion is all tending toward a uniform minimum in which it will be evenly distributed all through the physical universe. Where you have a great rate of motion, that motion will impart itself to the other molecules about it, and that to still other molecules, and gradually there will be an evening up. If there is more motion in one place than in another, there will tend to be a situation in which the amount of motion will be the same everywhere. Thus, temperature can be conceived of as streams of water which are all running down toward an entropic ocean, where the motion will be at the lowest degree but the same everywhere. The whole world seems to be running down toward that result.

While that conception still remains, it has lost a good deal of its interest. We are now approaching the scientific problem from another standpoint; and the conception of entropy, while still retained, has not the import that it had before. We are now stating our problems in terms of waves, not of heat. The question of entropy was one that arose out of the appearance of the machine. And, as we have seen, in a certain sense the machine dictated the conceptions which science itself should utilize. That is, industry wanted a unit that would answer to work done. Industry was interested in work. It divided its work up into single units, steps, such as the foot-pound. That became the accepted unit of work. Now look to nature, where we are seeking for forces to drive our machines, and see if you can find something to answer to this unit of work done. Society, as I said, came forward with a problem, that of controlling the forces of nature as they appeared in machines. These machines worked. If we can get a simple unit, this work can be expressed in any instance in which we find it. We will look in nature for forces which will do work, and we will state them in terms of units of force. It is very interesting to see how society set up this problem for the scientist. The former had its job on hand—that of introducing machines—and it wanted a scientific statement of nature that it could utilize for that purpose. With its task of getting a certain amount of work done, it looked into nature for something that answered to that work; and this was supposed to be energy. There might be gradation of energy. This particular telephone here at my side represents a certain amount of gradational energy. If I let it drop, it will do a certain amount of work.

From all this you see that science becomes really quite fluid instead of being a fixed dogmatic structure of the world. It becomes a method, a way of understanding the world, so that we can act with reference to it. And the problems that arise are those involved in our conduct with reference to the world. That conduct has a great many phases. It is not simply the conduct involved in driving machines. It is also our conduct with reference to other members of society. Religion, for example, undertakes to interpret the meaning of the world. It calls for a certain type of conduct on the part of those who accept religion. Science may come in to determine whether the concepts which religion embodies are in accord with what we call the "facts." It then faces another problem.

Such a situation arose, as we have seen, in the case of evolution. The accepted religious doctrine stated that all the different forms of plants and animals and physical things were given by fiat of the Creator. They were made just as they were by God, and they remained in the form that he gave them from the day of creation. Science examines the origin of species. It shows that there is no strong evidence that the forms of things arose in the creation of a day. God, of course, may have been responsible for their life; but he did not, if this statement of evolution is correct, create the forms as such at a particular moment. Well, science presented evidence to us that the forms themselves arose in the life-process, and then it came into conflict with the dogma of the church. And it was necessary that the dogma of the latter should be restated if man were going to continue to govern his conduct by science. Inevitably, in the end the dogma will have to be restated, because people are controlling their lives by science.

If you want to deal with disease and with the various technical problems presented to us—those of transportation, of communication with distant people—you must deal with them in a scientific manner. You cannot have two methods of conduct which are separated from one another. In the end your scientific conduct will be dominant, so far as dogma is concerned. It is not, you see, so much a question as to whether or not science can demonstrate a theory of the world. It is a question as to whether people are going to act in accordance with scientific technique.

I must insist again that scientific interpretation does not set up one dogma in place of another. What it sets up are postulates. It sets up hypotheses on the basis of which we act, and we will continue to act on them as long as these hypotheses work. They will be reconstructed when exceptions are found. Back of these postulates, however, lies the constant assumption that the world is intelligible. That is, if we abandon one hypothesis, we at once set about to build up another. From the point of view of dogma, this procedure would be a confession of failure. It is like people continually building cities under volcanoes: they are repeatedly overthrown, only to be built up again. But science is not stating dogma. It is giving us a method of conduct. The only thing that science accepts without question is that the world itself is intelligible. When a scientific law has been proved to be incorrect, it is reconstructed. The process of intelligence, then, is one of conduct which is continually adjusting itself to new situations. Therefore, it is continually changing its technique. That is what we mean by "intelligence": the control over conduct by past experience; the ability to adjust one's self to a new situation; adjusting one's past experience to meet this new situation. If there were no new situations, our conduct would be entirely habitual. What we term "consciousness" would disappear. We would simply become machines. Conscious beings are those that are continually adjusting themselves, using their past experience, reconstructing their methods of conduct. That is what we are doing all the time. That is what intelligence consists in, not in finding out once and for all what the order of nature is and then acting in certain prescribed forms, but rather in continual re-adjustment. The theory of evolution, you see, was a statement of this from the point of view of life.

Science, then, is not simply an advance from one theory to another, is not the erecting of a structure of laws simply to pull them down the next moment. Science is an expression of the highest type of intelligence, a method of continually adjusting itself to that which is new. You can immediately see that this attitude involves a different view of the universe from that which is presented by dogmatic disciplines. As far as our experience is concerned, if everything novel were abandoned, experience itself would cease. That is, our conduct would become habitual. Just as we pay little attention to our food, just as we walk along the street without being aware of the process, or as we carry out so many of our customary tasks without giving attention to them, so in a world without novelty that in the experience of the individual which we call "consciousness" would sink toward zero value. Experience itself would cease. Our experience involves the continual appearance of that which is new. We are always advancing into a future which is different from the past. In fact, if it were not, the very meaning of the passage would disappear. The conception of the mechanical statement of the universe which Newton gave was of a universe made up of physical particles governed by very few and very simple laws. There were movements of these particles; but they were tending, as we have seen from the conception of entropy, toward a condition of stagnation, of very slight movements. Changes were tending to balance each other; they were moving toward a situation in which there would be no change at all. That mechanical statement, as everybody felt, took the meaning out of life. If you state the world in purely mechanical terms, then you have a single law for the whole of it, and it is practically the same. The same kind of energy can be somewhat differently distributed, but it is uniform. It gives a static sort of picture of the universe. The point of view which comes in with scientific method implies that, so far as our experience is concerned, the world is always different. Each morning we open our eyes upon a different universe. Our intelligence is occupied with continued adjustment to these differences. That is what makes the interest in life. We are advancing constantly into a new universe; and, not only is the universe that we look forward into new, but, as we look back, we reinterpret the old universe. We have continually a different past. Every generation re-writes its history. Novelty reaches out in both directions from each present experience.

CHAPTER XIV

SCIENCE RAISES PROBLEMS FOR
PHILOSOPHY—VITALISM;
HENRI BERGSON

THE evolutionary phase of the scientific conception of the world got one of its philosophic expressions in the philosophy of evolution of Henri Bergson. I wish now to turn to an examination of that philosophy. Life is a process of continued reconstruction involved in the world as experienced. The new is always appearing, with the consequent appearance of new forms answering to that reconstruction. Bergson recognizes what the office of intelligence is in this immediate adjustment, and he saw that it cannot look ahead and see what the order of the world is going to be. But we have assumed that we can prophesy the future, at least in certain details. For example, the astronomer can figure out all the eclipses of the sun for a number of centuries ahead; and we utilize the same sort of data for determining certain events in the past. We can date past events from certain eclipses which occurred at certain recorded times. And we can go ahead and predict them for the future. But these eclipses are stated in terms of the laws of Newton, and these laws are being continually re-written. While the differences may be minute, the statements of the laws are not exact. There are changes taking place which those laws do not take into account. Even such fundamental facts as that of the relative motion of heavenly bodies with reference to each other cannot be stated once and for all. If the function of intelligence is to previse the future of the world, it is a failure. And Bergson took that view. He said, like all the rest of the world, we are en route to something which we cannot foresee. We do not know where we are going, but we are on our way. Intelligence undertakes to tell us where we are going, and it cannot do it. Intelligence is in that sense a failure. It does enable us to direct our immediate steps; but it cannot tell us the meaning of the world. The onward movement which we discover in it is not one directed by our intelligence. There is some force in nature, which Bergson called the *élan vital*, which is pushing us on; and yet we do not know where it is going, what it is going to do. We adjust ourselves to it at the moment as best we can. This means that we trust ourselves to that force without trying to see into the future. So Bergson decried intelligence. He was an anti-intellectualist. He undertook to show that our reflective view of the world always distorts the world. It does it in the interest of conduct, it is true; it does enable us to accomplish our daily tasks; but it does not give us the picture of the world as it is. If you ask Bergson how we are to get a picture of the world as it is, he says by means of immediate intuition. And there his philosophy becomes quite unsatisfactory.

It is the evolutionary phase of science, as interpreted in Bergson's philosophy, that we will consider first, that part of his philosophy which emphasizes the forward push, the *élan vital*. It emphasizes a progress which takes place without any given goal. I have spoken of evolution as in one sense having reached the goal of human society. There is always the relationship of form to environment. The control may be on the one side or on the other. In human societies forms are reached which do, in a very large degree, control the conditions under which they live. But, while you can say that that is a goal which in some sense has been reached; while there is always an effort on the part of every living form to control its environment, as far as it can; the ways in which that goal can be reached, by the development of sense organs, of means of locomotion and of communication, never stands outside of the process. It is reached in the struggle, in the effort to control. The form it takes is something that can never be prevised. And that is true not only of separate forms but of social development as well.

We can never tell what inventions are going to put us into closer communication with each other, what industrial methods will be worked out for closer economic connection with other people in the world, what means of communication will set us in actual intercourse with people thousands of miles away so as to make of society a universal interrelationship of people. All these are ways in which we get ahead, and not ways of approach to a given, fixed ideal. Bergson interpreted the movement of development as anti-intellectual. He assumed that reason, in the control of conduct, simply served immediate purposes. And it served them by distorting the world. Forward movement does not come from a rational, reflective element but from an impulse that lies behind, a blind impulse as far as reason was concerned. What Bergson failed to realize is that there is nothing so rational, so self-consciously reflective, as the application of scientific method to immediate conditions, and that the use of this method is just the means, under these conditions, that the human race is using for advancing. The anti-intellectualist attitude of Bergson represents a failure to grasp the import of the scientific method, especially that it puts the environment under the control of the individual. It is always true that we get ahead and keep going without knowing what the goal is toward which we are moving. But we are free to work out the hypotheses that present themselves and test them and so solve the immediate problems that we meet.

In a certain sense, Bergson's position is one which was an outcome of the theory of evolution, as I have already said. The philosophy of the Renaissance had as its background a view of nature which got its expression in Newtonian mechanics, that is, a physical world which was determined in all its movements by certain simple laws and which gave an account only of the positions of these physical particles. The result of this was the bifurcation of the world, the putting of other characters of the world of our experience into consciousness while it left the world of matter and motion to the statement of a mechanical philosophy. The doctrine of Bergson is one which implies that there is a process of evolution going on in nature, a process in which there is a constant creation of that which is new. There is in the traditional statement of nature, at least of the mechanical theory, practically nothing that is new. While there is a shifting of energies from one field to another, there is the same amount of energy, the same kind of motion and of matter. These always remain the same. And the doctrine of entropy assumes that everything is moving toward a state in which there will be practical stagnation, at least only slight movements taking place among molecular bodies. This was the picture which the mechanical view of the world gave. It abstracted from everything except matter stated in terms of inertia and the motions of these particles. In consciousness arose the various experiences of the world that we know, different objects with the sensuous characters which belong to them in experience. What the mechanical doctrine was able to do was to state the conditions under which these conscious experiences arose. But the characters which belong to objects and their nature as objects belong only to the conscious experience, if the doctrine is carried out consistently. The world itself, from the point of view of the mechanical philosophy, is simply a congeries of particles all being related to all others. There was no justification for unifying certain groups and saying that these existed by themselves. There were really only two objects in the universe: one the physical particle, the other the universe as a whole. The lines drawn between separate groups of physical particles were arbitrary, determined by the process of consciousness. The very interest which, for example, an animal would have in certain groupings of them as over against other groupings would, in Bergson's statement, be determined by his perceptions. That is, he would see those characters of the object, as this appeared in his experience, which were of importance for his own conduct. He would see that which was dangerous and would then run away. He would see food and run toward it. He would regard only those parts and characters of the physical universe which are of interest to him, so that perception would be responsible for the actual structure of the thing itself. Perception would be, in that sense, the determiner of the object.

But Bergson assumed that the nature of things themselves was to be found not only in perception but also in the world. Our thought or perception—so-called "consciousness"—really belongs to the nature of things. The conceptions that we form of things are, as he indicated, determined by the usage to which we are going to put them. We think things out in terms of plans of action. These are the characters that belong to the things themselves. We want to see the world as it is and as it will be when we are going to act in a certain way. We recognize, as fixed, the ground upon which we walk. The object toward which we are acting is fixed or moving in a certain direction. We see things as conditions of our conduct. We fix the world as much as we can, because that will enable us to act with reference to it. In reality the world is not fixed. We are simply selecting out the characters which are of interest to us for our conduct and holding them in a static condition before our eyes because the changes taking place are unimportant as far as our conduct is concerned. Actually, everything is in motion. Things that seem to be fixed are really in motion, but the motion may be so slight that it is unimportant. Or the motion may belong to a whole group of objects, so that relatively they are at rest with reference to each other. The earth is moving about the sun in this manner, but for our conduct it can be dealt with as at rest. Such a statement of things in certain fixed relations, Bergson said, was a special statement. And this special statement freezes the world, so to speak—catches it at an instant and holds it there. It is not a statement of things as they really are. They are really changing always. And their change is not simply motion from one special point to another. There is change going on within the objects themselves, just as there is change going on within ourselves; there is an inner change, and, as a result of this, there are outer changes. That fundamental process going on in all things Bergson said appears in what we call "time," or duration as distinct from space. And one of the fundamental tenets of his philosophy is that this duration, this process which is going on, can never be presented adequately in spatial terms. Any statement of it in purely spatial terms is always bound to be a distortion of reality.

When he looks for an instance of what he calls pure "duration," as distinct from mere motion in a fixed space, he goes to the inner experience of the individual. If we look inside ourselves, we find a process going on in which there is interpenetration of what takes place at one moment and what takes place at another moment. You cannot cut off your ideas, feelings, sensations, and fix them at a certain point and say that one belongs to this point and another to another point. Your feeling is something that pervades a whole experience. Such a phenomenon, for example, as a melody is illustrative of what Bergson refers to. You can deal with the melody simply as a set of notes, if you like; and you can hang those notes up on the bars and think of each note as answering to a certain vibration. But there would not be a melody if there was a sound at this moment, another at the next, and so on, each taken by itself. And if your experience was only of that sort, it would not be one of a melody. What is characteristic of the melody is the fact that the note which you are hearing and singing extends on, endures into later notes. It is a relationship between the different notes that makes up the melody. There must be an interpenetration of the different notes in order that there may be a melody, and that is what is characteristic of all our thought. Duration, as such, always involves this interpenetration, not only in the sense that what is taking place extends over into what is coming into existence and anticipates what is coming on, but also that it gives the meaning and value to things. It is the use of the table that makes a table of it. If there is no use for it, it is nothing but a lump of wood. It is our attitudes of conduct that give to even such a thing as a work of art its beauty. It is a sort of response that is aroused in us that calls out the aesthetic feeling. And in our attitude toward more abstract things, such as a concept of a table as a unit that is already there, we find that that constitutes the import of it as an object. When you cut things off and place them in special cubicles, an injustice is really being done to reality. The "knife-edge" point of view assumes that all our experience takes place at instants—instants that are not spread at all. These instants have the same relation to time that a point has to space. As a point has no magnitude, so an instant has no duration. It is succeeded by another instant, and so on. The mathematician breaks up not only space, but motion, into an infinite number of points; he breaks up the temporal phase of it into an infinite number of instants.

Now you can see that, if our experience of anything taking place was really confined to an instant, then pushed aside and another experience put into its place; if our experience was simply that which takes place at one instant and then at the next instant, and none of these instants had any spread; then there would not be any experience of change at all. Then the world at one instant would be completely wiped out by the world as it is at the next instant. There would be no connection between the two, no real duration; there would be only substitution of one instant for another. This statement of time in terms of separate instants Bergson calls a "spatial statement of time." And what he insists upon is that this spatial statement of time does not anticipate each duration as we actually experience it. What the mathematician does, you see, is to give an account of time which is spatial. If he draws a line which represents the path of a motion, one of the co-ordinates representing time, another space, he can draw a curve which determines the velocity of the moving body; he can mark off a certain point on one co-ordinate and call it a certain moment, the next point the next moment, and so on. That is a spatial statement. What is of importance from Bergson's point of view is that each moment in time includes any other, just as any point in space includes any other point in space. The exclusion of the parts of duration is what Bergson denies. They do not mutually exclude each other. If they did, duration would be nothing but a set of separate experiences which could have no temporal relationship to each other at all.

Put in different terms, but with practically the same meaning, is the statement that our experience is always a passing experience, and that this passing experience always involves an extension into other experiences. It is what has just happened, what is going on, what is just appearing in the future, that gives to our experience its peculiar character. It is never an experience just at an instant. There is no such thing as the experience of a bare instant as such. The psychologists have termed this the so-called "specious present," a term which implies that it is not a real present. It is experience dealt with as if the present were instantaneous. Of course, the present is that which is going on; it is a spatial image. To this present psychologists have hitched memory on as a memory image, and the future as another image, something anticipated; and they have dealt with these images as if they existed in an instantaneous present. You can see that your memory of something is something that exists now. You remember now what you did an hour ago. So the psychologist makes up the present out of an instantaneous experience, plus an equally instantaneous memory and an equally instantaneous anticipation, all fused into a present instant. And they say that these images, fused into an instant, give us the impression of a specious present which extends.

Well, of course, experience does extend. If you could get it into a single instant and then simply replace that by another instant, there would need to be no such thing as duration. You would be living only in the present. And the difference of the presents would be a difference not of duration but of substitution. Actually, our experience is one which includes both past and future. What is going on is something that is slipping away, plus something that is just coming up over the horizon. Part of it has just happened, part is just coming to be; and in order that it may have happened and that it may be an experience, it must be past and future. Our present is the fusion with both past and present in the experience itself. The specious present is not the present. The present is something that is happening, going on; and in this going-on what does happen is related really, actually, to what is taking place, and what is taking place is really related to what does happen. Of course, our present is chopped off into very small portions. We can represent only a few seconds perhaps. At times it is so chopped off that we cannot effectively connect the different portions of it. An illustration of this has been given of a person who is riding in a train with telegraph poles flashing by. Suppose he tries to relate these. He is counting them. They go by very rapidly. He finds himself dealing with sets of such short intervals that he cannot connect them, think of them consecutively. One experience is replaced by another so rapidly that he cannot think them separately. But if he can stretch himself out on the grass in the sun, with things moving slowly—the swoop of a bird, the wind in the trees—where there is an extension, he can get a longer present than in the railroad train. One part of experience merges into another, and you have really the interpenetration of Bergson.

This is something you do not get in a spatial statement. It is the very essence of space that any position excludes any other. A thing cannot be in two places at once. If you are going to represent time in this spatial fashion, then your experience cannot be at two separate instants. But our experience, our feelings, our sensations, are extended over our present; and one present extends over another so that there is a flow in which the past is really reflected into the future, and the future back into the past. That, Bergson says, is the nature of reality. It is not that which can be expressed in points and instants; it must be expressed in duration. And what he insists upon is that we should take time seriously. The impression we have of this continuity and of this interpenetration is not something simply to be found in consciousness while the real world is made up of happenings.

separate instants at separate points, in which the past and the future are not actually present. If the future is in the experience it influences it. That is, of course, the nature of our so-called "intelligent conduct." What we are going to do is determined by what we are doing. Our ends are there, interpenetrating all the world in terms of means. If time is taken seriously, as Bergson says it must be, then what is going to happen can actually affect what has just happened. You can get final causes into nature. The future can influence the present just as it does in our own conduct. If that is the nature of what takes place, of duration, the future can enter into it. The world is not simply a process of the readjustment of physical particles with reference to each other, a situation that remains always the same; it is a process that is going on, always moving on into a future which lies ahead of it, which is just appearing, and, as it appears, influencing what is taking place.

For example, a person finds, in crossing a street, that the automobiles are going by at great speed; and he suddenly stops or turns. It is only after he has actually stopped or turned, or means to stop or to turn, that he is aware of what it is that is responsible for his action. That is, his adjustment to what is taking place comes earlier than the impression of the situation itself. You find that frequently it is the beginning of your own motion that first apprises you of the object itself in regard to which you are moving. It is particularly true of the impressions which have reached the periphery of the retina as over against the most sensitive point of vision. We turn with reference to a moving object, and then see what it is. The motion comes first, with reference to something which is already there. But it is our adjustment to it that is first given in experience. That is the sort of picture of the world that Bergson presents. It is always moving on toward a future which is just arising. What it is you cannot tell until it does arise. But it is always coming into experience, and we are always adjusting ourselves to it, finding out what it is by the very process of change. That is the sort of evolution which is taking place, a process ceaselessly going on with continued adjustment, with a future actually affecting that which is taking place. Well, as I said, what Bergson has insisted on is that we should take time seriously, that is, that we should take into account pure duration, and that that involves not simply the past but the future as well.

The past which physical science gives us is of something that has happened. We are always looking back at something that has happened, in so far as we are observing things scientifically. The event must have taken place, must have left some definite record, must have fixed itself in some definite way; and then, after it has fixed itself, we estimate it. Scientific data are the records left. All that has happened, all that is taking place, is fixed in a spatial framework in which every element excludes every other element. But that is not the nature of reality according to Bergson's statement. From his standpoint, reality is something that is always going on, and that which is taking place is always reacting on what has taken place and acting ahead upon that which will take place. The novel is always there affecting us, always affecting what is taking place.

In a sense, of course, Darwinian evolution expressed this. Something happens and affects the form, selects out that which is adapted to the new situation. It eliminates those forms which are not adapted. This process, going on all the time, is one in which what is taking place has something of the future in it. If you take a geological picture of the world, you get a picture of it looking back over what has taken place, and the continued influence of that which is going on over the future is lost. The view of evolution which Bergson recognized is a view in which there is this interpenetration in which the future can affect the present, in which there is continued adjustment, but an adjustment which is due to what is taking place.

But this view is one which can never be given in spatial terms. What is just taking place is continually belying what we are thinking. Our thinking is just such a process of putting things into a framework as the mathematician's process of dealing with motion. In thinking, we are putting things into different cubicles and separating them from each other. It is the very nature of thought to tear things apart, to cut out the things that are important, to pick out only one particular character of the thing and relate it to something else that has the same character and then put these into the same cubbyhole. It is a process of classifying things in which we are continually breaking them up. That, says Bergson, is of service to us in our conduct; but it does not give us the reality of things.

His philosophy then, while it looks toward the future, looks toward a future that is always novel, toward a future which cannot be conceived, which cannot be presented in terms of perception. Any picture which we make of the future, as we know, is always belied by that which really happens. You go to meet somebody and anticipate the meeting. It may be a disappointment or it may be beyond your anticipation, but it is always different. You never can present it to yourself exactly as it is going to happen. You can only say that such things have happened in the past; they have had such and such a fixed character; so I am justified in assuming that the same sort of thing happening in the future will also have this character. But there is always something different. All this fixed conception can do is to direct our conduct; but when we use conceptions to give us the nature of things as such, we are always discarding them, according to Bergson. And we know that the future will always be different from anything we can actually present to ourselves, so that an intellectual view of the world, a conceptual, reflective view, is, apart from its use in conduct, a distortion. Thus, Bergson is an anti-intellectualist. The true view of reality, says Bergson, has to be got by intuition, in which you are able in some way or other to catch the something that is going on and hold on to it as a reality. He is very vague, unsatisfactory, in the picture of reality which is grasped in a sort of metaphysical intuition.

Of course, so far in this discussion I have done no more than suggest certain phases of the Bergsonian philosophy. What is of importance to us is this taking of time seriously, for in a certain sense this is an anticipation on the philosophical side of the relativistic doctrines which have set up a space-time in place of an absolute space and an absolute time. And what is also important is that Bergson's philosophy arises out of a point of view of the world which is evolutionary as over against mechanical. And evolution as such is a process that is continually going on. Bergson's term for this process is an *élan vital*. Anything that is continually going on cannot be stated simply in terms of that which can be put into an instant. What evolution has done is to present to us the conditions out of which new forms can arise. It has given us those conditions; and our thought, our interpretation, of them implies constant appearance of new forms. If we turn back to a mechanical statement of the world, what we get is simply a distribution of physical particles now at one instant and now at another. In all these situations what we have is practically the same. We have the same amount of energy, the same kind of motion. Everything is interrelated with everything else. The new form that arises means simply the redistribution of physical particles. It is only our interpretation of it that makes the new animal, the new plant, out of this shift of positions. What Bergson does is to insist that this process of change that is going on, with the appearance of that which is novel, is the reality of things, and that our philosophy of nature should be an evolutionary philosophy which takes into account a theory of change. This change involves duration. His is an approach to the interpretation of the world from the evolutionary point of view which takes into account the whole of our nature.

From another point of view we may say that Bergson's approach is the same as that of Kant.[1] You will remember that the latter found his problem arising out of the statement of Hume. Hume came back to the reality of states of consciousness but failed to find in them the world which science had been describ-

---

[1] From this point to the end of the chapter the material has been taken from class notes of Mr. George A. Pappas. They are from a course in "The Philosophy of Bergson," as offered during the summer of 1927.

ing. The uniformities of the scientific description dissolved into a succession of conscious states held together by laws of association which, being subjective, tell us nothing of the nature of an objective world. Against this Kant proposed to find the necessity for science within consciousness itself. Whereas for Hume knowledge had no other basis than that of habit, for Kant concepts were themselves essential, they were the precondition of knowledge. Prior to dealing with the spatial attributes of reality you must have a concept of space. The necessity of the great mathematic structure which was the basis of the science of the time was something that came from the nature of the mind itself. Since the mind had this formal capacity, it was perfectly possible to develop a rational and universal science on the basis of it. Of course, you will remember that this science applies only to the world of experience, the world of phenomena. There is no bridge from it to the other world, that of noumenal reality. But within the former there was necessity, uniformity, and universality, because the mind required that. The mind being what it is, these characteristics of our science could not be avoided.

Now Bergson is Kantian in the sense that he too takes his departure from the results of science and builds up his position in terms of what he sees to be the implications of these data. He, like Kant, was convinced that, while science was exact within the field of experience, there was another phase of reality that science itself could not come into contact with; and, in somewhat the same way as his predecessor, he felt that this latter was more important than the former. The fundamental distinction between the two is that the science in which Kant was interested was mathematical while Bergson turns to the implications of biology and psychology.

Mathematical mechanics, the mechanics of Newton, had broken the world up into ultimate elements. In this statement we have the universe as a whole, on the one hand, and the infinite number of particles that compose it, on the other. This view pays no attention to the particular groupings of these particles into smaller units, objects or organisms. These can be of no special interest to the physicist, because the groupings are not necessary. They are the result of the operation of certain physical tendencies, and any group that may be formed can be broken up until finally the ultimate elements are reached. When these are obtained, it is seen that the temporary groupings of them are wholly incidental from the point of view of their nature and have nothing to do with the character of the physical forces.

This is not the picture as the biologist presents it to us. It is still less the presentation of the psychologist. In biology the most important factor is the structure of the particles, not in their isolation, but as they appear as structures. Kant himself realized this; and while he was primarily interested in presenting a philosophical defense of the Newtonian science, he recognized, in the *Critique of Judgment*, that things had to be dealt with in biology which were of no importance from the physicist's point of view. The first of these was that the biologist has to conceive of particles as related in wholes; and second, that to understand these wholes, ends and purposes had to be admitted into the picture. Biology, like art, is teleological.

Kant had accomplished in philosophy what Newton had in science: he had given it complete intelligibility. That is the suggestion that came to Bergson. He found the mechanical explanation inadequate. When you turn to the world that had been unfolding under the influence of the growing interest in biological phenomena, particularly after Darwin, you find that the early statement of science is not adequate. You cannot take biological structures and describe them in Newtonian terms. Thus, Kant's intelligible world is faced with a serious difficulty. His problem must be worked out again. It is this that Bergson, in a certain sense, undertakes to do. He proposes to start with the nature not of physical but of biological and psychological phenomena.

His interest in the data of psychology indicates another root in Bergson's thought, one that goes back to Descartes. Psychology became important in the nineteenth century. It does not start with the physical particles of the mechanical statement. It starts with the organism which is there as the condition of experience. The organism in some sense is there before consciousness appears. Of course, this is not the Cartesian statement. For Descartes, mind and body were distinct substances neither of which depended upon the other for its being. His fantastic treatment of the pineal body must not be thought of as implying any functional relationship between mind and body. It was simply a device for dealing with an acknowledged situation, the reciprocal influence of mind on body, and vice versa. Not even the English empiricists saw the problem in terms of a functional relationship. Their psychology was a philosophy. It undertook to give a statement of the structure of things which at the same time left the things "out there." Hume left the world in the form of impressions and ideas, of states of consciousness. It is to this situation that the words "subjective" and "objective" ordinarily refer. But gradually a new meaning appeared. With the psychology of the nineteenth century these terms apply to a functional relationship within experience. The mind is no longer something here, something inside, which gets impressions from something there, something outside. The inner and the outer, the subjective and the objective, are phases of a single process and point to differences of perspective, not to absolute differences of locus. This new approach is that of what may be called the scientific, the "new," psychology, as over against the philosophical psychology of the earlier period. It develops out of the recognition that the physiological organism is the condition of the appearance of states of consciousness. Just as there is a functional relationship between the organism and its environment, so there is one between what is "in the mind" and what is "outside." It is a reconstruction of psychology which starts off with the assumption that there is a world "out there" and a world which is the precondition for the states of consciousness.

According to this functional point of view, the mind itself creates new worlds, not in the Kantian sense of determining the forms, the categories in which experience must be interpreted, but in the sense that each new perspective gives rise to a new creation. The mind is a part of a creative process which is responsible for the world itself. Appearing within this process, the mind is functionally related to all other aspects of it. It is no longer possible to stand by the bifurcation of the world into outer and inner.

With this new position Bergson is in hearty agreement. Indeed, in it we find one of the clues for the interpretation of his whole position. If the world out there is the condition of what is within, it brings the possibility of the within being created of what is without. Thus Bergson turns his attention to that which lies within experience; and he, like Kant, finds in this certain factors which must be dealt with before the nature of reality can become clear, before the problems of the philosopher can be satisfactorily dealt with. The thing in subjective experience to which he gives his attention particularly is its flow, that is, its temporal aspect. He finds the same thing in consciousness that the biologist finds in dealing with organisms, namely, that it is impossible to reduce either to ultimate elements. By means of this process of reduction physical science had destroyed the significance of particular objects. The world of experience, in so far as it contained wholes, was broken up into an indefinite number of elements. The world in inner experience had been broken up into a series of atomic impressions by the English empirical thinkers. In each case something is left out. In the former, it is the essential unity of certain groupings of particles; in the latter, it is a certain penetration of the experiences into one another. It is this which is of especial interest to Bergson. He goes back to his experience and finds that what takes place there is an interpenetration of experiences. Take the notes of a musical scale, for example. A melody is something more than a mere accumulation of separate tones. The E, G, C of the scale have no musical significance in themselves. It is only as they interpenetrate that they form a musical unit; it is only as the tones interpenetrate that the melody is presented.

VITALISM; HENRI BERGSON

The experience of the present moment is what it is because of what took place just before it, and of what is about to take place. That which will be in consciousness in a moment is connected with that which is present there now. All our experiences share this character of interpenetration. But it is especially true of our indefinite states of consciousness. The subjectivity to which Bergson returns, then, is one which shows us a content rather than a form. In this there is a distinct cleavage between him and Kant.

It is in terms of the interpenetration of particles in objects, on the one hand, and of elements of conscious experience, on the other, that Bergson proposes to build up his philosophy. That is, whereas Kant took his problem from mathematical physics, Bergson attacks the philosophical question from the point of view of biology and psychology. The procedure of the scientist of modern times differs from that of the ancient scientist in that the former starts from specific problems whereas the latter developed his procedure from the point of view of certain given characters. The practical significance of this is that modern science is hypothetical. It is true that Kant tried to give science a categorical form. But he did not succeed in this. Although he did not realize it, the categories, the universality, the necessity, which he set up are themselves only hypothetical. Even though the form of the laws might be universal, they were still only hypothetical in character. Galileo's statement that velocity varies with time and Darwin's statement that species have arisen under the influence of the process of natural selection and the survival of the fittest are both hypothetical.

One of the hypotheses of the mathematical point of view was that organic structures could be broken up into their ultimate particles in exactly the same way as could inanimate objects. But the biologist found this could not be done. He had to deal with his objects as individual things. The parts must be conceived in their relationship to the whole, for apart from that relationship they have no significance. In dealing with the problems of this science and with those of psychology, we cannot come to the simplicity of the mechanical statement. If we attempt to do so, we destroy the object with which we are dealing. The organism must be thought of in terms of its processes as a whole and not in terms of its particles, just as states of consciousness must be dealt with in terms of their actual interpenetration and not simply as a flow of atomic sensations each of which is distinct from, and can be dealt with independently of, others. One result of this is, of course, that neither biology nor psychology is as accurate as physical science. The mechanical science builds up the whole from the parts, and there is no reason why one whole should be built up rather than another. Biology, on the other hand, deals with wholes, and the parts have meaning only in so far as they belong to the whole. If you look at them from the point of view of physical science, they cease to be parts; they become atoms and electrons. Thus you have to pay a price for the exactness that you get in the mechanical statement.

The inadequacy of this statement of reality greatly impressed Bergson, and to offset it he turned to the nature of the process of consciousness for his clue. The terms "extensive" and "intensive" have no significance for mechanical physics. All particles are alike. Consciousness does have a definite intensity and a definite extensity. What is its inner reality? What is it that one does realize in this field of inner experience, and what is the relation of the judgments that refer to it and those which science uses in referring to the outer world? Bergson finds a number of characters which pertain to this inner world which have no significance for the outer. The most important of these are two that have already been mentioned: the experience of the interpenetration of our states of consciousness, and the reality of intensity and extensity in inner experience.

The statement that one experiences a certain brilliance has no meaning for the physicist. He cannot deal with brilliance any more than he can deal with color. Experiences of brilliance are qualitative experiences. You cannot say that your experience of the brightness of a light is equal to your experience of the combined brilliance of three lights. In regard to certain experiences attempts have been made to carry on such analyses. In weights it has been found that the addition of a certain fraction of a weight—I think it is one-fourth, according to the law of Weber—is sufficient to give you a qualitatively distinct experience. But even here it is impossible to get any constancy of statement from the point of view of inner experience. It is impossible to completely control all the conditions outside and then ask what is going on in consciousness. You have to go to consciousness directly. And when you do that, you find the elements of your experience related in ways different from those used in dealing with the outer world. The fundamental difference found between these two types of experience is that the inner experiences interpenetrate. That is, they have a span, they have duration. This sort of consciousness has a peculiar disregard for certain important philosophical problems. It ignores the epistemological difficulty. It refuses to take account of a bifurcated world. Bergson approaches the problem of knowledge from the point of view of biology, and what he finds is that knowledge answers to a stream of interpenetrating states of consciousness each of which draws into itself the nature of the past and projects its own nature into the future. Thus they achieve a span, a *durée*.

But of what importance is this duration? First of all, it determines the nature of time. Time is not simply the sum total of an indefinite number of temporal units. It is a process, and must be conceived as a process or its essential character is lost. In the second place, this being the distinguishing character of our inner experience, the relation of penetration which characterizes it passes over into the character of the object. This means, of course, that time has a new significance in the outer world. The basic philosophical question, as Bergson sees it, is this: Shall we take time seriously, shall we recognize the import of duration in experience itself? The answer which he gives to this question is affirmative. The fact of an event in the time series means the recognition of duration as a reality in itself, as something that is going on. A passage which is always taking place is the necessary precondition for the appearance of parts. You could not single out individual temporal events unless there were a continuous passage, a duration, in which they appear. Here, again, we meet the necessity of recognizing the whole as the condition of the parts. This reality which is going on, says Bergson, has to be taken seriously. It cannot be presented in terms of mathematical analysis. In the latter, all we can do is to break up the series into minute elements and look at these as points. But this is not the process. Thus Bergson tries to seize upon an inner process in reality which will correspond to the process in our inner experience.

But the mathematician will ask if Bergson has been fair with him. Is it not possible for him to take time seriously in the Bergsonian sense? Is not his description of reality one in which processes are recognized and dealt with as important aspects of the whole? Let us substitute for the older concept of space such a one as Whitehead's. The only thing that you can say about extension is that it extends over. Such a statement obviously is about a continuum. Now, a continuum can be broken up. Take this table, for example. It is a continuum; you can break it up into parts. Now add to this idea of extension, of a continuum, the idea of time as a fourth dimension. What you get then is not merely a spatial spread but a temporal spread. That is, you get duration. In this latter case we now have an actual process in nature. Thus, Bergson's insistence that duration is an attribute of inner experience only, and that since the world outside, at least as presented by science, is a static world it cannot be the source from which this inner duration is obtained, is not wholly adequate. The mathematician has presented us with a picture of a world which has just the type of spread, of duration, that Bergson says is requisite if we are to get at its real nature. The thing that Bergson dislikes in the scientific procedure is essential to it only for purposes of description and analysis. In this aspect, it is true that science, and particularly mathematics, gives us static independent particles.

For example, one of the most useful of all mathematical concepts is that of the limit. The ultimate element to which the mathematician retreats, as Whitehead points out, is the limit. As an object we deal with the table as having extension. It has not only extension in space but extension in time; its extension lasts through this hour. We conceive of the table as a part of a world of passage. It is passing; in its temporal dimension it has an extension that cannot be defined in an instant any more than its spatial extension can be defined in terms of points. But when we undertake to analyze this table in terms of certain scientific problems, we find that it can be broken up into successively smaller and smaller bits of extension. We reduce this extension by getting something that extends over, something which is apart from the table. To take the analogy of boxes, we get boxes which are contained within other boxes until we finally approach a limit. We never get the limit because we can always think of another box being within the smallest that we have thought of up to that time. Thus, if you take a certain portion of extension and consider its quantitative characters, whether this extension be of a table, an electrical charge, a momentum, or what not, you can successively take smaller and smaller portions of it. These can be constructed into a quantitative series which approaches a limit. This limit is never reached; it is ever more closely approached.

Now the mathematician does his best to state his law of the series in terms of such limits. They can never be gotten in our experience, but they can be thought. Here you are dealing with an ideal situation. The mathematician realizes that it is ideal. But he can get a better statement of what is going on in the process through this method of postulating an ideal situation which can never be found in actuality than he can by turning to the immediate process as it is going on. These ultimate, static particles against which Bergson utters so severe an indictment are ideal particles in terms of which we get the laws which we find in nature. There is no such thing as a point or an instant in the static sense. They are constructs which we use in so far as we are seeking a certain sort of simplicity, a simplicity that makes it possible to get a statement of a law. The law is discovered in the ideal situation, but it is then tested in reality to see if it works. It is taken out and put up against the object, against the process it is designed to describe. Thus, when we come back to the table, we see it described as at rest, as an object in which the particles have no velocities added to them. But after the scientist has gotten hold of his law in this way, he comes back to the table and deals with it as an object whose particles are in motion, as an object which itself revolves around the sun, for example. It is an object which has a passage. Thus we get the Bergsonian duration in the external world. It is not duration in the Bergsonian sense, because it is not duration from the standpoint of an inner experience. The duration with which the scientist deals is an objective duration. It belongs to the object. The object may be fixed as we look at it; to see it we may have to stop the process. But that reflects a limitation in our method. It does not imply that process, passage, duration, are excluded from the nature of things and made subjective.

Whitehead comes back to somewhat the same problem that Bergson faces. But, whereas the latter tries to seize upon an inner process, the former tries to present the picture without the distortion which the other emphasis implies. The world of the physical sciences, in so far as they are analytic, is a world of external relations. But that is not the picture of what lies outside us. Nature is composed of structures: atoms, stellar galaxies, tables, living beings—all these are organisms, the reality of each abiding within itself. The analysis, the quest for limits carries us back to elements out of which the whole may be thought to be built up. But these are not the whole. It is something that lies within each thing; it is a process. The characters of the object are not present without it. The atoms carry no ions unless there is a process; the living thing does not live unless there is a process. Natural science deals with a reality of such structures whose essence involves process. The reality of the atom abides within itself. It is not affected by any process of dissection, of analysis. Natural science continually brings us back to a reality in which there must be process if reality is to have the characters which belong to it. Physical sciences, even, are dealing with processes which are going on. But they find they can most effectively get hold of them by setting up ideals such as the idea of limit. Whitehead sums the whole question up by saying that any structure which we find in nature is an organism. If this statement is correct, if this is an adequate account of the reality with which the physical scientist is dealing, then Bergson's position that it is only in an inner process that we find processes as such is incorrect.

The world at an instant is a pure fiction. The natural order is an organization of perspectives. We have to recognize that these perspectives exist in their relationship to organisms. Process must be preserved as an ultimate part of reality. How the process appears depends upon the position of the organism from whose perspective it is reported. These perspectives can be got only in terms of a process in which they have their locus. All these aspects are essential to reality, the latter being nothing more than the sum total of the former. It is my opinion that you have to recognize not only the organism but also the world as having its reality in relation to the organism. The world is organized in relation to each organism. This is its perspective from that point of view. Reality is the total of such perspectives. Now Bergson is right in insisting that if there is such a thing as life or consciousness, anything to which a rhythm belongs, we have to think of this as being in the nature of reality. The point at which he deviates from Whitehead is his inability to discover this process elsewhere than in the inner experience. Bergson's point of view is justified when we realize that there is, in the physical processes, a distortion which is due not to the recognition of qualitative changes but to differences of velocity It is his desire to get inside this process, and he finds his clue in the process of inner experience as distinct from the statement about reality which is presented by the exact sciences. These sciences distort reality through their quantitative presentation of it. The real is qualitative, and you cannot get quality at an instant. It occurs over a period, whether it be color, melody, or the ionization of an atom.

For the same reason that he finds the static statements of the exact sciences inadequate, Bergson also turns away from the associational psychology. This describes the conscious life as a series of separate, distinct units. It attempts to account for the fact that a certain book happens to appear in memory through mere association; it seeks to find the causes of an act in terms of similarity, contiguity, and so forth. But this is inaccurate. Thought, as well as conduct, presumes an organization prior to its eventuation. Neither can an act be explained in terms of pleasure and pain. These belong to the end of the act. Statements of this sort are superficial. They are useful in determining certain relations of things in thought, just as the static picture of the world has its use in the physical sciences. But when you get below this surface account, you find that the mental states interpenetrate each other. You can always separate that which is characterized by this interpenetration, but the relationship of states of consciousness is not that of mere contiguity. So you see, from every point of view the Bergsonian statement is one of interpenetration. All you have is a set of processes. The real is a set of continuities.

This takes away the element of determination which has been a constant charge of the philosopher against the scientist, as Kant indicated earlier. Here Bergson turns again to an inner experience, this time to the experience of the living organism. It has freedom in the determination of its goal. The question is whether or not this freedom is an expression of an accumulative set of experiences which work from behind, or whether in some sense this freedom is the result of future conditions, that is, is influenced by ends still hidden in the unrevealed future. According to the mechanical statement, the past is gone and the future is not yet here. Therefore, the future cannot determine what the change is going to be. The mechanical statement is unable to give us the reflection of the future into what is going on. And yet this is the essence of conduct. It is directed toward goals, ends which, while not yet actual, are operative in the determination of the directions which conduct shall take. The organism is free in the selection of its goal. Conscious selection is quite as really influenced by what is yet to be as it is by what has been. This leads Bergson to turn again to experience to see just what it really is like. He finds that in its characteristic interpenetration there is no sharp, knife-edge separation between past and future. The interpenetration of experience does go into the future. The essence of reality involves the future as essential to itself. In this way he rescues freedom. The coming of the future into our conduct is the very nature of our freedom. We may be able to get the reason for everything we do after the act, according to the mechanical statement; but to see conduct as selective, as free, we must take account of that which is not yet in position to be expressed in terms of a mechanical statement of events which follow one another as a series of atomic experiences.

But, again it seems that Bergson has failed to recognize that this process upon which he lays so much stress must be recognized wherever an effort, a process, is essential to the nature of the object. Thus the description he makes must hold for the atom, for which the present is just as much weighted with the future as it is for more specifically "organic" structures. In his *Matter and Memory* he again deals specifically with the psychological problem of the mind and body. Here we have the question of the function of the nervous system. Nerve cells may answer to the seat of certain excitations. But there is, as yet, no discovered relationship between a certain sensation of color and the excitement of a certain nerve cell. There is nothing in the path of nerve current from one cell to another, and then to another, and so on, which answers to the appearance of color as such. The functional process is one of action, and here you have nothing which answers to the static character of the sensation itself. Bergson points out in reference to these static contents of sensation, the reporting in consciousness of successive qualities, that the response in each case serves as the selection of the stimulus. In other words, the older statement, which put the stimulus first, made it the condition, the cause of the response, had, so to speak, put the cart before the horse. You cannot deal with psychological data adequately if you insist on the causal, associational statement in regard to them. We are at any moment surrounded by an indefinite number of possible sensations. Which of these will be picked out is de-decided in terms of the response that is already being made. There you have the future, the conclusion of the act, implied in what is now going on but which is not yet achieved, coming in to set up the conditions in terms of which stimuli shall arise. This mechanism selects certain responses; it selects the stimuli which shall be effective. The inadequacy here, as I indicated a moment ago, is that this is an account not only of living organisms but of every object which involves a process. It can be said equally of the atom. Out of the total field in which the object may respond in terms of processes that are already set up within it, are the conditions for its acting in one way or another.

Partly through this limitation, this failure to extend sufficiently his doctrine to include all processes in reality, Bergson has to face the alternative of stating his world not in terms of what is going on but in terms of images. We cannot get to reality in any other way, according to him, because, when we try to think our way into it, we stop the process which is requisite to its being. In this, his approach is not unlike that of Locke. Bergson is interested in the organism which as such has this selective character. On the one hand he sees the world of the physical scientist, a world which he describes as a world of physical particles. On the other hand is the experience of the individual through which he reaches the hypotheses which the scientist sets up as a thought structure. This is the idealistic picture. Both of these Bergson tries to avoid by turning to a world of images. Our perceptive world is one which centers about the organism. The more distant the object imaged, the more indifferent its characters. Take the illustration of your perception of objects from a moving train. The objects near at hand change with rapidity, while those which are far away are relatively stable. The real process is revealed to us in immediate perceptual experience. But over against this we have a world of objects which is independent of the organism and by which we correct our perceptual experience. This latter world, the world which science analyzes, was there before the organism appeared. How does Bergson set about to fit these two worlds together?

The perceptual world, says Bergson, is a world of knowledge. It appears as a representation in the cognitive sense. The image is a cognitive representation of something. All the conduct of the organism is mapped out in your central nervous system. There are an enormous number of possible reactions. But there is nothing in the central nervous system which answers to the structure of the representation. You cannot find the representations there; you find sensitivities. You find nothing in it which answers to the representation of this table as such, for example. The table is not in our heads. What is there is what we are going to do about it: read on it, sit on it, eat from it. Whenever I change my position, I change my perceptual world. All the stimuli change because of the relation of the organism to them. They are expressed in terms of our reactions. We make the world from the point of view of our reactions to it. If you state the organism in terms of a mechanism, you get the logical relationship between the perceptual world and the scientific world. Your perceptual world is a statement of the scientific world in terms of your possible reaction to it. This is Bergson's approach. The sensation is a clue; it helps us to pick out the memory image which we will use in action. This memory image had no place in the scientific world. Yet it plays a great part in the determination of stimuli; and this determines the world to which we shall respond, the world which will be presented in our perceptual representations at the present and which will become the memory images of the future. These images will then play the same rôle in regard to the multitudinous stimuli from which our conduct will select those which are pertinent to what is then going on. Thus the future image, which has no place in the scientific world, plays a great part in actual experience. Bergson starts off with a freedom which is there for all the world of images. This gives the world the meaning it has for us.

By including within this world of images the future as well as the past, Bergson hopes to have established not only the fact, but also the efficacy, of freedom. But we must examine into the nature of these images a little more deeply. How does it happen that we have perceptions and yet only incomplete representations of reality if, as Bergson contends, these perceptions are really representational? Perception is a restriction of experience, he says. Thus he has to bring in other aspects than those which he has thus far stated. The problem, he says, has been to add to the perceptual experience something that is not there. This is an insoluble problem. It is far easier to diminish the content of what is given than it is to add something to it that is not there. Thus, in undertaking to explain how our perceptions are called out from reality, he starts out with what he calls "pure perceptions." Perceptions arise only in so far as objects affect the bodily organism. These perceptions represent the interrelations, the interconnections, of the rest of the universe. He accepts the theory that every particle of the universe is interrelated with every other particle. Perception represents the passage of the different forces of the universe. The vital organism is distinguished from all other objects in that it is an indeterminate center which serves as a focal point for the processes in reality. When certain processes, certain activities, reach the nervous system, they are checked. This checking of the processes which are going on in nature seems to Bergson to be the essential character of the living form. This characteristic involves not simply the selection of stimuli but also a stoppage of the process of experience itself until a decision in regard to future activity has been reached. He does not elaborate the ground for this stoppage, but it may be stated in terms of a conflict of the different sensibilities. The organism has tendencies which would lead it to react in different ways to different stimuli. Out of these different tendencies arise conflicts which require deliberation. This deliberation means that the life-process has got to be held up, so to speak, until the various possible responses have been held passive long enough for a selection to be made among them. This is the difference which will be most immediately noticeable in comparing a living organism to a stone. The part of the response which is held up in this way, Bergson says, constitutes the representation; in other words, it is the conscious perception. If it were not for the checking, we would perceive the whole universe.

Thus we are really brought to the core of the whole doctrine. The implication clearly is that our conduct, in so far as it is not conscious, in so far as it simply goes on as a part of an inclusive process, is sensitized, so to speak, to the whole of reality. Could we catch it in that condition, we would see the nature of things as they really are. But the way into that vision is not through conscious reflection. That stops the process. Consciousness arises only when our impulses lead us into conflict—conflict that must be solved before conduct can go on effectively. As long as conduct is held up, we get conscious representations of the stimuli which are relevant to the solution of the present difficulty. But we have representations only of these. In selecting some, we neglect and ignore others. If we are to catch reality at its core, we must turn to a more instinctive level. We must catch it while the process is going on. Since this is impossible in consciousness, Bergson says that consciousness is inadequate. Through this we are directed to pure perception, that is, to the perceptions which would show us the total interpenetration of things, were we able to become aware of this inner process. Conscious perception arises only when the process is checked, and thus never gives us the "inside" of it, so to speak. We must use "intuition." Only intuition can save us from the distortion which comes with reflection. In other words, Bergson is interested in intuition as opening the door to another type of metaphysics than that which can be gotten through reflection,

through scientific description. This is why his system is ultimately an irrationalism.

Paralleling this field of pure perception is another, the field of
pure memory. Here again, as in the case of pure perception, if
the influence could go through, there would be no image, no consciousness. Just as there are many objects about us to which
we adjust outselves without perception, situations to which we
give only slight attention, so there are memory images which
are present, as if there were an undifferentiated field of memory
which never rises to the level of reflection. These images are
present as a part of the ongoing process, but their efficacy is not
required in setting up the process by which stimuli are selected
out; they are not required as means to the direction of our conduct. Therefore, like pure perception, pure memory represents a
deeper, more fundamental aspect of the basic process. Our conscious memories are an expression of the selection that we make
among the stimuli presented. Pure memory, on the other hand,
answers to the whole of our experience, as pure perception answers
to our instinctive contact with the whole of reality. It is not
connected with our central nervous system. It must be independent of this system, for the central nervous system is itself
simply one of the images. Pure memory is, of course, as different from memory as it enters into our experience as pure perception is from ordinary perception. The function of the central
nervous system is the same in each case—it is a selecting and
dissecting organ.

This brings us to another individual and interesting point of
Bergson's position. This dissection of experience that goes on
under the influence of the central nervous system and which
gives us the world of ordinary perception and which calls up
our usual memory images is a materializing process. His doctrine involves an assumption of a world of images over against
the customary psychological doctrine, which assumes that sensations and memory images are functions of the central nervous
system. This is, of course, true of ordinary perception and memory in so far as each is a result of the process of selection which

is carried out in the central nervous system. Even here, however, the relation is not the one ordinarily presented. The selection of which Bergson speaks is something very different from the process that is implied in the idea of the functional relationship of the central nervous system and the images presented. The images are a part of the process of pure perception and pure memory, which are themselves not the result of any structure within the organism but a part of the world of images in which the representations of the organism and of the central nervous system are included. These particular images are caught at one moment and then another. Having been selected, presenting, as they do, the stoppage of the process, they are mechanized bits. Using Bergson's illustration, they are the dead fragments of an exploded shell through which the process must keep pushing on, only to reach a new point of conflict in which the same materialization occurs again. The process itself is the complete interrelation of the parts of the universe so that all share in a common reality. According to Bergson, the philosopher has been led astray by the analysis of the scientist into thinking that the conceptual object is a clue to the real nature of things. On the contrary, these are not concepts of anything; they are a part of the process of the materialization which occurs in perception. The object is there as a reflection back of the process. I must confess that what this "reflection back" is I am unable to isolate.

It is interesting in this connection to note that the world of images which Bergson presents is adequate for scientific statements. Scientific objects are objects of hypothetical character; and, as such, they have imaginable contents which are essential to the hypothesis to which they belong. At least this is the way I see it. Scientific hypotheses vary constantly. The test of them comes back finally to the test of our own experience. Now the question is whether or not conceptual objects appear in our hypotheses without any imaginable content. I do not see any reason for abandoning the imaginable world with which Bergson deals. Our scientific experience always implies the distance experience and the contact experience. What the distance experience is, is immaterial to the imagination. The microscope and the telescope extend our powers of contact in two very notable directions. But imagination goes beyond them. The electron, if not the atom, is conceived in the imagination. These are not, at least as yet, contact experiences. This simply means that some sort of distance experience is essential. The problem, then, is of the nature of these concepts. Concepts are not supposed to involve any necessary imaginable stuff. The concept is defined in terms of the conditions under which a process of analysis is carried on. Here you get a conceptual account without filling your concepts out with stuff. Does the reality of the object involve the effective occupation of space as revealed by the contact experience? You cannot have a concept which is itself an object. It is a concept of something, conceivably of a matter that occupies space. The contact experience would give the material stuff which answers to the distance experience. But at least we are sure that we can give no exact statement of size, for example, of the stuff of the contact experience. It is Poincaré who points out that there is no absolute size to which the material universe could be reduced. Then, too, the scientist sets up a noumenal world which lies beyond contact experience. It is true that some of the relativists, notably Einstein, assume that our spatial time world is entirely relative to the individual. Such a doctrine gives to each individual his own world. But among these worlds we find uniformities which seem to lead us even here to the necessity of setting up a noumenal reality the events and interrelations of which lie beyond our own experience. It is this problem which Bergson proposes to meet through his doctrine of the world as images; and, as I said before, I do not see any reason for abandoning this imaginable world.

Where Bergson gets into his greatest difficulty is in failing to see, or at least to state adequately, that the reflective part of consciousness, which is the source of our inadequate representations of reality, is only one part of the whole process which he identifies with analysis. Bergson insists that objects are in experience—in pure experience, so to speak—without our being aware of them. Becoming aware of an object is an analytic process. Of course, if your fundamental position is that when we know things we tear them to pieces, then you are going to have distortion. But if you have objects in your experience which you can enjoy as well as analyze, the necessity of the intuitive relation seems, to me, to disappear. In other words, Bergson's immediate intention furnishes the blind spot in his philosophy. He fails to see that the flow, the freedom, the novelty, the interpenetration, the creativity, upon which he sets such store, are not necessarily limited to the interpenetration of experiences in the inner flow of consciousness. They may also be gotten in an objective statement just as soon as we see that the objects of experience have the same type of interpenetration, the same essential spread, as that which Bergson discovers in our inner experience; as soon as we see that the ideas which we get in reflection, the objects which we get in science, and against which Bergson is particularly vehement, are the result of analysis and are not presumed to be reports of the nature of the objects themselves. It is this correction of the Bergsonian philosophy which, it seems to me, Mr. Whitehead has most effectively made, up to the present at least.

CHAPTER XV

SCIENCE RAISES PROBLEMS FOR PHILOSOPHY— REALISM AND PRAGMATISM

W E TURN now from the Bergsonian philosophy to the realistic movement and its reaction on modern science. This realistic movement is, in a sense, a continuation of the rationalism of the eighteenth century, that which went back to the logical structure of the object of knowledge. Over against this rationalism was the empirical doctrine represented by the English school—Locke, Berkeley, and Hume. The empirical doctrine dealt with the structure of the object as it appears in our qualitative experiences. It was interested in the content of the object rather than in its form. And this school attempted to get the structure, the form of the object, out of the relation of the different elements as they appeared in sensation, in impression, in experience. The rationalistic doctrine started with a certain structure which belongs to the object itself; and, of course, the mind was supposed to have immediate knowledge. The empirical school started with the experiences that came through the senses, and tried to find in the association of such experiences the details of the structure of objects.

That structure was largely expressed in two conceptions: one of cause and effect, and the other of substance and attribute. The critical doctrine of Kant, you remember, recognized both elements. And still, Kant's leanings were more toward rationalism than toward the empirical side. He assumed that the mind must give the form to the object, but this structure was one which was simply a form of the mind and not a form of things-in-themselves. The mind had the forms of the categories, twelve in number, of which the important ones were substance and attribute, and cause and effect. The empirical school had attempted to show how mere association of the different experiences with each other would lead to the appearance of such conceptions as that of cause and effect and of substance and attribute. Kant recognized that these must be logically antecedent to the object. There could be no object except in terms of substance and of cause.

The recognition that these forms came from the mind led to the idealistic school that undertook to regard the whole of the world as a structure of the mind, applying not simply to categories already fixed in the mind but to the very evolution of the categories themselves. The evolution in this case was that of a self that thought the universe.

When we come to the situation after this Romantic idealistic school, we find that people had abandoned this conception of the self that thinks of the world, but that they retained these two phases of experience, the form and the content. The realistic school undertakes to come back to the formal side of the object, only it approaches it from the standpoint of a new conception, that of the more modern mathematics and logic. These conceptions are of the relations which lie between the ultimate elements of things. They were conceived of not as forms of the mind but as relations that exist in the world. Neither are they regarded as the association of states of consciousness with each other, as the empiricists conceived of them. Until we get to the skeptical statement of Berkeley and Hume, the empiricists assumed that there were relations which answered to the relations which arose in the mind, that is, relations in the world, such as cause and effect, that answered to the association of one experience with another. Of course, they could not prove any such connection, and Kant's critical philosophy came in to present another point of view.

The realists, on the other hand, as distinct from the proponents of these two positions, believe that the relations of elements with each other are directly cognized, directly perceived. They are there. And the relations form some of the elements which are discovered in analysis. If you take an object of knowledge and analyze it, break it up into its content, you will find not only the substantive content, the impression in experience, but also definite relations. And what the realist does is to attempt to present both of these contents, those which appear in sensuous experience and those which we think, as relations given in the world. The assumption is that we have direct knowledge of these elements and of their relations in the world itself. The relations are no longer dealt with as acts of thought. In the idealistic school the relations were always the impressions of the realizing mind, so that relations were taken back to the thought of the self. Our own selves were parts of the Absolute Self. The realist, on the other hand, assumes the relations as simply there. We think them; and if we think them, they must be there, for we must be thinking something. The something we think is Being. Whether it has existence or not depends on whether it is located in our spatial, temporal experience. Existence is the relation with reference to which other relations are found actually in spatial, temporal experience. But we can think relations which are not in these forms. We can think of various relations existing between things but which do not exist. They must have being, otherwise we could not think them. We have, then, direct relationship or cognitive relationship with the objects of experience and their forms.

The interest of the realist has been in this process of analysis, of breaking up the object of knowledge into its various elements, with the isolation of the connection as well as of the things themselves, carrying with this the doctrine of the external character of relations. The relations do not exist inside of that which is realized; they exist between relata, between elements that are connected with each other. Realism is indicated by the term which implies that that with which we have cognitive relations is real. It is not phenomenal. It is just what it appears to be in experience. But, to find out just what it is, we must discover it as it appears in the analytic, rather than in the synthetic, phase of experience. The synthetic phase of experience was dealt with by the empiricists under the head of "association." If experience B follows after experience A, it becomes associated with it, so that in the future when we have experience A, or one similar to it, the other experience, B, which had been associated with it, arises also. It is purely a mental affair, a connection of these various states with each other.

Thus realism gathers about the world-old problem of epistemology. The form which that problem took, you remember, was dictated by the very development of Renaissance science, which, as finally formulated, set up a world of physical particles moving with reference to each other in accordance with fixed laws. The rest of the world had to be put over into consciousness. While there was supposed to be a world of these physical particles moving in accordance with natural law, the question at once arose: How does man get outside of the world of consciousness? How do you know there is anything else but what you have in your own experience? The epistemological problem has been thought out in this way, on this issue.

As I said, the answer of the realist is to give another statement of knowledge. Knowledge is finding a relationship between an object that lies in consciousness and an object that lies outside of it. If you say, for example, that the table here is nothing but a congeries of your own perceptions and images, you have a table anyway. That is an object. You know it. What you ask is how you can get from such an object which lies simply in your consciousness over to the group of electrons which constitute, as you say, the reality of that table. And the question is practically unanswerable when stated in this way. There is no way of getting from the inner to the outer. All is inside your experience; all is consciousness. What the realist says is that this is an improper statement of what knowledge means. Knowledge is not going from an object already in experience over to something that lies outside of experience which by definition you must reach. It is simply the relationship between the mind and that which it senses, that which it perceives. It is thought in a direct relationship, and that is all that you can say about it. It is a fundamental, connotative, relation which exists between the mind and that which is known. We have no problem of getting from the object which is in the mind over to an object which lies outside of the mind. What knowledge consists in is this relation between the mind and its object. It is that shift in the conception of knowledge itself which is characteristic of the realistic doctrine. You see this is not the particular form of the question which I have said was practically unanswerable, namely, "How can one get from consciousness over into something that is not consciousness?" That form of the question arises out of Renaissance science. The realist said the relationships between the mind and the object is an immediate, given relationship.

This was anticipated by the so-called Scottish school, who said knowledge is immediate intuition. But their statement was bound up more or less with the earlier form of the cognitive doctrine. They still kept the object in consciousness as the immediate object of knowledge, and they still set off reality beyond it. The realists said the object is simply the relationship between the mind and the object, a direct cognitive relationship. That relationship in a certain sense guarantees the object, and one of the great problems of the realistic philosophers is, therefore, the problem of error. If knowledge is given in the relationship of the mind and its object, how can there be error? And, of course, there are errors.

What has been of still more importance, perhaps, from the standpoint of the realistic doctrine has been its recognition of the objects of thought as they appear in the process of analysis. The realistic philosophy is one whose method has been analytic. It has sprung from mathematics—mathematics used, however, in the large sense of that term, the sense in which logic and mathematics come together. The earliest of the group, as you might call Leibnitz, goes way back to the Renaissance period. He at least sketched out the implications of the realistic doctrine. He was one of the great mathematicians of the world, one who had an implicit faith in the possibilities of analysis. If, he said, you could take objects of knowledge and analyze them so that you get back to the ultimate elements, as, for example, in mathematical problems, those immediately given to you, those which in one sense cannot be defined, which can be set up as indefinable but which can be specified in the sense of having their outlines given so that you can combine them with each other, you would be able to build up all possible combinations. You could have charge of the ultimate elements, and all the relationships that lie between, if you just pushed your process of analysis to the limit and got these elements spread out before you, as a watchmaker spreads out the parts of his watches. Then you could get all possible combinations of things.

It is this method with which the realist operates. He wants to get back to those ultimate elements which are just there, given in immediate cognitive relation, and of which there is no question. If you could get back to those ultimate elements, and particularly to the relationships that lie between them, they would be the basis in terms of which you could make all possible combinations. If you can discover those which are not contradictory, those which are tenable, you have the same assurance of your results as in the immediate experience of the ultimate elements themselves. The realists came back, for example, to final definitions of ultimate elements in the world—elements which we make use of in thought itself, the so-called "logical constants." They came back to these ultimate elements and then defined the relationships which could exist between them, and in this way they could build up logical structures which could not be questioned. They found out what the possible relationships could be between all these different elements. This has a very abstract sound, and the achievements of these mathematicians and logicians are abstract in the highest degree, but they are very penetrating; and they did, as I said, bring together the fields of mathematics and logic.

They carried with them a doctrine which for a while belonged to the realistic field but which is not so certain now. This is the doctrine of the so-called "externality of relations." I have said the realist analyzes, takes his object to pieces, comes back to ultimate elements and the relationships which exist between them. He isolates the relations from the elements themselves. In this activity the relation is something that we will say is like a wire that connects two different objects together. You can put up a wire and set up different relations between objects strung on it. The relations as such do not affect the object. The relata are connected by means of the relations, but the relations do not exist by themselves. This emphasis upon the externality of relations was brought out in contests between the realists and the idealists, especially the neo-Hegelians of the latter group.

From the standpoint of that latter group, the relation was an internal, not an external, affair. It was not simply a connection set up between different objects, separate relata, but something which affected the very thing related. These relations grew inside of things rather than being connections between independent elements. Take, as an illustration, the Hegelian doctrine of the social individual. We speak of him as having certain relations. He stands in his social group as a citizen, as a member of a family, of this and that group; and all these groups represent various social relations. We might speak of him as a point through which any number of social relations pass. Now, these relations of the man to the people about him are just what constitutes the man. His relations to the members of his family make him what he is. We cannot say that the relationship of father to son is one that lies outside of the character of father and son. We cannot say that here are two different objects connected by means of paternal and filial relations. We cannot substitute something else for this. It lies within the individual, makes him what he is. It is an internal relation so far as the object is concerned. And, not only is it internal, but it makes every individual entering into the relationship different from what he was before that relationship was entered into. You form an acquaintance with someone; it becomes a friendship. That relationship changes both of you. You are different beings from what you were before. Now the

Hegelian took this situation over into the whole of social and spiritual reality. For him relations are internal, they are thought of as being the very nature of the Absolute Self. The relation is a process of relating. Relating is a process of thinking in the Absolute Self in which our minds are simply finite aspects. Thus relations lie in the very nature of things themselves.

Over against this doctrine, the realists set up one in which relations are external. The process of analysis takes things apart, sets up ultimate relata; and the connections between them, the relations as such, never change the character of the thing related. You can say that new characters arise, but they are simply the expression of the relations existing between the separate elements. The separate elements themselves can never be changed. Connect one number with another number, and perhaps the result gives you a larger bank account, or it may indicate that you have overdrawn your account. Those are very important facts. But they do not change the character of the numbers that are connected with each other by addition and subtraction. These are ultimate elements which remain always what they are. And the relations that exist are what they are. You do not change the relata by their being related.

Thus the realists accept cognition as a simple relationship between the mind and its object. Nothing can be said about it except that it is an immediate relationship between these two. Therefore, in so far as it exists, it presumably carries with it the import of cognition, that is, it carries knowledge, and so the truth of the experience.

But this knowledge has as its fundamental principle that of analysis, a principle which, as I have said, it had taken from mathematics. It is a process which leads to the breaking-up of the object of knowledge into its ultimate elements. The difficulty which the realist got into on this basis was to account, not for knowledge, but for error. In the older theory the object was given in consciousness as the immediate object of knowledge. That is, the organization of one's percepts, ideas, images, meanings, as they lay in consciousness, into the immediate object of knowledge is where the epistemological problem was found in setting up some sort of a relationship between this immediate object of knowledge and the supposed real object outside. That is what we would consider as answering to our perception of a table, for example. If we state the table in terms of our ideas, or our perceptions, we can say that it constitutes an object of knowledge, but that it is not the real object. The real object is a congeries of physical particles that do not get into experience at all. From the point of view of the realistic philosophy, with its analysis, knowledge is of the ultimate elements in the experience itself. And thus the problem becomes one of accounting for error, for mistakes. The experience of the ultimate elements themselves is evidence of the object's being there; otherwise it could not be experienced. Knowledge is the relationship between mind and these ultimate elements. Given this relationship, both mind and the ultimate elements are there. Meaning and cognitive value, as well as other values, are also objects of knowledge. And they, too, have to be related and organized.

Remember, the external character of relations is a fundamental point in the position of the realist. The relation does not lie inside of the object. It is simply the connection between the ultimate elements. The so-called "meaning" of the object is nothing but an organization of the relations that lie between these different elements. For example, we have the relationship of distance which exists between different objects and our conduct in experience. The groups of distance relations which we find in experience give us the surface of this table, for example. The groups which represent the relation of the individual to each corner, to the different lines, the different spots of color on the surface, taken together, give us our general sense of the distance of the object, as an object, from the organism. It is an organization of the relations which, together, go to make it up. If we want to deal with the meaning of the object, we come back to the various relations which compose it, and get them in their perspective. We may make mistakes in the organization of these relations, in the meaning they have. We see an eagle soaring over our heads as we lie in the grass, and after a while we become aware of the fact that it is nothing but a gnat a few inches away. There are mistakes also so far as the immediate experience goes, that is true enough. But we may also make mistakes when we organize them into ultimate relationships.

But this leaves yet another group of elements in that experience. The eagle to which I referred is, after all, something more than a set of separate experiences. It is not only something more than that; it is something universal. It is something that is recognized in any eagle that we see. It is the same, the concept of the eagle, the universal eagle; and it is not only a universal, but it is a unity. We may break the unity up into separate parts, but it is something that belongs to the concept of the eagle. These ultimate universals have to be recognized in their relationship to mind, especially the fundamental universals that appear as logical constants. Not only concepts of this character, but also those of our sensuous experiences— the reds, the blues, the high and low sounds—are all universals; and we have to deal with them as such. They have to be recognized from a realistic standpoint as something that is there because we think about them. If we think about them, there must be something there to think about.

In the earlier statement which was given, the concept was dealt with as a mental structure of some sort; it was thought of as something in the mind itself. We assume that that which lies in the mind answers to something outside. The realist assumes that our knowledge of the universals is, so to speak, the contact between the universals and the mind; we must put them in the mind, but they must also have their existence outside. And yet, many of these universals do not have an existence, in our ordinary use of that term. We imply that a thing is at some point and at some definite time when we say that it exists. If we say a man exists, we locate and date him. If he exists, he does so somewhere and somewhen. But the idea of a chimera, for example, does not exist anywhere or anywhen. It does not exist. That is very characteristic, of course, of the chimera as such or of any other mythical animals, dragons, and what not, that have played such large rôles in mythology and in the imaginations of men. They do not exist, and yet we think about them. If we could regard them as just constructs of the imagination and locate them in people's minds, we could account for their being mere mythical objects. You say there are not any such animals; they do not exist; they are just mental pictures which people have had of possible animals which proved to be impossible animals. But if you take the realistic viewpoint, there must be something to think about—some universal, at least—to which our mind turns and about which we are thinking. There are a good many other things we think about which do not exist. We puzzle our heads over them for a long time, over perceptions which prove to have contradictions in them. And yet we have been thinking about them. After all, there must have been something. We talk about such things as "round squares." They could not exist—they are contradictions in terms—and yet we can discuss them. As long as we can think about anything, there must be something that answers to the process of thought, and yet many of these things cannot be put into existence.

What this led to on the part of this realistic approach was the recognition of a real being which generally goes under the name of "subsistence" rather than of "existence." There is a world which subsists, but does not necessarily exist. You can have thought occupied in the recognition of the response to all the elements in experience, and not only to these but to everything we call "idea," that is, any universal. These subsist; some of them exist. Thus, some of them do appear. To apply one of the terms that is used, they have "ingression" into events. This is Whitehead's term for the process. These eternal objects, in the sense that they are outside of time, have ingression into certain events in so far as they constitute things. What you see taking place is the emptying-out of the whole content of the mind, as the Renaissance philosophers dealt with it, into the world. It is a setting-up of mind as that which has cognitive relationships with all these different elements, allowing the construction to take place through the action of the mind.

But the realist has not been very strong on the constructive or synthetic side. His interest has been in analysis. To understand this interest we have to go back, as I have already indicated, to a mathematical background. One of the greatest of the realists is Bertrand Russell; another is Alfred Whitehead. What they were interested in at first was the perfection of mathematical theory. They were interested in carrying back the mathematical process behind the immediate objects of the physical world that we follow through their various changes. Back of this lay the development of our modern mathematics. Mathematics, for Kant, stood on a basis of Euclidean geometry on one side and of the traditional arithmetic on the other. Kant, you remember, believed that the forms of mathematics were the forms of the mind. Well, not long after the time of Kant two mathematicians undertook to work out geometries which contravened the Euclidean axiom in regard to parallels. It was a question of whether more than one line could be drawn parallel to another line through a point outside that line. They took different points of view, such as that there could be no such line drawn or that there could be a number of them so drawn. The interesting thing was that, starting off with such an axiom, that no lines could be drawn parallel or that there could be an indefinite number of them so drawn, they could build up perfectly consistent systems of geometry. This was not, of course, going back to experience to find a world in which they were true. Neither of these propositions, if true, conforms to the Euclidean axiom. Nor does actual physical experience conform as far as that goes. Of course, this does not go very far. You cannot actually measure the distance between lines so constructed. One mathematician actually undertook to see whether the experiment of setting up triangles or parallels which could be measured on the surface of the earth would hold, but he did

not measure with sufficient accuracy to get any absolute conclusions. What these people wanted to do was not to find
parallel lines which act like rails as you look at them. It was a
question of seeing whether you could assume that there could
be an indefinite number of parallel lines drawn to any line from
points outside that line, or if you could assume that there could
be no parallel lines. Whichever side you took, you had the basis
for a possible geometry. Whichever geometry is right in the
sense of describing physical nature, you can prove all the propositions in one or the other. If you come back to experience, so-
called, it is, after all, that of one geometry only. Why cannot
there be others?

And then, of course, there is always the question as to whether
space is curved. We cannot actually follow lines any great
length or distance. Do they actually tend to meet? We could
never tell if they did. We have another interesting speculation
about people who live in a two-dimensional space. Supposing
a person were of no thickness at all and lived on the surface
of a sphere. Then, if one started to throw something forward in
a straight line with sufficient force, it would hit him in the back
of the head. How can we tell whether the space in which we
live is of one sort or another? Supposing, for example, to give
another illustration, we say space is of indefinite extent.
What we mean is that, given (or setting up) any limit in space,
we imply something beyond it. It is indefinite. Or, supposing
we lived in a world which got cooler as we went away from
its center, and that in accordance with these conditions the
dimensions of things changed, so that the diameters would
shrink as they got farther away from the warm center. And
assume that the diameters of all objects shrank proportionally.
Then as we walked away toward the periphery of the world, we
would get gradually smaller and smaller as we got cooler and
cooler, and our steps would get shorter and shorter. In such a
system we could never reach the limit of the world. We could
have an indefinite world inside of a definite one; we would never
arrive at the limit; and yet we would never stop. Everything

would become proportionately smaller as we went away from that center.

The value of such an illustration, which is given by Poincaré in his *Science and Hypothesis*, is simply to show us that our spatial world, which has a right and left, an up and down, is something that is entirely dependent upon our experience. And we have no way of telling whether the world of our spatial experience corresponds to one geometry or another, whether the world is actually Euclidean or non-Euclidean. It is something that is not open to any proof, because our experience will always lie inside our own world. What are these irrefragable difficulties, then? They are proofs for a geometry, provided that the axioms of that geometry are true. We can never tell whether they are true or not. We say a straight line is the shortest distance between two points. We have some difficulty in defining a straight line, but we cannot set it up as indefinable, and it comes back to the statement that it is nothing but the shortest distance between two points. You have to assume it to define it. You come back to certain postulates you set up. On one basis you will set up a Euclidean world; and you can prove certain conclusions in that world, prove that there is such a world. All judgments are necessarily hypothetical judgments. Whether or not there is a Euclidean world we cannot tell. We cannot tell whether the world actually has the dimensions that we think it has or the dimensions of a billiard ball. You could just as well set up all the relationships which you have in the world in one the size of a billiard ball, provided you reduce your units. Why not? Your proofs are dependent upon certain given postulates. It is much easier to prove the Pythagorean proposition if you actually have lines drawn in a Euclidean fashion, a number of them, and work them out. But you are not sure that there is such a Euclidean world. Well, now, is there anything in that Pythagorean proposition which would be true if there were no such Euclidean world? Would it be possible to prove propositions of geometry, and of all mathematics, without actually accepting the postulates of our empirical world about us?

That is the problem the mathematicians were working on, and what they did was to set up symbols which would be most general and universal and just as few in number as possible. And by means of these and by using the simplest processes of logic, it was possible to prove a whole mathematical science without introducing the postulates of our empirical experience. You can find this done in the *Principia mathematica* of Russell and Whitehead. In it mathematics is presented in propositions worked out in so-called "symbolic logic"; and the propositions there are propositions which, if translated into Euclidean geometry, would give all the propositions of that geometry, but give them in such a form that they are free from the fixed postulates of our sensuous experience. We free ourselves from all that to a certain degree. We say that the world which seems to have up and down, right and left, really does not have these characters. What we mean by "up and down" is the relationship between the object on the surface and the center of the earth. In this symbolism you come back to a larger, more effective analysis than that worked out in the past, in which you have symbols that refer to universals and the smallest possible number of indefinables. With these you work out propositions that would be true in any world. You do not know, for example, if they are true in the sense that they actually exist. That is the interesting thing, says Russell, about mathematics. You do not know whether what you are presenting is true, and you do not know what you are talking about. You abstract from the content of your postulates. You set up certain indefinable elements and put relationships between them; and then you say that, if such and such a thing exists, a certain result must follow. It was this most generalized form of mathematics which was worked out by these mathematicians; and in accomplishing it, they went beyond the logic of Aristotle, for example, in introducing the so-called "logic of relations." They produced a symbolic logic which was a more powerful instrument than the Aristotelian syllogism is. And they reduced the content of our exact scientific knowledge to the simplest form in which it could be expressed and to a form which is valid in any sort of world to which you may wish to refer.

They were somewhat excited about their success. This was natural enough. If you can take the whole of the object of mathematical science and trace it to a set of formulas which look very much like the marks of which a stenographer makes use, condense the whole of that to a relatively small number of pages, and have all the content there, you are justified in getting excited. You get a symbolic logic which is very much more effective than the older logic. If you invited twenty people to dinner and some belonged to one religion and some to another, some to one political faith and some to another, and some of them disliked others, and yet you had to seat them about the table so as to have everyone at peace with his immediate neighbors, you would have quite a job on your hands. If you ever have such a job, I advise you to familiarize yourselves with symbolic logic, for that will enable you to state just what the possible combinations are that you can make. It will enable you to arrange your guests in such a way that there will not be any unpleasant experience at the dinner. There are certain situations of that sort which make us aware of the practical value in the use of symbolic mathematics. But I must confess that beyond that, so far as practical things are concerned, its use has been very slight. The achievements which symbolic logic makes in the realm of thought are very impressive, indeed. But we still go on thinking in terms of what has been called the "logic of things," the logic of inference, that is, the logic of Socrates and immortality: all men are mortal; Socrates was a man; therefore Socrates was mortal. That is logic built up on the inherence of certain qualities in certain substances. Well, now, the world we live in is a world of things, and the logic we will continue to utilize will be a logic of things. Symbolic logic gives a powerful discipline, an apparatus which enables us to deal with relations. But if you continue to work in a world of things, I do not think that symbolic logic will be of any particular value except in such problems as I suggested above.

What I have been trying to bring out was the background of these realistic philosophers. They try to get rid of the epistemological problem by simply recognizing that knowledge is a cognitive relation between mind and the elements. And then they try to state the so-called "objects of knowledge" in terms of their ultimate elements and the relationships between them. And in order to do that, they have to assume the externality of relations, that is, that there is a set of ultimate elements which are related to one another as if by wires or strings. If you want to handle such a number of ultimate elements and their relations, you have to have a very powerful sort of technique, such as that which the symbolic logic gives you. So all these go along together. The realists assume that knowledge is just a relationship between the object and the mind. Then by analysis they break up the object into all its elements, set up cognitive relations between mind and these elements and their relations, and then connect them all together. They give you a technique which enables you to handle these factors.

It is in this field that the realist is occupied. Things are, or at least they have being. Elements, anything we think about, have being; and our problem is, not to determine whether some things have being and others not, but to determine the relationships between these elements of being. And the relationships between these elements also are actually given. They are realized. Things are real. There are different sorts of reality. That of existence, for example, of something located at a certain point at a certain time. But things which do not exist have being, that is, they have subsistence; and the problem is to determine what that means. In this philosophy the problem of the universal as out there has to be recognized as present because universals can be thought about. The problem of the universal, as far as our sensuous experience is concerned, presents some difficulties. The forms in which these universals appear among different relata are different. For example, Whitehead refers to them as eternal objects. Another group, the so-called "critical realists"—Santayana, Lovejoy, and others—refer to them as "essences." And the question of the appearances of these essences, these universals, in the object and the presence of them in the mind becomes a somewhat difficult question. We say, for example, that there is something which constitutes a table. I know what you mean by this term, otherwise we could not talk about the object in question. We attach a particular word to it. We may call it by any word. But there is something we think about, and it is universal. We also assume that it is in this thing. What evidence have we of this? There must be such a thing; otherwise we could not think about it. How do we get it into this relationship? That presents problems which we are not undertaking to follow out, but to criticize this philosophy I want to give you the point of view of a group of influential philosophers whose doctrine belongs to this period. If you want a further account, take Santayana's *Skepticism and Animal Faith*. These realists had something of the same confidence in the mathematical technique that Kant had in the achievements of Newton.

Philosophy has in this as well as in other centuries occupied itself with the interpretation of what science has accomplished. In modern times science and philosophy are separated from each other. Science reaches certain results. It tests them. We can act upon them. Philosophy has been occupied with the question of meanings. Some philosophers feel that philosophy goes further and can criticize the propositions, the presuppositions of science. But as a general rule it can be said that what philosophy has been doing, especially since the time of the Renaissance, is to interpret the results of science. Well, now, mathematics has been going ahead at a frightful rate during this last century, and the realists represent an attempt to interpret it from the point of view of its own technique. You get very strange results looking at this development of mathematics from our empirical point of view.

Alongside of this realistic philosophy we find another—pragmatism—which has developed out of a different aspect of the scientific movements of the period. This doctrine has two outstanding figures: one of them is William James, the other, John Dewey. There are differences in the formulation of pragmatism on the part of these two men. That of James is to be found in his volume entitled *Pragmatism;* that of Dewey, in his earlier statements in his *Essays in Experimental Logic,* and in a more elaborate statement in his more recent book, *Experience and Nature.* Back of the work of both lies the common assumption of the testing of the truth of an idea, of a hypothesis, by its actual working.

Our problem now is to put this statement in relationship to the doctrines which we discussed earlier. In them the test of truth lies in the coherence, the orderliness of ideas, the way in which ideas fit into a general logical structure as it arises in the mind, a mind which is not only a mind but also a creator of the world, all minds being simply phases of a more general, an Absolute, mind. From this standpoint the world was the result of the thought process of the Absolute. Our thinking is but one of the finite and imperfect elements of this process—imperfect because a mere phase. It would be impossible for us to think of the world in a true fashion because of our finite character. But in proportion as our thinking is coherent, to that degree we can assume that our mind approaches truth.

The point that needs particularly to be recognized in an approach to the pragmatic doctrine is the relationship of thinking to conduct. The undertaking of the Romantic idealists and the rationalists was to present thought as that which discovered the world. It had the distinct business of finding out what the nature of things is. That is, cognition is a process which arose, so to speak, for its own sake. One is curious, one wants to know the world; and knowledge is a simple getting of the nature of the world. Its tests lie, from that standpoint, in the product or in the nature of what is known. This is a copy theory of knowledge; one has in his mind the impression of that which exists outside; or one may have a coherence theory such as that to which I have referred above, that which fits into a structure which lies outside. The function of knowledge in either case is to give as close a resemblance as possible to something which lies outside the mind.

If we approach the world from the standpoint of the sort of experience with which the psychology we have been presuming deals, we can see that intelligence in its simplest phase, and also in a later phase, really lies inside of a process of conduct. The animal, even the plant, has to seek out what is essential to its life. It has to avoid that which is dangerous for it in its life-process. A plant shows its intelligence by driving down its roots, in its adjustment to the climate. When you get into the animal kingdom, you find much more adjustment and an environment which involves more dangers, in which the getting of food, the avoiding of enemies, the carrying-on of the process of reproduction, take on the form of an adventure. Intelligence consists in the stimulation of those elements which are of importance to the form itself, the selection of both positive and negative elements, getting what is desirable, avoiding what is dangerous. These are the ways in which intelligence shows itself.

For example, the intelligence of the human form is one which has arisen through its ability to analyze this world by discrimination, and, through significant symbols, to indicate to other forms with which it works and to the form itself what the elements are that are of importance to it. It is able to set up such a structure of symbols, images, which stand for the object that it needs. Thinking is an elaborate process of selecting, an elaborate process of presenting the world so that it will be favorable for conduct. Whatever is its later function—it has one of knowledge, which is for its own sake—in its earlier phases we have intelligence, and then thought, as lying inside of conduct. That is, the test of intelligence is found in action. The test of the object is found in conduct itself. What the animal needs is its food, freedom from its enemy. If it responds to the right stimuli, it reaches that food, that safety. The animal has no other test as to whether it has made such a proper selection except in the result attained. You can test your stimulus only by the result of your conduct which is in answer to it. You see, that takes the research method over into life. The animal, for example, faces a problem. It has to adjust itself to a new situation. The way in which it is going brings danger or offers some unexpected possibility of getting food. It acts upon this and thus gets a new object; and if its response to that object is successful, it may be said to be the true object for that stimulus. It is true in the sense that it brings about a result which the conduct of the animal calls for. If we look upon the conduct of the animal form as a continual meeting and solving of problems, we can find in this intelligence, even in its lowest expression, an instance of what we call "scientific method" when this has been developed into the technique of the most elaborate science. The animal is doing the same thing the scientist is doing. It is facing a problem, selecting some element in the situation which may enable it to carry its act through to completion. There is inhibition there. It tends to go in one direction, then another direction; it tends to seek this thing and avoid that. These different tendencies are in conflict; and until they can be reconstructed, the action cannot go on. The only test the animal can bring to such a reconstruction of its habits is the ongoing of its activity. This is the experimental test; can it continue in action? And that is exactly the situation found also in science.

Take such a problem, for example, as that of the radiation of the sun or of the stars. It is assumed that that radiation is due to the compression which comes with attraction. Then, knowing what the mass of the star is, what the direction of attraction is, and the compression that follows from it, one can figure out how much heat the star can radiate. On that basis it was figured out some forty years ago that the sun has not been in its present condition for a period of more than twenty million years and that it might be perhaps seventeen million years before it became dark and cold, so far as the earth is concerned.

Geologists, on the other hand, were turning back the pages of the history of the earth and working out its history. In this process they got various tests as to what the time periods had been. And all these tests called for far longer periods than the astrophysicist was willing to grant. The former dealt in terms of a hundred million years. In recent research we have discovered a new test which is perhaps the most accurate of all; that is the radiation of radioactive bodies. We know, for example, that bodies of this type are continually breaking down. We can see them doing it. In the dark we can see the sparkling which represents a continual discharge of energy, the breaking-down of higher atomic structures into lower. At first this process seemed to be indefinite; but when it was worked out, it was found that such a process in radium might last for several hundred years. The rate of disintegration could be figured out. We know something about the elements, the parts of the earth, that are radioactive; and in that way we can determine what the rate is at which certain minerals which result from such a disintegration as this could have formed, how long a time would be necessary to build them up. Taking this and all the other tests, the scientists set up their theory of the history of the world—the geologist writing his history on one time schedule, and the physicist writing his on the basis of another. We get a clash here. One calls for a period of several hundred million years; the other denies any period longer than twenty million years. There you get a typical scientific problem.

What I want to point out is that it stops the scientist in his process of reconstructing the past. You are reconstructing it on one doctrine or the other. You cannot use both of them. And yet there are facts which lie behind each of them. What is the source of the energy of the sun? It is not burning up coal. It undoubtedly produces heat by the very compression that follows from attraction. That is the only source of heat which can be found. On that basis the age of the earth is twenty million years. And yet, here we have a history which the geologist and the archeological zoölogist and the botanist have been writing on the basis of other data. And the two stop each other. The process of writing the history of the earth cannot be continued, because the two theories are in conflict with each other. You have these exceptional situations arising over against each other. What is taking place is the recognition that there is another source of energy which has not been attacked, so to speak, in the doctrine of the scientists themselves. This very energy, which is found in the process of radiation which we make use of in our radium watches and clocks, represents a source of energy which the suns may themselves be drawing upon. In its process of radiation, the sun is actually turning out more than four million tons of energy per square yard every few minutes. It is using itself up. Its mass is passing over into the form of radiation. We know that light has weight. Of course, that weight represents just so much mass. Mass must come from the radiation of the sun. The sun is breaking down its own atoms and getting the energy that is in them. We do not know just what the exact process is by which this takes place, whether it is due simply to the immense crushing power of such a great mass as that at the center; but we know that there is much energy in an atom. If you could explode an atom, I think it is said that you could carry the S.S. Leviathan across the ocean on the amount of atomic energy found in a drop of oil—perhaps it is two or three drops if you like, I have forgotten the figures—but there is an enormous amount of energy shut up in the structure of the atoms themselves.

Given such a problem as that, what does the scientist do? He proceeds to start to write his history of the stars as he finds them, the giant and the dwarf stars, the white and blue and red stars, in their different stages of evolution. He starts to write of them on the basis of the hypothesis that these suns have been continually expending the energy involved in their atomic structure in the form of radiation. And that is brought, of course, into its relationship with the geological and biological history of the earth. Could one go on writing the history of the stars and of the surface of the earth so that they do not come into conflict with each other? It was found that there is plenty of time provided under the now recognized form of expenditure of the energy of the sun—a hundred million years or so, instead of twenty million years. So the process of interpreting the world, working out the scientific statement by means of the new hypothesis, could be continued.

Now, what constitutes the test of the hypothesis? The test of it is that you can continue the sort of conduct that was going on. It is the same sort of test which the animal finds. If it finds itself in a difficult situation and sees escape, it rushes off in that direction and gets away. That is a fair test, for it, of what we call a hypothesis. It did not present ideas to itself in terms of significant symbols, but it was a good working hypothesis. It could continue its action of living that way, where it could not have continued it otherwise.

Well, in the same fashion, from a logical standpoint, the scientist is engaged in stating the past history of the world, and he comes up against this blank wall of insufficient time. Now, when he collates the history of the surface and the history of the radiation of the sun, he gets a clue—a hole, so to speak—which will let him escape from that difficulty. That constitutes the test of the truth of his hypothesis. It means that he can continue the process of stating the history of the world within which he is living. And, of course, the process of stating the world, stating our past, is a process of getting control over that world, getting its meaning for future conduct.

That is the importance of the pragmatic doctrine. It finds its test of the so-called "true" in hypotheses and in the working of these hypotheses. And when you ask what is meant by the "working of the hypotheses," we mean that a process which has been inhibited by a problem can, from this standpoint, start working again and going on. Just as the animal no longer stands there, dodging this way and that to avoid its enemy, but can shoot away and get out of danger, so the scientist does not simply have to stand before a history which allows him only twenty million years and a history of two or three hundred million years. He can now continue the process of giving the history of the world, having this conception of the source of energy which had not been recognized before. Putting it into behavioristic terms, what we mean by the test of the truth is the ability to continue a process which had been inhibited.

A certain statement of the pragmatic doctrine implied that a thing was true if it satisfied desire. And the critics of the doctrine thought that this satisfaction meant the pleasure one could get out of it. That is, if a hypothesis was pleasing to an individual, then it was true. What I have just stated is, however, what is implied in this doctrine—that the test of truth lies in the continued working of the very processes that have been checked in the problem. It is a pleasant thing to get going again after we have been caught and shut in. It is a pleasant thing to have a new planet swim into our ken. But it is not pleasure which constitutes the test, but the ability to keep going, to keep on doing things which we have been trying to do but which we had to stop. That is one phase of the pragmatic doctrine—the testing of a hypothesis by its working.

The other phase I have touched on earlier. You see the attitude of which I have been speaking brings the process of knowing inside of conduct. Here, again, you have a relationship between pragmatic doctrine and the behavioristic type of psychology. Knowing is a process of adjustment; it lies within this process. Cognition is simply a development of the selective attitude of an organism toward its environment and the readjustment that follows upon such a selection. This selection we ordinarily connect with what we call "discrimination," the pointing-out of things and the analysis in this pointing. This is a process of labeling the elements so that you can refer to each under its proper tag, whether that tag is a pointing of the finger, a vocal gesture, or a written word. The thinking process is to enable you to reconstruct your environment so that you can act in a different fashion, so that your knowledge lies inside of the process and is not a separate affair. It does not belong to a world of spirit by itself. Knowledge is power; it is a part of conduct that brings out the other phase that is connected with pragmatism, especially in Dewey's statement.

This phase is its instrumentalism. What selection, and its development into reflective thought, gives us is the tools we need, the instruments we need to keep up our process of living in the largest sense. Knowledge is a process of getting the tools, the instruments. Go back to the illustration I have used above of the atoms as a source of energy. This concept becomes a tool by means of which the length of the life of the stars can be estimated. And when you have that, you can relate it to the age of life on the surface of the earth.

Perhaps the best statement to bring out the importance of this instrumentalism is the term "scientific apparatus." We think of that generally as the actual tools of the scientist; but we know that the term "apparatus" is also used for the ideas, the units, the relations, the equations. When we speak of a scientist's apparatus we are thinking of the very ideas of which he can make use, just as he can use the things which he has in his laboratory. An idea of a certain type, such as that of the energy of an atom, becomes a tool by means of which one is able to construct the picture of a star as a source of energy. There, you see, the object as such is a means which enables one to carry on a process of reconstruction such as is given in scientific doctrine.

Well then, the sources of the pragmatic doctrine are these: one is behavioristic psychology, which enables one to put intelligence in its proper place within the conduct of the form, and to state that intelligence in terms of the activity of the form itself; the other is the research process, the scientific technique, which comes back to the testing of a hypothesis by its working. Now, if we connect these two by recognizing that the testing in its working-out means the setting-free of inhibited acts and processes, we can see that both of them lead up to such a doctrine as the one I have just indicated, and that perhaps the most important phase of it is this: that the process of knowing lies inside of the process of conduct. For this reason pragmatism has been spoken of as a practical sort of philosophy, a sort of bread-and-butter philosophy. It brings the process of thought, of knowledge, inside of conduct.

Because pragmatism has these two aspects, it will be well to spend a little more time in their consideration. The first phase is that of the motor psychology. We have referred to its development into behaviorism. The other phase of the problem is that of the scientific method. The rationalistic philosophies assumed a certain structure of the object as being given in the nature of the object itself, a certain structure of knowledge which the object has and which also lies in the mind—as some thought an innate idea, others a something which the mind could directly perceive. The psychological approach of the empiricists translated this structure of the object over into the relations of states of consciousness to each other. Substance and attribute, cause and effect, and the other so-called "categories" were stated in terms of the mere association of different states of consciousness with each other. If they happened to be associated in a certain way, certain structures arose; if associated otherwise, other structures would have arisen. But they were not structures directly, not objects as such. They were mental structures, subject to mental laws. It was generally assumed that there were structures of things that answered to these mental structures, that lie behind them, as illustrated in the so-called "causal theory of perception," the theory that our mind is causally affected by things and that these things impress themselves on the mind and that with these impressions come not only the sense qualities but also the relations of these qualitative elements to each other. That is the structure of the object. Both rationalism and empiricism assumed that there are certain structures in the object which the mind gets hold of, and that it is through these structures that one can know the laws of causation, the laws of the relationship of qualities to substances, and so on. Particularly, however, it was in the law of causation that science and philosophy found the reality of things. What were the uniform successions of events to each other in a causal series? Everything, as far as possible, was carried back to causal laws or uniformities.

The history of science since the Renaissance is really a history of the research process. At first this research was conceived of, and still is largely conceived of, as a simple discovery of something which is out there. Discoveries followed each other closely, so that one statement of the object was rapidly succeeded by another statement. This seemed only natural, because men were finding out more about the world through the scientific method. And this new scientific method carried with it another criterion than that which belonged to the older period, the criterion of experiment, of experimental tests, of experimentation that included observation. Exceptions arose, we have seen, and a problem was formulated, and then a hypothesis for the solution of the problem was presented, and then this solution had to be tested. That is, one had to see whether or not this new hypothesis would work. If it did, then the hypothesis became an accepted theory; if it did not, a new one was substituted for it and subjected to the same test.

This test or experiment—the research method—in some sense took the place of the mathematical method in which one proceeded seemingly by demonstration, by deduction. At least the assumption of the latter was that, if one had all the ultimate elements of things, one could deduce from their mathematical relations what the structure of the world is. This was essentially the position of Descartes. He assumed that he could conceive of the world as made up of ultimate spatial elements which were moving with reference to each other, and, given this motion and the spatial elements, could work out what the structure of things must be. He identified matter with space itself and assumed a great whirl of this, with the consequent movement of all the different particles in relation to each other; and he undertook to show how the world arose out of such simple motions. He undertook to do this by means of the mathematical laws of physics. Leibnitz also assumed that, if one could only get hold of these ultimate laws, it was conceivable that one could work out the nature of things from them. In fine, the rationalist went on the assumption that there were certain structures of things of which the mind got hold.

The practice of research science, which I have described at some length above, was continually to approach, continually to seek for, new problems, and with these new problems to find new hypotheses. And these new hypotheses brought with them new worlds which took the place of the old worlds. The test of them was one which lay in the experience of man. It was to be found in the actual process of cognition as it lay in experience itself. The test became the ultimate test, and from this standpoint the mathematical theory simply presented an apparatus for working out hypotheses, for determining what the situation must be within which the test could take place. But the assurance in regard to new hypotheses, with their new structure of the world, rested upon the test of experience itself. It is this scientific method, which finds the test of the truth of a hypothesis in its working, that has got its philosophic expression in the pragmatic doctrine.

This doctrine is nothing but an expression of the scientific method, which is an experimental method. It has advanced by the positing of hypotheses. It has advanced from problems toward their solution, and these problems have called for analysis. And in the case of changes that we have been describing, this analysis is of the type mentioned above. But, besides these analyses, it is necessary that the scientist should present some hypothesis as a solution to the problem. The hypothesis is not simply a statement of the ultimate elements and the relations between them. If that were the case, one's thinking would be mere deduction, mere demonstration. Given the elements and their relations, we can see that possible combinations can be made and conclusions deduced. That leads to the curious situation that Poincaré has pointed out, that in mathematical science we seem to advance simply by drawing the necessary conclusions from the premises. In that case there should be nothing in the conclusion which was not in the premises; and yet these sciences have advanced from one achievement to another, discovering that which is new, reaching results which are foreign to the positions from which thinking started. Mathematical science has not been simply a recording of the necessary results which can be drawn from a set of given premises. It has been an achievement such as that found in the physical sciences. For example, within mathematics itself we have seen the development of so-called "transcendental numbers." How shall we explain this: that we get, by a purely deductive process, results not found in the premises? Actually, the conclusion that we have to reach is that we are not using simply a deductive process. For, after stating our problem by means of the most penetrating analysis, we reach a point at which a reconstruction of thought takes place. The scientist, including the mathematician, presents a hypothesis and then tests it. In mathematics this testing of the hypothesis is generally hidden, covered up. The way in which the mathematician or mathematical scientist justifies himself is by giving a necessary line of reasoning, and one loses the point at which the hypothesis is made.

Put it in this way: If you should take any other view of the world than our own—such as that expressed by the Ptolemaic theory, the geocentric theory of the world—on the basis of that account you could state the positions of all the different planetary bodies; you could tell where they would all be, could predict eclipses, and other relations. Up to some time in the eighteenth century you could have covered the whole field of astronomy by a Ptolemaic account of the world. But, by working out that doctrine with all its implications, you could not have deduced from it the Copernican, the heliocentric, theory. By the most complete set of deductions possible you could not have reached the latter theory as a necessary result of the former. When one has accepted the statement of the Copernican theory that the sun is the center, then you can show why the conclusions that you drew from the Ptolemaic theory were accurate. You can show why it is that, when the sun seems to revolve about the earth, you can get the same statement of the relative positions of sun and earth and the other planets whether you regard the earth as revolving on its axis or the sun as revolving about the earth. You can take the geocentric theory with the heavens revolving about the earth, or the heliocentric with the earth as revolving about the sun, and show that in either case you get the same relative positions of the different bodies. That is, you can deduce the results of the Ptolemaic theory from the results of the Copernican theory. But you could not move in the opposite direction at the time when the Copernican theory took the place of the Ptolemaic. To put it in a more general form, later hypotheses which you present and accept must be able to take up into themselves all the facts gathered before, all the results which have been attained; and they must be able to show how these results were reached. But you cannot advance by a mere process of deduction from an earlier to a later hypothesis. Of course, if your later hypothesis is merely a correcting of errors, you can. If a statement of your bank account is not right, you can go back and find the mistake. But you cannot deduce later theories from earlier ones. You cannot deduce the theory of electromagnetism from a theory of solid atoms. But, given the theory as it is being worked out, we can state mass in terms of electromagnetism. From the standpoint of mathematical science, we seem always to have only a process of deduction; and the point at which the new hypothesis comes in is one which is very apt to be completely hidden. It is not realized that this has taken place in the mind of the scientist who has a new idea, for, just as soon as he has a new idea, he states the whole in terms of a set of equations where the results follow necessarily from the premises. And in this way he covers up the hypothesis that he has fashioned. Actually, the hypothetical method is essential to development even inside the field of exact mathematics.

Mathematical technique has shown itself peculiarly powerful in dealing with problems which science has approached. It succeeded, for example, in dealing with the problem of change.

That problem was never attacked by the ancient world, that is, the problem of change while it is occurring. The ancient world considered change in terms of qualitative elaboration, in terms of degeneration and decay, but always from the point of view of the result being attained. Motion, in particular, was studied in terms of spaces which were in the past, in times which had elapsed. The ancient thinkers never undertook to deal with each change while it was going on.

Now, that is just the problem that presented itself in dealing with what in modern mathematics are called "acceleration" and "deceleration," that is, increase and decrease in velocity. How can you estimate the change that is uniformly taking place within change itself? You have a body moving toward the earth. You can measure the length of the fall and the time of the fall. But this fall is not one in which velocity has been constant. On the contrary, its velocity has been uniformly increasing. That seemed to mean that the ratio between the distance passed over and the time elapsed is itself continually changing. And yet this ratio always means a certain distance passed over in a certain elapsed time. That is, you have to take a certain distance and a certain time as uniform. We say that a body has fallen so far in a half or in a thousandth of a second, and that its velocity is such and such. That means it has passed over this fixed portion of its path in this fixed time. Then the next portion may represent a ratio which gives a greater time or a greater space. But each portion of it has to be treated as if it were fixed. The problem of the falling body is the problem of a process in which the velocity is uniformly increased. It is that problem that the "infinitesimal calculus," as Leibnitz termed it, or "fluxions," as Newton called it—terms which refer to identical methods at bottom—was invented to solve. These are the methods which mathematics has used for dealing with a seemingly insoluble problem. What Leibnitz and Newton did was to find a way of stating numbers in terms of infinitesimals, of distances that are so slight, times so short, that they can be neglected. A more accurate statement was one in which these distances were stated in terms of the law of change. A still more satisfactory treatment was a statement in terms of limits. That is, it was found out that as one approached a certain limit a certain law was indicated. And it was assumed, then, that this law must be true of the limit itself. What was true of the different situations as you approached this limit, so to speak, must be true of the limit itself.

There are different ways of stating a mathematical procedure by means of which, as I have said, the scientist was able to deal with the law of change while that change itself was occurring—of getting at the law of the change of a change. It is this that has enabled science to get inside of, and to deal with, a process that is going on. The method is one of analysis which goes farther and farther and discovers laws by means of this continued analysis. It was the effectiveness of this analysis which gave prestige to mathematics. It was no longer simply a static science of Euclidean geometry, no longer a mere statement of equations between static quantities; it was a method by means of which one could get inside the processes which were themselves going on, and get the laws of those changes which were occurring.

As I have said, the realistic philosophy has been a generalization, in some sense, of this mathematical method which has been so remarkable in its achievements. It has enabled the scientist to enter all sorts of fields—those of the changes of air, of fluids of all sorts; those of the changes with which physics and chemistry have to deal; those of the changes of heat, for example. It was a method which, by its analysis, was able to get back to ultimate elements—ultimate at least for the time being —and get relations existing between these elements even when the relations were changing. Knowledge, then, seemed to consist in getting hold of ultimate elements and the relations between them and also the study, as I have said, of the relations of relations, the changes of changes. It seemed to consist in getting hold of the ultimate elements and relata and the relations between them. That has been the goal of realistic thought.

This movement and the pragmatic are the two which are peculiarly characteristic of the modern period, for both of them grow out of phases of the scientific process: the one arises out of the mathematical technique which has been greatly generalized, so that it goes into the field of pure logic in which mathematics and philosophy are brought together; the other is a development of the technique of experimental science and the recognition that the test of a hypothesis lies in the successful solution of a problem and that human advance consists in the solution of problems, solutions that have to be stated in terms of the processes that have been stopped by the problem. Progress is not toward a known goal. We cannot tell what the goal is toward which we are moving, and we do not test our movements or direct them according to any fixed goal that we can set up. What we do do, in the face of difficulties or problems, is to seek solutions. We seek a hypothesis which will set free the processes that have been stopped in the situation that we call problematic.

There has been a neo-idealism in our modern philosophic thought too; but it has not played a very important part, and I will not complicate the picture by introducing it.

CHAPTER XVI

THE PROBLEM OF SOCIETY—HOW WE BECOME SELVES

WHAT I have wanted to make evident in the last few chapters is that science itself has been advancing at a great rate and has become conscious of its experimental method, which latter seemingly has been the source of its advance. It has been natural that philosophy should take these phases of the scientific advance as a basis for its interpretation of life, for science, as we know, is not a thing which exists by itself, even though it uses abstruse mathematical methods. It is an instrument by means of which mankind, the community, gets control over its environment. It is, in one sense, the successor to the early magic that undertook to control its environment by magical methods. It is a means of control. Science is something that enters into all the minutiae of life. We cannot brush our teeth without it. We cannot eat or drink without science coming in to tell us what should be eaten, what vitamins in the upper part of the alphabet ought to be used, how they can be obtained in the orange juice and the spinach that is on the menu. It tells us how to blow our noses and indicates with whom we may shake hands and whom we should avoid. There is hardly a point in life at which science does not tell something about the conduct that is an essential part of our living. It is, in a way, independent of the community, of the community life. It goes on in separate institutions, in universities that cloister themselves from the community, under separate foundations that demand that this work shall be entirely free so that the scientist may entertain whatever view he cares to hold, use whatever methods he has worked out. The scientist demands a freedom in his operations which is greater than that which anyone else in the community can demand. He seems to stand outside the community; and yet, as I have said, his statements, the directions which he gives, enter into the whole minutiae of social life. Society is feeling its dependence upon scientific method more and more, and will continue to do so if it is to go ahead intelligently. The control over community life in the past has been a control of situations. The control, as such, has been almost inevitably conservative. It has preserved orders which have established themselves as social habits that we call "institutions." A conscious social control has taken on this form: The law must be obeyed; the constitution must be honored; the various institutions such as the family, school, courts, must be recognized and obeyed; the order which has come down to us is an order which is to be preserved. And, whenever the community is disturbed, we always find this return to the fixed order which is there, and which we do not want to have shaken. It is entirely natural and, in a certain sense, entirely justifiable. We have to have an order of society; and, if what is taking place shakes that order, we have no evidence that we will get another order to take the place of the present one. We cannot afford to let that order go to pieces. We must have it as a basis for our conduct.

The first step consciously taken in advance of this position is that which grew out of the French Revolution, that which in a certain sense incorporated the principle of revolution into institutions. That is, when you set up a constitution and one of the articles in it is that the constitution may be changed, then you have, in a certain sense, incorporated the very process of revolution into the order of society. Only now it is to be an ordered, a constitutional revolution by such and such steps. But, in any case, now you can change the order of things as it is going on.

That is the problem of society, is it not? How can you present order and structure in society and yet bring about the changes that need to take place, are taking place? How can you bring those changes about in orderly fashion and yet preserve order?

To bring about change is seemingly to destroy the given order, and yet society does and must change. That is the problem, to incorporate the methods of change into the order of society itself. I do not mean to say that society has not always recognized that change could take place, but it did not undertake to find a process by means of which this should go on. It simply assumed that change was going to take place toward some fixed goal. If you are going to have a society in which everyone is going to recognize the interests of everybody else—for example, in which the golden rule is to be the rule of conduct, that is, a society in which everyone is to make the interests of others his own interest, while actually each person seems to be pursuing his own interest—how can that goal be reached? It was assumed, of course. that this was to be done through a religious current, through a change in the heart of the individual. But in the last analysis that goal was to be reached in the world to come, not in this one. That was the religious solution. The order we find is one given by God for this world and must be preserved. The final perfect society was to be a New Jerusalem that belonged to another world. The religious goal was one of otherworldliness. We have other conceptions, councils of perfection set up, such as that of a society in which you should bring liberty in the sense of everyone's respecting the rights of everyone else, one's liberty being in that sense only circumscribed by intrenching on others' liberty. That is more or less an abstraction. To take a practical illustration, how are you to determine where the liberty of a man in the control of his property is to be restricted? He needs controlling. We will say that he, or rather a group of men, own shares in a railroad, and that they choose to deal with rates in a fashion which will serve their own interest. Well now, if they are to have complete control over their property, and then the community comes in and says that theirs is property of a different sort, that their acts must have the approval of the community, how are we to determine where the restriction in the control over the property is to take place?

THE PROBLEM OF SOCIETY

How is society to find a method for changing its own institutions and still preserve the security of those institutions? That is, in general, the problem that presents itself in its most universal form. You want a society that is going ahead, not a fixed order, as the religious solution would have it. You want a society that is progressing. Progress has become essential to intelligent life. Now, how are we to get ahead and change those situations that need changing and yet preserve the security of them? You see this is an advance in which we cannot state the goal toward which we are going. We do not know what the goal is. We are on the way, but we do not know where. And yet we have to get some method of charting our progress. We do not know where the progress is supposed to terminate, where it is going. This is a seemingly insoluble problem.

Science does, in a sense, present the method for its solution. That is, it recognizes that progress is of the nature of the solution of a problem. What these problems present are inhibitions, the checking of conduct. And the solution of the problem stops this checking process, sets it free so that we can go on. The scientist is not looking ahead toward a goal and charting his movement toward that goal. That is not the function of the scientist. He is finding out why his system does not work, what the difficulty in it is. And the test of his solution of the difficulty is that his system starts working again, goes on. Science is occupied with finding what the problems are that exist in the social process. It finds what the problems are, what processes have been definitely checked. Then it asks: How can things be so reconstructed that those processes which have been checked can be set going again? The illustration which I have given from the field of hygiene is as good as any, but you can find similar illustrations elsewhere.

Take, as another example, the social problem of recreation, with all the dangers that gather about its various forms, particularly about commercialized recreation. Shall we recognize the legitimacy of the expression of the play instinct, the freedom for the play one wants, when at the same time we recognize that dangers go along with it? You do not set up an ideal form of recreation. You find out what the dangers are, just what it is that finds expression in play, what the freedom is that is demanded there; and you see how you can combine the control or avoidance of danger with the freedom of expression. That is the sort of problem we are meeting. We have to let freedom of activity go on, and yet dangers must be avoided. And what science does is to give a method for studying such situations. Again, on the social side, or on the biological side in dealing with questions of disease, we have the question of how we shall deal with these problems. As a further instance, take the question of crime. What are the conditions out of which crime itself springs? How, on the one hand, can you protect society against the criminal and yet, on the other hand, recognize those conditions which are responsible for the criminal himself? What procedure can you set up by means of which you can guard society against the criminal and at the same time protect the individual against unfair conditions under which he has been living? Here we have a series of clashing problems, and what we have to do is to get a way which will recognize that what we feel is essential in each, so that the problems can be adjusted and the essential processes of life can go on. When we get such a method, we have the means for the solution of our problems. Let me illustrate this further in the problem of juvenile crime, so-called. There we have a situation in which certain definite habits embodied in our institution of the court prove unsatisfactory. The child is brought before the court by the police. The social habit left simply to itself would condemn the child to the penitentiary and thus make a confirmed criminal out of him. But it is possible to modify those habits by what we call the "scientific method."

What I wish to point out is that the scientific method, as such, is, after all, only the evolutionary process grown self-conscious. We look back over the history of plant and animal life on the face of the globe and see how forms have developed slowly by the trial-and-error method. There are slight variations that take place in the individual forms and occasional more pronounced variations that we call "mutations." Out of these, different forms gradually arise. But the solution of the particular problem of an animal—the food problem, we will say—is one which may take thousands of years to solve in the gradual development of a certain form. A form which passes, let us say, from the eating of meat to the eating of vegetables develops a type of stomach capable of handling this latter kind of food. Here we have a problem which is met gradually by the appearance of some form that does commence to develop an adjustment to the problem, and we can assume that from its progeny those particular forms will be selected which are adapted to such digestion. It is a problem which has to be met if there is to be development, and the development takes place by the seemingly incidental appearance of those forms which happen to be better able than others to meet the peculiar demands set up. If we put ourselves in the same place, there is the same problem. The food problem faces us as it does all other animal forms. We have to get our food from both the vegetable and the animal kingdoms. But if it is a question of our being able to get the food that is shut up inside a cellulose covering, we do not wait through long periods until we develop stomachs which will be able to digest this substance. We work out a milling process by means of which we set free that which is digestible. That is, we solve the problem directly by what we call the "scientific method." Here is a certain necessity: the food which we need is shut off from us by a cellulose covering. We work out a mechanism to get rid of this covering. There is an evolutionary problem made self-conscious. The problem is stated in a definite form; this, in turn, excites the imagination to the formation of a possible hypothesis which will serve as the solution of it; and then we set out to test the solution.

The same process is found in social development, in the formation of great societies among both invertebrates and vertebrates, through a principle of organization. Societies develop, just as animal forms develop, by adjusting themselves to the problems that they find before them. They have food problems, problems of climate, just as individual animals do; but they meet them in a social fashion. When we reach the human form with its capacity for indicating what is important in a situation, through the process of analysis; when we get to the position in which a mind can arise in the individual form, that is, where the individual can come back upon himself and stimulate himself just as he stimulates others; where the individual can call out in himself the attitude of the whole group; where he can acquire the knowledge that belongs to the whole community; where he can respond as the whole community responds under certain conditions when they direct this organized intelligence toward particular ends; then we have this process which provides solutions for problems working in a self-conscious way. In it we have the evolution of the human mind which makes use directly of the sort of intelligence which has been developed in the whole process of evolution. It makes use of it by the direct method that we call "mental." If one goes back to a primitive society, one finds the beginnings of the evolution of what we call "institutions." Now these institutions are, after all, the habits of individuals in their interrelation with each other, the type of habit that is handed down from one generation to another. And we can study the growth of these habits as we can study the growth and behavior of an animal.

That is where science comes in to aid society in getting a method of progress. It understands the background of these problems, the processes out of which they have developed; and it has a method of attacking them. It states the problem in terms of checked processes; and then it has a test of the suggested solution by seeing whether those processes can continue or not. That is as valuable—in a certain sense more valuable —a contribution of science as any of its immediate results that we can gather together. This sort of method enables us to keep the order of society and yet to change that order within the process itself. It is a recognition that intelligence expresses itself in the solution of problems. That is the way in which evolution is taking place in the appearance of problems in life. Living forms have found themselves up against problematic situations: their food gone, the climate changed, new enemies coming in. The method which nature has followed, if we may speak so anthropomorphically, has been the production of variations until finally some one variation has arisen which has survived. Well, what science is doing is making this method of trial and error a conscious method.

Up to this period the so-called "social sciences" have been gathered about the more or less dogmatic theory of certain institutions. It was assumed that each institution as such stood upon certain rational doctrines, whether those of the family, the state, the church, the school, or the court. The early theory was that these institutions were established directly by God. The divine right of kings was simply the assertion that the state had as divine an origin as the church; and, of course, it was assumed that God was also responsible for the ordering of the family and the other institutions. They all came back to a direct structure which was given to them. If the theories did not place this structure in divine ordinance, they brought it back to certain natures in the institutions themselves. And it was assumed that you could work out the theory which would determine what the institutions ought to be. The development of evolutionary doctrine had as great an effect in this field as any it had in biology. Spencer, and others following immediately in his path, carried over the evolutionary theory into the development of human institutions. People went back to primitive societies, which at first were regarded as much more primitive than they were, and then undertook to show how, out of the life of these people, different institutions arose through a process of evolution.

I pointed out earlier that a certain part of the stimulus which directed this thought came from the Hegelian movement. The Hegelian doctrine was in one sense an evolutionary one. At least it was particularly interested in the development of what we term "self-consciousness," in the process of thinking where that arose. And it was the Hegelian thinkers who turned to the study of human institutions, but they did so on the economic and the political side. On the economic side, we have the Marxian doctrine of the human institution in the economic process. On the political side, we have the development of the state, especially the city-state. Hegel's son Karl was quite a notable author in the early study of the city-state, particularly of the way in which it developed. The whole study of so complex a dogmatic structure as the Roman law, for example, was brought back to an evolutionary consideration. Later, attention was directed toward social forms as social forms, apart from any dogmatic structure that lay behind them.

Take, again, the attitude of the community toward crime. On the evolutionary side, you go back to a situation, we will say, of blood vengeance. A man from one clan kills a man from another. Immediately there arises within the injured clan a man who is determined to revenge the death by killing someone from the other clan, and the next of kin sets out to kill the slayer. When he accomplishes this, he sets up at once the need of vengeance on the part of the first group. Again, the next of kin goes out to slay in his turn. And this process goes on until, we will say, the clans are nearly exterminated. Well now, when clans were brought together in a tribe in order to defend themselves against other tribes, such a decimation of fighting members of the group became a serious matter, and the tribe came to consider how this problem could be met. A court was worked out in which vengeance took the form of paying a fine. And some sort of a court had to be constituted which should pass upon obligations. In this way a means was gradually built up of getting rid of blood vengeance. There you have an evolutionary process in which the court arises.

When it is carried through and it becomes necessary to organize society more exactly and fit the penalty more definitely to what is felt to be the character of the crime, there arise all the penalties which belong to a court of law. And we get the institution of criminal law which still carries over some of this sense of vengeance which is to be enacted. There must be some suffering on the part of the man who has gone against the interests of the community, who has trespassed on the rights of others. In the older, medieval state the community was called together to witness the suffering of the individual who was being punished. The community thus got satisfaction out of the vengeance, particularly any specific individuals who were themselves injured by the so-called criminal. That element of vengeance in a sense demands that where some particularly outrageous crime has been committed, the community feels the need for somebody to suffer. And under such circumstances it is difficult to get impartial justice. It becomes more important to the community that someone should suffer than that the specific individual should suffer. So in our criminal law we have this motive of exacting suffering, and we have a partially worked-out theory which states that where a person has committed a crime he should pay by a certain amount of suffering for the wrong he has done. If the wrong is great, he must suffer more than if it is a lesser wrong. So we inflict punishment by putting him in prison. If the sin is heinous, he is put in for ten or twenty years; if lighter, for perhaps only a few weeks or months. We fit the punishment to the crime.

But we know that that process does not work at all. We have no such exactly measured sets of sufferings as to be able to put them accurately over against wrongs. When the sense of vengeance has died down, we are not sure whether we want the other person to suffer at all. We want to get rid of crime. And so we change our theory from wanting the person to suffer for a wrong he has done to seeing that we keep him from doing the same wrong again. So we have retribution, not in the sense of vengeance but as repression of crime itself. But you know how difficult it is to work those two motives together, trying to find out just how much repression of crime does take place through the action of the law. And when we come to juvenile offenses, we feel the situation should be approached from an entirely different standpoint. So we put aside criminal law, and we have the judge sitting with the boy or girl; we get members of the family, perhaps some person interested in social service, possibly the school teacher, and they all talk it over, and try to find out just why what happened did happen, and they attempt to discover some sort of situation by means of which the criminal can be got back into a social position and be kept from doing the sort of thing he has done in the past. Thus we try to get rid of crime by a social process. That parole system has been carried over from the juvenile court into the adult court. Very good results have been obtained where politics has not come in to corrupt the process. There we have the development of an institution from both ends, so to speak. You can see how, out of the attitude of vengeance, the court itself has arisen, and then how, out of the operation of an institution of that sort, one having conflicting motives in it, such as repression of crime on the one hand and a demand for vengeance on the other, that institution can be approached from the standpoint of reinstating the individual in society. There is a social problem here, the problem of an individual who has abused the rights of somebody else but whom we want to put back in the social situation so that he will not do it again. There we have the development of a social process by a real scientific method.

We try to state the problem as carefully as we can. Here is a boy who has allied himself with a gang and has been carried away with the sense of adventure and has committed a burglary which could send him to the penitentiary for years. But that would be absurd. It would make a criminal out of him, and no good would be accomplished at all. It is very questionable whether it would even keep other boys from doing the same thing, for, of course, the sense of adventure makes the attitude of the criminal something attractive in itself. It is astonishing how, when we are somewhat relaxed by an attack of grippe or disease, we turn to criminal tales for our relief! If you go through the hospitals of the city, you will find such tales being read in great quantities. The creation of crime taken in itself can be looked at from the point of view of adventure, especially for the adolescent. If you approach things scientifically, you can see what the attitude is. You can see that the boy has approached it from this attitude of adventure, does not realize its import; and if he is made to realize it, you can make a very good citizen indeed out of him. What you want to do, then, is to state your social situation in such a fashion that you can reconstitute the boy as a normal citizen, give him opportunities for play in which he can express his demand for adventure with a recognition of what the rights are that make a possibility of citizenship. That has to be brought home to him. He wants to be a citizen in the community, and he has to see that he must have the same respect for the rights of others that he claims for himself. And at the same time you must have a situation where the boy can lead a normal life. Work out specific hypotheses, and by means of them you may get the boy back into society again.

Take any institution as such and look at it from the standpoint of evolution, the way in which that is determined in society, and then you can see the development in society itself of a technique which we call the "scientific technique," but it is a technique which is simply doing consciously what takes place naturally in the evolution of forms. I have been pointing out that the process of evolution is one that meets such a problem as that of blood vengeance, where members of the tribe are at work killing each other as fast as they can. And the community works out there—in a somewhat bungling fashion, if you like—a court which undertakes to meet this situation. It becomes established, acquires a dogmatic structure, holds on to motives which belonged to the earlier situation. But finally we see the situation as one in which we try to do with self-consciousness what took place by a process of evolution. That is, we try to state the problem with reference to a particular child; we want to see what can be done toward bringing together what was a healthful expression of adventure on the part of the boy with rights which he himself claims. So the juvenile court represents a self-conscious application of the very process of evolution out of which the courts themselves arose.

What I am trying to do is to connect this entire evolutionary process with social organization in its most complex expression, and as that within which arise the very individuals through whose life-process it works, giving birth to just such elements as are involved in the development of selves. And, as I have said, the life-process itself is brought to consciousness in the conduct of the individual form, in his so-called "self-consciousness." He gets a much more effective control over his environment than the ox can get over its. The process is one in which, in a certain sense, control is within his own grasp. If you think of it, the human being as a social form has actually got relatively complete control over his environment. The animal gets a certain slight kind of control over its environment; but the human form, in societies, can determine what vegetation shall grow, what animals shall exist besides itself; it can control its own climate, erect its own buildings. It has, in a biological sense, complete control over its own environment. That is, it has attained to a remarkable degree an end which is implied in the whole living process—the control by the form of the environment within which it lives. To a degree human society has reached that goal.

It has often been pointed out, of course, that evolution does not reach any goal. The concept means simply the adaptation of a form to a certain environment. But adaptation is not simply the fitting of the form into the environment, it carries with it some degree of control over that environment. And in the case of the human form, of human society, we have that adaptation expressing itself in a very high degree of control. Of course, we cannot change the chemical and physical structure of things, but we can make them over into those forms that we ourselves need and which are of value to us. That is possible for us; and, as I have said with reference to the question of food and to the question of climatic influences, we can in a very large degree determine that control. So there is, within limits, a development toward complete adaptation where that adaptation expresses itself in control over the environment. And in that sense I think we can fairly say that human organization, as a social organization, does exercise control and has in that sense reached a certain goal of development.

Well now, this social process I have been sketching in these broad strokes has become of increasing interest to reflective thought throughout this whole period. Of course, to some extent it has always been of essential interest to man in the social situation in which he lives. What I am referring to specifically is the character of the social organism—its organization, its history, and the conditions under which it can be controlled. The statement of the functions of the different parts of the social organism is that study which we have in a so-called "social science," and more particularly in sociology. This had its inception in the thought of Comte, and then was enriched by the idea of evolution as brought in by Spencer. From that time on, the attempt to understand human society as an organization has been of increasing interest to the Western world. Men have been trying to see the habits out of which society has arisen, to find out under what conditions it operates, and how problems that arise in it can be definitely controlled. This involves looking at human institutions from the standpoint I have suggested, that is, as social habits.

While during the century there has been this increased interest in the study of the social organization, there has been a corresponding interest in the experience of the individual. Part of this is due to our scientific attitude. As we have seen, it is the unique experience of the scientist that presents the problem, and it is in the mind of the scientist that the hypothesis arises. It is not only in the scientist as such that this uniqueness of the experience has been recognized as of importance. After all, the scientist is simply making a technique out of human intelligence. His method is the same as that of all intelligent beings, even though it involves a simple rendering in self-consciousness of the whole process of evolution. That in the experience of all individuals which is peculiar to the individual, that which is unique in his experience, is of importance; and what the last century increasingly recognized was the importance of these unique individual experiences.

The emotional side of these experiences, as we know, registers itself in the folk poetry, in the lyric expression of the self—a registration of values from the point of view of the individual. There have always been some neat ways of scientific observation, although accurate presentation of it belongs really to the modern world, that world which has grown up since the period of the Renaissance. But what I am particularly calling attention to is the interest we have in that which is peculiar to the individual as it is revealed in our literature and in our journals, our newspapers. The curious thing about the newspaper is that it records happenings to individual persons; and it assumes that it is of interest to us to know that a certain individual at a certain time was run over by an automobile or that a certain person fell down, hurt himself in such and such a way, and that John or Jane has had such and such an experience in such a place. It is curious to note the interest that centers about individuals as such, and the assumption that the world at large will be interested in these happenings.

Well now, what I want to connect with this journalese interest in happenings to particular individuals is the character of our literature, not simply in its lyric poetry, where the emotion of the individual is presented so that it can be handed on to others, but particularly in our novels and the drama. In these we have this interest in the experience of the individual as such presented as it has been during the last century, because it does answer to some very profound interest on the part of all the individuals who take up their morning and evening papers, who read all sorts of stories and novels, go to movies, listen to the radio, get those experiences of other individuals which, as I say, have an interest for us which is rather astonishing when one just stands off and looks at the situation. They seem to be so unrelated. We seem to be interested in just a particular occurrence.

We speak of it as sensational and perhaps are apt to regard it as an attitude not entirely helpful on our part when we are interested in this fashion.

What is the import of this interest? I wanted to bring this up in sharp contrast to what I am going to develop later, that is, that the human self arises through its ability to take the attitude of the group to which he belongs—because he can talk to himself in terms of the community to which he belongs and lay upon himself the responsibilities that belong to the community; because he can recognize his own duties as over against others—that is what constitutes the self as such. And there you see what we have emphasized, as peculiar to others, that which is both individual and which is habitual. The structure of society lies in these social habits, and only in so far as we can take these social habits into ourselves can we become selves.

We speak of this interest on the emotional side as "sympathy" —passing into the attitude of the other, taking the rôle of the other, feeling the other's joys and sorrows. That is the effective side of it. What we call the "intellectual side," the "rational side," is the recognition of common stimuli, of common emotions which call out responses in every member of the group. And in so far as one indicates this common character to others, he indicates it to himself. In this way, of course, by taking the attitude of the others in the group in their co-operative, highly complex activity, the individual is able to enter into their experiences. The engineer is able to direct vast groups of individuals in a highly complex process. But in every direction he gives, he takes the attitude of the person whom he is directing. It has the same meaning to him that it has to others. We enter in that way into the attitudes of others, and in that way we make our very complex societies possible. This development of a form that is able so to communicate with others that it takes on attitudes of those in the group, that it talks to itself as it talks to others, that imports into its own life this conversation, and sets up an inner forum in which it works out the process that it is going to carry on, and so brings it to public consideration with the advantage of that previous rehearsing, is all important. Sometimes we find that we can best think out an argument by supposing that we are talking to somebody who takes one particular side. As we say, we have an argument to present, and we think how we will present it to that individual. And as soon as we present it, we know that he would reply in a certain way. Then we reply in a certain fashion to him. Sometimes it is easier to carry out such a conversation by picking out a particular protagonist we know. In that way in the night hours we are apt to go through distressing conversations we have to carry out the next day. That is the process of thought. It is taking the attitude of others, talking to other people, and then replying in their language. That is what constitutes thinking.

Of course, conditions are different in a human society than in simpler situations. I was pointing out the difference between a human society and a society of invertebrates. The principle of organization is not that of physiological plasticity, not that of holding the form itself physiologically to its particular function; it is rather the principle of organization as found in the form of human intercommunication and participation. It is what the human individual puts into the form of significant symbols through the use of gestures. He is then able to place himself in the attitude of others, particularly into just such attitudes as those I have spoken of as human institutions. If institutions are social habits, they represent certain definite attitudes that people assume under certain given social conditions. So that the individual, in so far as he does take the rôle of others, can take the habitual attitude of the community over against such social situations as these.

As I have pointed out, he does this in the process of indicating to others the important elements in a situation, pointing out those elements which are of importance in the social process, in a situation that represents one of these social habits, such as the family situation; one that involves the rights of different individuals in the community, such as a political situation. What the individual does is to indicate what the important characters in a co-operative process are. He indicates this to other members of the community; but as we shall see, especially in the case of vocal gestures, he indicates it to himself as to others; and just in so far as he does indicate it to himself as to others, he tends to call out in himself the same attitude as in others. There is a common attitude, that is, one which all assume under certain habitual situations. Through the use of language, through the use of the significant symbol, then, the individual does take the attitude of others, especially these common attitudes, so that he finds himself taking the same attitude toward himself that the community takes. This, of course, is what gives the principle of social control, not simply the social control that results from blind habit, but a social control that comes from the individual assuming the same attitude toward himself that the community assumes toward him. In a habitual situation everyone takes a certain attitude in so far as it is habitual, in so far as the habit is one which all have taken, that is, in so far as you have what are called "institutions." If, now, the individual calls out this attitude in others by a gesture, by a word which affects himself just as it affects others, then he will call out the same attitude in himself that he calls out in others. In this way he will be acting toward himself as others act toward him. He will admonish himself as others would. That is, he will recognize what are his duties as well as what are his rights. He takes the attitude of the community toward himself. This gives the principal method of organization which, as I have said, we can study from the standpoint of a behavioristic psychology, a method which belongs to human society and distinguishes it from social organizations which one finds among ants and bees and termites. There one finds societies that run up into the millions; and we find these as finely organized as human societies are, and so organized that individuals' lives are largely determined by the life-process of the whole. We get far more complex and intricate organization, of course, in human society than among the invertebrates. For this principle to which I have referred—organization through communication and participation—makes an almost indefinite organization possible. Now the study of the way in which this organization takes place, the history of it, the evolution of it, is what has been opened up to the human mind in the last century. We now see the way in which out of a primitive group there can gradually arise the very highly organized societies of the present day. We can study that process in the evolution of institutions, and we can see how that process is modified or may be modified in the presence of problematic situations.

This evolution also takes place in human society, but here it takes place not through physiological plasticity, not through the development of peculiar physiological functions on the part of the separate individuals. It takes place through the development of what has been referred to on the logical side as a universe of discourse. That is, it takes place through communication and participation on the part of the different individuals in common activities. It takes place through the development of significant symbols. It is accomplished almost entirely through the development of vocal gestures, through the capacity of the individual to indicate by means of his own gestures to other forms and also to himself, those elements which are of importance in co-operative activity. So far as we can see, the stimuli that keep the invertebrates occupied are those of odor, contact. But we find no evidence of any language among them. It is through physiological development and plasticity that their very complex communities operate. But the human form, subject to no such development as this, can be interwoven into a community activity through its ability to respond to the gestures of other forms that indicate to it the stimuli to which it is to respond. We point things out. This pointing-out process may be with the finger, by an attitude of body, by direction of head and eyes; but as a rule it is by means of the vocal gesture, that is, a certain vocal symbol that indicates something to another individual and to which he responds. Such indication as this sets up a certain definite process of pointing out to other individuals in the group what is of importance in this co-operative activity.

The peculiar importance of the vocal gesture is that it affects the individual who makes it just as much as it affects the individual to whom it is directed. We hear what we say; if we are talking with our fingers we see what we are saying; if with attitudes of the body, we feel what we are saying. The effect of the attitude which we produce in others comes back on ourselves. It is in this way that participation arises out of communication. When we indicate something to another form, we are calling out in that other individual a certain response. The very gesture we make calls out a certain sort of response in him. If that gesture affects us as it affects him, it has a tendency to call out some response in ourselves. The gesture that affects another, when it is a vocal gesture, is one which may have the tendency to influence the speaker as it influences others. The common expression of this is that a man knows what he is saying when the meaning of what he is saying comes to him as really as it goes to another. He is affected just as the other is. If the meaning of what he says affects the other, it affects himself in the same way. The result of this is that the individual who speaks, in some sense takes the attitude of the other whom he addresses. We are familiar with this in giving directions to another person to do something. We find ourselves affected by the same direction. We are ready to do the thing and perhaps become irritated by the awkwardness of the other and insist on doing it ourselves. We have called out in ourselves the same response we have asked for in another person. We are taking his attitude. It is through this sort of participation, this taking the attitudes of other individuals, that the peculiar character of human intelligence is constituted. We say something that means something to a certain group. But it not only means that to the group, it also means that to us. It has the same meaning for both.

There is a certain, what we would call, "unconscious direction" that takes place in lower vertebrate forms. A group of animals is said to set up a sentinel. Some one form is more sensitive than others to stimuli of danger. Now the action on the part of this one which is more sensitive than the rest, the action of running from danger, for example, does cause the other forms to run also. But the first one is not giving a signal in the human sense. It is not aware of giving such directions. Its mere running constitutes a stimulus to the other forms to run in the same direction. It works in the same way as if the form knew what its business was, to catch the first evidence of the enemy and go give the evidence of it to the whole group, thus setting them all going. But in the experience of the animal there is no such procedure, no such content. The animal does not influence himself as he influences others. He does not tell himself of the danger as he tells it to others. He merely runs away.

The outstanding characteristic in human communication is that one is making a declaration, pointing out something that is common in meaning to the whole group and to the individual, so that the individual is taking the attitude of the whole group, so far as there is any definite meaning given. When a man calls out "Fire!" he is not only exciting other people but himself in the same fashion. He knows what he is about. That, you see, constitutes biologically what we refer to as a "universe of discourse." It is a common meaning which is communicated to everyone and at the same time is communicated to the self. The individual is directing other people how to act, and he is taking the attitude of the other people whom he is directing. If in this attitude of the other person he makes an objection, he is doing what the other person would do, and he is also carrying on the process which we call "thought." That is, you indicate to somebody else that he is to do something, and he objects to it. Well now, the person might in his attitude of the other make the same objection himself. You reply to the other person, trying to point out his mistake or admitting your own. In the same way, if you make some objection, you reply to your own objection or admit your mistake to yourself. Thinking is a process of conversation with one's self when the individual takes the attitude of the other, especially when he takes the common attitude of the whole group, when the symbol that he uses is a common symbol, has a meaning common to the entire group, to everyone who is in it and anyone who might be in it. It is a process of communication with participation in the experience of other people.

The mechanism that we use for this process is words, vocal gestures. And we need, of course, only a very few of these as compared with those we need when talking to others. A single symbol is enough to call out necessary responses. But it is just as really a conversation in terms of the significant symbols of language as if the whole process were expressed. We sometimes do our thinking out loud, in fully organized sentences; and one's thought can always presumably be developed into a complete grammatical unit. That is what constitutes thinking.

Now, it is this inner thought, this inner flow of speech and what it means—that is, words with their meanings—that call out intelligent response; it is this that constitutes the mind, in so far as that lies in the experience of the form. But this is only a part of the whole social process, for the self has arisen in that social process; it has its being there. Of course, you could carry such a self as that over to a Robinson Crusoe island and leave him by himself, and he could carry that social process on by himself and extend it to his pets. He carries that on by himself, but it is only because he has grown up in society, because he can take attitudes and rôles of others, that he can accomplish this.

This mental process, then, is one which has evolved in the social process of which it is a part. And it belongs to the different organisms that lie inside of this larger social process. We can approach it from the standpoint of evolution; and we can approach it more particularly from the standpoint of behavioristic psychology, where we can get back to what expresses itself in the mind. We also can get somewhat underneath the experience that goes on in the self in what we term "pathological psychology," a psychology that enables us to get hold of the various processes that are not themselves evidenced in this stream of inner conversation to which I have referred. The term "pathological" simply means that this type of psychology has been pursued largely in dealing with pathological cases. It is a study, for example, of the way in which our special world arises in our experience through our distance senses and our contact experiences, through the collation of the elements which we reach through vision with the elements which we reach through the tactual sense, the process by which we have built up an implemental world by the use of our hands; for a particular instance, the process by which, for purposes of food, we reach with the hand for a distant object. Man comes into that process and gives to the organism a physical thing which is not the food, not the consummation, whatever it may be, but a physical thing. Our world is made up out of physical things. We deal with things as if we could handle them. We think of things as being "pulverized," broken up into parts so we can get hold of them. A physical thing is a unit into which we break up our environment. The process by which we build our world of physical things is a process, too, of which we are not immediately conscious. The child, the infant that is uncertainly groping toward a ball, is gradually building up a world of such physical things; but the process takes place underneath the level of our own consciousness. We cannot get at it in its immediate inception, only indirectly by this type of psychology, a psychology that does enable us to get into the workings of the individual process as it lies inside of the whole social process to which it belongs.

And this is what constitutes the self as such. A self which is so evidently a social individual that it can exist only in a group of social individuals is as much a result of the process of evolution as other biological forms. A form that can co-operate with others through the use of significant symbols, set up attitudes of others and respond to them, is possible through the development of great tracts in the central nervous system that are connected with our processes of articulation, with the ear, and so with the various movements that can go on in the human form. But they are not circumscribed within the conduct of a single form. They belong to the group. And the process is just as much an evolution as is the queen bee or the fighter among the ants. In those instances we get a certain particular evolution that is taking place, belonging to a certain particular society, one which could exist only in such a society. The same is true of the self. That is, an individual who affects himself as he affects another; who takes the attitude of the other in so far as he affects the other, in so far as he is using what we term "intelligible speech;" who knows what he himself is saying, in so far as he is directing his indications by these significant symbols to others with the recognition that they have the same meaning for them as for him; such an individual is, of course, a phase of the development of the social form. This is a branch of what we term "behavioristic psychology," one in which we can see how the self as such has developed.

What I want to make evident is that the development, the evolution, of mind as well as of institutions is a social evolution. As I have just stated, society in its organization is a form, a species that has developed; and it has many forms developing within it. You see, for example, at the present time in reference to the question of food that the problem is one which is met by very intricate social organizations. Where the individual himself responds simply to the odor or sight of food, we recognize it as a biological process. When the whole community responds to the need of food by the organization of its industries, its methods of agriculture, of milling, of transportation, of cooking and preparation, we have the same process, only now not by separate individuals but by a social organization; and that organization is just as really an evolution as the stomach of the ox. That stomach is very complicated. The evolution of a social mechanism by which grain is sowed and reaped in South America and North America, is carried to great milling establishments and there converted into flour, and then carried and distributed by dealers so that the individual groups can get hold of it and prepare it in such fashion that it can be readily assimilated—that is just as much evolution as the development of bacteriological laboratories in the digestive tract of an ox. It is a process, however, which takes place much more rapidly than it is taking place in the case of the ox. There we have something that answers to a physiological plasticity in the case of invertebrates—the adjustment of different organs within the body to accomplish what we accomplish by mechanical means. It is this ability to control our environment that gives us what we term "mind."

What we attach to the term "mind" particularly is its privacy. It belongs to the individual. And what takes place there takes place, we say, in the experience of the individual. He may make it accessible to others by telling about it. He may talk out loud. He may publish. He may indicate even by his uncontrolled gestures what his frame of mind is. But there is that which goes on inside of a man's mind that never gets published, something that takes place there within the experience of the individual. Part of it, of course, is what answers to what is going on in the physiological mechanism there, the suffering that belongs to one's teeth, the pleasure one gets in the palate. These are experiences which he has for himself because they are taking place within his own organism. But, though they are taking place within his own organism, and so no one else can experience the same thing, the organism does not experience it as its own—that is, it does not realize that the experience is its own—until a self has arisen. We have no reason to assume, for example, that in lower animals there are such entities as selves; and if no such entities, then that which takes place within the organism cannot be identified with such a self. There is pain; there is pleasure; there are feelings which are not exactly painful or pleasurable, such as heat and cold. These various feelings belong to the organism, the tensions of the various muscles, the movements of the joints, so essential in our intelligent social conduct. These belong to the organism in a certain sense. But the individual animal does not associate them with a self because it has no self; it is not a self.

A self can arise only where there is a social process within which this self has had its initiation. It arises within that process. For that process the communication and participation to which I have referred is essential. That is the way in which selves as such have arisen. That is where the individual is in a social process in which he is a part, where he does influence himself as he does others. There the self arises. And there he turns back upon himself, directs himself. He takes over those experiences which belong to his own organism. He identifies them with himself. What constitutes the particular structure of his experience is what we call his "thought." It is the conversation which goes on within the self. This is what constitutes his mind. For it is through this so-called "thought," of course, that he interprets his experiences. Now that thought, as I have already indicated, is only the importation of outer conversation, conversation of gestures with others, into the self in which the individual takes the rôle of others as well as his own rôle. He talks to himself. This talking is significant. He is indicating what is of importance in the situation. He is indicating those elements that call out the necessary responses. When there are conflicts, the problem gives rise to the hypotheses that form in his mind; and he indicates them to himself and to others. It is this process of talking over a problematic situation with ones' self, just as one might talk with another, that is exactly what we term "mental." And it goes on within the organism.

CHAPTER XVII

MIND APPROACHED THROUGH BEHAVIOR— CAN ITS STUDY BE MADE SCIENTIFIC?

WHEN the scientific method we have been describing was brought into the problems of psychology, it was recognized that association could not be maintained as the fundamental principle in terms of which they might be solved. We speak naturally of certain elements as associated with each other. Why are certain experiences associated rather than an indefinite number of others? When we come back to account for their strong association, we find we come back to attention, to interest. We are interested in certain connections, and these get fixed in our minds. We give our attention to certain elements in experience, and that fixes them in the order in which they occur. But association is itself something that needs to be explained. Why is there selection in experience? Consciousness is selective; we see what we are looking for. There is a character of conduct about experience that determines what the relations are to be, or at least determines between what elements the relations are going to lie. This recognition of the importance of conduct as determining what the connections shall be within experience itself is the characteristic of the latter psychology. It has gone under various names.

The older psychology was structural. That is, it took experience as we find it to pieces and found certain relations between the various elements of it. These it explained through association. The latter psychology is functional rather than structural. It recognizes certain functions of conduct. We get experiences of distant objects, and their import for us lies in what we are going to do about them. We are hungry, and we set about getting food. We have become stifled with the air in the room, and we get out-of-doors. We are acting, and in our actions we determine what the relations are going to be between the various elements in experience. The structure of the act is the important character of conduct. This psychology also is called motor psychology, as over against the older psychology of sensation; voluntary psychology, as over against the mere association of ideas with each other. Finally, the development of these different phases got expression in behavioristic psychology, which gives itself to the study of this conduct to which I have referred. It undertakes to approach the mind from the point of view of the action of the individual. As a psychology, behaviorism has turned away, then, from the category of consciousness as such. Accounts of consciousness had been largely static in character. There were certain states of consciousness, certain impressions —the imagery men had in a spiritual substance that was impressed from without by certain experiences. The senses were the organs through which impressions were made on a substantial entity called "consciousness," and they were made in a certain way, in a spatial, temporal order. Consciousness was dealt with as a sort of substance which received impressions. Following upon this came the fruitful statement of Professor James.

For James, consciousness is not to be regarded as a static substance receiving impressions from without. It is rather a stream that flows on. And this stream has various characteristics, those that we express by its substantive and transitive character. It gathers about a certain experience and then passes on from that to another. Another analogy that James used was of the bird that alights on one branch and then flies to another, continually moving from one point to another point. The transitive phases of experience are those answering to relations; the substantives are those that answer to what we call the "things we perceive." If one is speaking, relating something, and says "and" and then stops at that point, we have the feeling of being ready to go on to something else. The feeling is just as definite an experience as that of yellow or red, of hot or cold; it is an experience of "and," one that is transitive, that is moving on. And these experiences are qualitatively different from each other. If, instead of saying "and," the speaker said "but," we should have an entirely different attitude toward what is to follow. In fact, our whole grasp of what we are hearing or reading depends upon the feelings we have for these different relating articles. If we come upon a thought with a "though" in it, we have one attitude toward what is to come; if "also," a different attitude. We are ready for a certain sort of content. We have a definite sort of experience answering to these relations which appear immediately in experience.

There is also another very important phase of experience which Professor James emphasizes, that which is represented by the spotlight of our attention as over against the fringe of the experience. If one gives his attention to something immediately before him, there lies about this experience a fringe which is very important in the recognition, in the value of that to which one gives attention. For example, when we are reading, we often have the experience of a world which is not immediately before us. The eye in moving over the page has caught a word several lines below. We have to hunt for it to find out what it was. It lies there in the fringe of our immediate experience, and we are ready for it when it appears. But still more, these different attitudes which are connected with the different particles, the "and," "but," "though," "also," also represent the fringe. We are immediately considering something, but we are already going on to something else. And the beginnings of that something else to which we are going on are already forming in the realization of our experience. They are taking place, and they represent the fringe of experience which comes in to interpret that to which we are giving attention.

These conceptions of James's which were so fruitful for the psychological consideration of experience do represent definitely a process which gets its whole statement in our conduct. We are going on to something besides that which is before us. And the structure of the experience itself depends on what we are going on to do. If we see something, we have at least aroused in the organism a tendency to meet it, or to avoid it. And it is this experience of what the contact will be that comes in to give the meaning to that which we actually see. We are continually interpreting what we see by the something that is represented by possible future conduct. So, to understand what is appearing in experience, we must take into account not only the immediate stimulus as such but also the response. The response is there partly in the actual tendency toward the object and also in our memory images, the experiences that we have had in the past. And this relationship of the response to the stimulus is one of very great importance in the analysis of our perception.

Professor Dewey brought out that fact in a memorable article on the stimulus-response concept. He pointed out that the very attitude of being acted upon by a stimulus is continually affected by the response. We start to do something, and the process of doing it is continually affecting the very stimulus we have received. A familiar illustration is that of the carpenter who is sawing on a line. The response of the organism to the stimulation of the line is there to determine what he will look for. He will keep his eye on the line because he is continually sawing. The process of listening is a process in which we turn the head in such a way that we will be able to catch what we are hearing—the listening is essential to the hearing. The process of responding is always present, determining the way in which we shall receive our so-called "impressions." That is, the organism is not simply a something that is receiving impressions and then answering to them. It is not a sensitive protoplasm that is simply receiving these stimuli from without and then responding to them. The organism is doing something. It is primarily seeking for certain stimuli. When we are hungry, we are sensitive to the odors of food. When we are looking for a book, we have a memory image of the back of the book. Whatever we are doing determines the sort of a stimulus which will set free certain responses which are there ready for expression, and it is the attitude of action which determines for us what the stimulus will be. Then, in the process of acting we are continually select-ing just what elements in the field of stimulation will set the response successfully free. We have to carry out our act so that the response as it goes on is continually acting back upon the organism, selecting for us just those stimuli which will enable us to do what we started to do.

Out of this stimulus-response concept has developed be-havioristic psychology. Now, there are two ways of elaborating the general point of view belonging to behaviorism. One is to consider the process itself in an external way, or, as the psychologists would say, in an objective fashion; just consider the act itself and forget about consciousness. Watson is the representative of that type of behaviorism. The behaviorist of this type is interested simply in the act. He is particularly interested in the act as it can be observed from the outside. Watson is representative of the so-called "scientific psycholo-gist" who is observing that which can be observed by other scientists. It is a type of psychology which was developed first of all in the study of animals. There you are necessarily shut off from any so-called "field of consciousness." You cannot deal with the consciousness of the animal; you have to study his actions, his conduct. And these psychologists carried over the method of animal psychology into human psychology. They carried over from the study of animal psychology a new and, what seemed to be, a very fruitful conception, that of the reflex which could be, in their terminology, conditioned—the idea of the conditioned reflex.

This goes back, as most of you know, to Pavlov's dog. Pav-lov was an objective psychologist who was studying the con-duct of animals and endeavoring to make a complete statement of that conduct without bringing in the element of conscious-ness, that is, without having to refer to what was called "intro-spection" to understand the act. He took a dog and, by putting food in its mouth, collected the saliva that was secreted. If a piece of meat was brought within the vision and the sense of odor of the dog, then saliva was secreted. The dog was all ready to eat the meat, and the glands in the mouth were preparing for the process of mastication. Now, taking the dog in that way and bringing the meat, he was able to determine just what the effect of this stimulus was in the production of saliva. Then, when he brought the meat to the dog, he also rang a bell. He kept this up long enough so that the two experiences would be associated. He did not speak of it as the consciousness of the dog but in terms of the process of the nervous system; and then he found that, if he rang the bell without presenting meat, the same effect was produced, that is, the excess of saliva was secreted without actual sight or odor of the meat. This particular reflex, then, the secretion of saliva, was conditioned by the association of the sound of the bell with the smell of meat, so that, when the meat was not presented, the sound of the bell actually acted as a stimulus in place of the smell of the meat itself.

This conception of conditioned reflex is evidently one that can be carried over into all sorts of fields. I will refer to some of them by way of illustration. First, take the cry of a baby who, for example, is shown a white rat with which he has played before without any fear. If the rat was associated with a loud sound, the sound, especially if not seen, was a natural stimulus of fright. If the white rat was presented to the child when this sound was produced, the child became frightened; and afterward, when the rat was brought to the child and the sound not made, the child was still frightened of the rat. That is, this particular reflex of the fright of the child was conditioned by the sight and feel of the white rat. This can be carried over to a whole set of situations. Take another example from our conventions. We expect a person to act in a certain sort of way. We expect him to be dressed in a certain sort of way. This conduct goes along with a certain type of manners, and these manners go along with a certain type of individual. If we meet a person whose manners are not those we expect, we have an attitude toward this person as one who lacks those particular characteristics. We have conditioned our reflexes by these particular conventions, many of them entirely external and having nothing to do with the character of the man. We assume that certain manners represent courtesy. A great many of the manners have nothing to do with courtesy; but they have become so related to it that if we find a man who has rough manners, we perhaps do not expect courtesy of him. We can carry the conditioned reflex over into other fields, such as that of language, where we have a set of arbitrary symbols. Certain experiences call for certain responses. We can associate with each experience a certain arbitrary symbol, a sound, a written word, and we can become so conditioned that when we hear the sound, see the word, we get the attitude which goes with the original experience.

The conditioned reflex, then, was brought in and used by Watson in his attempt to analyze conduct. You see, this makes possible analysis without bringing in consciousness as such. You do not have to deal with introspection; you do not have to go back and ask the person what he thinks, or feels, what imagery arises before him. One studies simply his conduct and sees what the stimuli are that act upon him under certain conditions. And a sort of an analysis can be made of conduct from his standpoint. What is of importance in this method is that this type of analysis goes back to the conduct of the individual, goes back to his behavior, to what he is doing—not to what he is thinking and feeling, but what he is doing.

The other approach is that of Professor Dewey, also from the standpoint of the conduct itself, which carries with it the various values which we had associated with the term "consciousness." There arose at this time the question which James put so bluntly: Does consciousness exist? He wrote an article under that caption. Is there any such entity as consciousness in distinction from the world of our experience? Can we say that there is any such thing as consciousness which is a separate entity apart from the character of the world itself? The question, of course, is difficult to answer directly, because the term "consciousness" is an ambiguous one. We use it particularly for experiences which are represented, we will say, by going to sleep and waking up, going under and coming out of the anesthetic, in losing and regaining "consciousness." We think of it as something which is a sort of entity, which is there, which has been, under these conditions, submerged and then allowed to appear again. That use of consciousness is not essentially different from the shutting-off of any field of experience through the senses. If one, for example, turns out the lights in the room, he no longer experiences the sight of objects about him. We say he has lost consciousness of those objects. But you would not speak of him as having lost consciousness. He is simply unable to see what is there. If he gets farther and farther away from a sound, or the sound becomes fainter and fainter, he loses consciousness of that sound; but he does not lose consciousness in the other sense. If we closed up his eyes, shut off his nostrils, ears, mouth, shut him off from a whole series of different stimuli, even those coming to him from the surface of the body and from the visceral tract, he would probably lose consciousness, go to sleep. There, you see, the losing of consciousness does not mean the loss of a certain entity but merely the cutting-off of one's relations with experiences. Consciousness in that sense means merely a normal relationship between the organism and the outside objects. And what we refer to as consciousness as such is really the character of the object. That is, the object is a bright object. If now you close the eyes, there is no bright object there any longer. We would say that you have lost consciousness of it, or simply that the bright object is not there. When the eyes are open, you have access to it; when the eyes close, you have access to it no longer. You see, there are two ways of looking at this having consciousness of the object. You may regard consciousness as a something that exists inside of the organism somewhere, upon which the influence of certain stimuli come to play. You may think of consciousness in terms of impressions made upon this spiritual substance in some unexplained fashion in the organism. Or you may think of it simply as a relationship between the organism and the object itself.

James in his answer to, or his attempted answer to, the question, "Does consciousness exist?" lays stress on the relation between the experience which the individual has had, that which has gone before, and that which follows after. He took the illustration of a person going to a house and entering the first room. Now that room and its furniture is an experience. You can say that it enters his consciousness, if you like; and still you think of the room as something there with its pictures, furniture, whether he came in or not. If now, the house is burned up by a fire, this particular room with its walls and pictures and furniture has disappeared. The experience which the individual has had of the room, however, is not burned up. He remembers it, remembers how the pictures were hung upon the walls. This, says James, is a cross-section of two histories. And the cross-section is identical. The room belongs to the history of the house. It has been there since the house was built. It is in that particular history. When the person comes into the room, that particular room with its furnishings becomes a fact of his history. He had been elsewhere yesterday. He comes into that particular room, and that room is now a part of his experience; he goes out, and it is related to his former experiences. He had been in other houses, seen other furniture. He compares pictures. Each is related, you see, to his history. On the other hand, this room also belongs to the history of the house, of the architect, of the carpenter. Thus this question of consciousness, according to Professor James's statement, is a question in what history this particular entity, so-called consciousness, lies. From this point of view the consciousness a man has of the room is a cross-section of his history, while the room in the house regarded as a physical affair is a cross-section of the history of the house. Here we have a single cross-section answering to both of these series. Or there is a coincidence of cross-sections. In that case what we would say is that the consciousness of the man in regard to the room in the house is nothing but a statement of that room as it lies in relationship to the man's own history: taken in its relationship to the history of the house, it is physical; taken in its relationship to the history of the man, it is a conscious event.

These two are not the only implications or meanings of consciousness. That which represents mental activities of one sort or another—of volition, of analytic and synthetic thought, of purpose and intention on the one side, and on the other side certain contents—has been stated in the past in associational psychology as states of consciousness. On the one hand, as we have seen, the active side can be stated in terms of conduct, while that which might be referred to as the passive definition of consciousness can be regarded as belonging to the object itself. So far as such a division of the spoils takes place, consciousness as a private affair seems largely to disappear. There are other phases of it, as I have said, which we will not refer to now; but these two phases, these two conceptions of consciousness, I wanted to bring out. One is an active, the other a passive, statement. And what I have said is that this active phase, that involved in the motor, volitional side, as well as in the process of analysis and discrimination, can at least be stated in terms of conduct, of the act; and this act can be stated in terms of the organism as such. What we refer to as the passive side, the content side, is found to lie in the object. It can be regarded, of course, in its relationship to the individual. It does belong to his history, though not simply to his history but to that of the object as well. When the man is in the room, the room is stated in terms of his experience. It is interpreted in terms of memory, of his own anticipation. But still it is a room. Without attempting to discuss the various philosophic implications of this, I am pointing out that on the one side you may speak of consciousness in its passive sense and at the same time be thinking of the object, the room itself.

In some fashion, if we turn to the active side we have impulse as perhaps the most fundamental phase of activity; and impulse certainly can be given a statement in terms not only of acts but also of the organism. There are various fundamental physiological impulses, that of attack and flight, those which gather about hunger and sex. These are lodged in the organism itself. James's celebrated theory of the emotions comes back to the reaction to the motor attitudes of the organism itself in conditions such as fear, hunger, love, joy. That is, fear represents our response to our tendency to run away; hatred represents our response to our tendency to attack. The emotions as such are responses of the organism itself to its own attitudes under certain conditions. These responses are expressed in more or less violent action.

What is further involved here, that which James did not bring out which Dewey does, is that there is always some inhibition of these actions. If one could actually run away before the terrifying object, if one could keep ahead of it, so to speak, give full expression to the tendency to run, one would not be terrified. If one could actually strike the very moment one had the impulse to strike, he would not be angry. It is the checking of the response that is responsible for the emotion, or is essential at least to the emotion. Even in the case of joy, if there were no hesitancy about the way in which one expressed his happiness, there would not be that emotion.

We can approach the emotion, then, from the point of view of our own responses to the attitudes of the organism. Here the James-Lange theory recognizes the visceral, as well as the motor, responses involved in the act. We spoke of the emotion as our effective experience of these attitudes. The impulse is something that can be stated at least in terms of the response of the organism itself. It is, of course, out of the impulse that desires, intentions, arise. What is added to the impulse and desire is the image of what we intend. And here we seem to find ourselves in what might be regarded in an unassailable field of consciousness as such. By its very definition imagery would be not the object, but some copy of the object; not the past event, but some memory of the past event; not future conduct, but a picture of future conduct. If you ask, now, where this image is, you would be at a loss to locate it. The easiest thing is to say that it is in consciousness, whether you put that consciousness in your head or say that you cannot locate it spatially. In any case, it is a relationship to something in your head. At least, the assumption of our physiological psychology is that an image answers to the excitement of certain nerve elements which have been excited in past experience. A cruder form of physiological psychology assumed that pictures of what had happened, were lodged, so to speak, in nerve cells, and, if the organism pressed a button, these pictures would come out. But further study revealed the fact that the nerve cells were no more than paths and junctions of paths. They should not be regarded as cubbyholes in which memory images or any other images are stored away. Just where the image is, is, I say, questionable. But you cannot say that the image is not in the objective world, for many of them are.

Here again I am not discussing the various philosophical implications of this analysis, but merely referring to the fact that every book you read has on every page of it your own memory images of words you have read before. Your own eye touches a line of print perhaps only twice. You take in only a relatively small portion of the actual printed line on the page, and the rest of it comes from memory images. I have referred to the attitudes represented by particles, adverbs, conjunctions, prepositions, the "ands," "buts," and "thoughs," which put us in certain attitudes of anticipation of a certain sort of word that is expected. The context we have gone over gives us a pretty definite anticipation of what is going to be there, so that our mind fills in from past experience. We have not time enough to read each word by itself. There are people, children particularly, whose eyes are bound to the page. They have to read word by word; and if they cannot be freed from it, they are slow readers and can accomplish little in this medium. What we have to do is to make most of what we read a contribution of our own. We fill out what we see. That, of course, is evident not only at the time. You suddenly find yourself in a snarl. You see something which is not there. The proofreader has trained himself to notice the words and letters and not the sense.

Well, that is true not only of the printed page. The faces of our acquaintances are largely filled in by our memories of them. We notice very little in the outlines of a face with which we are familiar. The rest of it comes from memory images. If we are seeing a person for the first time, we regard the features in detail, look at the whole face; but even then what we see in each case is in some sense a sort of type. You could not tell what the types of the human face are that you recognize. Yet, there is something about every human face that is in some sense typical, and you fill in there. A considerable part of our perceptual world, the world existing "out there," as we say, is made up out of mental images, the same stuff that comes before us in revery, only in that case we are looking at it from the point of view of imagination. These images actually go to make up objects we see and feel.

The imagery cannot all be put into a consciousness that is distinct from the world about us. It goes back, as I say, to James's question as to whether consciousness as such exists. We have again a type of experience which from one point of view belongs to the external world and from another point of view to the history of the particular individual. Without attempting to discuss the question further, I simply want to emphasize the fact that the former is the passive side of our experience, which we ordinarily term "consciousness," but which under various conditions we do not consider as consciousness but as the object. If you should take away the so-called "imagery" from what you say you immediately see, from that which answers to what falls on the retina, to the sounds you actually hear, you would find that you have bare skeletal elements; most of the flesh and blood, of the content of the world about you, would have been taken out. What you call the "meaning" of it will go also. The distinction you make between what we call "consciousness" and what we call the "world" is really a functional distinction. It is not a static one. You cannot, then, cut off any particular field of content in our ordinary experience of the world and say, "This is my consciousness as such. This is a certain stuff which belongs inside of my head and not to the world." There are times at which it is inaccessible. But the printed page you see you hand to your friend, who reads it also. A large part of what he reads is his mental image, and what you read is your mental image; and yet you say you are reading the same page.

If one approaches the problem of psychology simply from the standpoint of trying to find out what takes place in the experience of the individual as an individual, you get a surer clue if you take the man's action than if you take certain static contents and say these are the consciousness of the man and that these have to be approached by introspection to be reached. If you want to find out what the man is doing, what he is, you will get it a good deal better if you will get into his conduct, into his action. And you come back there to certain of his impulses, those impulses which become desires, plus his mental images, which from one standpoint are his own but from another standpoint represent certain of his past experiences, or part of his future experience. So-called "objective" or "behavioristic" psychology undertakes to examine the acts of the man from outside without trying to get them by introspection as such, although introspection, as I shall show, has a certain definite meaning even for behavioristic psychology.

I have already referred to accessibility. There are certain very genuine experiences which belong to physical objects and yet which are accessible only to the individual himself, notably, a toothache. There is an aching tooth, no question about it; and yet, though others can see the tooth and the dentist can tap it, it aches only for the individual in whose head it is located, and much as he would like to he cannot transfer that ache to somebody else. There are, of course, a whole series of experiences of which that is typical, which are accessible alone to the person having them. What I want to point out is that you have no question about the aching tooth, no question about the members of your body. Your hands have certain definite characteristics for you. They can be seen by others, but you have the only inside approach to them. And that feeling is one which is just as genuinely a feeling of an object as is that of a table. You feel the table, and you feel your hand. Your hand is softer and warmer than the table. Your hand is not as large as the table. All sorts of distinctions can be made. You are feeling your hand as a physical object, but one having a peculiar character, and that character which it has is one which is accessible only to yourself. Nobody else can get that feel of your hand which you have, and yet that does not make you regard it as less genuinely there. You do not put the feel of your hand in your brain. You may assume that that feel is dependent on what is in your brain, but what the hand is involves the actual character that it itself has. Well now, if anybody else comes up and feels the table, he has a sense of the same table; but this approach to the feeling is peculiar to the individual. The mere fact of the accessibility to the experience you have of parts of your own body does not lodge them, so to speak, in a consciousness which is located in the brain or somewhere else. It simply means certain objects are accessible to you which are not accessible to anybody else.

There are various phases of nature which lie betwixt and between. Take the beauty of a landscape as an instance. From one point of view it is the response of the individual himself and seems to be accessible only to him, but the painter and the poet succeed seemingly in making it accessible to those who enjoy the picture and the poem. This is more or less debatable. All I want to insist on is that mere accessibility is not in itself evidence of something that belongs to a consciousness. It is much safer, even in such fields as these, to come back to the conduct of the individual if you are going to study him than to come back to something he reports to you by means of introspection.

Without discussing the various logical and metaphysical snarls involved, we will say that the space about us is public. We are all living in the same spatial world and have experiences of the same world. When it comes to a question of color, the thing seems to be dubious, for one man does not see certain colors which another man does see. We seem to have a case there where the color is private while the space is public. And yet, you cannot possibly separate the space from the color. And, while you may say that the space which one person perceives has a different degree of brightness from another, we would not hesitate to call those spaces public. But there is also something definitely private. Take a man's intentions, for example. We do not know what he is going to do. He has an advantage over us on that account. This is notable in the case of warfare, or in the case of a man who is making a feint when he is boxing. The intent which the person has is not evident to the other person. He may make a guess at it, but it is only the person who is going to strike who knows definitely what he intends to do. This is also true of intent not simply in such a situation but in all our intercourse with other people. We have a pretty genuine idea, as a rule, of what we are going to say when we are talking; but the person to whom we are talking probably does not. He may guess from past experience; but, as a rule, what a person is going to say would in some sense present a problem to the other person while it would be present in the mind of the one who is going to say it. It is not public property.

That is also true in very large degree of certain types of mental imagery. There is a field, a sort of an inner forum, in which we are the only spectators and the only actors. In that field each one of us confers with himself. We carry on something of a drama. If a person retires to a secluded spot and sits down to think, he talks to himself. He asks and answers questions. He develops his ideas and arranges and organizes those ideas as he might do in conversation with somebody else. He may prefer talking to himself to talking to somebody else. He is a more appreciative audience, perhaps. The process is not essentially different in these two cases, that is, of thinking and of talking to somebody else. It is essentially the same sort of a process. But the activity, such as it is, is not of the same sort. When you do talk to yourself, you do not ordinarily do it out loud. Sometimes you do talk out loud, and somebody else hears you. But, as a rule, when you talk to yourself, you depend on subtle motor and muscular methods of articulation. Supposing that conversation which takes place by such imagery as that is only accessible to the man carrying it on. He takes different rôles. He asks questions and meets them; presents arguments and refutes them. He does it himself, and it lies inside of the man himself. It has not yet become public. But it is a part of the act which does become public. We will say he is thinking out what he is going to say in an important situation, an argument which he is going to present in court, a speech in the legislature. That process which goes on inside of him is only the beginning of the process which is finally carried on in an assembly. It is just a part of the whole thing, and the fact that he talks to himself rather than to the assembly is simply an indication of the beginning of a process which is carried on outside.

Well now, that process of talking to one's self—of thinking, as we say—is a process which we speak of as involving discrimination, analysis. Analysis may be a very physical affair. We can smash up an object by means of a hammer and analyze it. We can take it into the laboratory and use more subtle methods of disintegration. But we are analyzing the object either way. We may analyze a thing for somebody else. He wants to find something in it which he cannot see, and we point it out. We point at the particular part of the object he is to take hold of. Now, that pointing is a process of analyzing the object. For him it is the selection of some part of the object to the neglect of other parts, so that he can get hold of it. Indicating by the finger is just as much analysis as breaking up by a hammer or by chemical reagents. There are various ways of pointing at things. There are people among certain native tribes who can point at things by their own features, their lips, eyes, the way in which they turn their head. I have seen people carry on rather elaborate conversations that way. The ordinary way in which we do our pointing is by means of vocal gestures. Pointing of the finger is a physical gesture.

Words are gestures by means of which we indicate things;

and, just in so far as we indicate things by means of our gestures, we are analyzing just as really as if we put them into a test tube of acid or as if we took our hammer and smashed the thing up to find out its different elements. It is a process of analyzing some element by means of our conduct. Thinking, as such, can at least be stated. I am finding all sorts of problems which can be brought up. Even the most recondite intellectual processes come back to the things we do; and, of course, for an intelligent human being his thinking is the most important part of what he does and the larger part of that thinking is a process of the analysis of situations, finding out just what it is that ought to be attacked, what has to be avoided. We have to take the situation to pieces, think it out; and that process may be a process of pointing or of vocal gestures which indicate certain elements in it. Those vocal gestures are the indication of the elements which will lead to certain responses. One of the principal differences between a dog and a man is that, as a rule, we cannot point out to a dog what we want him to give attention to. If you can find out what the dog's interests are, you may be able to point something out to him; but if you want to have the dog tell time, you can never get him to look at a watch and notice where the hands of the watch are. Even if a person does not know what a watch is, you can indicate to a human individual the face of the watch and get him to see the meaning of it. That part of our thinking process, the power of analysis by means of gestures, is the most important part; and we can say, if you like, that we carry that on inside of our heads. The sense in which we do that is to use these pointers, these vocal gestures, the words which we utilize, to point out certain features in a situation; but we do that inside of ourselves. Occasionally, people do hear us. We talk out loud. But as a rule they do not hear us, and we reply to the gestures that we make with other gestures; and in that fashion we get our plan of action made for ourselves.

Well, that is the way in which behavioristic psychology, if carried out consistently enough, can cover the field of psychology without bringing in the dubious conception of consciousness. There are matters which are accessible only to the individual, but even these cannot be identified with consciousness as such because we find we are continually utilizing them as making up our world. What you can do is to get at the organism as something that you can study. Now it is true that you cannot tell what a man is thinking about unless he chooses to tell. If he tells, you have access to that as well as he has; and you know what he is going to do, and it can enter into your own conduct. You can get at your own conduct and at the conduct of other people by considering that conduct in an objective sort of fashion. That is what behavioristic psychology is trying to do, trying to avoid the ambiguity of the term "consciousness." And what is of importance about this psychology is that it carries us back, as I have said, to the act as such. It considers the organism as active. It is out of the interest in the act itself and the relationship of thought to the act itself that the last phase of more recent philosophy dealt with above, that is, pragmatism, arises. Out of the type of psychology which you may call "behavioristic" came a large part of the stimulus for a pragmatic philosophy. There were several sources, of course; but that is one of the principal ones.

CHAPTER XVIII

INDIVIDUALITY IN THE NINETEENTH CENTURY

I WAS referring in certain preceding sections to the social mechanism through which the individual registers that which is peculiar to his own experience, a mechanism which is most strikingly illustrated in the newspaper, in its giving of news, news being regarded peculiarly as something that happens, something that in itself is novel. Now, that which is novel must appear in the experience of an individual as an individual. The rising of the sun, its going down, the ordinary courses of the seasons—these happen to us all, take place for us all. There is no necessity of bearing testimony to them from the point of view of any particular individual. But when something strange takes place, it can only be validated through its introduction into somebody's biography; it must be said of it that John Smith or A or B had this experience at such a time and such a place. That is, we cannot give universal value to that which is individual. It just happens; it is something that we can state only in terms of the fact that it happened to somebody, at a certain place and at a certain time.

I have already referred to the import of this in the exceptions to laws which make the basis for the scientific problems and the formation of new hypotheses. It is the observation of the scientist that is essential for the establishment of such an exception. I do not mean to say that the statement is confined to a single individual. On the contrary, what the scientist does when he has experienced such a novelty is to state the conditions under which it has occurred, so that others may have the same experience. But it comes to them also as a separate experience. The data of science, especially the exceptions that are noted, are dated and located with reference to individuals. When we come back to those precious events which are the starting-point for the testing and carrying-out of the scientific problem, we come back to the experience of individuals as such, experiences which are the so-called "hard facts" of science. What is meant by their being "hard" is that they just happen when they are not expected. You stumble over them and scrape your shins against them. They are something there that you are not adjusted to, and they have no universal value as yet; so you have to state them in terms of your own experience only.

All this shows again the two sides of the scientific experience: one, its laws, which give meaning to the world; and the other, the experience of individuals just as individuals. Both must be kept clearly in mind. They are the two poles, the foci about which the orbit of science runs. What I want to point out is that even scientific observation of this individual sort is essentially news. That is what constitutes news. It is that which gives import to so-called news. What is of interest is not the mere fact, of course, that it has taken place in the experience of a single individual. That is going on everywhere all the time. The important thing is the fact that that which is going on in the experience of the individual in some way runs counter to that to which we are accustomed. For example, the result of the measurements of the positions of the stars about the sun during an eclipse was news when it started the hypothesis of Einstein. The flourishing of a new star in the heavens is news. And if it is recorded, that record has to be in terms of the experience of individuals. It has to be known just who the people were who made the observations. It could not be any Tom, Dick, or Harry; it has to be a competent person, from our standpoint, in order that his experience may be of importance. It is necessary to know when it took place, the exact second and fraction of a second, as well as the location which gave the conditions for the proper observation. The time at which it took place has to be stated. And it has what we may call from the journalese standpoint "sensational value." The data of science, if they can be brought out so that people can realize their merit, are all sensational. When murders and divorces are recorded, they are sensational just in so far as these immediate experiences run counter to the customs and habits, to the valuation of the group to which the persons involved belong. They are sensational for the same reason that the records of the positions of the stars about the rim of the sun were sensational. The same data which are presented in the sensational press become scientific data when a competent social scientist studies them, examines them, gets them into such shape that they can be evaluated. There is nothing we may assume that is improper to appear on the front page of a paper which does not have its perfectly legitimate place if only it is reported by a competent person who can evaluate it. But what I am insisting on now is that what gives it its importance is that it takes place in the experience of the individual.

I have perhaps given sufficient emphasis to the reason for this. Just because it is in some sense exceptional, you cannot state it in terms of uniformities. You have to state it, then, in terms of somebody's biography. It just happened to him. Well, what modern experience has succeeded in doing is to get control over these exceptional experiences and make use of them. Look through the literature of the ancient world, through such a really marvelous book as Aristotle's *Habits of Animals*, which sums up the biological knowledge of the ancient world. You will be struck by the fact that there is not a reference to a proper name, to an individual, as a basis for the accounts which are given of the animals with which Aristotle's treatise deals. He refers to a number of philosophers whose opinions he is combating; but when he comes to the statement of the character of animals he is describing, he never once refers to any individuals as having made this observation or that. He does not rest the value of the thought he is presenting on the testimony of anybody. On the other hand, if you are to look, for example, into that natural historian, Pliny, you will find recorded observations, statements of events with seemingly no basis for criticism of the value of the evidence. He gives you a remarkable account of the overwhelming of Pompeii, of the eruption of Vesuvius; and the facts he cites are such that any school child would discount. There is no basis for the criticism of the value of what we term "observation." The ancient world did not utilize what we call the "scientific method." It organized the experience and works of men such as Aristotle—the experience of the community—and put it in more or less systematic form; but there was no mechanism for its reconstruction, no mechanism for the test of the experience of the individual, and for a statement of the scientific problem, for the formation of hypotheses and the testing of these, which constitutes our scientific method.

It is because we do utilize this method that these experiences of individuals qua individuals have come to have such supreme importance in our lives, and I am calling your attention to the fact that the newspaper is simply the popular expression of just this fact. And that which appears in the newspaper is logically of the same character as that which appears in scientific magazines. We can just as well refer to these magazines as constituting newspapers. They record observations, happenings, experiments of scientists, which are things that happen to certain individuals; and the importance of these events lies in the fact that they have happened to just these individuals, that they can be put into the experience of this man whom we know to be competent, who can state just what the custom or law or theory is that this particular event has contravened. Consequently, we can state the problem and the ideas of the individuals that are brought forward. The hypotheses are brought forward not in the form of the newspaper editorial but as the interpretation of events. The newspaper editorial in some degree, of course, does this same thing. It undertakes to give the interpretation of what has happened. It takes the events of the day or of the preceding day and picks out what is peculiarly important, and interprets it either in terms of older laws or of some new idea. There is not the scientific control, of course, in the editorial that you have in the scientist's hypothesis; but the newspaper editorial does put before us the community problems. And what appears in the editorial is an attempted interpretation of them in some sense, giving the meaning of them so far as they are novel, implying that some change, some reconstruction, ought to take place in order to deal with them.

Our whole literature from the period of the Renaissance has become increasingly more journalese in its character. We have become distinctly interested in biographies, for example. Go back again to the ancient world, and you have in Plutarch the biography of the ancient world. Read his *Lives*, and you find that he presents his figures either as typical heroes or typical villains, one class or the other. They embody the attitudes and the views, the values, of the community to which they belonged. Or they stand out as striking criminals, people of the type of Alcibiades. But, on the other side, you have the person who is essentially of the hero character. These figures present what is characteristic, that which represents the virtues and the vices of the community. What we fail to find in these biographies as contrasted with modern biographies is just that which commonly goes under the caption of "local color." They do not try to record experiences just as they took place; there is no reference to the form of, say, the food the hero ate, nothing of particular interest in the matter of clothes, or his golf score, the elements which we bring in by way of making a person seem real to us. These elements are all omitted. What the modern biography does is to try to reproduce as far as possible those little things which enable you to put yourself into the situation of the individual so that you get his experiences and experience them.

To get an analogous contrast, go to the Louvre and see the statues which have come down from the ancient world— "Venus," "Hermes," in their calmness and perfection; and then step across to the Luxembourg to see modern statues. You get a sense of life, of movement. The one with that perfection of the type which ancient art has given and which has never been given in any such transcendent type since that time. When we undertake to represent that which is typical, we always present what is abstract. Look at the statue we have put on the Chamber of Commerce building, which represents "Commerce." Compare it with the ancient statue "Hermes"; or the statue on the Courthouse representing "Justice." The ancient world was able to take that which is typical and give it the content and the meaning which belongs to such a philosophy as Plato's. What we present is that which is immediate, living, because we are able to utilize that, because we can take that which occurs to the individual and utilize it for the interpretation of life.

A great expression of this, of course, is in the novel, which undertakes to present the meaning of life in terms of its occurrence to the individual. You can see that the novel and the newspaper belong to the same picture. They are taking happenings and putting the meaning of life not into a moral theory, not into a social theory as such; they are trying to give life as it actually happens to individuals, to men, women, and children. It takes place there; and when a person is able to see exactly what it is that he gets from the novel he is reading, he feels in some sense enriched when he has read an admirable one. His life has had content added to it. He has been given a new point of view, a new approach, a new way of looking at things; and the novelty involved in it leads to a richer experience, just as novelty in some way makes us feel that the meaning of the social problems which we face has been revealed to us. It makes us realize that our consciousness as such is a continued meeting and solution of problems, or an attempted solution of them. This is not abnormal; it is just the nature of consciousness itself. And, as I have insisted, the problem has to appear in the experience of the individual. The problem never appears in a generalized form. The solution we work out and test becomes universal. The problem itself is always individual.

The place of the individual as an important, extremely valuable, thing comes into our thought by way of religion. The preciousness of the human soul was made central in modern experience in religious terms. The soul was that which was to be saved, and saved from an eternity of suffering. That was the yardstick, in some sense, by which one estimated the value of the individual. But we have another sense of the import of the individual as such, namely, that the problems with which our reflective consciousness deals are in the experience of the individual. They must appear in the experience of the individual; and for the individual they come in some sense as a new view of life, as an aspect of life peculiar to him. If we do not get this, we lose a certain kind of experience, a certain amount of it. There are problems that arise, as we all know, in the lives of every one of us; and in so far as they are not mere mistakes, they represent an onward movement. Progress, as I have pointed out, even from the point of view of evolution, is the constant meeting of problems and solving them. It may take nature five hundred thousand years to solve a particular problem in digestion. But the problems that appear in the experience of each individual represent the poles of life itself. This is what we are doing: we are solving problems, and those problems can appear only in the experience of the individual. It is that which gives the importance to the individual, gives him a value which cannot be stated. He has a certain preciousness which cannot be estimated. You cannot tell what will happen to him, what must happen to him. Take cattle, on the other hand; one is like another. There is nothing represented in the experience of one ox that is peculiar to him. But a human individual, when he is a self, has this capacity to state and meet problems peculiar to himself. There is something that takes place in his perspective that does not occur for anybody else. Each one of us has an outlook on the universe which belongs to each one of us alone, and it appears in so far as we have in us a reflective consciousness in which life seems to be interpreted.

We do not write epics in our day; or, when we do, nobody reads them. We write novels, and we write dramas, which represent life and its import in terms of that which happens to an individual as such. Of course, this makes the individual invaluable in the sense that we cannot evaluate him—not in terms of the eternity of suffering, or of more or less abstract blessedness, but in terms of what his function is as an individual in the community, that function which belongs to him in his particular perspective. I have brought in the term "perspective" both because it expresses this point of view which I was presenting and also because it brings us into this latest expression both of science and philosophy, "relativity."

From the point of view of the most abstract of physical sciences, it has been recognized that the world, taken from the point of view of any particular physical particle or any particular physical structure, even such as that of an atom of iron, is shifting. If you think of it for a moment, it is really astonishing the change that has taken place recently in the mechanical sciences from that in which every physical particle could be given its place in an absolute space and time. By the mere development of physical science itself, especially through the theory of electromagnetism and the analysis of the spatial and temporal conception, we find abstract physical science taking this most extremely novel point of view: if you give a certain velocity to a certain particle, the world from the point of view of that particle is a different world than it is if the particle has another velocity; the time is a different time; and the space is a different space. That is, you cannot regard the universe except from the point of view of this particular particle in its essential characters. Well now, perhaps that particle does not exist by itself. There is a consentient state, a group of other physical particles which have the same velocities. Take them at rest, and the whole world has a certain value from that standpoint; put them in motion, and it has another value; change the motion again, and again the value changes. What we had assumed was that such a relative statement could always be read over into an absolute statement. We realize that we cannot take the revolution of the heavens as a presentation of the real movement of things. We put ourselves in the position of the sun and see that the earth is moving about its axis; and when we come to the position of the sun with reference to other stars, we see that it is moving; and so we set up so-called "co-ordinates" of the fixed stars. But we know there is no such thing as a fixed star. Thus, in the end we have nothing to which to attach our Cartesian co-ordinates. We cannot take our point of view and the point of view of a man from Mars and that of a man in the sun and reduce them all to a certain absolute space in which we can tell what the real mass of a body is. All we have is an indefinite number of perspectives. From the point of view of the physical sciences, that shift of perspectives is analogous to what we have been presenting from the point of view of society. That is the reality of the world: it is an organization of the perspectives of all individuals in it. And every individual has something that is peculiar to himself. Our science has grasped that precious peculiarity of the scientist that enables him to get hold of the problem whose solution gives a new heaven and a new earth. And we realize this in our daily talk and conversation, where we see that each one of us has his own value and own standpoint.

Now, from an earlier point of view that meant what the philosophers called "solipsism." It meant that the real world had to be translated into the perspective of each one, and that there was no way of getting out of one's perspective into that of somebody else. That is, it means the defeat of any universal philosophy or, seemingly, of science. And, of course, there have been all sorts of philosophical battles waged over this. What I want to point out is simply that science itself has never been disturbed by this sort of so-called "subjective idealism." It has gone on utilizing that which is peculiar to the individual, seeing the world in terms of the individual, getting the problem involved there and then obtaining a solution which is one that belongs to the more inclusive consentient set, which belongs to the community of which the individual is a member. The individual himself is, after all, there only in so far as he arises in the community, as his own particular perspective arises in that community. In some sense you may say that that represents the form of the philosophical problem which has been presented through relativity.

Another striking phase that has arisen in modern scientific and philosophic thought is found in the category of emergence. From such a relativistic point of view as we are stating, people will recognize, for example, that there is such a thing as color in the world. It belongs to the perspective of people that have normal retinas. If your retina is not normal, then your color perspective is different. The color does not exist in your "soul"; it exists in the relation of your self to the world. It is a different world in its relation to you than in its relation to me. There are slight differences if you like, and there are other differences which we can interpret as real differences. Well now, if that is true, when retinas appear, in their relation to the central nervous system, color appears. It is presented not in the consciousness of these particular forms, but it appears in the relationship of the world to organisms that are endowed with retinas. When the canals, which developed into an ear, appeared in the side of the head and enabled the form to orient itself to sound, noise and music appeared. It did not come to exist in the consciousness of the individual as such, but in the relationship to the world of the organisms endowed with such apparatus. When individuals with appreciation for beauty appeared, beauty appeared. It did not reside in the consciousness of these individuals but came into existence, emerged, through the relationship of the world to the individual.

The problem which faces thought, then, is the problem of the relationship of individuals to each other, or the perspectives of these individuals to each other. These philosophical problems appear in terms of relativity. It may be that it presents an attempted solution in terms which are thought to be consistent with Einstein's statement, as is the case with Bertrand Russell's book called *Philosophy*, which still leaves each perspective more or less in the consciousness of the individual but does set up some unknowable world outside. This is one philosophical attempt to solve that problem. Or it may be attempted from the point of view of Whitehead, with his recognition of an organization of these perspectives themselves.

I will just call your attention again to the fact that the statement we have given of the self as it arises in the human community is one which does definitely represent such an organization of perspectives. That is, the individual comes to realize himself just in so far as he can take the attitude of the group to which he belongs. He can approve or disapprove of himself in those terms. He stands on his own legs just in so far as he assumes his own perspective, criticizes it, and reconstructs it. Other people can put themselves in his place, as in the novel and newspaper; and then the same reconstruction can take place. There you seemingly have just this organization of perspectives going on. What society represents is exactly this. The community as such is the organization of the perspectives of all. They all belong to the same consentient set. But it is an organization of the perspectives of real individuals. Each one has his own perspective, and he can assert it against the group.

And the scientific method is that by means of which the individual can state his criticism, can bring forward the solution, and bring to it the test of the community. We do have in social consciousness—or, better, in social experience, since "consciousness" is an ambiguous term—a real organization of perspectives. That is what takes place. Whether that can be taken over and made the basis for a philosophic solution is another question. But the problem as it lies is whether to take it in terms of relativity and of a space-time world or whether to take it in terms of the lives of individuals in a human community. Whether in terms of scientific advance in any direction, the problem is definitely one of this organization of individual perspectives and the finding-out of what is universal, but with the recognition that, when we do find that out, the very character of one's self as an individual lies in discovering some exception to the universal and going on to the formation of other universals. It also requires the recognition that this is not simply a series of revolutions but the very quality, the very nature, of reflective experience. It is that which distinguishes each individual from every other in the whole group to which he belongs. That is the form of the problem, then, which science, philosophy, and reflection approach at the present time.

There is another phase of it I wanted also to call to your attention particularly. As I have said, a subjective idealism takes the content of the world and puts it into the consciousness of the individual. And as you remember, the romantic idealists took the meaning of the universe as a whole and put it into the consciousness of an Absolute Self of which our separate consciousnesses were mere aspects or phases. They took the whole of the world and put it into the consciousness of the individual. I have referred again and again to the ambiguity of this term "consciousness." What the modern movement is doing is taking what has been the consciousness of the individual and carrying it out into the world again and realizing that it belongs to the latter, and yet keeping this relationship of the world to the particular individual. The world is a different world to each individual. That does not mean that the consciousness inside of me is different from yours, but that the universe from my point of view is different than it is from your point of view. Those are genuine aspects of the world as such. The relationship of the universe to the separate individuals is genuine. One can, from this conception, return the stolen goods to the universe, give it back its color, its form, its meaning and beauty, which had been lodged in the consciousness of separate individuals. They can be returned to the world when we realize that the universe has a different aspect as it exists over against each separate individual.

What science has always assumed, whether we have been able to give a philosophic statement to it or not, is that the universe has a definite import in its relationship to separate individuals. And in some way we have to get an organization of those differences in the whole, the meaning of which shall be different from that of absolute idealism. Absolute idealism tried to solve the problem by uniting all these different individuals into a single Absolute Self, and the attempt broke down, because it never could state the scientific method as such. But the scientific method goes on. And the continued reconstructions of the world go on—reconstructions not only of the future but of the past. The history which we study is not the history of a few years ago. We cannot say that events remain the same. We are continually reconstructing the world from our own standpoint. And that reconstruction holds just as really with the so-called "irrevocable" past as with reference to a future. The past is just as uncertain as the future is. We do not know what the Caesar or the Charlemagne of the next century will be. We look over histories which have dealt with Caesar, but we find a different Caesar portrayed in each one. A dozen different Caesars have crossed the Rubicon. We are continually reconstructing the world, and that is what our consciousness means; it means this reconstruction from the standpoint of the individual.

Stating it in as broad a form as I can, this is the philosophical problem that faces the community at the present time: How are we to get the universality involved, the general statement which must go with any interpretation of the world, and still make use of the differences which belong to the individual as an individual?

APPENDIX

FRENCH PHILOSOPHY IN THE NINETEENTH CENTURY

I

THE background of philosophy in France in the nineteenth century is, in one sense, the background of all philosophy in the nineteenth century, that of revolution and the varying reactions to it in the different communities of Europe. One reaction was found in Germany in the Romantic idealism of Fichte, Schelling, and Hegel. In England the reaction was determined by the so-called Industrial Revolution. In France the background was that of a defeated Revolution—a Revolution that had suffered a double defeat. The undertaking to establish a society or a state on a rational basis, an enterprise for which Rousseau's *Contrat social* furnished a model, broke down because it was found impossible to build an adequate concrete political structure on the abstract rights of man. It was defeated in the second sense because the imperialism which sprang out of this failure got its expression in Napoleon's military genius. This produced a reaction in the whole of Europe in the form of an attempt to turn the clock back. It is this double defeat more than anything else, perhaps, that characterizes the peculiar atmosphere of France during the last century.

In one respect the Revolution had been a success from the point of view of the French. It had put the land into the hands of the peasantry. The land was and remained the great source of wealth in France. The French peasantry had been fighting to get control of it. They had been carrying on lawsuits with the feudal owners of the land. And it was the peasant who was successful in the cultivation of the land. There was a marked difference between agriculture in France and in England. In England, successful agriculture was carried on by landowners who farmed large tracts. The whole tendency was to break up the small holdings and bring them under the control of a single man who would put through the improved methods of agriculture which were characteristic of England in the latter part of the eighteenth century. In France, on the other hand, the owners of the land took no interest in the cultivation of it. They were absentee landlords; they sought only the rents, which they spent in Paris. Agriculture fell back to the peasant, and he was eminently successful in his agricultural processes. He had an intense love for the land itself. He wanted to get it for himself. The whole class of yeomen had disappeared in England, and there was no passion on the part of the English peasant to get hold of the land and work it himself. The French peasant had this passion, a love for agriculture; and when he got the land, he worked it successfully. The passage of the land into the hands of the peasantry was one of the most fundamental and important results of the Revolution in France, and it was a result which could not be overthrown or put aside. In many respects it was possible to return to the old order, but even the rulers themselves with all their armies could not take the land away from the peasant. He remained in possession.

This was a result of importance to France in determining the attitude of the French nation, but it did not show itself in the reflective processes of the French nation. Those of the French people who were articulate, who could express themselves in art and literature, in philosophy and science, were not immediately touched by this change. It did not affect them.

The changes that took place in England were changes that put the control of the land into the hands of the large landowners, the men who were the controlling political body. The landowners were represented in Parliament. They had been in control of England ever since the Revolution in 1689. This party, with its control over the land, was the controlling power in England and gave the cue, in one way or another, to all the thinking, to all the artistic expression, to science and philosophy, during the eighteenth century. It was a minority of the

English people, but it was a minority that was in control and that regarded itself as having got its liberty through a marvelous constitution. Its advantages were almost lyrically sung by Burke. It was the constitution of a monarchy, but of a monarchy which was under the control of Parliament. And this Parliament represented the nation, but secondarily the landowners, who bore the prestige of the people themselves. Parliament had the possibility of developing in the direction of democracy. Its possibilities worked out later in the extension of the franchise in England. But at the end of the eighteenth century the power was in the hands of the squirearchy itself, which owned the land and held the power.

Growing up in England, however, was a new class, a class which had put itself in opposition to this control of the squirearchy, the class of industrial entrepreneurs and financiers. The Industrial Revolution that was going on in England was one which, while it increased the wealth of the nation and brought groups of men into prominence and a sort of power, still left the control in the hands of Parliament and of the men who made efforts to buy holdings in order to become a part of the controlling squirearchy of England. So the ideas and ideals of the eighteenth century about the control of the land were maintained during the years of the nineteenth century. The reconstruction that was taking place was not deep; but it was through the class of mill-owners and manufacturers and financiers that this change, such as it was, took place at all. It was brought about through the labor movement which began early in the century and which presented a new social problem to England.

That is the picture that we have of the development which was taking place in England as over against what was occurring in France. In France the land itself had passed into the hands of the peasantry, out of the hands of the nobility. The nobility were largely deprived of the land they had had in the past. They became a landless aristocracy. Many of them were provided with estates; but as a class the aristocracy was ousted from the land, and the peasantry came into possession of it and it was the first source of wealth in France. Land being the primary source of wealth, and being so effectively cultivated by the peasants, the wealth from it increased. The land itself, with the wealth that went with it, represented the inarticulate part of French society, a group that had espoused revolution to get control of the land. It had been swept on by the abstract ideas of Rousseau, but its interests lay not in political reconstruction but in rights that the peasants themselves had got by entering into their new holdings. The peasants having attained that result, their interest in the Revolution largely subsided, after the excitement of Napoleonic imperialism.

Thus the changes that took place during the early part of the nineteenth century in France were changes that were not motivated by the mass of the French people. They were largely revolutions in Paris; they took place in Paris and the other large communities. There was no interest in them that took hold of the French people as a whole. The people had planted themselves on the soil and were, for the time being, satisfied with the exploitation of their new possessions. This situation did not lead to any profound reconstruction from the point of view of the thought of the world, such as that which took place in Germany, in Italy, and in England during the Industrial Revolution. The people themselves had changed the attitude when, from being feudal tenants, they had become the owners of the soil, and their attention was turned back to the political movements going on. That is the feeling one has with reference to the changes that took place in France. They were superficial in character, for the great number of the people in France were not interested in them. The thought out of which they developed, the expressions that were given to the national life, were expressions which did not reach down in the great masses of the French people themselves.

The changes that had taken place in Germany were more profound, because the Revolution continued to be felt in Germany. The small states—the small dynastic states—were too numerous to be reconstituted. Many had to pass over into the control of the larger states. Here a political change was going on which affected the mass of the community in a profound fashion. Particularly, it brought liberty to the great states in the German part of Europe. First of all to Austria and then to Prussia, those two states which became rivals. That movement went on finally to the formation of the German Empire. It was a movement which was profound because for the first time it was bringing German nationalism to articulate expression. It is that which lies behind Romantic idealism. France and England and Spain had attained nationalist sentiment and consciousness two centuries earlier. But Germany was divided up into dynastic states. The principle of the organization of these states was dynastic, not national. It did not turn about the national heritage of the people. They were of the same race, had the same traditions. But they were subjects of different dynasties, and it was about these that the organization of the communities gathered. For a time an attempt was made to turn the clock back through control of Europe by Metternich, backed by the czar. This control laid emphasis against all these small dynasties and their communities; but the map of Europe could not be reconstituted as it was before the Revolution and before Napoleonic pressure in the Rhine districts. The small dynastic states had been broken down. Their people had been affected by their contact with the French. The ferment of the Revolution had been more active there than elsewhere in Europe. People in that part of Europe continued to feel tendencies toward that national expression which, during the war of liberation, found its most effective expression through the Prussian state. It was a Prussian state which was a means of bringing to successful consciousness a sense of nationalism.

The great exponent of nationalism at that period was Fichte in his addresses to the German people. These were not to the Prussians as such; they were addressed to the German people. Fichte undertook to bring to the German people the awareness that their peculiar nature was a part of their peculiar heritage.

He pointed out what their task in the civilization of a feudal world was and was to be. It was the efficiency of the Prussian administration that gave a certain popular character to this up-lift which took place in the struggle to throw the French out of Germany. The Prussian state could take over the institutions and developments as though they were the expression of the German nation, though they were not such politically. Prussia could give instruction, and the army could be made a national institution. The schools and the army were the two institutions by means of which the Prussian people and the Germans in general, so far as they were affected by what was going on in Germany as a whole, got control of governmental authority. This authority was in direct control. It was in control in so far as it fostered the spread of intelligence, the development of public schools, and the undertaking to make the intelligence of the community in some sense the director of the life of the state itself. Frederick the Great undertook to develop a state which was eminently intelligent. But a new end was brought into the life of the people with the institution of a national army which should take in all those that were capable of bearing arms. As was the case with the school, the whole of the youth of Germany should be brought into the army, in which they would be trained for their national life. Prussia, therefore, although it was an autocratic state, although all the power belonged to the monarch, as such, was a state which was undertaking to train its citizenry not for fighting alone but for intelligent political life. During the period of the war of nationalization there was an intense national life which spread from Prussia throughout Germany. That was the spirit which got its expression in the Romantic philosophy. Thus, while this philosophy was a system of great profundity, while it lay beyond the comprehension of the masses of the people, it was also an expression of the spiritual life that came up from the people themselves.

On the other hand, in England we have a development in which the national movement was brought into the life of the community, of the masses, not through those that owned the land but by the urban laborers, the factory laborers. They had been brought together in organizations, in trade-unions, that gave a sense of understanding which the masses of the people had never had before in England. The labor movement reached all the way down into English society. It was a movement which got its expression in industrial strife, and that industrial strife got its expression in Parliament. As a result, the development of English democracy throughout the nineteenth century had been what it so evidently is today, a national movement. That movement also got its expression in a philosophy, that of the utilitarians, Bentham and the Mills. It was a philosophy which was capable of a simple statement; it was one that could find its place among the trade-unions themselves, one that could get its expression in the movement toward free trade, in the demand for cheap bread, and the demand for internationalism by way of free trade. It was a movement that was connected with the political and philosophical thought of the community itself, reaching out beyond England to other communities.

It is in contrast with those two countries—England and Germany—that I want to put the French community. The result of the political revolution was of profound importance for the French people. France, like Germany, was affected in some degree by the Industrial Revolution. But France was not as much affected as Germany. In Germany there arose the socialist theory which took hold of the masses of the people, for in Germany the factory system worked itself out earlier and gave the background for the development of the Marxian doctrine. But in France the wealth lay in the soil. The manufacturing in France was of luxuries. The products did not get into the wholesale markets. In England the peasants had been loosened from the soil. They were free to go to the city. When England began the development of coal and iron, she had a supply of labor that was glad to work at starvation wages. In France the peasantry were satisfied to remain on the soil. There was little of the large production which was essential for the development of the national labor movement as such. This movement got its expression in trade-unionism in England and in socialism in Germany. Both were popular movements; both got into politics. But the labor of the French peasant was not affected by the political situation. It was only in so far as taxation bore on him that he was interested in the political situation as such.

As I have said, the attempt during the nineteenth century was to put the clock back. In France men returned to the spiritual order of the church, the Catholic church. Nationalism, so far as it expressed itself, was a chronological expression. France went back to the medieval situation, not exactly as the Germans went back to it or as the English went back to it, in a romantic attitude, but to find an expression of the society of France itself. The Revolution had been a failure politically. From the point of view of its transfer of the land to the peasant it had been a success, but politically it had been a failure. It failed to reorganize society on the rational lines that had been its goal. The religion of reason, which went with the French Revolution, had a life of only a few duties, and, when the latter failed, men drifted back to the church, which again became the center of the life of the community as such when men turned back in a romantic fashion to the medieval period, but with the sophisticated attitude that belongs to the beginning of the nineteenth century. They went back to rediscover in the medieval period something which they felt they had lost, something which was different from the experience of those who lived during the medieval centuries. That life had been a direct life. The attitude of the romanticist when he returned to it was one of appreciation and enjoyment. It was an aesthetic reaction. All the paraphernalia of the religious service was looked at from the point of view of men who had been estranged from it and returned to it, and who undertook to appreciate it with the new attitude that they had gained. They were playing the rôles of people in the medieval period.

Another phase of the Revolution in France must be kept in mind. France exhausted itself emotionally in the Napoleonic period. The enthusiasm in the French armies had arisen out of the sentiment of defense against the outsider. Here you have the peasants with the same sentiment as that found later in the Russian peasants, who, without interest in the government as such, were determined to hold on to the land which they had secured. They were ready to fight battles against invaders and protect themselves. They proved themselves the most effective infantry in Europe, and they had a great general. Out of this arose Napoleonism in France. It became identified with Napoleon himself. He was not a dynast; he did not represent the history of France. The justification for his position was that he made possible a larger community that otherwise would not have existed. He brought together people separated socially, geographically, but who still recognized themselves as belonging to the same community because they were subjects of the same monarch. The dynast, the emperor, had been the center of the social organization during the medieval period. He was the symbol of Europe as a single society. While having slight politi cal power, he stood as an impressive symbol of a larger community—a community that was surpassed only by the church, one which might take in the whole human race, which was organized about the church. The dynast in the position of the emperor was the political symbol of that larger community.

We must go back to France or England in the feudal period to realize what the monarchy meant. Means of communication were slight, customs were different, different dialects were spoken. There was no organization, no France, no England as a whole; but through the monarch it was possible for the feudal tenant, the serf, to recognize himself as having a relation to everyone else inside the national bounds. Running up the line to the monarch was a community made up of parts, of different elements, that were hostile to each other. Thus, only the monarchy made possible national life in Napoleon's opposition to the feudal order. In France the Bourbons, and in England the Plantagenets, were able to root out the feudal order and make a national life possible. We must remember this in order to recognize the importance of the dynasty Napoleon wanted to step into. This would have identified France with himself. But he could not do it, for his hold on the people was not a historic hold. He represented a revolution; he had overthrown the old state and broken down the principle of authority; and when he undertook to place himself on the historic throne of France and make himself the representative of the line of the oldest dynastic family in Europe and to make his peace with the people which had the longest tradition in Europe, he failed. All the emotional life that he was able to arouse had been spent in the glory which victory produced, in a sense of enlargement that came with the enlarged empire. It was impossible that this should remain. The country broke away; and when France came back to its own boundaries, Napoleon was a stranger. He could not be the symbol of national life. He undertook to carry over the efficiency of the Prussian state. He showed a genius comparable to his military genius in the reorganization of the state on the basis of an autocracy which undertook to control everything. The schools were turned into barracks. There was the same training of the child that there was of the soldier in the army. The whole state was organized with great efficiency, and Napoleon was the center of it all. He undertook to pass over into the field of the arts, to get an expression for the principle of his state in the field of philosophy, to direct the life of the community itself. He gathered about himself literary men and women. The philosophers, he thought, could be utilized in the organization of France as the monarchy of Napoleon. But in all this he failed.

The one hold he had on the community was that of his military genius and success. The Revolution had done its work. It had overturned the earlier state, and Napoleon could not set up that state again arbitrarily. The emotion of the French people was exhausted. They had been on a long military debauch. Their operations in the field, the glory of their victories, the plunder they had brought back from Europe, were the signs of that debauch, and they were exhausted. The one pre-eminent change which had taken place besides the breakdown of Napoleon's hold was the passage of the land into the hands of the peasant, and the peasant was now indifferent to what went on. The masses of the people were outside of the life that went on among the intellectuals. There was no connection between the literary, philosophical thought of the time and the mass of the French peasantry. Napoleon had almost decimated France by filling his army with those who could bear arms; he had materially weakened her physically; he had decreased the population of France by his continual warfare. But those who were left remained on the soil and were satisfied, so that when the Bourbons were put on the throne and undertook to turn the clock back they found that France was exhausted and the mass of the citizens were indifferent to what went on. Thus, while there was a rich life in Germany and nationalism expressed itself in vivid ways—a national literature sprang up there and science flourished in a remarkable degree—in France there was the deadness of the morning after. There was the interest of the people in the soil itself. They were looking down and not up. They were satisfied with what they had and were not looking ahead. They did not wish to carry on the life of the old Napoleonic state. I think it is necessary to appreciate this situation in order that we may realize the comparative poverty of spiritual development in France as compared with that which took place in Germany and in England.

II

The enthusiasm of the Romantic period, as it turned back to the medieval period, was expressed in England and in Germany. In France what occurred was the return of an army which was melancholy and defeated. The great expression of the romantic movement in France was religious. In this connection there are two or three figures of importance for the time. De Bonald and De Maistre represented a return to the philosophy of the people —an attempt to restate the medieval philosophy, that which belonged to the period of the twelfth and thirteenth century. They restated it from the standpoint of France in the nineteenth century. They were both men of imagination, men of very great intellectual power and of supreme devotion. They took the fact of the religious organization of the community most seriously. What they undertook to show was that no community could exist except through religion; that the only bond that could hold men together was the church; that the church was the presupposition of society. They found themselves not in touch with the historical development of the church in France itself however. The Gallican movement in France, which answered to the Reformation, left the monarch in power within a national church. That movement was, of course, entirely outside of the conception of life represented by De Bonald and De Maistre. They fell back onto the conception of the Holy Roman Empire as representing the single community of Christendom. In its time it was the oldest possible organization of Christendom as such. Europe had been broken into feudal states which were more or less hostile toward each other. Only from the point of view of the church could all the tenants, the serfs, the underlings, conceive of themselves as belonging to a single community. There was, in the medieval period, the presupposition that society must have a religious basis. Only the church could make Christendom possible. However, the further the development of this organization went, the more it tended toward the national church, and rulers undertook to get control of it within their own boundary. So far as the church represented the spiritual organization of the community, the state insisted on having its hands on it. So Louis XIV and Henry VIII were acting logically when they undertook to set up national churches inside the Catholic church. That was possible in France; in England it was not possible, and a complete separation took place. The return of De Bonald and De Maistre to the Catholic tradition, their attempt to revive the conception of the thirteenth century, was an inevitable failure. They influenced religious schools and convinced those who did not need to be convinced, but the mass of the people was not touched by them.

Chateaubriand came forward with a work which was superficial as compared with the arguments of De Bonald and De Maistre. He presented Christianity as a civilizing power, a humanizing power; he appealed to the aesthetic phase of Christianity and called out the aesthetic response in the process of worship itself; his was essentially a sentimental reaction. For the time being, however, it had very considerable influence in Paris among the intellectuals. It was distinctly a romantic movement, but not one which had its roots in the past life of the community. Chateaubriand failed to connect with De Bonald and De Maistre. The latter were undertaking to bring back the church of the thirteenth century; the former, to bring men into the church of the nineteenth century, a church which was Gallican, national, and opportunistic in its relations to Napoleon; a church which had lost the philosophy of its earlier life; a church which did not have the consciousness of being the organizing principle in the whole of Europe. That proud consciousness did belong to the people, and its hierarchy could be aroused again in the nineteenth century. But the only approach Chateaubriand could make to the church was on the sentimental side. De Bonald and De Maistre represented an interest in the development of the church itself. Their doctrine was planted in the dogma of the church; Chateaubriand appealed to the ritual.

III

The philosophy of the French Revolution was represented in the pre-revolutionary days by Voltaire and Rousseau. The group of men who gathered about them were called Encyclopedists, after the Encyclopedists who represented the Enlightenment in France. The philosophy which lay back of them was imported from England. Voltaire had carried over from England the philosophy of Locke and put it on French soil. In this period those who were found within this school were called "idealogues." They stood for the ultimacy of a state of consciousness, an impression, a sensation. What Locke undertook to do was to analyze experience into simple elements, and then to find how our experience, especially our collective experience, arose.

It is interesting to see that it was the philosophy of Locke that was carried over to France rather than that of Berkeley and that of Hume, both of whom represented developments of the Lockian philosophy. But the transplantation of this English philosophy by Voltaire and others was taken from Locke. To see this is to see that the hold French thought got of this philosophy was superficial. The development that went on from Locke through Berkeley and Hume was an essential, logical development. The contradictions which were involved in the Lockian statement came out in the subjective idealism of Berkeley and in the criticism of Hume. For Locke, all our knowledge falls into sensations and impressions—those of the outer sense, and those of the inner sense. The outer appears to us in our sensations and contacts—those of color, sound, taste, and odor. The inner impressions are those that come from our processes of thought, from our emotional life, from the action of desire and of will. From Locke's standpoint, the mind is a mosaic of these impressions. His interest was to take our ideas, or presuppositions of thought, and break them up into ultimate elements, and then to show the connections that lie between these ultimate elements. The first orientation was that of a philosopher who is fighting the doctrine of innate ideas, a sort of superficial neo-Platonism of the time, one which was used by the church and by political philosophers. This philosophy lost the profundity of the Platonism from which it sprang. It located the idea, as such, in the mind and presented the mind as a tablet on which were written certain fundamental ideas. Locke's ideas were oriented by his opposition to the doctrine of innate ideas. His position was that there was nothing in the mind that had not previously been in the senses. Everything was reduced to sensations, to impressions. The memory had impressions of the outer sense and also the inner sense.

Ideology and the philosophy which it presented in France

were brought over from England through the translation of the works of Locke, without the recognition of the development which had taken place as represented by Berkeley and Hume. The emphasis lay upon analysis, so-called. The interest behind this was the elimination of the abstract idea. You remember, in one sense, these three were all nominalists. They assumed that the abstract idea, the universal, had no further existence than was found in the association of certain symbols with different individual things. The problem involved in the similarity between particular things was passed over. They insisted that in the process of thinking the mind was dealing with particulars and with the association of these particulars with each other.

The interest in the problem which the French of this period had was in getting rid of the abstractions about which religious, ecclesiastical, and governmental theories gathered. Was there such a thing as absolute divine right? Were there such things as transubstantiation, ideas of which could only be presented in terms of particular objects? The theology, the political science, of the period dealt with speculations from these particular objects. Did these abstractions have a unity in themselves, or did one have to come back to particular experience? The Idealogues welcomed a philosophy which analyzed experience into ultimate elements of sensation, which came back simply to particular experiences as such and advanced the abstractions which were built into the theories and political doctrines of the time. The ideological philosophy was regarded, then, as the philosophy of the Revolution. It was used by Voltaire in his attacks on the church; by Rousseau, and those who were influenced by Rousseau, in showing that the state was actually an organization of individuals. As they conceived of it, the state existed only in the contract between individuals. There was no such thing as the unity of the state as such. There were the individuals that made up the state and the relationship that existed between these individuals. You see how this simplified the problem, especially as it involved an attack on the whole institution. From the standpoint of the medieval period there were universals. These universals existed in the mind of God; on earth, in our own minds. About these universals the whole doctrine of the church and state was gathered. If one could attack those universals and substitute for them individuals and their experience and the relations that existed between them, one could exorcise those abstract units and come back to what seemed the immediate situation, that is, to men and women associated in various ways. The universals were to be found in the images of these men, in their particular relations. These were to be brought into the mind. Institutional organizations were to be analyzed into the physical relationships of people. The problem of empirical philosophy as it appeared in England and in France was, then, essentially this.

That this philosophy did not bring about political revolution in England, as in France, was due to the difference in the political situation. In a certain sense, that revolution had been going on in England ever since the Puritan Revolution. The people were conscious of a change taking place. There had been the institution of Parliament, with its representation in the counties. However inadequate that might be for the absolute power of the crown, the crown was no longer necessary for holding together an English community. Parliament with its powers accomplished what the crown had accomplished. The revolution was taking place. Furthermore, England was, after all, a Protestant community. There was a state church; there were also dissenting bodies; and a large proportion of the population of England was found in these dissenting churches. They were free to carry out their own process of worship. There was no organization or group of people in an ecclesiastical organization that undertook to determine what their ideas of the world should be. The people were free to formulate their own theology. They were, of course, subject to various political disabilities, but still they could carry on their own religious life. That battle had been fought through; and they were left, in that sense, free. The revolution had, in its essentials, taken place in England.

The French thinkers were satisfied with the application of this empiricism. This does not mean that the French mind was less profound in itself. You have only to turn back to the period of the Renaissance to realize how profound a philosophical power the French mind has. This attitude indicates that the interest of the French mind was turned toward the revolution, a revolution which, as I have said, had in its essentials already happened in England. The problem, then, was a different problem. The philosophy was one which could be used by individuals, by the revolutionists, for the disintegration of the institutions which they were trying to pull down. It could be used for the theory of the reconstruction of the institutions that they proposed to put in their place. Philosophy existed in their minds for that purpose; and when they had mastered the idea enough to be able to use it in this analysis, they had no further interest in it. Their interest lay in the revolution they were undertaking; it did not lie immediately in philosophy itself.

IV

After the revolution, when the restoration took place, there appeared philosophies of the church, reconstructions of the doctrine of the institution built on the previous ideas of the church and state. These were formulated by De Bonald and De Maistre, as we have already mentioned; and they were consistent and very able doctrines. They turned on the empirical philosophy of the time and insisted that it was skeptical, that it made knowledge impossible, that it reduced man to a simple congeries of separate sensations. It was known as "sensualism" instead of the philosophy of sensation. Man was reduced to the sensations out of which he was built up, and nature was reduced to the set of experiences that people had.

For a time, ideology remained the philosophy as far as philosophy existed in France. It had sunk to a very low ebb. It almost disappeared from the universities. But where it was taught, it was taught in terms of ideology. There were, however, those that were interested in carrying this philosophy through to certain skeptical results like those of Hume. But even they were rather interested in the psychological problem and wanted a psychological analysis revealed. Cabanis and De Tracy pointed out that there were elements in experience of which Hume took no account, elements which did not appear in the analysis of substance and of cause. This content was the content of activity. If the analysis had been carried through to that point, it would have gone on to criticize Hume's skepticism as reducing experience to a set of instantaneous presents. These men made their statement in terms of factors present in activity itself and in an analysis of conception as involving something besides passivity. They recognized that in perception we are passive so far as the qualities of sensation are concerned. But, they said, our knowledge of these involves an act, and this act is something more than mere association. In that respect they were taking a step in advance. They were advancing toward the psychology of education as distinct from the psychology of association. In one sense they were advancing ahead of their time. In England it is not until after the period, or during the later period, of John Stuart Mill that the theory of education is recognized.

The interest in this type of analysis in France took quite different forms. The sensationalism of Condillac was the philosophy of the Revolution. It was an attempt to get back to ultimate elements so that they might be reconstructed. His interest was in the analysis of the governing ideas in the French community. What was wished was to get back to more primitive, immediate elements so that a plan of reconstruction could be set up. The reconstruction of the Revolution was a failure, of course. The analytic discussion of the older ideas was successful. It is this difference in attitude which one must keep in mind in comparing these philosophies. The result, from the philosophical standpoint, was that the position of Condillac seems superficial. He was not interested in such problems as Hume was interested in. He was interested in the immediate application that could be made of this analysis in testing and overthrowing the structure of church and state. After the revolution, with its failure, came the restoration and the philosophy of the reaction. That philosophy was expressed by men who did not simply accept ideas but who undertook to formulate them with their implications. It had, however, a definite political and practical social interest at that time, just as the philosophy of Condillac had had a political and social interest. The later philosophy was naturally the direct opposite of the revolution. It denied the rights of man—there were no such things as rights which inhere in the individual; it denied the independent existence of the individual; it went back to a society which was organized for the church on the authoritarian basis. It was quite powerfully presented. It represented, however, the philosophy of reaction; and, beyond its rather successful attack on the philosophy of sensationalism, it had no political effect in French thought. It was succeeded by a new movement whose chief figure was Guyau, with a connecting link in Royer-Collard.

V

Royer-Collard was a lawyer by profession. He became a philosopher late in life. What he brought to French thought was the attitude of the Scottish common-sense school, the school of reason. This school was that of the individualists, and was the dominant philosophy in American colleges fifty years ago. As indicated by the term "common sense," it appealed to the common judgment of the community as carrying with it a conclusion which should be accepted, and accepted as final, as that which is always true. Of course, there must be some sort of philosophical background in so abstract a statement as this; and this was found in what was a different statement of the process of knowledge itself. The doctrine of knowledge as it appeared in the empirical school is found in the relationship of impressions and ideas. In the first place, the empiricists would say that having an idea or impression and knowing an idea or impression are the same thing. It is there in consciousness; that is all there is to it. It carries its own existence with it. The impressions are connected with memory images. By the process of association they are connected with other impressions that occur at the same time. If one sees an object with which he is familiar, there arise other impressions with which he is familiar and which are like it; there arise impressions of other things that have been associated with it in space and time in the past. When one observes a place, certain memories of persons he has seen there appear. This relation of ideas and impressions to others comes to take the place of knowledge, or what we mean by knowledge. Knowledge is reduced to the relations of the impressions and ideas to each other as they lie in the mind.

It was assumed by the rationalists that we have, besides that knowledge of things which is present in the mind, knowledge of things to which this refers. Beyond our immediate experience there are things that appear in that experience. For example, there was the assumption that we know there is such a thing as "matter." Our experience of matter is only in our sensations. They lie in the mind. But there is back of these sensations some substance that we call "matter." We experience our own experiences. We have memory of our own experiences. But we are supposed to know that back of these states of consciousness lies a mind, a conscious mind, a substantial spiritual something in which these experiences inhere. And we are supposed to know that there are causal relations, as well as substantial relations, in the world. We have a set of ideas such as those of unity, multiplicity; we have all the logical concepts as such; and we are supposed to know that they unify our knowledge. And from these ideas and concepts we deduce results that follow or not because of the nature of the laws indicated. That is, it was assumed that we have a knowledge of what lies beyond the impressions. What the empirical school did was to carry back, step by step, all this inference of something beyond experience to the simple relationship of impressions and ideas that lie inside of experience.

The most striking result of this analysis was Hume's attempt to show that the causal relation of things was nothing but the pictures that arise in our mind—a succession of impressions one after another. If in the past we find one event following another and this has been repeated, then we expect that it will happen again. That is all there is to the law of causality. It does not show that every cause must have a certain effect, every effect a cause; that there must be like causes for like effects; that there must be an adequate cause for every effect. We do not know this as a law of the universe. What we find is this fixed expectation—an expectation that comes so frequently, so unconsciously, that we are not aware of it. When the sun rises, there will be day; when it sets, there will be night. If we follow the course of these events, there will be only certain anticipated results. You can see the result of all this was to resolve knowledge as such into the mere relation of impressions and ideas to each other, remembering that I am using the term "idea" in Hume's sense as merely the copy of the impression. Every image must, of course, be of the same character as the impression itself.

The change that is involved in the position of Reid and the Scottish school is to bring back knowledge as the immediate relationship between the mind and an object. Reid recognizes what has been called the "inner sense." According to Reid, we can have knowledge of something that is not given in the state of consciousness itself. The intuitional character of the Scottish school of philosophy lies in this: With experience we have an immediate knowledge of something that is not given in the state of consciousness, in the mind, at the time. In this sense the school seems to hark back to Locke's position. What the intuitional school said was that we have an immediate intuition of the table as extended and as solid; that this knowledge as such is an immediate relationship between the mind and the object. There is no association of common impressions and ideas with other impressions and ideas. There is a cognition of something that is not in a given state of consciousness. If the Scottish school were asked to explain this, they would say you cannot go behind it. We just know. Ask them to explain seeing, or vision, or color, or sound, or taste, or odor. They are there; we know them. That is a position that you cannot over-throw. But this school had to recognize that matter does not have the characters which appear in our vision, in our hearing, in our taste, in our sense of temperature. That which answers to color is motion; that which answers to odor is change; what answers to sound are vibrations of the air. Now these physical characters are not what appear in experience. Color, sound, taste, and odor are not motion; they are not chemical structure. So, the Scottish school had to answer the assumption that these lie in the mind and are applied to physical things that we immediately know. In these experiences we are subject to all sorts of possible errors. The extended matter is there; sound, color, taste, depend on surroundings. Put it in one surrounding, and matter has color; in another, it has not. There are possibilities, then, of error; and the Scottish thinkers had no way of accounting for them.

Royer-Collard carried over into French philosophy the doctrine of common sense, but he gave a somewhat different interpretation to it. He dealt with common sense in so far as there is uniformity in everyone's judgment. This recalls Kant's assumption or implication that minds have universal character. It is not simply that they have common forms but that there is some general consciousness of which all the different minds are different expressions. This is an implication of a good deal of the Kantian doctrine, although Kant himself did not carry it out. He avoided these implications so far as he could. Something of this sort becomes evident in the statement which Royer-Collard made of the common-sense school. He comes back to the statement, to the assumption, that we have immediate knowledge of that which is outside of ourselves and that that knowledge is simply given; it is there. We can verify what is immediately given by common sense—that in which everybody else agrees. This French transportation of the doctrine of common sense across the channel carried with it an assumption of a common consciousness in which different minds agree, from which, in some sense, different minds arise. The characteristics which belong to this common experience are given, in a certain sense, in advance of that which takes place in the separate experience. Thus we have a statement in France of the Kantian transcendentalism—the logical priority of certain characters of the mind. That is one striking difference between the doctrine of the Scottish school of Reid and his followers as it appeared in the British Isles and the doctrine as introduced in France.

There is another character also that belonged to this philosophy and which became emphasized later. That is the element of activity, especially in our normative states. This arises in some sense out of a criticism of the empirical school. As we have seen, for the empiricists having an idea and knowing it or having an impression and knowing it are the same thing. There is no difference. So far as our impressions are concerned, what they insisted on was that we are passive. You open a door to enter a room. If you have never been there before, you do not know what you are going to see, what the furniture will be, what the decorations will be. Furthermore, you have no initiative in the matter. You open the door, there is a light in the room, and you see what is in it; but you are quite passive in that experience. The experience which will come to you is something of which you will be aware, but you will have done nothing about it. Having sensation and knowing are the same thing from the point of view of the empirical school.

What the French school insisted on with growing emphasis was the distinction between cognition and perception. They admitted that, as far as the sensations are concerned, we are quite passive. No one can, by willing, have a sensation of a certain type any more than he can add a cubit to his stature. If the object is there and the eyes open, one will have a sensation; one is passive in regard to it. The act of cognition, on the other hand, is not passive. It is knowing. If my relationship to this table is not simply the presence in my mind of a set of impressions but is a knowledge that the table is there, then that knowledge is the result of an active process. It is not a simple report of a set of sensations. What that means is that the mere having of a set of perceptions is different from knowing the table. In the latter the analysis must be carried on farther if one is to say that the case is correct. Getting a glimpse of a face, one sees an acquaintance. When he meets the person he finds it is someone else whom he has never met. He has made a mistake. Our perceptual process and conceptional processes are passive in regard to the elements over which we have no control. But we are continually building things up. If we are taking certain experiences from the past, we have at the time relatively few impressions that are immediate. We are experiencing what the last impressions meant and what they imply for the future. We start off with an image, a sensation; and we expect something. We bind the whole thing in our perception. We set up the objects we look for next.

There were, then, these two elements in this French school; the taking-over of the Scottish school with its immediate knowledge of something, the acceptance of common sense, as, in a certain sense, the criterion of that which we are sure we know; and, in the second place, the emphasis on the presence of activity. It is these factors that distinguish the sensationalists of the period and represent the difference between them and the Ideologues on the one hand and the eclecticism of Cousin on the other.

VI

One point I want to impress on you is that all French philosophy of the period had a political bias. It is only natural that that should be the case. France had been overthrown by political speculation in a certain sense. The French Revolution was called the revolution of the philosophers—Rousseau, Voltaire. They were the philosophers of revolution. When the Revolution had been carried out, the reaction came, and with it a philosophy that undertook to put back the old world. Then there grew up a liberal school that tried to establish something on the political side like that already achieved in England. In England you find a philosophical detachment. The constitution seems to reflect a permanent political order. There were relative freedom and development. People were at liberty to speculate without asking for the political implications of their speculations, but that was not the situation in France.

I want to call your attention again to the fact that the stream of French life was flowing not through Paris but through the experience of the peasants. They represented the mass of the French people, and through the revolution they had got the soil and were occupied in the cultivation of it with a passion that belonged to the life of the French peasants. In this they are different from the English peasants. They were satisfied. They were not interested in what was going on in Paris. Thus, much of the thought of the period was superficial, as far as the consciousness of the French as a whole is concerned. This is characteristic of the whole period in France. The changes taking place in England went all the way through; and although there the expressions are the expressions of the upper class, they were felt by the whole country. A minority was in control, but their control affected the life of the whole group. They carried the community with them, and they had a sense of the racial life that they were directing. The profoundest experience in the French public lay below the surface; and what took place on the surface, while it was picturesque and had back of it men of talent and ability, did not represent the deeper currents. It has been only very slowly that the French people have passed over into political life, passed over by means of institutions which were brought in from the outside, which were not their own.

The movement from this earlier position to which I have just referred took place by way of Royer-Collard. He made a common consciousness, rather than a common assent, the characteristic of the process of knowledge. It was a movement, as I pointed out, that lies within the Kantian movement. It goes back to something that is transcendent. It implies a common character which belongs to all consciousness, to all intelligence—something which is logically there in advance of cognitive experiences themselves. This was not worked out in any such metaphysical theory as it finally received in the German idealists, but it is definitely implied; and what Royer-Collard came back to in his lectures is something that is common in the attitude of everyone, something that is common in consciousness itself. It was a test of what is true.

The other feature of his philosophy to which I have referred and which was emphasized by other writers was that of activity, and here he was in advance of the English movement. His emphasis was placed upon the ego, upon the self. For him ego has substance, which is soul. If you deal with it in terms of substance, it is that in which states of consciousness exist. But the soul is more especially that which organizes experience or that which is a statement of a process of organization. The soul, you may say, is an ego; but it is a substantial ego in which inhere the different states of consciousness whose faculties express themselves in the conduct of the individual. But the soul lies back of the states of consciousness as a substance which is unknowable and as a function whose faculties express the soul lying behind the idea. The act of volition takes place; the man is responsible for what he does; but the process of volition itself is the self. The self has wanted; has felt; has been affected. That is the ego of the older metaphysics, especially with its teleological implications. This principle of the activity of the soul comes into the process of consciousness as something that is going on, not as something that is simply an expression of a substantial entity that lies back behind the sensation. It is something that is going on.

Here Royer-Collard simply gives an emphasis to a phase of experience; he does not work out his doctrine. We have only a report on his so-called "second year" in philosophy, and his influence was one that came to those who listened to his lectures rather than those who read his book. But he makes a connecting link between the philosophy of the revolution, which was destructive in character, and the latter thought. The point at which he may be said definitely to depart in his emphasis, at least from the philosophy which he had taken over, was in this conception of a common consciousness and common will, and not in the concept of an activity going on in experience itself which, therefore, is not stated in terms of associations which are already there, and which is not to be stated in terms of a substance. For the psychology of association the process as such has already taken place; the association is simply an inference of organization which is already there. You bring up things by association. You are allowing a relationship which is already in existence to apply itself. You have met a person at a certain place; you pass the place, and the memory of the previous event comes back to you. You are allowing the structure which is already there simply to express itself. It is not a process; it is not an activity in itself. The psychology of Royer-Collard, as it expressed itself later, comes back to what is going on. It is the impulse that is taking place expressing itself. That is found in attention as such. It creates relationships, sets up relationships, or, in finding relations, organizes them. It is active in a manner in which activity cannot be found in the associational statement. But it is this activity which is emphasized at this period.

It is the activity which gathers about the ego, the self, as it represents an interest in the study of the self in its psychological experiences, which has been characteristic of French thought from that time on. We find also, an interest in memoirs, an interest of the sort which gets expression in Montaigne; but that is a characteristic of the French of an earlier period. They, too, were looking for an activity which goes on in the inner life of the individual. They make use of introspection, but as a different process from that used by John Stuart Mill. The difference has to do with emphasis again, with the sort of problem for which introspection is used. Introspection is still used by the English school in the interest of the solution of the epistemological problem. It comes back to an analysis of sensation and perception. The interest in the French school comes back to the life of the individual himself, at this period to the salvation, the glorification, the affirmation, of himself. It took account of the record of the experience of philosophy as it goes back into the past. That interest in history is also characteristic of the Romantic movement. Introspection as we connect it with this earlier psychology is a distinct affair. It has to do with experimentation that starts off with extreme abstractions and qualitatively susceptible differences. It is a different affair from the introspection of the English thinkers and writers of this period. Those who were working under the general idea of introspection were endeavoring to get back to their own selves, to find out what they were, and to try to evaluate themselves. It represents a process of evaluation of spiritual experiences rather than the process of locating certain cognitive experiences.

VII

Every philosophy and every philosopher appearing in France during this period has a political status. This is notable in the figure Cousin. He had a career in which there was difficulty. He expressed the attitude of the monarchy of Louis Philippe and the school of the bourgeoisie, of those who were seeking security and still were attempting to hold on to that which was valuable from the standpoint of the Revolution. They did not break with the Revolution, as the reactionary school had. They insisted that what it undertook to achieve—liberty—was essential to the life of the individual, to the life of the soul. But it was a liberty which had to be stated in terms of conditions under which it could be expressed. It was a school which was endeavoring to gather together what was valuable in the thought of the period that had gone before it and also another French school that was moving outside of its own border to get what was valuable in the thought of other nations. It took over not only the empiricism which the philosophy of the revolution had brought in from the English empirical school but also the interpretation of the Scottish school's doctrine to which I have referred. Then Cousin went farther afield into Germany and studied the new Continental philosophical doctrine that was arising, and undertook to get the outline of the philosophy of Kant and also to realize what was going on in the German Romantic school. This school set up what, in the sense that I have already indicated, you may call a "transcendentalism." This was presented in the philosophy of Royer-Collard. There is a certain structure of things belonging to a common consciousness which is a presupposition of the act of knowledge. It is something given in advance in the mind that determines the character of the object itself. The French thinkers did not take this doctrine in the skeptical sense in which it is presented in Kant's *Critique of Pure Reason*. It was taken as the test of that which could be verified; in the sense in which it was presented in the Scottish school—what is common is true.

The figures in Germany that most attracted Cousin and other writers of the time were Schelling and Hegel. It is interesting to see the different reactions to the Romantic philosophers. In England a class movement fastened on Fichte, rather than Schelling, although Schelling had a reverberation in Coleridge. Carlyle responded to Kant and Fichte; Cousin, to Kant and Schelling. There is perhaps an outlet of the French aesthetic nature in the philosophy which gathered about the aesthetic response as presented by Schelling. It was, however, also a presentation of nature as having the objectivity of the mind itself. This made the philosophy of Schelling attractive to Cousin and other thinkers of the time.

The other expression to which I have referred, that of activity, found its statement in a psychological method which was affirmed as the method of this philosophy. It is the expression, of course, of Romantic idealism. This was developed in Germany in the affirmation of the absolute philosophy, in the statement that our own selves are simply aspects of the Absolute Self. This carrying-back of experience, objective experience, to the self found its expression in French philosophy in the assumption that the philosophical method is essentially a psychological method. If one did make a consistent philosophical system on this basis, he would find himself in the position of the German Romantic idealists, as that appears in Hegel's phenomenology. This metaphysical statement, however, was not taken over and made use of by the French philosophers. They insisted that the study of the self as it appears in introspection is the method of which philosophy makes use. This philosophy had, in some sense, fortified itself with the Kantian position. The structure of the mind determines the structure of the world. The problem of getting from the mind over into the world it knows is a problem which must first be faced; but it presumably has built its bridges by means of the Kantian assumption, connected, of course, in a certain sense with the assumptions of the Scottish school. It has already made its established contact with the world. The structure of the world and of the mind are in some sense the same. The former will be studied, then, in the mind, as it can be got at most readily there. The method given is psychological. That is the French interpretation of Romantic idealism as it was seen in Germany. That idealism, of course, had a late after-birth in England in the neo-Hegelian movement. But the influence of Hegel, as it appeared in Carlyle and Coleridge and men of that sort, was literary. In France the definite inference from this idealism came especially by way of the Kantian philosophy of Cousin, but it had none of the air of abandon of the Romantic idealistic philosophy in Germany. It was carefully regimented. It dealt with a mind which has definite faculties. It takes over the problems which Kant had thrown up in the doctrine of a common consciousness in which are given the forms of mind which are also the forms of matter. By this method men could turn back to study themselves with a feeling that the study of the self was also a study of the world; that the same drama was present in the mind as in nature; that nature was free, an odyssey of spirit. One could study nature, its reality, its structure, in some sense, in our own minds.

Another characteristic which was present in this school, one which led to greater fruitfulness, was the interest in history. The Romantic school affected all Europe in this same fashion. It was the essence of the Romantic movement to return to the past from the point of view of the self-consciousness of the Romantic period, to become aware of itself in terms of the past. We have a Romantic interest expressed in Voltaire in the renewed interest in the more primitive conditions of society. We have it in the reaction of a national consciousness, a national soul, which definitely has that which is comparable to the history of the individual. The work of Hegel in going back to the expression of racial and national community consciousness expressed itself early in philosophy. The interest of the school of Royer-Collard in the history of philosophy also reflected the same spirit. But it is not a history of philosophy which is the statement of the other side of a theory of metaphysical logic, as was the case with Hegel. Hegel presented the development of the categories as they take place in our thought and the development of these categories as they take place in history as two sides of a single process. The study we find in France has more feudal interest behind it. It is interested in men, and it led to very important advances. It is an acute critical study of Greek philosophy, particularly of Plato. It was interested in the building-up of a school of philosophical thought that was not committed to a metaphysical interpretation. Its statement was not the reflection of a single philosophical doctrine.

The philosophical doctrine of Cousin, on the other hand, was tenuous and superficial. It never seriously had a real interest in the study of earlier philosophy and in the presentation of it on the basis of actual documents and their interpretation in terms of historical criticism. You find that sort of systematic interest existing in German philosophy that has gotten beyond the period of Romantic idealism. Something of the spirit of that idealism is still found in such a work as Zeller's *History of Greek Philosophy*. It also passed over into the interpretation of history in the Marxian movement. It has its reflection in the interpretation of history in the formulation of the Hegelian doctrine of the state. It has less detachment than French history of philosophy, as reflected in the uncertainty of the philosophical presuppositions of the French thinkers.

VIII

There is another figure of more importance to us than Cousin, though he made relatively little stir at the time. This is Comte, I have presented Royer-Collard and the philosophy of the revolution. Comte has his connection with the philosophy of reaction, that of the church in the reactionary period. He has his revolutionary aspects, but it is the other that is the taproot of his philosophy. If we are going to understand the man, we must realize that.

The philosophy of the early period, the philosophy of the revolution, that of De Maistre and DeBonald—the philosophy of the Restoration, that of Royer-Collard—which was the philosophy of the bourgeois monarchy, were all practical in some sense. Another element, however, was forcing its way in and was setting the temper for the later philosophical thought. This element was science, a science which was not political. The connection between philosophy and science is a connection which may be made either through a cosmology (a theory of the physical universe) or through methodology (the attempt to present the world as a whole, to organize all the different sciences into a single science, to criticize the concepts of the different sciences from the standpoint of others). This attempt is one which we find in all philosophy. The scientist is occupied with his own particular field. This is especially true of modern, specialized science. And the very restriction of the fields of the different sciences set up what may be called "organic relationships" between them. You cannot consider a biological field by itself without putting it into relationship with the physical environment in which the organism is found. You cannot concentrate your attention on the digestive tract of an animal without taking into account the whole life of that animal. You must relate the one in its organic functioning with the other. You cannot, in a physical sense, take up the consideration of physics as over against chemistry without setting up relationships between the different fields. Thus the scientists themselves feel the necessity of this interrelationship. It gets its fullest expression on the philosophical side, and in every generation there have been philosophical scientists or philosophers who are familiar with the science of the period. There have always been those who endeavor to present a concept of the world as a whole, with the interrelationship of the different sciences.

It is possible, however, for philosophy to approach science not through a conception of the different scientific fields but from the point of view of the scientific method. The scientific method in the Greek period was not different from the method of philosophy. Plato was educating his young men, so that they would become guardians or philosopher-kings, by giving them work on geometry. The method of geometry was the method of the philosopher. It was a process of deduction from the very nature of the ideas with which the geometrician or philosopher dealt. Aristotle, entering the field of biology, carried into the philosophical field a new method, the development of a teleological concept of matter as potentiality and substance, as the realization of matter in form. This concept he brought over from science. It was a conception which he used both in his studies of animals and plants and in his consideration of metaphysics. He drew no line between philosophy and science, as far as method was concerned. Both Plato and Aristotle regard themselves as philosophers in so far as they are astronomers and biologists. There was but a single field with a single method.

The Renaissance introduced a new method which was distinct from the philosophy of its time. Bacon presented it as an inductive method which was not one of Aristotelian induction. It appeared sharply in the work of the great scientists of the period as the experimental method. What was peculiarly scientific in it, as distinct from the philosophical method of the time, was that it dealt with that which was taking place not in terms of the substance of things but in terms of events as they took place. Galileo registered this in his statement of it as a new science. He called it "dynamics." Aristotle's treatment of falling bodies was that the nature of heavy bodies was to move toward the earth. He deduced their velocity from their weight: the more they weighed, the greater their velocity. He started with the object and deduced from that what the nature of the process must be. What Galileo undertook to do was to find out what the velocity of the object was in fact. If you take that method over into biology, you come to a statement of the physiological organism in terms of its functions. You ask what a digestive tract is. Instead of starting off with the form of the stomach, you start off with the digestive tract and state its nature in terms of the function it has to carry out. Then you can see why it has a certain form, why it has a different function. You state your problem in such terms that you can define it in terms of the process going on. This is just the opposite of what you find in the Aristotelian science and philosophy, where you get the nature of the object first and define its processes in terms of the nature of the object itself.

What I want to point out in this connection is that our modern scientific method abstracts from the things which had been philosophically, metaphysically defined, and occupies itself with what is happening. It has brought on what we now call the "event" as the object of observation. We do not observe, as Aristotle observed, to see through the process to what the nature of the object itself is. We observe to see what changes take place, what motions are going on, and at what velocities. That is the character of the observation; and that is also true, of course, in the biological world as far as it has its modern expression in evolution. Observation can be directed toward that which is taking place and can, to that extent, be abstracted from the nature of the thing itself. That is, it can ignore metaphysics. Aristotelian science was bound up with its metaphysics. Our biology, until evolution set it free, was bound up with metaphysics. It could explain species only in terms of creation. But an evolution which explains the development of form is free from such a metaphysical statement. Well then, the point that I am making is that modern science is interested in what happens as distinct from the thing which was supposed to be responsible for the nature of the happening. And when it comes to the statement of the thing, it defines it in terms of the process going on. It is free from metaphysics.

Now, the reflection of this in philosophy appears in positivism. Positivism is the statement of reality in terms of so-called "phenomena." These are the things that happen, that which is going on. Positivism abstracts the process, the event, from the nature of the things that are involved in what is going on. That such a process of knowledge should be possible is, of course, due to the experimental method. This method presents a test by means of which you can consider by themselves what the philosopher calls "phenomena" and still standardize your knowledge. These are the two characters of scientific method which put it in such an independent place as over against philosophy: it can abstract from the nature of what is involved in the process of the world; it can in that way free itself from metaphysics in so far as it studies phenomena. The philosopher has no method by means of which he can contest its claims. The experimental method set the scientist free from the philosopher.

The attempt to carry this method into philosophy is found in positivism, which undertakes to deal with phenomena. They are called "phenomena" in the philosophic sense; "facts" in the scientific sense. A fact is something that happens, takes place. There is no problem of a certain "nature" in what is taking place. Put it in philosophical terms, and it is something happening that has a relation to a noumenon that lies back of it. Positivism deals with what is there, what is positive and directly experienced, whose processes the mind can follow. It was Comte who undertook to carry over this method into philosophy. He was by no means free from metaphysical taint, but he is the one who gave the first definite philosophical statement to the more descriptive aspect of science. He was the first one to make the attempt to build up philosophy along the lines of the scientific method.

It follows, of course, that such a method is hypothetical. What one does is to follow a curve, so to speak. On the basis of observation, one assumes or makes the hypothesis that the curve is of a certain character. If it is of that character, then a body moving in such a path would have to be at such and such a point at such and such a time, and one could observe and make sure that the body was at that point in its process. The hypothesis is justified, in so far as that movement of the body is concerned; but there may be something in it that the scientist has not been able to determine. In that case it may later be necessary to reconstruct the hypothesis. That is, the scientific method is essentially hypothetical. It is a method of extrapolation, a way of determining what the result may be and justifying one's theory by means of that result. Of course, one can never make a complete statement of all that is involved in anything that happens. In some sense everything is involved in everything that happens. Consequently, the theory must be hypothetical. The experimental method, as applied by science, always implies that a theory is hypothetical.

What positivism undertook to do was to deal with that which falls within the field of philosophic thought as we deal with scientific data, in terms of scientific method. There we deal with the event as it appears. The event as it appears for the scientist, the observer, is the sensation in consciousness. The scientist takes the event as something by itself. Then he finds out what other events are connected with it, finds what uniformity may be discovered, and forms a hypothesis of the way in which these events will be associated with each other. He tests this hypothesis by future events and establishes a theory, but a theory which still remains hypothetical in character. The assumption here is that knowledge is to be obtained only through the observation of events and the testing of hypotheses as they appear in experience, and that the immediate object of knowledge is the event and the thing. Here we have a philosophy which is positivistic in character. If we cannot treat entities in terms of metaphysical things, we can deal with them at least as far as our experience is concerned. The matter that lies back of the qualities of the chair is something that does not enter into experience. It is not positive knowledge. This is a statement which is of the same general character as that of Hume. As far as his account of what we have in our cognitive experience is concerned, Hume comes back to impressions and ideas and the analysis of them. In thinking of the substance of things, he says we have uniformities which reveal themselves in our experience in terms of habit; and that is what Hume was interested in—the relation of events in experience to the so-called "laws of nature."

In the case of positivism, of the form in which it was espoused by Comte, the interest does not lie primarily in reducing nature and its uniformities to associated ideas. What Comte was interested in was the relation between the events as they take place. He did not bring up the question as to where those events take place, whether in the mind or in the world, whether there is something that answers to them as they take place in the mind. He said here are the events; we call some subjective, some objective. Let us find the uniformity of their happening, not only for an observational science but also for philosophy. Comte was particularly interested in the appearance of this method and its relationship to the formal metaphysical content which should lie behind it. He went back into the history of thought to the Greek period, with its metaphysical method, and asked what lies behind it. He showed the interpretation of the world in terms of gods, of magic influences of spirits, and then showed how Greek philosophy, becoming rationalistic, advanced beyond this concept of gods to the concept of certain natures which belong to things. Such a statement as that which Aristotle gives is partly theological and partly metaphysical. He assumed, for example, that the nature of the heavenly bodies is divine. He assumed that there must be some sort of a divine being that directs the motion of all planetary bodies. They are gods, such gods as the Greeks had conceived, but deprived of the anthropomorphic aspects we find in mythology. Aristotle conceived of them as responsible for the motions of the heavenly bodies, although he assumed that these bodies, by nature, move in circular orbits and with uniform velocities. On the face of the earth this teleological element largely disappears, and you have heavy bodies whose tendency is to move toward the center of the earth. Aristotle did not conceive of these as directed by divine beings. From the standpoint of nature, there is no very great difference between assuming that the growth of a tree is due to a dryad or to a certain metaphysical substance which belongs by nature to the tree. The growth of trees is such as it is. You can think of it in pictorial form, show it as it is, a living tree. You can think of the force of the tree as that which comes from a living being or from an inherent force of nature that tends to develop itself in a certain way. There is a certain nature in the acorn which, given an opportunity, will develop into a sapling and then into an oak.

A scientific statement is a natural development of the theological statement. The intermediate, metaphysical statement is, of course, free from all the anthropomorphic characters of the theological statement. It does not have to be brought inside of the sphere of magic. The mind is free in that respect. But still it is bound to the definition which it gives of the nature of the object itself. Having given that definition, it can deduce certain necessary qualities from it. So we find that the Aristotelian metaphysics regards not a growing science but a completed science. Aristotle was the Encyclopedist of his period. He gathered into his statements all that could be known, and put it in terms of the nature of the things that make up the world, things that we find in the world when put in their necessary logical relations to each other. Such a statement has a certain finality about it, provided it is carried out by a genius, like Aristotle, who is able to gather together and organize a great body of diverse material. If the summation has been a very complete one, there is no invitation to anyone to carry it further. That is what is striking, but with such a complete science interest lapses.

The type of problem which comes with the work of Galileo, as expressing the experimental method, is essentially one which comes from the method of research science, not from the science of the Encyclopedists, not from the type that we sometimes call "systematic." There are certain fields into which this new method has entered comparatively late. Biology, to go back for a generation or a little more perhaps, took into itself everything that men knew; and anything that they did not know, at the time, could be added to it. There were certain groupings of plants—the genera, the families, and their species and sub-species. There was a principle of organization, a principle which was worked out in the eighteenth century by Linnaeus. Into this system could be introduced any new species that might be found, but the system itself did not carry with it any proof.

That is not a research science. Research science has come into biology only with evolution, for the conception of evolution deals with species not as ultimate metaphysical entities but as something that arises out of conditions. Experience, instead of being of such and such a metaphysical entity, becomes a problem. That is, of course, presented to us in Darwin's great work. What is the origin of species? This question indicates a new line of approach. The earlier concept was that characters and species were given in the creation of the plant or animal. God gave to the plants and animals a certain nature for their preservation. The whole life-history of plants and animals shows the development of this nature. The cataloguing system enables us to give them their characters and place them in a complete science. A scientific problem is itself not a statement that here is the oak, the ox, the tiger. It is rather the question: "Why is the oak there; why is it oak instead of another tree; what is the meaning of this species?"

In what I have been saying, you have a very vivid illustration of the passage from the metaphysical over to what Comte would call the "positivistic state." There are, said Comte, these three stages of development, the theological, the metaphysical, the positivistic. And he said this is true not only of communities but of individuals. A child lives in a world of magical things and persons. He loves things that meet his wishes, and he hates things that hurt him. And then comes the later period when he gives up these magical implications and takes to hard and fixed definitions of things. The objects about him have certain natures. They are not to be looked at from the point of view of a fairy tale. It is a common-sense attitude if you like, but an attitude which in itself is metaphysical in that each thing has a certain nature that distinguishes it from other things. Because of its nature, it has certain qualities; and the child utilizes these qualities. It is the common-sense attitude which all persons of adult years reflect in regard to the objects about them. The natural definition of a chair is that it is something having certain necessary qualities—it has hardness, a certain form, and other qualities—inhering in a certain nature. That metaphysical statement is nothing but the abstract formulation of our attitude toward all things as they exist about us. Then we advance to the positivistic, the scientific, stage as Comte stated it. Such a statement as that which had been given of the nature of the chair is recognized as utterly incomplete. What is there that gives to wood its particular strength? For example, how does it compare with iron or steel? We depart from the metaphysical attitude when we ask: "What happens when we do this, that, and the other thing to the object?" We try to find certain uniformities by means of which we can determine what will happen. We have passed out of a world of fixed things as such and come back to data which we can get in experience. We have to distinguish between what the scientist refers to as "hard facts" and the objects about us. Persons are said to "come up against hard facts." Their theory comes in conflict with a fact. But the fact against which the theory comes in conflict is a happening of some sort; it is a happening which is not the happening that we anticipated from a certain theory. Given a certain theory, we expect certain happenings; and then something else happens. It is the contradiction in experience that is the hard fact of science.

That is the phase that we need to keep in mind in getting the scientific method as it appears in such a system as that of

Comte. What one is dealing with is a set of events that take place in experience. In those events you find uniformities; they never get a final statement, however. Given the statement, we have a theory; we are then able to determine what the results will be on the basis of that theory. If something else happens, then the theory must be reconstructed. The world is a world of events, of things that are going on. The scientist's attitude is the expression of the positivistic statement that succeeds the medieval statement. This exemplifies the three-stage theory of Comte. As communities and as individuals we pass through three stages —the theological, the metaphysical, and the scientific. From the point of view of philosophy, the importance of the view lies, you see, in the statement of the object of knowledge. Is one considering substance or is one considering events that are taking place, what philosophers would call "phenomena"? Is knowledge occupied with these or with something that these reveal? Is our observation a finding, an isolation, of a certain nature or form that lies back of it all? Or is it occupied with the phenomena themselves? It is a question as to what the function of knowledge is.

IX

The important characteristic of Comte's doctrine was its recognition of what we may term the "philosophical import" of scientific method. As I have indicated, the scientific method recognized the object of knowledge in the experience of the individual, in that which is ordinarily termed the "fact." If one is to identify the fact, he must do it in terms of his experience. It is, of course, true that the observer states his observation in such terms that it can also be made an object by others and so be tested by them. He tries to give it a universal form, but still he comes back eventually to the account which he gives of his observation as such.

What is not recognized in the positivistic doctrine is that the observation is always one that has an element of novelty in it. That is, it is in some sense unusual. It is observed because it is distinct in some way from the expected experience. One does not observe that which is to be expected. One notes it; one recognizes it. We recognize what we expect, and give attention only to that which differs from that which is expected. If one reaches for a tool that he is after and it is in its expected place, or for a book in its place on the shelf, all he gives attention to is that the object is of the type that he expects to find. He gives as little attention as is necessary in order to identify it. More than this would mean loss of effort and time. One does not stop to examine the expression of his friend unless there is something unusual about it. He sees only enough to identify him. Ordinarily, then, we would not speak of an observer as one who merely recognizes. Observation implies careful noting of all the details of the object. It is true that you do not observe everything about anything. What one does is to observe all that enables one to assure himself that the object is not exactly what one expects. One reaches for a tool, thinking he is going to pick up a hammer, and finds it is a chisel; and he pays attention to find why it was that he made the mistake. He observes the character of a plant that misled him. His observation is given to that which distinguishes it from the expected thing. These are the facts of science—those observations that enable us to determine characters that would not have been anticipated. One may also, of course, give attention to objects that seem quite familiar. That is what is implied. You are looking for something that will strike your attention as in some sense unusual.

The positivistic doctrine assumes that our objects are given in such observation, and that is the logical weakness of positivism. It assumes that the world is made up, so to speak, out of facts, is made up out of those objects that appear in the experience of the scientific observer. Most objects we regard simply as they identify themselves. The objects of scientific observation answer to a detailed analysis, which implies an interest of some sort. We can explain this position in terms of the method to which I refer, by saying that the objects of science do not always have behind them implicit or explicit problems. In other words, science is really research science. Research always implies a problem. Where there is nothing of this sort, we are not engaged in research. There is a type of thinking which is not problematical—that of carrying out a habitual act, of attending a machine with which you are familiar, for example. That sort of concentrated attention is given simply to those stimuli that will enable us to carry out a well-formed habit. There we have concentrated attention, but it is not occupied with the proceedings of our research science. It is occupied in a world where one is awake only to the next stimulus that is necessary to carry on an activity that more or less runs itself.

A further step which Comte did not recognize, because it belongs to a later period, is the evolutionary one which undertakes to see how these forms, these experiences, arise. Evolutionary doctrine started off with the life-process, and undertook to account for the appearance of species themselves. It carries us back to a world in which the nature of the object, the experience as such, arises. Neither Comte nor John Stuart Mill, who would be the corresponding figure in England, was influenced by evolutionary doctrine to any great degree. Mill was also, to all intents and purposes, a positivist. He, too, assumed that the analysis that the scientist makes of an object reveals the characters of things, reveals the elements of things, the parts of things; and if we want to know the world, we must discover these elements which the scientist finds. Mill, as you know, embodied this doctrine in his logic in which he undertook to state the logic of science. It is by no means an adequate account of scientific procedure; but his theory of induction and of the inductive process in science, his method of agreement and difference, are definitely attempts to state the scientist's procedure. They are really methods of distinguishing rather than of forming hypotheses.

What I am attempting to make clear is that the positivistic doctrine was one which undertook to give the philosophic implications the form of scientific method. But neither Comte nor Mill gave a competent account of the scientist's procedure.

They did assume that science—what we would call "research science"—was the most efficient method of knowing. They did recognize that this type of science was one which was an advance over metaphysical science, while the metaphysical was a natural successor to theology. We have, then, in the French thought of this period, the reconstruction of science as presenting the form of the philosophic problem.

The step which positivism represents is that of stating a problem so that it is put in the form of a method rather than of a result. Is the method of science the method of philosophy? Can one make the method of science the method of philosophy? One great, somewhat grandiose effort to solve this problem was made by the Romantic idealists. Hegel, who was most complete in his statement, undertook to show that the method of science and the method of human thought in all its endeavor and the method of the universe were all the same, the method which he represented by his dialectic process. His philosophy was in one sense a philosophy of evolution; but the same process, the same method, the same logic, lay back of physical nature, back of moral effort, back of human history, back of all that science presents. It was, as I said in other connections, a grandiose undertaking which was a failure. Particularly, it was unable to present the scientific procedure within each field. It could not successfully state the method of research science. This is the problem, then, that is presented in positivism. For positivism metaphysics is past; it is gone. Just as metaphysics was supposed to have wiped out theology, so the positivists were presenting a method which could be immediately applied, and through which we could get rid of metaphysics.

X

Comte had as vivid an interest in the relation of his philosophy to society and its values as any others of the period. He looked for the forms of a society of the human race whose values should determine the conduct of the individual. But, as far as the process of knowing social values was concerned, it would be the same as in the physical and the biological sciences. He assumed that there could be a study of society which could be undertaken in the same way as the study of the physical sciences. That was the most striking character of his doctrine in its immediate impact. The church had a metaphysical doctrine behind it. And this is no less true in this period of what we may call "political science," the theory of law, of ethics, of education. That is, each of them had essential doctrines. The sovereignty of the state, in the attitude of an English community, is to be found in the individuals that form the republic. Sovereignty was a dogma. It was that in the state which exercised absolute power. And the state had to be conceived of in terms of such metaphysical entity as that. Similarly, the family was a certain definite entity, and the school was a certain definite entity. One argued from the nature of the sovereign, of the family, of the school, what the position of the individual under it must be. In each case the attitude was essentially metaphysical. What Comte presented was the demand for the use of positivistic method in the study of society. He presented sociology as a new field. What I want to emphasize is that we do not think of it as another science. We have economics, education, political science; and here comes sociology, another science covering the same field and yet claiming to be different. It has been, in very recent times, a great question as to whether there was any such thing as sociology. And I have seen theses presented in this university for the degree of Doctor of Philosophy in the field of sociology upon the problem of whether or not there is any such thing as sociology. What is characteristic of Comte's position is his demand that society and social events should be approached in the same fashion that the study of plants and animals and moving bodies are approached. He was breaking away from the metaphysical attitude and presenting another science, that of society. As he conceived of society, it inevitably includes the whole human race; and he thought there could be one science of it. Sociology, then, was the attempt to apply the method of positivism, the method of science, to the field of society, an attempt to displace what was, at that time, an essentially metaphysical approach, one which started off with the definition of the state, with a study of the processes of social changes going on in various institutions. Comte undertook to approach human affairs in the way of the scientist who simply analyzes things into their ultimate elements in a positivistic fashion and then from that finds the laws of their behavior. But there lay in the back of Comte's mind pictures of a medieval period, only he would have substituted society for the pope. He was not freed from that. This other side of Comte's doctrine is one that harks back to the medieval period.

I pointed out that early in the century, during the period of De Bonald and De Maistre, reactionary philosophers sought to go back to the church as the source of all authority, as that which must give an interpretation of life. Their statement, however, was different from the medieval statement. They were particularly impressed with the society of Europe in the twelfth and thirteenth centuries, the period which is best represented by Dante. It was a period in which the world realized itself as a single community, in which everything could be explained by the doctrine of the church. There was no difficulty in the explanation, because this world was so created that man can be moral; and, if he can be moral, it must also be possible for him to be immoral. It is a world in which sin has a legitimate place; and if man sins, the punishment of sin follows. The world at that period was entirely comprehensible from the point of view of the church theology. It included everyone. Anything that happened that was undesirable could be explained by the fact that God was using it to bring about the great good, including the good of man. The Western world was conceived of as a single society. It took in nearly the whole of the human race. It was organized through the church. The church took over the statement that St. Paul gives, you remember, of the church as the body of which Christ was the head. In his concept of a unified society everyone has his place and everything can be explained from the point of view of the theory of the church.

It was to that conception of a society which was a world society, an organic society, and a society which answered to the immediate impulse of the individual that these philosophers, De Bonald and De Maistre, went back.

Comte was never influenced by this account. His positions freed him from the dogma of the church, but he still looked to such a picture of the whole society of man as representing the idea that should be realized. The curious thing from our standpoint is that he should have copied to such an extent the characters of the church. His idea, too, was that society should be an organic whole. It must then have some organized value. What Comte presents, instead of welfare by the church, is the welfare of the community as a whole. This community as a whole comes to take the place of the glory of God, which, as spoken of by the church, is the end of all existence. For the positivist it is not the glory of God but the good of mankind that is the supreme value. That is the supreme value in terms of which everything should be stated. This point of view is stated in less emotional form in the utilitarianism in England during the same period. Bentham and the Mills are, in a sense, companion figures to Comte. Their idea of the ideal society is one which achieves the greatest good of the greatest number. This welfare of the community transcends the good of any particular individual. This is something all should see, and man's attitude toward it should be a religious attitude. This should be recognized as the supreme value that determines all others. And Comte recognized that an emotional attitude was essential.

John Stuart Mill said that everyone finds himself and his conduct constantly influenced by others. Each can retain his own pleasure by recognizing others in the pursuit of their pleasure. The individual feels continually the presence of the community about him forcing him to recognize the interest of others. It seems a skeptical account which Mill gives of the origin of virtue. Comte would put up the good of the community itself through an emotional expression which should be essentially religious in its character. That is, men should actually worship the Supreme Being in the form of society. Society as an organized whole, as that which is responsible for the individual, should be worshiped; and on this basis Comte undertook to set up a positivistic religion. Now, this religion of positivism had some vogue among the followers of Comte. There was a devoted group of this sort to be found in England. It never attained any size. A wag, referring to a dissension among them, said of the sessions, "They came to church in one cab and left in two." It never became a widespread religious movement, but the undertaking to set up such a religion which should find the highest value in society and fuse that into a unity which could be worshiped was characteristic of Comte. He thought and looked for a society that could be organized in the same fashion as medieval society had been by the church. And he attempted to work out in some detail how this sort of ordering of society would take place. He did not try to substitute the value of society itself for the Deity, but tried to take over the religious attitude toward the Deity into the religious attitude of members of the community toward society itself.

This phase of Comte's sociology was not a lasting one. What was of importance was his emphasis on the dependence of the individual on society, his sense of the organic character of society as responsible for the nature of the individual. This is what Comte put into a scientific form. It had already found its theological statement, as I have said, in Paul's account of the relation of men in the church to parts of the body and to the church as the whole. That is, he conceived of the individual as determined by society as an organism, just as there are different organs which must be conceived of as dependent on the organism as a whole. You cannot take the eye as a separate reality by itself. It has meaning only in its relationship to the whole organism of which it is a part. So you must understand an individual in a society. Instead of thinking of society made up of different entities, Comte thought of it in terms of a union of all which was an expression of a certain social nature which determined the character of the individual. There are two characteristics of

Comte: first, his recognition that society as such is a subject for study; and second, his conviction that we must advance from the study of society to the individual rather than from the individual to society.

XI

The next point I want to emphasize is that in France the philosophic mind was dominantly psychological. It was psychological in a different sense from that in which English empirical thought was psychological. It was also different from the psychological position of Reid and the so-called Scottish school. For example, it recognizes activity as a fundamental characteristic of the experience which science was studying, and not simply the content of experience, not simply states of consciousness. It recognizes that the process of knowledge is not simply the passive reception of impressions, but that it is an organized process in knowledge. In sensation one can say that the mind just has impressions. But in perception you have a reaction of the mind upon its own sensations, and perhaps on the objects which were supposed to be responsible for these sensations. Activity, then, forms part of the content with which the French psychologists were occupied. They were also much more interested in the affective side of life, the emotional side. They were not, however, any more interested in the personality, the ego, the self, from the psychological side than were the English empiricists. The Germans, of course, in their philosophy came back to the self as basic. It is central to their whole doctrine. But their interest was metaphysical rather than psychological.

The interest of the French psychologists was in the actual stream of life of the self rather than in the psychology of the other groups. These others regarded psychology as the method of philosophy. This gave to their philosophy that character expressed in the term "spiritualism." That is, it assumed that what is revealed in our study of ourselves is in accord with nature itself. In one sense, Comte agreed with this position; in another sense, he did not. In his adherence to science and the conception of the individual as a product of social forces he did not. The emphasis of French philosophy was upon the experience of the individual. In this it went back to its psychological method. Royer-Collard, for example, in taking over the Scottish form, comes back to our immediate intuition. He relied upon those experiences with which psychology deals. That is, he, like Reid, did not come back to immediate experiences in the sense that Descartes did. Descartes came back to the immediate experience of his own existence as a self, as a substantial being. Reid came back to that experience in its immediate psychological character. In our immediate experience we are in contact with objects that we know. This is the aspect of experience to which Reid came back. And French philosophy laid particular emphasis on this same aspect of the individual. Its method was that of psychology. Comte turned away from that and tried to reduce psychology to biology. He denied the possibility of a science of psychology.

If we are to relate the French philosophy to that of its neighbors in England and Germany, it is essential to recognize this essentially psychological interest. The whole interest of the English analysts was in carrying the division of experience back to that which was common to everyone—back to common sensations, common impressions, common memory images— back to that which was psychical in the sense of being private not only in that it lies within the experience of an individual but in the sense of having that particular character which belongs to one's own inner life as distinct from that of anyone else. What the French felt and expressed on the philosophical and the literary side was the need of an active self to which these experiences came back. Among the Germans we have seen thinkers coming back to a logical process which is identical with experience, for both are expressions of the single ego. But in that single ego it is difficult to get to the common character which belongs to the individual life, that in which sensations are identified with the life of the individual. This disappears in so far as it is known to the experience of others and the infinite movement of minds that are common to it. From the logical standpoint, that which is peculiar to the individual lacks reality. What is universal and necessary is real. John Stuart Mill definitely presented his philosophy in a psychological form. So did his father. But they were interested in the analysis of the object of knowledge. They proceeded on the principle that if they could get back to the elements of knowledge they could determine the character of objects. They find these in what were called "impressions" and "ideas," which are located by the individual in his own experience. Their method, then, was that of introspection. What the school was interested in, and what it placed emphasis on, was the object of knowledge as such. Thus their problem was essentially the epistemological problem.

The interest of the French philosopher was not in the epistemological problem. It lay, rather, in the attack on certain institutions. They were interested in pulling down the theories of the church and state. This problem was first attacked by the "sensationalists," as their opponents called them. This was essentially a revolutionary school. It was recognized as having that political bias. When philosophy was being established on more definite philosophical bases, when France was endeavoring to get itself out of the situation which had been left by the Revolution, a turn was made to the philosophy of Reid, taking over his position that one has immediate knowledge of that which lies outside, and particularly emphasizing the test of that knowledge which Reid had insisted on, the test of common sense, a sense which is common to all. This left the experience of the individual as a field which was of deep interest in itself. It was no longer simply the field within which the object of knowledge was found. It was that in which the experience of the individual was found. The object of knowledge is common. It is only in so far as it is public that it has validity. On the other hand, it lies in the experience of the individual. The emphasis of the empirical school had been on that object as it was supposed to exist in the experience of all; and, while they recognized that it appeared in the experience of the individual, their interest centered in finding out what was the import of its being common property. If one sets this doctrine up as the theory of knowledge, it implies that the mind itself has direct acquaintance with its object. It has, in some sense, cut the Gordian knot. You cannot ask how you know; the fact is that you do know! That leaves the field of the experience of the individual as a field which may have interest in itself. And it was this interest which the French took up.

As I have said, they were following out what was characteristic of the French mind and its genius—its memoirs, its study of the experience of the individual, as found, for example, in Montaigne. That interest belonged peculiarly to the French. They were interested in the experience of the individual just as an individual, and in the recounting of that experience. As I said, they took the position of Reid; but they took it in a somewhat different form. Their position approached that of Kant. They assumed a general experience which was common in some sense to all, something answering to the transcendental ego. The forms of the mind, which were common to all individuals, are the Kantian reply to the position of the English empirical school and their skepticism; and French philosophy took over this answer. It is this interest that characterized French thought and its psychology. And this interest gives a certain definite turn to French psychology and to the philosophy that depended on it.

To get that angle one must realize the development taking place in Germany. After the development of the Romantic school the Germans also turned to psychological investigation. We have, first of all, the philosophy of Herbart, which may be said to answer to the tendency among the French. Herbart undertook to establish his philosophy on the basis of ideas as they appear in the minds of the individual. The principal application of this Herbartian psychology was in the field of education. Herbart was himself a theorist in the field of education. He looked on the mind from the point of view of the increase of knowledge. The organization of ideas in the mind answers to the Lockian idea, a state of consciousness which has a reference to something else, that out of which the intellectual life, as over against the affective and volitional life, is built up. What Herbart was interested in pointing out was that it was the organization of these elements in the mind that made the mind able to isolate others. Taking over the Kantian term, he called this organization "apperception," and not simply "perception" in the sense of immediate experience—not simply the organization of that experience in terms of association but a perception which is a unified grasp of the sense in experience. Now this Herbart referred to as an "apperceptive mass of ideas." The gist of the doctrine was that grasping anything, taking it over into the mind, is dependent on there being given such a mass. There must be a group of ideas to which one might look for connective factors which give ideas their essential relations. The value of this theory was to be found not only in the application of it to education but also in the beginnings of the science of language. In those two fields the Herbartian psychology remained significant long after its influence had been lost elsewhere.

There is a certain community between the French and Germans in connection with their interest in psychological content. But another distinction must be made. German psychologists, especially Herbart's successors, were laying stress on the organism and its structure. This resulted in a significant physiological psychology. If you study what takes place in experience in terms of the central nervous system and the nervous mechanism in general, you will find that which is common, universal. The technique of your study will be to isolate what your experience has in common with the experience of others. But suppose you get a curious experience like color blindness, where one person fails to distinguish red from green. Even this may be isolated, at least hypothetically, in terms of certain color spots which should be present in the eye but are not. In this way you get a more or less universal statement of the unusual experience. Just because this psychology was so interested in the organism as such, it was stated in terms that belong to all organisms. The study of the experience of the individual was put into the same terms. Such an approach would select out of the experience of the individual that which is common in the experience of all. French psychology lays emphasis on that which is individual and peculiar, on that which introspection reveals. The German school passes over this, perhaps. Its interest is in the problem as it appears in the organic responses and mechanisms of experience in the individual.

XII

The psychological problem that came to have the largest meaning for the French philosophy, that about which other problems were gathered, was that of mechanism and determinism as over against voluntary acts and free will. We have seen that French philosophy had oriented itself with reference to fact. Comte had given expression to this in terms of scientific method, as over against simply scientific results. He brought over a scientific method into philosophy and undertook to approach the problem of common reforms from the standpoint of the method of science. Is there any place for common choice in the world which science discusses? Can the worlds of will and of law be brought together? That is the problem that fixed itself in the mind of the French thinkers.

They accepted a scientific statement that did not open the door to the sort of miracle which you find in the statement of Descartes, which assumes that God in some fashion enables consciousness to react on the organism. They did not take that course. They tried to find a place for consciousness in the world as science presents it. There was no criticism of the scientist's statement in his own terms; but they tried to find a way by which choice could be brought into a mechanistic universe, a world in which causal relations are dominant, in which one can state, from the point of view of the causes, if he had them all, what the effects must be. It was the sort of a picture suggested by Laplace in his world-equation in which one would have only to introduce the variable of time and solve it in order to find just where every particle must be at any given instant. If that is your conception of physical science, is there any place, any meaning, for human spontaneity, human freedom? That was the problem which interested the French thinkers because of their concern with their own inner experience. You do not find this sort of problem dominating thought in England or Germany. It was peculiarly a French approach.

In the case of the English, we have the analysis of the object of knowledge in terms of impressions and ideas, or sensations and images, the interest lying in the treatment of the epistemological problem in reference to the content of the object of knowledge as related to the states of consciousness of the individual. On the German side we have, first of all, the approach from the standpoint of the personality, the self, and the metaphysical conception of the Absolute Self, of which the individual self was regarded as a phase. The interest there lay in the metaphysical identification of the personality of the individual with the Absolute Self of the whole universe. The later development from this period of German Romantic idealism was found in the physiological approach, in which the attempt was made to find what answers to the stimulus in what takes place in the organism, especially in the central nervous system. An attempt was made to set up a relationship between the stimulus and the response of the organism to it. It was inevitable that the interest should be guided by that which could be actually isolated in the study of the physiological process. A central nervous system is a complex structure whose elements are so mixed that they can be reached only by microscopic study, and the complexities of the structure are so great that it was with very great difficulty that any entrance at all was made into this field. It was inevitable that investigators should fasten on that which could be got hold of. Beyond that, they were left largely in the field of speculation and were thrown back on what introspection indicated plus the hypothesis of nervous processes and structures that would answer to what introspection revealed. The sense organs themselves were, of course, there for study, analysis, and anatomization. These could be identified as having definite relationships to stimuli from without. It was possible to approach the theory of color, for example, from this standpoint. The photochemical substances in the eye could be regarded as answering to particular vibrations without.

When it came to following the nerve tracts back into the central nervous system, the field was so intricate that it was difficult to follow out the paths. Simple reflex automatisms or paths could be found or were supposed to exist running through the sense organs back to the muscles and glands, and it was possible then to approach the central nervous system from the point of view of these reflexes. The earlier assumption had regarded these elements in the central nervous system as in some sense answering to certain characteristics of the object. They even pictured the nerve cells as that which would answer to a group of ideas. The study of the central nervous system showed that it consisted of a set of paths among the nerve cells. But you got nothing but a set of paths. There is nothing static in the central nervous system. You could not find anything there that answered to an idea of a static entity. One simply finds connections between the end-organs and the muscles and glands in which the nerve processes finally terminate—a field of fibrils and nerve centers which are intricate but remain in the paths. You had, then, an approach from the point of view not of statics but of dynamics. A physiological psychology inevitably emphasizes what we call the "active side" of psychology, and this leads back to the study of what goes on in the experience of the individual.

Now, there was no place within this process into which one could insert a conscious process; the most that one could do was to define a certain correlation. It was this interrelationship between what was going on in different nervous mechanisms and what belonged to the experience of the individual that interested the German psychologists particularly.

The interest on the French side was one which belongs to the field of introspection first of all. Physiological psychology was not neglected there. Some very valuable work was done in

France in the study of the phenomena of light. Many of the subjects which were dealt with by the psychology of the period were examined in the laboratory by the French psychologists. But their approach was from the standpoint of the individual rather than from the standpoint of the physiological system. I have already pointed out the positions of Royer-Collard and Cousin. They came back to the immediate experience of knowledge as that in the experience of the individual which is ultimate. I have indicated the difficulties connected with that, but the position is characteristic of the French school. They held on to the experience of the individual.

When we advance to the philosophical problem involved in such an approach, we find it centers in the problem of the freedom of the will. Science assumes that everything that happens can be explained because it must necessarily follow from previous events as an expression of natural law. The intelligibility of nature is dependent on our assumption that there are uniform laws that can be depended on. If nature were a chaos of events that had no necessary connection with each other, it would be impossible for science to unravel any of its mysteries. Our knowledge would be confined to particular experiences, sensations. Unless we can find connections between these, knowledge is utterly impossible. The intelligibility of nature presupposes natural laws. Science, in its faith in the intelligibility of the world, is committed to the necessity of its happenings. It is natural, therefore, that science should emphasize this necessity and that it should sweep everything within this field of necessity, at least in so far as it knows it. And that, of course, took in the human body; everything that happens there must be in accordance with natural law. There are laws for the circulation of blood as for the movement of planets. Each can be known. It seems that what takes place is necessary. In terms of this, the succession of our states of consciousness as they succeed each other seems to be necessary. The behavior of human consciousness is as necessary as the movements of the heavenly bodies.

XIII

Cousin's reaction against this assumption was a superficial one. He undertook to check the statement of the necessity of physical science against the active nature of the self and thus tried to find a place in which you could insert the freedom of the individual. The approach of Renouvier is somewhat different in character. He emphasized the hypothesis as it appears in science. Science approaches its field with postulates which, we say, are based on a certain phase of experience. One of these assumptions is that the world is knowable; another is that the world is in some sense necessary, that is, that we can predicate events. Now, if we can predicate events, we must know the reason why things are going to happen. But the hypotheses with which we approach these problems are hypotheses which arise in our own minds. The hypotheses are themselves in nature. We must find that which answers to nature by the form in which it appears in human thought, and what Renouvier insists on is that in the alternatives which we have between hypotheses it is possible for the human mind to enter as a determining factor. There are alternative hypotheses, especially when we recognize how small a part of the whole field of knowledge is really brought within the range of our scientific study. We know very little— so little that we feel like a child on the seashore gathering pebbles while the ocean of truth lies beyond. Renouvier insisted that in the selecting of hypotheses the human will plays its part; the mind plays a part in the structure of knowledge.

This comes out in another form when we get to Boutroux. Still a third answer was suggested by some who came back to parallelism in a somewhat different expression than that of the physiological psychologists. The physical and the mental side of the world are parallel. That implies some common content. The attempt was made to approach something that was both physical and mental; and it laid that which was more fundamental in the mind. It was an attempt to go back from parallelism to something that lies beyond it. This parallels Boutroux's statement, and indicates that we have here a reflection of the positivism to which I have called your attention in Comte.

You remember Comte undertook to get away from metaphysical presuppositions. That which we know is what appears in experience—it is phenomenal. Our knowledge of that is positive and direct. When we go back to a substance that lies back of this, we are making metaphysical assumptions that cannot be established. Knowledge should confine itself to the recording of experiences and the relationships which we find lying between them. We cannot say that there are certain physical bodies, entities, substances; the most that we can say is that there are certain experiences which we have interpreted in this metaphysical fashion. We cannot say that there is a force which acts with necessity in the world; the most we can say is that there are certain uniformities in motion and change. We can determine this but we cannot get back to any forces. When we speak of a force as operating from an object, when we allow ourselves to use our imaginations and think of the sun as pulling the earth, then we get a sense of a necessity which impels the earth to move toward the sun. If, on the other hand, we observe the movements of the earth and sun with reference to each other and we find that these movements agree with Newton's law that velocities are proportionate to masses and indirectly to the square of the distances, we are noting certain uniformities in certain changes; and these uniformities present a different experience from that which was implied in the idea of a force.

It is Boutroux who undertakes to analyze what is involved in this conception of knowing. You must remember the sort of problem with which we are working: Does the necessity which science implies as found in the world include also the action of the human mind? You set up the mechanical universe and posit the human body as a part of it. If you establish a strict parallelism between an organism and what takes place in the mind, you seem to reduce the mental process to a mechanism. What Boutroux undertakes to do is to analyze what this necessity means. He speaks of a metaphysical necessity in the first place, a necessity which expresses itself in the formula of identity: A is A, or, in order to put it in a form which we feel to be the most general, A is not-nothing. That is, given any certain reality, in so far as we can identify anything with it we can affirm the same thing of that which is identified with it that we can of the thing itself. If we can say anything about the nature of substance, because of a given effect, then anything that we can identify with substance can have the same thing attributed to it. That is the nature of substance. If you say anything of it in its relationship to an effect, then you can identify anything which occurs with that which makes possible the same affirmation in regard to the relation between cause and effect. In so far as you can get back to A as A, you can get back to cause as a metaphysical necessity. But the necessity that is indicated here does not go over to the characters of things.

We keep talking about the mechanical universe as a whole. But we have no knowledge of a whole. We have knowledge of various elements and speak of them in a metaphysical sense. We say the table has a certain nature which was there before and will be there after we are gone. It is substance that we identify in certain of our experiences. We can make the same affirmation about the universe that we make of the table. But we never reach the universe as a whole. Our metaphysics necessarily is confined to those situations in which we identify the nature of one thing with the nature of something else. If we could get hold of the whole universe, we could get a statement which would identify everything with the universe and give to it the characters that belong in the universe. But we cannot do that. Necessity from the metaphysical point of view is a necessity that is affected by contingency in regard to the object about which we make our affirmation. For one man a substance, an organism, is certain states of consciousness. For another it is a form of a phenomenal mind and does not apply to the noumenal reality. For a third it is a phase in the logical process of development. It is a fact that there is a certain matter out there in the world that is immediately given to us by knowledge and has a certain range of contingency; but if we go beyond our field of experience, we find the contingency which the positivists emphasized.

We see that the laws of nature are necessary. They are the record of happenings that have come within the experience of ourselves and of others who have recorded their experiences. They state simply the fact that B follows A in our own lives and in theirs. That is all the necessity that there is: A itself is contingent and B is contingent. When A has occurred and B has then occurred, we form, if you like, a habit of expecting B when we find A. We strike a match and expect a light, but the relationship between the striking of the match, as science distinguishes it, and the light is certainly a contingent relation. Suppose you can follow out in detail the process that goes on in the explosion of the match: the waves of radiation that reach the retina of the eye; the disintegration of the photochemical substances there; the effect in the central nervous organism following that; the movement from the nerve centers to the muscles and back to the eye; and the resultant winking of the eye. There we have a necessary succession of events. What about the light? The light is not a chemical explosion; it is not the waves of radiation; it is not the disintegration of photochemical substances in the eye; nor is it the excitement in the central nervous system. The events that take place in nature are events which, as events, are contingent. They happen. No scientist can sit down and evolve nature, from any ideas, any metaphysical entity. He can experience objective nature and accurately record it and know certain relationships which are there, but that which happens is contingent. The uniformities which we discover are in themselves contingent. That is, the law of nature does not exclude contingency any more than metaphysical laws or laws of logic exclude it. In order that we may observe anything, something must be happening. The whole point of the position in question is that it is the unexpected that happens, and there is much truth in it. If a thing happens at all, it is in some way unexpected. It is not entirely the sort of thing that we could prophesy. There is always some element in that which takes place which is different from anything that we could anticipate—a bit of novelty attends the recurrence of even ordinary events. That is true as far as our observation of it is concerned. It has got to be something different from anything we could hold in the mind or we would be unable to identify it. Our discovery of uniformity implies that which is not uniform. What Boutroux was interested in was in reducing an event which is different from another event to a certain identity with it.

To have uniformity you must have it in that which is not uniform; that which the genius of research is able to get out of the world are uniformities in the midst of that which is not uniform. You cannot have the one without the other. We come into a world which is pluralistic, as far as our knowledge is concerned. We are overwhelmed with a multiplicity of things that cannot be identified with each other, and then we set out on a scientific approach and select something which we think may be a clue to identities. In order to select that element, we must ignore other characters. If we are going to consider a given peculiarity, we must not give attention to others; and if we have good fortune when we follow the peculiarity out, we may discover it elsewhere. We might have had some other clue. A later scientist with better luck or greater penetration does find some other clue that is more important and builds up his theory on the basis of that clue. But a still greater genius may displace him. The undertaking is to bring order into something which is, in our immediate experience, wholly disordered. We must get a method for doing this: following out clues which are involved and ignoring what we do not know. It has been pointed out that ignoring is an essential part of knowledge. You can only know a thing in so far as you can ignore something else. We generally think of this in terms of getting rid of that which is not essential to the thing. It was Boutroux who insisted that scientific procedure is directed by the interest which we have in the process of knowledge and is dependent on the choices that we make of the hypotheses that we form out of contingent interests. I want to leave that in your minds particularly, because it appears in somewhat different form in the later statement of Poincaré in regard to the conventional character in which mathematics is presented. Boutroux also turned particularly to mathematics to show in what sense his statement was correct. A man in mathematics gets the highest degree of abstraction. In that subject you can consider things only in terms of the content of their certain, definite relationships. You must abstract everything else. But the knowledge you get is at the expense of everything else.

Boutroux, and the point of view which he represents in the development of French philosophy, indicates the reaction to the method and psychology of science. As I pointed out, science had given a control over the world which went beyond that which could be obtained by philosophy. The striking result of scientific work, its research, and the establishment of its results by observation and experiment lay, among other things, in its presenting that which is recognized by all who are competent to recognize what the scientist is doing. That is the difference between science and philosophy. One belongs to one philosophical school or another; he is an idealist, a pragmatist, a realist. One does not, on the other hand, belong to one scientific school or another as far as the results of science are concerned, if these results are established by observation. If the hypotheses are consistent and logical, they are accepted even where there is a difference of opinion in regard to the value of any certain one of them. They are taken as working hypotheses; and, in so far as they work, they are accepted. There is, on the whole, unanimity among the scientists in so far as results are concerned. Of course, in regard to the questions of accuracy of observation, of the adequacy of absolute tests, and of the interpretation of these results there are wide differences of opinion. But in so far as one gets a hypothesis that is recognized as consistent in its structure, one that answers to the problem which has given rise to it, and the hypothesis is supported by tests, it is accepted. It must be accepted to get that sort of unanimity which science presents but which is in contrast with the attitude of philosophers. The temperament of the man himself, his background, may determine the philosophy that he adopts. There is, of course, rational development of it from his mere opinion. It is criticized by himself and by others. One must accept certain types of criticism, but in the end one does take the point of view which answers to the personality, the interest, the background, of the man himself in his philosophic creed. Thus, science has stood out in contrast with philosophy in certain respects. It has an authority which philosophy does not have. During the medieval period philosophy expressed the attitude of the authoritative church, with its affirmation of divine inspiration; and hence it was able to speak for science. But with the appearance of experimental science you have an authority which is different from that of philosophy.

I wish to call that to your attention in order to indicate the attitude which philosophy took. It felt that it had to recognize science; and the relationship of science to philosophic doctrine became, in one way or another, the really important problem of all nineteenth-century thought. The Romantic idealists undertook to bring science within philosophy itself. They did not succeed, but they stated the scientific method in terms of the dialectic. If they had succeeded, then there would have been a philosophy of science which should have been more or less in harmony with both science and philosophy. The point of conflict between science and philosophy in England was the epistemological question. Science tells us what we know. And what the epistemological school did was to criticize knowing as such—not the result of science, but the process knowing. What does knowing amount to; what does it tell us? The Germans, of course, recognized this problem; but their interest lay in the carrying-out of science, particularly along the lines of physiology and the relationships between the organism and states of consciousness. There was an interest in finding that interrelationship through the development of psychophysics.

Fechner thought that he had found a mathematical relationship which could be set up between the intensity of the stimuli and that of the responses. He found out that you had to increase a stimulus by a certain percentage of itself in order to produce a difference in the response or in the sensation itself. If you were to take up a weight, for example, you would have to add a certain percentage, a third, of the weight to itself before you would recognize that you had a heavier weight in your hand. Similarly, a light would have to be increased by a tenth of itself. Fechner went on the assumption that these just-perceptible differences were elements in sensation which were equal to each other. The assumption then would be that sensation is made up out of elements which appear in just-perceptible differences. It is a composite. You can break it up so that you have elements which are just perceptibly different. If that is true, you can say that you can set up a mathematical relationship between the stimulus and the sensation. You add a certain percentage of the stimulus to itself in order to get a just-perceptible difference. If you work that out, what you get is a logarithmic equation. This seemed to be an open door for the mathematical analysis of so-called "consciousness." It seems possible, by means of mathematical analysis, to get back to ultimate elements in sensation itself. Fechner designated this as the field of psychophysics.

You can see at once that there are all sorts of assumptions here. For example, in the instances to which I have referred, it is assumed that the sensation can be broken up into just-perceptible differences, and that a difference in one case is equal to that in another. These assumptions are without support. Particularly, the theory runs frankly against the data of experience. One's sensation of weight is a unit; it is not made up of a number. You can lift a series of weights and, after that, can see, we think, that some of them would feel equal. Suppose we have a pound weight. That would be a guess which does not mean that the sensation you have when you lift the pound weight is equal to, can be divided into, twelve or sixteen different parts. The experience, the unitary experience, cannot be divided as the object itself can be divided. And then, of course, there is the question of just where the equation which is made use of is to be applied. What you get is the response of the individual which indicates that he feels that this weight is heavier than another. Now, what has happened? A stimulus has come in, has traveled around through the central nervous system, and has come out in the process of feeling. That represents a very intricate pathway in the central nervous system. Does the equation represent a relationship between the increase in the stimulus and the response of the nervous system? Have you a relationship there between the stimuli and consciousness, between the stimuli and the response in the central nervous system? This is a question which you see—when you once get over the sense of triumph at having gotten mathematics into the field of consciousness—involves assumptions that run counter to the actual data of experience. And, on the other hand, you have got the relationship which may apply to the organism in its response instead of the relationship between consciousness and the stimulus. So, the field of psychophysics lost its interest rather shortly. There has been a revival of it at the present time from another standpoint, however. I brought it up as an illustration of the type of interest that was dominant in Germany—the interest in the study of our consciousness and experience through the study of the organism as science deals with it. That is where the interest fastened in Germany.

XIV

Now, in France you have the interest in the relationship of the individual as an individual, as a personality, to science. What is the bearing of the scientific doctrine on the experience of the individual as a personality? What science gives is a world that is seemingly independent of ourselves—at least as far as science presents it. And, as I have indicated, Boutroux says it has necessity—the necessity which science predicates in its statements, if not one of a metaphysical character. The scientist qua scientist does not state that the changes must take place in the order in which he thinks they will. He has not got back to a necessary structure of the universe which can be dealt with. I have already said several times that the necessity which science postulates is practically synonymous with the intelligibility of the world. The only way in which you can know the world is in terms of uniformity. It is only in so far as you can get a law that you can get that which is uniform, that you can get that which can be known. Science does not state that it has discovered laws which are themselves fixed and certain. Its statements are always hypothetical. If the relationship between the mass, distances, and velocities of bodies is such as stated in Newton's law, then such and such results must be true. If the law of the pressure of gases is as it has been worked out, then such and such results must follow. That is where the necessity lies. It is a necessity of a hypothetical presupposition. A hypothetical proposition is a solution of certain problems which has met the test of observation. That is why we can go ahead on the basis of it. But science does not maintain that those hypotheses are necessary. It maintains, as I have said, that they are legitimate solutions for the problems which people have met and that they have been tested in the sense that action can continue on the basis of them. We can work out such things as stresses and strains, can determine when motions will occur. We do not hesitate to make these statements with the recognition that there may be some more satisfactory statement. But, as far as the situation is given, we are justified in accepting this hypothesis. Now, if we do use a certain hypothesis, it necessarily follows that such and such results will be found. If the hypothesis is correct, the eclipse will take place at such and such a time. That is the scientific necessity.

Boutroux approached the question from the point of view of a metaphysical necessity and asked what the justification for this metaphysical necessity is. He pointed out that there are always contingencies even in the metaphysical state. I think we can see that the contingent to which Boutroux referred is just that which I have pointed out in the hypothetical nature of the scientist's judgment. After A, B must follow. This is contingent, never dogmatic. On the contrary, the scientist is looking for events which will lead him to another problem. We can regard Newton's statement as an approximation and Einstein's as more accurate. Newton was the last person to maintain that there was absolute assurance in regard to the law of gravitation. He used the unfortunate expression that he had not used hypotheses. What he was referring to were the rather fantastic assumptions which the scientists of the time were making. They went beyond a possibility of testing. But his statement of the law was definitely a hypothesis. His hypothesis appeared in this form: he knew what the velocity of a falling body is near the surface of the earth; he had a rough estimate on the basis of which he could determine the distance of the moon, and he could figure out how much the moon falls toward the earth during a second; if it were not for the attraction of the earth, the moon would go off on a tangent; he could figure out how much the moon was drawn toward the earth during a second; if you take this relation in terms of the inverse square, then the distance the moon falls in a second, its velocity, would have a definite value; the moon should fall only 1/3,600 as rapidly as a body on the surface of the earth. That was the hypothesis which Newton set up, and he figured out on that basis what the velocity of the moon was and then saw that it was a certain fraction of the velocity of a body falling near the surface of the earth. That is thinking in a circle, and the first calculation was not entirely satisfactory; but he got a more accurate measurement of the attraction of the earth and found that it agreed exactly.

There you get the test of a hypothesis. You can continue to act on the assumption that the body is continually falling toward the earth with a velocity which is determined by this law. There is nothing that we now know that interferes with that assumption. All the facts are in harmony with it. If that is the law, then we can go on and state what must follow. That is the necessity that science can appeal to. If this law holds, there there must be such and such a result. If this law holds, there is a necessity which carries with it contingency. When Boutroux was criticizing the necessity of the law from the metaphysical standpoint, he was implying that the scientist was making a metaphysical assumption. Science, of course, always works with errors of observation; and science also works with reference to a method of limits. It does not get back to exact agreements, exact positions, exact congruence. What it does do, however, is to get a position which approximates these. The limit is never reached. But we get a series of which one can say: If the limit were reached, then such and such a thing would be true; and if that is true, such and such things must be true if we approximate it. We have, then, a method of approximation which enables us to state what the situation will be when you get there. But there is an "if" there, and the whole scientific method has this postulate behind it. Boutroux's assumption does not negate that. We cannot get back to the noumenal reality of the universe. Our knowledge is all relative knowledge. The space and time which are the basis for geometry and mechanics are relative to our own observations. All our observations have that sort of relativity behind them. What we find is a correlation between that which is given in experience and what we assume there as outside.

The possibility of getting such correlation is found, of course, in a field of thought in which mathematics and logic are dominant. Mathematics is a field of exact thought and analysis which has proved powerful. It has back of it certain definitions, certain presuppositions, certain postulates. Given these, its results are necessary results. Geometry has a postulate of parallel lines—that through a point outside of a line only one line can be drawn that will be parallel to it. Now you can set up another postulate, that through a point an indefinite number of lines can be drawn that are parallel to it, and you can construct a geometry on this basis. And as a piece of logic, the latter is just as sound a system as Euclidean geometry. You can make still other suppositions: that more than one line or a certain number of lines can be drawn through such a point, or that no lines can be drawn through it. You are at liberty to make any assumption on the basis of which you can build up a consistent geometry. If we say Euclidean geometry fits the experience we have of things, there is a great question as to how far it can be applied. Our measurements indicate that our local world is Euclidean. But we have never made any exact measurements which we tried to carry out to sufficient length to determine whether it is true that space is Euclidean. It is possible that our world is non-Euclidean. The assumption of Einstein is that it is non-Euclidean. We cannot prove that it is or that it is not. If we set up the assumption of its being Euclidean, then necessary results follow. Suppose you have a geometry which is non-Euclidean and one that is Euclidean. Which one is to be adopted? You will adopt the one that is most convenient!

Here you get the position of Poincaré, which is a development of Boutroux's statement, that our scientific theory and our mathematical theory are the most convenient that we can get. In the first place, we must abandon the space of immediate observation, the space in which we move up and down and right and left. What is real space? No one can tell. You can work out a geometry of one sort, or an infinite number of others, which could be applied to our experience, each having various of these different assumptions as to what the structure of the world is. Poincaré says we should adopt that which is most convenient. It is like getting persons of different races together and saying that the proceedings shall be in a certain language. You can find out the number of persons who speak the language that is most generally known, and you take that language as the medium of the gathering. In what language shall we express our observation of the world, Euclidean or non-Euclidean, or some other? That which is the most convenient! That is Poincaré's position. He said that our scientific theories are, after all, compromises. We never get back to the exact elements that science presupposes. There is always considerable leeway in the hypothesis, but the scientist proceeds anyway. We have never had knowledge of reality. We have a compromise, a working compromise.

But Boutroux did not go to the point of saying that statements which science makes are simply conventionalisms. That is the statement that Poincaré makes later. The former considered himself a rationalist. He said we can find out about the world so that we can get an agreement between the world as it is and the scientific statement we make. We can make a scientific statement that comes pretty close to the statement of the nature of things. Thus we can feel that we know something about reality. That was the position which Boutroux retained: we should believe that knowledge reveals something of the world. But he refused to recognize what he considered the datum of science in regard to the necessity of a scientific statement. As I have tried to point out, he was implying a necessity in the scientist's statement which the scientist does not claim. He was failing to recognize that all scientific judgments are, from the point of view of the scientist, hypotheses and that the necessity is only the necessity that you get in a hypothetical syllogism. If A is B, then C is D. However, A is B; so C is D. The scientist's laws are always of that form. If the square of the distances gives such and such a result, then a certain movement of the moon will be necessary if its motion conforms to the hypothesis of universal gravitation.

Boutroux represents a movement which comes to be more prominent in French philosophy, a movement toward the irrationality of our experience. He turned it in this direction, gave it an anti-intellectualist current. What he reached was the statement that science in its rational statement seems to get a necessary, ordered result which it does not really get. He criticizes what he considered to be the finding of science from the point of view of its own place. His interest in it was in showing that science is not justified—supposing it makes that claim—in saying that the unity of the individual is determined, that he has no free will, no spontaneity. The freedom of the will is a question. We do not know that the world is such a necessary texture of events that everything that takes place is determined by what has occurred before. He is interested in showing that the world is not such a necessary texture of events that everything that takes place is caused by what preceded it. He undertakes to show this by the analysis of the process of science itself, and by his assumption that what science presents is a sort of compromise. Boutroux comes to a definite conclusion that the realistic statement of science, as he interprets it, claims far more than it can establish.

That is a step in the direction of anti-intellectualism, and it is carried on by Bergson. Both Poincaré and Bergson represent a movement which developed along that line. In this, Poincaré was the scientist and Bergson the philosopher.

As I have already said, the principal figure in the movement in the tendency which introduced the element of irrationality in French thought is Boutroux, who criticized the conception of necessity as this appears in scientific doctrine and in scientific method. His theme was the presence of contingency in both the doctrine and the method of science. From the metaphysical standpoint he insisted that each postulate of science left the door open to contingencies. The axioms and postulates of mathematics and the sciences could not be reduced to identity; they could not be developed from the proposition that A is A. The universe could not be presented as necessary. Therefore, the findings of science are contingent.

From the standpoint of method, science proceeds inductively, discovering the laws which in their formulation are presented as necessary. But there formulations never exactly accord with the findings of observation and experiment. The point that Boutroux laid emphasis on was that the form of the law is one which is made by the mind. But this universal and necessary form does not exactly state what is presented in experience. Furthermore, the mind selects that form which seems to be the most satisfactory for the given situation. From Boutroux's standpoint, a compromise is made between the demand of the mind for necessary laws and the actual data as they come within the field of observation in science. This term "compromise" was the one that he used. There is an element of contingency here not only from the standpoint of the sort of data that comes within the range of science but also from the point of view of the mind itself in the selection that it makes of the hypothesis it uses. In the end, however, Boutroux conceived the universe as rational. He was not himself anti-intellectualistic; he did not come back to an irrational element. But, on the other hand, he did not believe that science was able to demonstrate a necessary rational order, that room was always open for the expression of spontaneity on the part of the individual. These were the principal points in Boutroux's statement. As you see, this study of science is made from the standpoint of contingency, with a view to leaving the door open to the freedom of the will, to the expression of the individual as an individual. That was the problem that more or less obsessed the French philosophic mind during the period under consideration. It has before it the seeming mechanical order of the universe which mathematical science presented and within which, at least in its formulation, everything that takes place is necessarily determined by that which has gone before. In such a universe there seems to be no room for the spontaneous individual, for the spontaneous mind, for our freedom or ability to determine our own conduct. This seems to be an illusion.

XV

The next figure of importance in this movement is Poincaré, the author of *Science and Hypothesis* and other significant works, and a cousin, by the way, of the one-time premier of France. He was an eminent mathematician and physicist. He was particularly important in the development of Maxwell's theory of electricity. He also gave a very acute and profound study of the meaning of scientific method. Born in the year of Comte's death, he parallels Russell and Whitehead in England. He belonged not only to the group of men we have considered but to these men who are our contemporaries. He is a connecting link between them. He took up the mathematical method as such and showed that that method is not one of deduction. So far as one has simply the principle of identity—that A is equal to A—as the principle of reasoning, no advance can be made. Nothing more can be found in the world than is presented in the premises. He sees, however, that advances have appeared in mathematical theory and asks what their source is. So far as arithmetic and algebra are concerned, he brings them back to a principle of mathematics which finds its expression in the number series, namely, the proof that anything true of n will also be true of $n-1$, and one goes on back until one reaches the position of unity itself. In such a situation the mind, by immediate intuition, realizes what the law of the number series is. That immediate intuition is not a mere reduction to identity. It does not come back to the principle that A is equal to A. It is a grasping by the mind of a process which, in its recurrence, exhibits certain necessary laws. In the field of geometry we have the fundamental assumptions of Euclidean geometry in the axioms, postulates, definitions. These Poincaré considers from the point of view of non-Euclidean geometry. The former geometry develops on the Euclidean axiom that only one line can be drawn through a point outside a line parallel to that line. What Poincaré points out is that we have here certain more or less arbitrary definitions. He discusses the space of our perception with its dimensions, its structure, and its position in relation to the space of mathematics and geometry; and he finds that the latter space is, in some sense, created by the geometrist.

I pointed out that it is perfectly possible to create other geometries which are non-Euclidean, geometries of what we may call "curved spaces." For example, we speak of a solid as the form of an infinite number of planes. We start from a line and reach the plane as an infinite number of lines; start with the plane and reach solids by an infinite number of planes. Now, suppose those planes, instead of being level, were bent, were slightly curved. Suppose the universe were made out of space that had a coefficient of curvature. The point can be made perhaps a little more concrete by the change which came about in navigation when it was recognized that the surface of the earth was curved. It came to be realized that the shortest distance between two points is not a direct line. Now, suppose that is true not only of the surface of the earth but that the whole of space has a slight curvature. Then the axiom of Euclid about the parallel lines would not be true. Such a space as that would require a geometry built on a principle different from that of Euclid. Such a geometry might be developed, and for every proposition in that geometry you could find a proposition in the Euclidean geometry, and vice versa. You could go on the assumption that you had a curved space with a certain coefficient of curvature, and build your geometry on that basis, and still you could utilize the Euclidean position as a particular instance. In other words, it is a matter of convenience whether we adopt one geometry or another. The reason for adopting the Euclidean geometry is that it has been found more convenient. And Poincaré said, suppose we should find that our space had some such curvature, that lines which are parallel tend to meet at a distant point. We would then probably find it more convenient to go on the assumption that there was an error in our calculation than to change our system of geometry. It would likely be that we would retain Euclidean geometry even in a non-Euclidean world because it would be the most convenient. In other words, our mathematical systems are conventional.

It is possible that people should live in a world not of solids but of fluids. Suppose one did live in a world of fluids. Then the form of this desk, as we conceive of it, when it had passed out through the fluid would be distorted. Or, take another illustration that Poincaré used. Let us assume that, as we move from a center in any direction, all dimensions and positions are proportionately decreased. This table, for example, would have a certain definite volume, a certain definite length. Now, if it moves away from this point, its dimensions would be altered proportionately. But not only would the dimensions of the table change, but those of the measuring-rods would also change. Not only that, but persons would also become smaller while retaining the same symmetry. The retina of the eye would be just so much smaller. Just as a body shrinks in the cold, every object would become proportionately less in all its dimensions. You can see that in such a world as that there would be no way of discovering this change, because the individuals and the units of measurement would change proportionately. What we have in science is a satisfactory language for stating the events and structure of things as they take place about us. Now, we could have another language; and if we did, we could express the relationship which exists in this world in one language or another. The system that is used is a conventional one. It comes back to the process of the mind of the individual. The whole mathematical system, then, is a conventional system. It does not give us a picture of the world as it is, but it does pick out certain relationships in it. And it states these relationships in terms of such convenient systems as that to which I have referred. Thus, the mechanical system of the universe, instead of being a structure lying outside of us in which we are helpless elements, is really a creation which serves to enable us to pick out those aspects that seem to be the important or essential features of the world and their relationships.

Here we have, as you see, a development of the conception of a compromise between the mind and the world which Boutroux had brought forward. Poincaré was not skeptical. He did not believe that it was impossible to know. What he was doing was reconstructing what he considered to be the limits, the actual content, of our knowledge. We have this same conception carried further among the neo-realists, like Russell, who assumes that the only knowledge that we have of a world outside of ourselves is of its logical pattern, and he thinks that there is a relationship between that pattern and the pattern of our thought. You have a certain pattern present in Euclidean geometry. You have another picture arising out of our immediate sense perception. You have still another pattern in the non-Euclidean geometry. Suppose there were creatures that lived in two dimensions only, and suppose they developed a geometry in that dimension. They have only those dimensions and move in that plane. Now, suppose there is a hump in that plane. These beings will be unable to state it in terms of dimensions of things. What they would find is that, as they approached the hump, in order to move around it in the shortest time they would have to make a curve. They might express that in different ways. They might assume that there was some sort of a force in the back of what we could call the center of this hump which drove them away. You would get the same sort of a picture if you were in a balloon and, looking down, saw people moving with lanterns where you could not see the contour of the earth. It would all be a plane. But you would see forms with lanterns going over the side of a mountain and notice that, when they got to a certain point, they went off in a curve instead of a straight line. You would have two different ways of stating that. If you could get the third dimension, you could state it in terms of this dimension or you could state it in terms of a force. How would you express it if you were sailing over the ocean and did not know that the surface was curved and found that you got to a certain point by taking a longer path? You could conceive of some repulsive power drawing you away when you take one way rather than another. You would have different ways of explaining your course.

So you can have different geometries. One geometry, the Euclidean, has proved to be the simpler way of stating our experience of spatial relations. You could state it in other terms. In the Einsteinian doctrine you get a particular statement which works out in a non-Euclidean geometry. That may be the simpler way of stating it. That may come to be accepted. It is the position in which one sees certain relationships which exist between certain events, something that is happening out there; and you presume the relationship between that and the patterns that you have in your own mind. You cannot get hold of those events out there, but you find a certain structure in them. The most striking illustration of that is found in the relativity doctrine. You can get a statement in terms of which you get what takes place in one space, then in terms of that which takes place in another. Now there is a certain interpenetration between events in your theory which can be given a definite statement, and that statement can be translated into any space. From such a standpoint you can recognize that your mathematical theory is only a link for bringing out relationships where you do not have the things which have these interrelationships. And you can get the correlation between that pattern and the pattern that you have in your mind. From the biological point of view, these patterns were all convenient. That is, they are definitely selected with reference to the uses to which one is to put them. They are selected for the sake of their convenience. That is what we mean by "convenience." But there are certain necessary relations. Thus, Poincaré was not skeptical. He was, as it were, simply loosening the mathematical theory of the world from the world itself, as it was presented by the physical scientist.

The latter had thought that the world was a mechanical structure of masses, of bits of energy, in motion. He thought of it as a great machine that ran in accordance with necessary law. Poincaré and the others were loosening this necessary structure from the world itself and lodging it in the mind. We can get a connection, a correlation, of the relations between the characters out there and those in your mind; but we have no such universe actually present in experience. We have only a way of getting hold of certain characters which are there. Do these characters reveal the actual structure of reality? In the matter of movement Poincaré came back to a certain intuition of the movement in dealing with the recurrence of the number series. Does that intuition reveal the actual relationship of events to each other? He believed it did.

The tendency here is to assimilate the nature of things to the mind. This is a tendency toward a certain type of idealism. But we have a fundamental break between the mind, on the one side, and what we call "matter," on the other. It involves the distinction between quantity and quality. Our experience tends to pick out that which is qualitative. Our mathematical technique, our scientific technique, picks out that which is quantitative. So, we speak of color in nature as a certain motion, of something with definite vibrations. We measure the world and deal with it as a measurable quantity, but no measurement gives us a control over it. The color, sound, taste, odor—the quantities of the world—tend to be put in the mind. That bifurcation of the world has been the most convenient to use. As Poincaré pointed out, it is a great convenience to have these statements; but the only thing we get hold of is certain definite relations in the world, and those relations from Poincaré's standpoint, as stated in terms of geometry, are, in a certain sense, a creation. What is the relationship of those statements to reality itself? Poincaré denied that the logic and metaphysics of identity could reveal to us the world as it existed, but he did speak of an intuition which could see through to certain essential relations. We want a world made up of events—one in which things have definite lengths, can be definitely measured—one in which objects can be put into geometric relations with each other, have perfectly definite successions, certain velocities, certain accelerations. That is the sort of world we want so that we can control it. In order to get such a world, we must abstract from our experience as it takes place immediately. This table is colored; it has a feel; it is warm; it is smooth. We cannot state its characters in these terms; but we can state them in terms of a geometry, in terms of a dynamics. We can utilize the materials of nature for this or that or the other thing, and by giving a scientific statement we can get control of reality. But to do that we must put this conventional framework of ours into the world.

XVI

We have in these conceptions, which follow from Comte up to Poincaré, the setting for the philosophy of Bergson. There is one important addition. The thought of Boutroux and Poincaré was occupied with mathematical physics. The problems of biology were only incidental to their discussions. It was assumed that life-processes could be stated in terms of the inanimate world; life could be dealt with in terms of chemistry and physics. This position could not be proved, but it was a legitimate assumption that the whole world could be included in such a mechanical statement. The justification for that is what Boutroux and Poincaré were discussing.

Bergson starts with the science of biology, particularly the theory of evolution. He is a true French philosopher in that his method is a psychological one. In his book *Time and Free Will* he starts off with the assumption that the universe and the field of our experience are fields of what he calls "imagination." They are the impressions that belong to a self, to a mind, an organized mind. You can see this is an idealistic statement; yet, it is not romantic, spiritual idealism, nor yet the subjective idealism of Berkeley. Bergson comes back to experience as he finds it; he recognizes the table as an experience that can be stated in terms either of physics or of psychology. And he chooses the psychological statement of it. He does not lodge objects in the mind. They can be in the mind or out of the mind but are the same in both cases. There is an identity of structure, or nature, as you like. The question whether they are in the mind or not is a question that does not necessarily arise. Suppose one takes the illustration I have given before of the face of a person that one sees and mistakes for an acquaintance. When one approaches the individual, he sees that he has made a mistake. In a certain sense he takes off the face that he sees and considers that it is a different individual. He has put something —the face, form, image, of his friend—on this person; and when he approaches, he sees that it does not fit. Where was that image that he saw? Was it out there, or was it in the mind? What is the meaning of any such question as that? We may say the image could not be there, for, when we come to study it, it is different and what was seen was only a mental image, and a mental image must be in a mind. But, for the purpose of experience the image is out there. That is a phase of experience of which French philosophy never lost hold.

Bergson presents himself at this point. His is a different approach from that which we have indicated was being made in Germany. The approach in Germany was to take the physiological organism over into the field of psychology. It states what corresponds to states of consciousness in terms of what goes on in the organism. And this psychology which wants to be scientific simply gets a parallelism between these two. As far as it can, it subordinates the mental to the physical, or rather the psychical to the physiological. If it can only get hold of what goes on in the central nervous system, the self, then it will have data of a scientific sort and will be able to interpret this much more uncertain field of the inner life. It goes from the ground of natural science into the psychical self. Bergson reversed this procedure. His approach was from the psychical side, and he attempted to deal with the physical and physiological from that standpoint. He does not, however, use the distinction as Berkeley did. Berkeley wiped out the distinction between the mental and physical and tried to state the problem in terms of association of ideas. The German, or physiological-psychological, school does not, of course, wipe out the psychical; but it looks at it from the point of view of the physiological. That is, the psychical tends to become phenomenal, merely a psychical shadow which accompanies certain physiological happenings. That which is given, the whole process, is found in the organism. Only a part of this reveals itself in consciousness which flares up here and there. If we want to understand states of consciousness, we must go over into the field of physiological psychology. That is the attitude which the scientific psychologists took, although a philosopher could interpret that attitude in different fashions. But the psychologists as such were demanding an attitude in which they interpreted the psychical in terms of the physical. They did not, however, say that consciousness is a secretion of the brain as the bile is a secretion of the liver. They had got beyond that form of crude materialism which belonged to the 1840's.

The position of Bergson is that the fundamental reality is given in mental experience, and that the statement of what we call physical and physiological must be interpreted in terms of the psychical, of the mental. He undertakes to treat the physical world, as science deals with it, as a phenomenal statement of what goes on in the psychological world. There is a distinction between knowledge and the real. It is a distinction which is legitimate. It is one which is undertaken in the interest of conduct, for the sake of utility. If one does not undertake to set up the experienced world as the ultimate metaphysical reality, there is no criticism to be made of our statement of it in such terms. But the content of reality is that which is revealed within, in that which is in some sense psychical. We have taken the realities that go on in our inner experience and have fixed them so that we can control them, but we must not assume that the petrification of these experiences is a living, pulsing reality.

The first question, of course, that would be put up to such a philosophy is: How do you know that this is the approach to ultimate reality? Science knows a world in so far as it can measure it, in so far as it can find laws of uniformity that are stated in terms of the relationship of things in space and time—and its statement in terms of time is, after all, spatial. If you ask the length of time that it takes to walk through the park, the answer is so many minutes. What is that? It is the representation of a certain distance on the face of your watch. If you are going to put the time that science deals with in measurable terms, you must put it in spatial terms. How can you get the different inner realities if what your science deals with is stated in terms of an outer physical world? It is in the former that you get to exact measurements, to ultimate realities. But how do you approach that inner world in which you say the outer is a distinct phenomena? What Bergson does is to set up a metaphysical method. He has rejected the scientific formula. He regards it as academic. He calls for an immediate return to inner experience, a return to that inner experience which does not take place in terms of what he calls "concepts." The field of distinctions and of reality are for Bergson special fields. And he places in the former not only what the measuring-rod deals with but also the whole of scientific technique. The only thing he can measure is something that he can put a measuring-rod on. You have the falling grains of sand in the hourglass, the drops of water in a water clock, the slow melting-away of the candle, the swinging of the pendulum of a clock. All these are spatial events, and the only time that science deals with is a time that can be petrified in such spatial form, that is, where one can apply measurement. Motion, to be measured, must be stopped. You measure a motion, and what you get is a simultaneity at one end of the line and a simultaneity at the other. You get the point on your watch at which the hand of your watch stands when the runner starts; and when he stops, you may reduce that and get back to an infinitesimal bit. If you are measuring in terms of space, your motion must be put in a spatial container. You have to stop your motion in order to measure it. As far as science deals with processes, then, it must petrify them in spatial forms.

Our concepts, says Bergson, have the same characteristic. What they do is to divide things off into discontinuities. Conceptualization breaks up processes and simply relates concept A to concept B. It analyzes the living object into certain quantities, and puts all these together; but it carefully distinguishes one from the other. It is this, that, and the other thing; and they must all be held separately. You take a reality to pieces and can get your conceptual view of what its nature is. It is made up of a set of situations which you describe in terms of movement, but a whole set of separate concepts would be required to define the thing. It is not as simple for Bergson to make his conceptual world spatial as it is for him to make his temporal world spatial. But he undertakes to show that our conceptual analysis inevitably stops the living process. It does not give the reality of something that is going on. If you are to know all this, know reality in terms of concepts, you must get it by the approach of intuition, by a sudden turning-back to the inner life, grasping it in its reality. Bergson distinguishes sharply between that reality and the spatial, conceptual statement which one finds of it. In that world of change, of process, of spontaneity, Bergson is able to preserve freedom. The other statement is that which science makes in concepts, in measurement. The former is the statement which you get in Bergson's volume translated under the title of *Time and Free Will*.

The ideal of a scientific statement is that you get in an equation the assurance of a reality of such sort that it makes no difference what happens—there is no accident in it. Everything must happen according to that which has taken place. That is the scientific ideal of accuracy. That is the picture that science undertakes to obtain. But, Bergson says, that does not carry with it the nature of duration, of what is happening. Under such circumstances, happening would cease. You would have absolute monotony, no way of distinguishing one moment from another. The scientist tries to wipe out all such distinctions. Bergson turns to the inner life for the expression of this other type of succession—a type of succession in which it is always the unexpected that happens, in which it is that which is universal that makes us aware of succession, of duration. You cannot recognize duration, happening, experience, except in that which is changing. There must be change in order that there may be awareness of what is going on. Duration, then, is something that lies in our immediate experience. But duration is not found in the world as science presents it, that is, not as mechanical science has presented it. Here you do not find that which is characteristic of this inner experience. It is the statement of this situation that Bergson faces, and it is more or less original with him. To Bergson there is for the scientist nothing but a succession of separate, instantaneous moments, one of which replaces another. Now that is not duration. What does characterize duration is a passage from the past into the present, and on into the future. Something is always taking place in which there is some past and some future. This is true of every experience. Whether that is to be called "interpenetration" may be a question, but that is the way in which Bergson presents it. The past is actually crowding into the future. The only way in which we can get that duration is by a sort of intuition, a sudden turning on one's self, grasping experience as it is going on. But, if you try to state it by means of analysis, especially in terms of the external world, you kill it. In such a statement you have to anatomize it. You can dissect it, but then you no longer have a living process there.

It is this attitude of Bergson which makes him an anti-intellectualist. Of course, Bergson is not an anti-intellectualist in the sense that he denied intelligence of a sort, but he says it has a particular function. From that standpoint Bergson may be called pragmatic. The function of conceptional thinking is action. It presents a world in terms of mechanisms. It is a mechanical thing and gives the mechanism by means of which we can control the content of experience. Man is a tool-making animal. He works by tools; and his concepts are tools, just as his machines are. They are legitimate for their purpose. But the purpose is not that of revealing ultimate reality. If you want to get ultimate reality, turn within, where you have experience itself. Bergson has the same difficulty in terms of philosophy and metaphysics as do the mystics. You get intuitions only in a glimpse that can be recognized now and then, and you cannot determine whether or not you are going to get them. In the very nature of the case there can be no conceptual theory of intuition. That is perhaps the most fundamental obstacle to the development of the Bergsonian philosophy. But the escape from this difficulty which Bergson presents is his identification of life with this reality which we have within us. I pointed out to you that in scientific development there is evolution, and the theory of life which appears in science is revealed in the Bergsonian philosophy. In other words, Bergson finds in life all the characters which he has identified in this inner experience. But what is life? As it is presented to us in the modern physiological statement, it is an interaction of process going on all over the body. The different elements must be there affecting each other in order that there may be life. You can kill a living form and get all the elements and get them into test tubes, but you can never get life. Life then is, from the point of view of Bergson, another illustration of that which we find in our own inner life, another illustration of reality.

We have seen that the center of Bergson's position is found in what he terms "intuition," the recognition of duration as it appears in the inner experience. This involves interpenetration of characters—intensity, rather than extensity, of qualities. This is a method which is given immediately, obtained through a conceptual analysis and construction. From Bergson's standpoint the reality of the world is that which is revealed in the inner experience. This inner experience belongs to the individual. It is not essential to the nature of reality. It indicates, rather, the path by which the individual gets this intuition. But that of which he gets an intuition is not a state of consciousness; it is of the nature of reality itself.

XVII

In discussing the relationship of mind and body in Bergson's doctrine we have seen that the center of reality is to be found in the psychical experience, as he indicates in the use of the term "image." These images answer in one sense to the impressions and ideas of the empirical school. For Bergson the center of reality is the psychical experience which is revealed in intuition, as distinct from conceptual knowledge and also as distinct from the organism of the spatial world. For Bergson the category of time, as he conceives time, is closer to reality than that of space. The time to which he refers is duration, *durée*, that which appears in the inner experience, that within which there can be different types of interpenetration. This he puts in sharp contrast with the spatial world, which is external, which is the state of quantity, while the inner experience is the state of quality;

which is a matter of extensive magnitude over against intensive magnitude. He refuses to recognize that this intensive magnitude can be dealt with from the point of view of the extensive magnitude. In Bergson's mind, concepts involve the same sort of externality which he criticized in the attempts to state our inner experience in terms of external stimulation. When we think of things in terms of concepts with the sharp differences of which they are capable, separating one from another, we are doing the same sort of injustice to reality as that to which I just referred in the relation of an extensive stimulation or an extensive physiological response in its relationship to the inner experience. Bergson does not say that a concept is a spatial event, but he says that it has just the same character of externality. Concepts are exclusive of each other, and that exclusiveness is almost externality. What Bergson finds in the world, especially in the biological world, is a creative process which grows out of that which has taken place but which is not itself given in that which has come before. Duration is always the happening of that which is novel. If you get a spatial statement of time, you get that which has no succession in it, at least no duration in it. Duration involves the appearance of something that was not present before.

The account which Bergson gives of this world, as against what he speaks of as a "distortion of reality," is in terms of the characters in which the organism, the mind, puts its experience. He assumes that the nature of the individual fixes the world, and fixes it in terms of the uniformities of an individual's past experience in order that he may utilize it. The mind selects out certain characters of experience on which it can depend, on which its past experience indicates it can depend, and states a world in these fixed forms. It is a pragmatic sort of procedure, a selection of characters which are relatively permanent and a statement of these in the interest of the solution of problems. The externalized world is, therefore, a fixing, a freezing, of reality in terms of certain uniformities that are applied to the world as if they dominated and expressed that reality. The mind, then, is that which within itself is psychical, and which fixes its own universe and its own organism for the purposes of conduct. The great instrument for this purpose is the central nervous system.

Bergson passes on from this sort of a statement which is in psychical terms over to a statement in biological terms in the notion of a creative evolution. Reality, in so far as it is living, is that which advances, that which changes in its own nature, that whose nature it is to change. In Bergson's sense, motion is something that goes on in the nature of the thing that is moving. It is not a mere change of position. It does not change that which is itself moving. Life is a change in the very nature of that which lives. In so far as we are living beings, we are not at any second what we were the second before. If we undertake to state life in terms of a permanent content, we have taken the whole meaning out of life as life. There is a physical, chemical statement available, but it is applied to inanimate things. It cannot be made into a statement of life, for our conduct is from one reality to another in which that reality is always changing. That, Bergson says, identifies life with this inner nature which our intuition reveals to us. Life is in that sense a sort of mind. It has the same relationship to its environment as mind has to its world and physical organism. It is selecting, it is petrifying its world in spatial terms in the same fashion that mind does. In an account of the process of evolution he gives this statement of an onward move that is creation, that is constantly changing, producing that which was not there before, changing itself but doing it by means of the physical world. This picture we must get from the outside, from what biology presents. But we interpret the form from within, for reality lies in our own experience. In our own experience we are cutting things up into homogeneous elements. That is, we want to have the same science for tomorrow that we have today. We do not wish to have to remember in detail. Therefore, we fix our world and become familiar with it.

Evolution is a process of constructing a world that is exactly parallel, in Bergson's sense, to our perception of it. Selection is going on. Processes are continued; and in this selection that which is novel is happening, making duration possible. That takes place in our conduct, too. Now, Bergson brings this over into a grand evolution in the development of life-processes. Life-forms in this fashion do just what we do in sense perception. They mobilize themselves. They maintain themselves by means of skeletons they develop, by sense organs which are produced by their environment, which bound it and analyze it into elements which can be regarded as relatively permanent. The organism does this sort of thing just as our perception builds up its field of perception and its objects. But this very world impresses life in just the way that habit impresses our own action. Man becomes the slave of his habits, of the exoskeletons which cover us. We can only see what we have habituated ourselves to see. We live in the world which is cut out by our past habits. This situation is presented from the Bergsonian standpoint on the side of evolution in its relation to an environment of organisms which have picked out that which they can eat, that which they can reach by their method of procreation, that by means of which they can avoid this danger and that. The organism has fixed itself, and it cannot go ahead. The man who is getting on in years loses the vital spark. Health is gone; he has nothing left but the fixed habits of life; he can see nothing but that which he has selected in his conduct; he has impressed himself, and there is no further advance for him; he can no longer be in a field of creation.

What I want to leave with you is a clue for the comprehension of Bergson's conception of the world—the parallelism of the perceptual process and the living process with this metaphysical assumption of process which he never fully worked out. He does not show us in any detail how the method does actually get stereotyped, nor does he show how life stereotypes its world. He appeals to the process of perception and refers us to that sort of intuition which is so difficult to get, and assumes that the same thing is taking place in the external world that is taking place from the standpoint of our inner perception. It is that to which he refers, as I have said.

Here, then, we have Bergson's solution of the problem he took over from Boutroux and Renouvier—the problem of freedom. If one accepts his statement, he has more than solved it. The only reality is this duration in which that which is novel is continually coming into being. Bergson's problem can be presented in this way. It is true that you can never previse what is going to happen. There is always a difference in what takes place and what has existed in the past. You cannot determine what you are going to be later. But the question is now: What is the relationship of means to ends? We are constantly stating the means. Bergson is correct in his position that, if we state an end in the form in which it is going to be realized, or if we state it in such form that we must stick to the account that we give of it, then we distort the thing. There is a story of James and Royce, who were out sight-seeing in a city. Royce had information of where they were going and told James what car they would take so that in the end they would get to such and such a place. They got to a junction where they had to change cars. James got on the wrong car. Royce corrected him, telling him he was on the wrong car, that the car he was on went to another point. "Yes," said James, "that is where I wanted to go." There he puts in acute form the present problem. Can we state the end of our own conduct and the end of creation; can it be stated in exact, definite form if the world is something that is moving on from that which is to that which is not? If that is the nature of reality, can the end toward which movement is to take place be stated in a conceptual form? Certainly we can say that it cannot be stated at any given time.

What Bergson overlooks in his treatment of science is that science does not undertake to make such a statement. It is continually presenting hypotheses of the world as it is, but science is a research affair and goes forward on the basis of the fact not only that the world will be intelligent but that it will always be different from any statement that science can give of it. That is, we are looking for an opportunity to restate any statement which we can give of the world. That is the implication of our research science. But that does not mean that we cannot think in conceptual terms. It means that we are always restating our restatement of the world. The same is true of our own ends and process in life. If a person could state to himself everything that is going to happen, his life would be unbearable. Life is a happening; things take place; the novel arises; and our intelligence shows itself in solving problems. But the solution of problems is by means of a definite conceptual procedure. The collapse of absolute idealism lies in the fact that everything is all accomplished in the Absolute. All that is to take place has already taken place in the Absolute. But our life is an adventure. And we can be intelligent in stating at every point the form which our conduct should take. We show our intelligence by giving as elaborate a statement of the world as we can. The realization of emergence in philosophy, the large acceptance of pluralism which you see, is involved in the assumption that the novel can appear by saying it is an enlarging of our finite imperfect experience. But there can be nothing novel in an Absolute. You can have a process of an infinite type, but it is one in which all the movements are determined. You can have contradictions, but they are always overcome. You have that which goes on; but it is going on in eternity, in an infinity in which the result is obtained already, but in which it does not appear.

It is this element that Bergson insists is involved in passage. That other statement is of a conception of the reality of the world in which everything is fixed in advance. It is its acceptance which Bergson is fighting. When you state reality in terms of a mechanism, it is an academic statement of nature. When you undertake to state your ends and problems, you fix and stereotype it. You stop advancing. Does that mean you cannot use the intelligence that enables you to get hold of means of stating the ends toward which you are moving? If this is true, Bergson's doctrine is correct, and we must draw away our intellectual control of life and give ourselves up to our impulses. But if you can state your end in terms of your means, with a definite recognition that that statement is one which you are going to change, that your life is a process of adaptation, you can have the full reign of intellectual life and the control that it gives and still not stereotype your experience.

That brings out the problem which Bergson presented in his philosophy. The problem is that involved in the opposition, if you like, the antimony, between a conceptualized statement of that which is going to take place, of that which we are going to do, and of that which does arise, that which we do do, that which takes place in nature. Is there any real duration? If there is, there is that in which the novel is appearing. We are passing on constantly to that which is new, and our conceptual statement is in terms of the situation in which we find ourselves. How can we state that which is not? That is the Bergsonian problem in its simplest form. I have tried to present it as it appears in perception, as it appears in mechanical science, in evolution, and in terms of social progress. We are moving on, in the very nature of the case, in a process in which the past is moving into the present and into the future. Can we use our intellects to get hold of and direct this movement? Bergson says that we cannot, because in the nature of the case that toward which we are going is not here yet and, if you do not have knowledge of the end to which you are going, you cannot travel toward it intellectually. You must depend on the wind blowing behind you. You cannot reach it by conceptual means. But there is another statement which can be made over against this: that the man who is finding his way toward a goal which he cannot state can make a tentative plan as he goes along; and then he can make that better, more accurate, more complete. But he has got to be in the attitude of continually reconstructing it and restating it. We do not know what the end of society should be, but we are sure that disease and misery in its various forms should be gotten rid of. How we are going to get rid of disease we do not know. How the values that have rested in it in the past, the care for the sick, and so on, fit in with the conception of a place where there will be no suffering we do not know. But we are stating in our conceptual way what the end is to be, and then we test our steps and restate it. What Bergson denies is the possibility of advancing by a set of hypotheses which are being continually reconstructed if they do not hold—hypotheses which are confessedly hypothetical. We have only the statement which we can give at the time, hypotheses which are open to unexpected happenings and which are ready for reconstruction, hypotheses that belong to a world in which things are going on, in which there is duration. What Bergson says is that this sort of intelligent control of our conduct and intelligent control over our comprehension of and appreciation of nature in the direction of the movements in society is impossible. He refuses that because any statement that is made at this time would be an absurd statement of what is going to be later. If we had to conduct the world by the hypotheses of the seventeenth century, we would not get along. They undertook to state the world as they gave it in conceptual terms. But that did not interfere with a continued restatement of them. The scientist is always ready to reconstruct, and it is by means of such refined statement that he gets ahead. If, of course, science had undertaken to give infallibility to any statement that it had and refused to reconstruct that statement, it would have been in a prison. But a restatement at every point possible is what science wants. Thus, Bergson's attack upon science represents a misconception of its method and ideal. His flight to irrationalism is unnecessary.

INDEX

INDEX

INDEX

INDEX

Postulates:
  Kant's, 119
  of science, 258–59, 265–91
Pragmatism:
  and Bergson, 502
  philosophy of, 344–59
  See also Dewey
Process:
  of entropy, 155
  life, 127–28, 161–68, 252–53, 260, 263,
    271, 289, 372, 377, 502–3, 505–6, 508
  natural, 158, 451–52, 500
  social, 148, 363, 370–73, 376, 381–85
  thinking, 129–30
Production, 218–20, 223–24, 231, 232–33,
    237, 245, 258
Profit, 218, 220, 223, 231
Progress, 411, 509. *See also* Evolution
Proletariat, 241
Psychology:
  behaviorism, 387–404
  behaviorism in pragmatism, 350–52
  behaviorism and society, 381–83
  in Bergson's philosophy, 305–10, 316–
    18, 322–23
  conditioned reflex, 391–92
  and consciousness, 387–88, 392–404
  and experience, 388–404, 435
  functional, 386–87
  in philosophy, 444–45, 446–47, 466–83,
    496–506
  stimulus response, 389
  structural, 386
Psycho-physical parallelism, 475–76
Psychophysics, 481–82
Ptolemy, 117, 137, 355–56
Pythagoras, 137, 339

Quantum theory, 117, 254, 256
Queen Elizabeth, 179

Radiation, 346–48
  Rationalism, 326, 344, 352, 437
  and Aristotle, 4–5
  and Christianity, 1
  of Christianity and science, 5–8
  and mathematics, 7–8
  in modern science, 9
  theory of the state, 12–24
  and St. Augustine, 2

Realism, 326–44, 358
Realistic movement, 151
Reality, 146, 269, 327–43, 352, 413, 467,
    476–90, 495–96, 499–510
  Abelard, 9
  Bergson, 300, 302–4, 308, 310–11, 315–
    19, 323–25
  Christianity, 10
  Descartes, 8
  Epicurus, 8, 9
  Kant, 35, 42–48
  quantum theory, 117
  Renaissance, 9–10
  romanticism, 82–83
  science, 9
  of self, 139
  substance-attribute, 82, 477
  See also Self
Reform. *See* Socialism, Utilitarianism
Reformation, 181, 182
Reid, Thomas, 438, 440, 466–68
Relation, 327, 343, 352, 386–87, 394–95,
    414–16
  cause and effect, 326–28, 437–38
  as knowledge, 437, 444, 454–55
  for science, 158, 243–44, 260, 449–50
  self-not-self, 111
  subject-object, 35, 73–75, 81–82, 87,
    97–98, 105, 130–31, 139, 163, 166–67,
    329–30, 393, 438, 481–82, 593–96
  subject–object relation and moral ex-
    perience, 98
  subject-object relation as process, 105,
    128
  subject-object versus substance-attri-
    bute, 109
  substance-attribute, 105, 326
Relativity, 140–41, 256–58, 303–4, 412–
    17, 487, 494–95
Religion, 176–78, 186–87
  and banking, 180–81
  and economic change, 181–83
  positivistic, 464–65
  and romanticism, 428–30
  and science, 247–49, 288–89
  and society, 362–63, 411, 425, 463–64
Renaissance, 1–24, 222, 248, 259, 275, 294,
    450–51
  as revolution, 12–24, 80, 137, 154
  social, 215–40

INDEX